FROM THE SANDLOTS TO THE WORLD CUP

INSIDE SEVEN DECADES OF AMERICAN SOCCER

By Joseph A. Machnik Ph.D.
aka 'DR JOE'

© From the Sandlots to the World Cup:
INSIDE seven decades of American soccer
By Joseph A. Machnik Ph.D.

©2025 Joseph A. Machnik

All rights reserved.

No part of this publication may be reproduced, stored, distributed, or transmitted in any form or by any means, including photocopying, recording, or other electronic or mechanical methods, without the prior written permission of the publisher, except in the case of brief quotations embodied in reviews, the worksheets at the end of the book and certain other non-commercial uses permitted by copyright law.

The information provided within this book is for general informational purposes only. While the author tries to keep the information up-to-date and correct, there are no representations or warranties, express or implied, about the completeness, accuracy, reliability, suitability, or availability with respect to the information, products, services, or related graphics contained in this book for any purpose. Any use of this information is at your own risk. All opinions expressed in this book are solely the opinion of the author.

ISBN: 979-8-9994840-3-1
Paperback

Book cover design and layout design by Simon Thompson

Honored to have my forty-five-year-old MISL Referee jersey on display at the National Soccer Hall of Fame.

Contents

Acknowledgements 6
Introduction: "Let's Bring in Dr. Joe!" 10
1. McCarren Park: "A New Excitement" 12
2. Brooklyn Technical High School:
   "So You Can Be The Goalkeeper" 18
3. The New York Ukrainians Sports Club: "TEMPO YCK" 24
4. Long Island University: "I Want the Job" 40
5. New Haven College/University of New Haven:
   "Becoming Dr. Joe" 78
6. USSF/US Soccer Coaching Schools: "Where It All Began" 106
7. The Major Indoor Soccer League (MISL):
   "You Can't Tell Smart People They're Stupid" 128
8. The American Indoor Soccer Association (AISA):
   "The Handwriting Was On The Wall" 166
9. No.1 Goalkeeper's Camp/No.1 Soccer Camps:
   "No.1 For A Reason" 182
10. NCAA Officiating and a NASCAR Career:
    "Let's See If Joe's Alright" 210
11. US Men's Five-a-Side '89 Bronze Medal
    and World Cup Italia '90: "The Long Wait is Over" 226
12. University of New Haven (Part 2):
    "We Will Truly Miss You" 262
13. Major League Soccer (MLS): "Please Help Us" 274
14. Fox TV Rules Analyst: "The Doctor Is In The House" 302
    Appendices 320
    Index 328
    Testimonials 342
    About the Author 344

Acknowledgements

As the first soccer games I remember watching were played in the early 1950's, there are literally hundreds of persons that I should acknowledge for contributing to my life during the past seven decades of American soccer. First acknowledgements, however, must go to my parents for creating an environment which encouraged me to have an inquisitive mind and a risk-free attitude regarding chance and new adventure. Thank you, Joe and Viola Machnik!

I would never have led the fortunate life in soccer without that fateful day a high school classmate in my sophomore year at Brooklyn Technical High School suggested that I try out for its soccer team. Thank you, Andrew Sheparovich, for seeing something in me worthy of your friendship and camaraderie not only for our two years of high school soccer competition at Tech, but also and perhaps more importantly for bringing me to your soccer club, the New York Ukrainians. There, I was introduced to a world that I knew nothing about but embraced with all my heart.

Thank you to my high school coach Mr. Arthur Peck who gave me a shot at playing at first for junior varsity and then on the varsity team that had a shot at the New York City (PASL) Championship. And mostly for recommending me to Gary Rosenthal, soccer coach at Long Island University (LIU).

And to my lifelong friend at Tech, teammate John Nussbaumer who also served to pique my memory and edit my manuscript. Thank you, John.

Gary Rosenthal was not only my Coach, but my first mentor. He led me to becoming a physical education teacher, introduced me to summer camp life, hired me as a graduate assistant coach and handpicked me to replace him as LIU Head Coach when he was promoted to Dean of Students. Most of all, he was adamant that I marry Barbara Otlowski, the future Mrs. Machnik before someone else did. He was Best Man at our wedding.

While playing at LIU, my teammate Ray Klivecka, also a Brooklyn Tech grad, and later an outstanding coach at many levels including the world-famous NY Cosmos, was scoring or assisting on most of our goals enabling the two of us to make All-American in 1962 and lead LIU to the first of its many NCAA Tournament appearances. Thank you, Ray.

While still a junior player at the New York Ukrainians, I marveled at the play of the senior team center forward Walter Chyzowych. Later I would be his teammate at the Newark Ukrainians of the ASL. We developed an appreciation of each other's talent and dedication. Walter would become my second mentor as he rose through the ranks of US Soccer as Director of Coaching and US Men's National Team Coach. He appointed me to his coaching staff for US Soccer's Coaching Schools, and to my role as Referee-in-Chief of the Major Indoor Soccer League and to the positions of Assistant Coach of the US Bronze Medal winning Five-a-Side Team and the 1990 World Cup team, the first to qualify for the prestigious world tournament in forty years. While working at his All-American Soccer Camp, I was motivated to start the No.1 Goalkeeper's Camp, the first of its kind on a national level. Thank you, Walter, for this and so much more!

At the Major Indoor Soccer League (MISL), I worked for Commissioner Earl Foreman who taught me so much about the ins and outs of professional sport leagues. I consider him my third mentor. He treated me like a son and shared so much of his experience not only as an owner in soccer but also with the NFL and of course, the ABA. Thank you, Earl.

I moved on to the University of New Haven in 1969 and recruited John and Tom Kowalski to play for the soccer team. John stayed on after graduation as an assistant coach and together we started the No.1 Goalkeeper's Camp. Over the years, John and I worked on many projects, and he invited me to serve as his assistant for the US team at the first FIFA Five-a-Side World Cup. We won the bronze medal. Thank you, John, for your friendship, loyalty and soccer understanding. I learned a lot from you and still do!

Thank you to the professors and advisors at the University of Utah which guided me through the Ph.D. process to graduate in 1973 and earn the title first given to me by New Haven baseball coach Frank Vieira of "Dr. Joe". And thank you Frank for the many coaching tips and for teaching me to be respectful of the press and other media.

Thank you to Bob Gansler, head coach of the US Men's National Team for having faith in me as his assistant during the difficult qualifying process for the 1990 World Cup.

And thank you to Debbie Chin and Allen Sack for bringing me back to the University of New Haven as women's soccer coach and Associate Professor in the Management of Sport Industries Department. Specifically, to Coach Chin who taught me further respect of female athletes and to champion their cause.

Thank you to Doug Logan, Bill Sage and Sunil Gulati for having confidence in me to manage officiating and discipline issues at Major League Soccer. And for friends Herb Silva and Esse Baharmast for easing that path. And to Ivan Gazidis and especially Alfonso Mondelo for sharing their immense love of the game and friendship. Thank you to Commissioner Don Garber for sticking with me through the many on-field issues that had to be dealt with in those early MLS years. And for my fifteen-year career at soccer's highest level. Thank you for making MLS what it is today.

Thank you to Michael Cohen for thinking that I had something to offer in the broadcast booth and to all the folks at Fox Sports TV for embracing "Dr. Joe" to the point of becoming a household soccer name.

Thank you to the many players who helped build winning records at two different universities. To Dov Markus, Carlo Tramontozzi, Arnold Ramirez and Mickey Cohen at LIU, to Roberto Taylor, Krys Furman, Peter Zimmerman, Carl Babb, Rick Kessel, Mario Oliva, Carlos Palencia at New Haven and Mireille DeRose and Christine Huber with the women's team, thank you. Of course, every player contributes, in thanking these few, I am thanking you all.

When I worked at three different pro soccer leagues, the referees became my team, but I was still a coach. Thank you to all the referees for putting up with me. I always looked at officiating through a different lens: as a player, as a coach and as a league administrator.

The fifty-year success of No.1 Soccer Camps does not happen without the work and dedication of so many staff members who made it happen on the field: Greg Andrulis, Rick Schweitzer, Frans Hoek, AJ Lachowecki, Tony Pierce, Bob Barry, Clark Brisson, Mike Potier, Todd Bramble to name a few. And the many camp graduates who went on to collegiate and professional playing careers inspired by what they learned at No.1 on and off the field, thank you!

No.1 Soccer Camps was a true family affair. Thank you, Barbara, for the years behind the scenes. You did all the real work: registration, housing, shipping, insurance, advertising and so much more. Daughters Colette and Janine helped as well, they traveled the country as young girls and teenagers, forfeiting many summers, but later worked on so many tasks at the camp office and at campsites. Sisters Madelyn and Debra ran the mail order equipment and supplies business. But a life in soccer, be it as a coach, referee, administrator or broadcaster meant lots of travel and time away from home. There are sacrifices made at every level. Thank you to my immediate and extended family for your understanding and goodwill. There were so many functions, gatherings and parties missed.

Thank you to the Andrulis family; Greg, Lorrie, Rob and Maggie for their leadership and management skills which enable No.1 Soccer Camps to remain at the forefront of the ever-changing soccer camp industry.

Thank you to the members of the various committees that have honored my work with induction into nine Halls of Fame and a host of other honors. It is good to feel appreciated!

I would not have been able to make sense of the past seven decades of soccer without the help of Harri Aston, my editor of Reedsy, a fabulous conglomeration of book writing and publishing talent. And my book designer, Simon Thompson for his artistic rendering, designing the cover and organization of the many images and other details.

Putting together a memoire covering seven decades provides an opportunity to pause and reflect on the many adventures, some harrowing, some taken at great risk that comes with pursuing a life in soccer, especially in those early years. My partner for those seven decades never questioned the challenges. "Through Thick or Thin-Better or Worse" does not even begin to describe the encouragement and support I have received from the former Barbara Otlowski. Even to the point of being the first proofreader of my manuscript leading to this publication.

At one point in time, I was able to say that Barbara Machnik saw more soccer games than any woman in America. She still might hold the record. We traveled the world together. I was proud to have her by my side regardless of the circumstances be it at Ukrainian Field where she was at times the only woman there or at our first World Cup together in 1982.

Barbara cared for injured players at our house, she hosted coaches, players and their parents, referees and strangers. She was often my social lubricant in situations I found uncomfortable. It is for these and so many other reasons that I am dedicating this book to Barbara, because she lived through almost every moment. There would be nothing to write about without her!

Introduction
"Let's Bring in Dr. Joe!"

From the day I first saw soccer being played in a local park, sometime in the early 1950s, I was enthralled by the sport. It reminded me in so many ways of ice hockey, which I had begun to almost religiously follow as a kid on radio and television.

Not only were there goals and goalkeepers, but the level of passion on display sometimes spilled over into physical confrontations that required a brave official to step in and separate the warriors.

Never in my wildest dream did I ever think I would someday be able to play, coach and officiate soccer with distinction, much less to be considered in later life as someone who positively influenced the huge growth and development of soccer in America.

Perhaps it was just a case of timing and being in the right place, as so many others also have experienced as they contributed their energy and enthusiasm, time and in many cases money to what was deemed their life's work.

Maybe it was just luck!

Regardless, when Fox Sports TV launched their FS1 and FS2 sports channels in 2013 - having secured the broadcast rights to major international soccer tournaments up to and including the 2026 World Cup, it seemed only natural that they follow the successful model they initiated on their National Football League (NFL) telecasts, using a "Rules Analyst" to explain controversial or otherwise interesting officiating decisions to viewers.

So much technology was coming into soccer at the highest levels - from the use of video replays to goal-line technology, as well as computer-connected balls and limb-tracking technology to help call offside - that it was rapidly changing the way the game was officiated and that needed on-air explanation.

Finding someone who could address various points of view from a playing, coaching, officiating and administrative background with sufficient experience in the game, and who also possessed teaching abilities, became their challenge.

In writing *From the Sandlots to the World Cup — INSIDE Seven Decades of American Soccer*, I have attempted to trace my personal observations and experiences in the many roles I have been privileged to hold.

Success is never achieved without the guidance, assistance and trust of others. Hopefully, I am able to explain and acknowledge that my story is no different. There was always a teacher, coach, friend, commissioner, TV executive and, most importantly, family members whose encouragement made the difference.

A lifetime of experiences from playing, coaching and officiating in the college ranks to serving as assistant coach to two successful national teams (including an appearance in FIFA's Italia '90 World Cup), working in three professional soccer leagues, and being recognized as the Fox Sports analyst "Dr. Joe" after covering multiple World Cups and other competitions; I think my story is unique and worth sharing. In many ways it is a window into how soccer in America rose from the sandlots to the World Cup.

So, "Let's Bring in Dr. Joe!"

Chapter 1

McCarren Park
"A New Excitement"

Straddling the border between Williamsburg and Greenpoint, McCarren Park is north Brooklyn, New York's largest park. Encompassing 35 acres, it is the center of the community. The park is divided by Bedford and Driggs Avenues and Lorimer Street, dividing it into several sections. Back in the early 1950s, when I first remember going "out the park" as we referred to the three blocks needed to walk there from where I grew up in my grandma "Nana's" eight family house on Clifford Place, the park was replete with facilities for most sports. Tennis courts which seemed seldom used; a full-scale baseball field where the semi-pro Greenpoint Greys played doubleheaders every Sunday; several softball fields; cement single wall handball courts which could be played on both sides; two very busy bocce ball courts which, if they had lights, would have been active 24 hours a day; a playground, a "kiddie pool" with sprinklers and NY's third largest pool with an adjacent 16-foot deep "diving pool".

Across Lorimer Street from the pool there was a full-size field for football (seldom played there) which was also used for soccer which was surrounded by a quarter-mile cinder track which was sometimes used for bocci when the bocci courts were flooded or there were lines of men waiting to play.

There were permanent goalposts without nets cemented in at each end of the field. The field was all dirt as this was a time before in-ground watering systems were in place and well before the advent of artificial turf.

The Crosstown trolley took us from Greenpoint to Ebbets Field, where the Brooklyn Dodgers played. Back then if you saved up or found ten "Elsie the Cow" Borden ice-cream pop wrappers, ironed them and mailed them to the Dodgers, you would receive a free ticket to an afternoon game.

We did that often, at least three times a summer. We regularly watched baseball legends Musial, Ashburn, Kluszewski and Brooklyn's "Boys of Summer". And it was the time of "Willie, Mickey and the Duke" so getting to Yankee Stadium or the Polo Grounds easily on the subway was also an option which we took advantage of.

I don't remember when I first became a New York Ranger hockey fan. I recall my father taking me to my first game in 1953 at the old Madison Square Garden, a 6-1 Ranger victory over the Toronto Maple Leafs, with my favorite Ranger player at the time, Ivan Irwin, scoring a rare goal from the blue line.

For some reason, the CBS televised Saturday afternoon *Game of the Week* was only able to show fixtures involving the four US-based teams. Rosters included only 16 players back then and with no helmets, a fan could easily remember every player by their face and number (never higher than 27 in those early days) and without the names on the backs of their jerseys.

During one game between periods, the play-by-play announcer Bud Palmer attempted to show new hockey fans how hard Ranger player Andy Bathgate could shoot the puck, a one inch by three-inch piece of frozen, vulcanized rubber. Palmer stood to the side of a goal and held a car door upright on the ice. Bathgate's initial shot missed the car door and rebounded off the boards, hitting Palmer in the back of the leg. Writhing in pain, Palmer proved the point. A second Bathgate shot hit the target, causing a huge dent.

Another great hockey moment on TV was when the Rangers traveled to the Rockefeller Center skating rink to take on the Steve Allen All-Stars which contained his regular Sunday night crew of personalities he would interview as "Man in the Street", namely Louis Nye, Tom Poston, Don Knotts and former Bowery Boy Gabe Dell. Allen hung a Venetian blind in his goal to hold out the puck. As far as I know, there is no video record of this event.

And I was there at the Garden when Andy Bathgate's backhander hit Montreal goalie Jacques Plante in the face, requiring him to return to the game wearing a mask. And the night Ranger players led by Vic Hadfield climbed the high glass behind the goal to protect their coach Emil Francis from an attack after he had left the bench to dispute a goal judge decision.

So, what has all this to do with soccer or even with McCarren Park? Patience, please!

I attended St. Anthony's Roman Catholic Parochial Elementary School which I was able to walk to from home and even walk home for lunch.

I played (if you could call it that) baseball for Brother Christopher's St. Anthony's team and McCarren Park was our home field. We had a permit! One night we had a road game at New Farmer's Oval on Metropolitan Ave., not knowing at the time that I would return there playing a different sport with a much more meaningful purpose.

I also played basketball for St. Anthony's and once scored ten points in a game; five two-handed set shots from the side corner; no backboard, no rim. Swish!

And I played in the very first year of Greenpoint's Little League Baseball program. My team was sponsored by Mutual Motors Pontiac while my best friend Tommy Cosgrove (Cossie) played for Von Dolen's Ice Cream Parlor. We played on two sandlot fields constructed on land donated in 1953 by the Brooklyn Union Gas Company near the northern most border of Greenpoint near the Newtown Creek.

Somehow, my baseball coaches figured out I really could catch, and I started out as a first baseman before moving to catcher where I seemed to flourish blocking wild pitches, blocking the plate and surviving collisions while holding on to the ball and generally having fun — except when it was my turn in the line-up to come up to bat! I was a no-hit wonder!

"Strike Three!" Once, I was told by a coach that the only way I would get my name in lights was to, "Change it to Exit!"

Cossie and I did everything together. Cossie lived at 21 Clifford Place, down the block from my number 11. And when I came home from Connecticut after visiting relatives in Old Lyme, a trip that brought me to my first stock car race at the Waterford Speedbowl in 1953, as a ten-year-old, I couldn't wait to tell Cossie all about it. It was then that we almost religiously started watching a filmed weekly program out of California called *Jalopy Derby*. And when the baseball Giants left the Polo Grounds in NY vacant, a racing promoter named Ed Otto (one of the founders of NASCAR) brought racing to that venue every Saturday night for three summers until the METS were born. Cossie and I did not miss a race! You could get there by subway!

My first job as a ten-year-old was to get coffee every night for the factory workers down the block.

In later years I made additional money in a variety of ways. I became the lead altar boy at St. Anthony's and that had benefits which went beyond the religious. Being assigned to a Saturday afternoon wedding, for instance, could generate a five or ten-dollar bill from a nervous groom or best man. That, for what was a 15-minute service. Weddings were always on Saturday, but funerals were during the week, usually at 10:30am, which meant getting out of class for at least an hour.

Then I was offered the chance to clean two floors of the Bingo Hall on Saturday mornings. That's another five bucks, but much harder work.

Sometimes, for additional money, I shoveled snow off the church steps or got to use the gas-powered snow blower to clear the sidewalks. I loved that assignment! I didn't like it as much when, because of the snow and mush, I had to mop up the tile aisles and vestibule using industrial cleaning fluid.

But the absolute best job I ever had was playing the 45 RPM records at the Wednesday and Sunday night church-sponsored "sock hop" dances at the parish hall. It was here that I first asked Barbara Otlowski to dance! I had made up my mind as early as then that she would be the future Mrs. Joseph A. Machnik. And this was the start of my love affair with doo-wop!

After serving the 12:30pm Mass on Sunday, I would go out to McCarren Park to kill some time before going to the traditional NY Ranger hockey game which typically started at 7pm.

On most Sundays, I saw nets on the soccer goals held down with stakes in the back and ropes to hold the net away from the cross bar. I used to like to stand behind the goal and make believe I was the goalkeeper. The skills the goalkeeper used seemed like something I could deal with; remember, I could catch. And there was angle play, just like the hockey goalies had to use, and an area of the field where they seemed to be able to use their hands to catch and hold the ball just like hockey's "crease", but of course much bigger.

And while penalty shots were rare in hockey back then (there was no tie-breaking penalty shot shootout), there seemed to be quite a bit more in soccer where the one v one challenge between kicker and goalkeeper (not goalie) seemed to have some comparison.

The game was officiated in a fashion like hockey, with one referee and two linesmen. I could figure out that the linesmen signaled when the ball went over the chalk boundary lines, but I had no idea what the other flags were for until I learned that, just like in hockey, there was the whole concept of offside. It would be many more years before linesmen's duties were increased and their title changed to Assistant Referees.

While hockey has the stationary offside blue line, soccer's blue line moves with the last defender (second to last if you include the goalkeeper). Really, a difficult concept. No wonder some 30 years later the North American Soccer League (NASL) experimented with a stationary 35-yard offside line.

If I could have seen the future back then, I would have paid more attention to the referee as officiating was to play an important role in my future employment in the Major Indoor Soccer League, Major League Soccer and Fox Sports.

Then one Sunday there were more than a thousand fans surrounding the field. The visiting team were wearing red and black striped shirts, black shorts and black socks with red stripes across the top. I learned they were the New York Ukrainians! There was an excitement in the crowd that I had not witnessed before. The crowd could hardly be restrained, they were two and three deep surrounding the entire field. I had company behind the goal. They spoke a foreign language. It sometimes sounded like the Polish spoken in my grandmother's house on my father's side of the family. I was a second-generation Polish American but I knew nothing about soccer. But that Sunday's memory lasts with me until this day. Was it just a coincidence with later life experiences or just a chance happening?

Greenpoint Little League... 1955 (age 12) standing second from left......good fielder but a "no hit wonder" as my father used to say. I hadn't yet decided to be a catcher.

With Brother Christopher's St. Anthony's team at New Farmers Oval. Kneeling second from the left. Note the catcher's glove (mit) and cut off sleeves imitating my favorite player Ted Kluszewski.

RARIN' TO GO—Perhaps a bit short on uniforms, the St. Anthony of Padua junior baseball team is every bit as long on talent and hustle. The young local crew competed in the Catholic Youth Organization Baseball League and made a fine showing for Greenpoint and their parish.

Chapter 2

Brooklyn Technical High School
"So You Can Be The Goalkeeper"

How I got into Brooklyn Technical High School is still a mystery. "Tech", as it was known, was one of New York City high schools for which there was an entrance exam. The others were Bronx High School of Science, Stuyvesant and Aviation. My father graduated from Stuyvesant.

Tech was a huge building, eight stories high not counting the radio studio on the ninth floor. Six thousand students at a time. Two huge gymnasiums, a swimming pool and just about every kind of shop you could think of: woodworking, machine, foundry, sheet metal and there was even a shop where, each semester, students framed a house. It was an all-boys school.

Tech offered many programs: Electrical, Mechanical, Aeronautical, Structural and Architectural Engineering. Coming from a parochial elementary school without a background in science, never having ever been in a shop or lab class or taken a physics class, I was advised to register in their most vanilla course of study, College Prep. I still had to take and pass all the shops (my first was pattern making) physics, chemistry, eight terms of math and four terms of Scientific German, which would later become important!

To say that I struggled at Tech is an understatement! I was up against brilliant fellow students of all ethnic backgrounds, some of whom were bringing early calculators in the form of a slide rule to class!

In the spring semester of my sophomore year in Mrs. Greenberg's English class (she was one of the very few female teachers at Tech), I had the good fortune to sit down next to fellow student Andrew Sheparovich, who I later learned was born in Lviv, Ukraine. His nickname was "Shep".

We started talking about hockey and after learning that he was from Ukraine, I mentioned that the Boston Bruins (NHL) had a forward line of

Johnny Bucyk, Vic Stasiuk and former Ranger Bronco Horvath. They called the line the "UKE LINE" although there was speculation that Horvath was not Ukrainian.

There were lots of named lines in hockey back then. One of my favorites was the Century Line of NY Rangers Edgar Laprade and brothers Max and Doug Bentley, whose combined age was over 100 years.

Shep asked me if I had ever played soccer. Of course, my answer was an honest "No!", but I did have that McCarren Park experience to fall back on and at least be able to engage in a semi-intelligent conversation (I thought) about the game.

Then Shep asked: "Would you like to try out for the team?" I really liked having my new friend and didn't want to disappoint or lose him. I told Shep that I had never played soccer. He then said: "So you can be the goalkeeper."

The team was practicing in the eighth-floor gym, and I knew that I had a chance to make the team because I could catch, and I knew angle play from hockey and watching the games in McCarren Park.

The players set up two gym poles the size of a goal and put down gym mats for me to stand on. Then they started taking shots from various distances. Of course, with angle play, I couldn't stay on the mat, instead needing to come off the line to reduce the angle. That meant getting hit with shots from close range, making kick saves (like a hockey goalie) where necessary and even diving on the wooden floor. I must have impressed coach Arthur Peck substantially enough to qualify for next fall's junior varsity (JV) season.

As an aside, and unbeknownst to me at the time, the varsity team members were practicing on the roof which at Tech was enclosed by giant covered screens so that a ball (or student) couldn't be propelled over the wall and wind up eight stories down. That outdoor play area became my home at Tech for the balance of my time there, four semesters of junior and senior years. Because if you were on the soccer team, you didn't have to go to gym class or study hall but instead you could go up to the eighth floor and "practice" with your friends. We used two metal doors as goals and knew the goal was clean from the sound of the ball hitting it square. The playing surface was roof tile, so there were lots of slipping and sliding but no one went to ground to make a tackle or block a shot.

Tech had no outdoor practice facilities. We sometimes ran at Fort Greene Park across the street and climbed the steps up to the monument there.

Our "home" field was in Fort Hamilton along the Belt Parkway, and you had to take the subway to get there. Many of our road opponents had their own field, however. The upside of being at Fort Hamilton at the time was being able to watch the Verrazano-Narrows Bridge being built, even if you weren't an engineering student. It was amazing!

One of the real advantages of being on a team at Tech was being assigned to a special "team homeroom". The soccer team homeroom was "T2" and my new homeroom classmates were not only Shep and the players I competed against while trying out the previous Spring but also members of the Varsity, the best team in the City at the time and NY City Public School Athletic League (PSAL) Champions in 1958. These guys were men, and although they pretty much kept to themselves, they were idols to us junior varsity (JV) guys. Most famous of that Championship team was Rimantis "Ray" Klivecka, who led the city in scoring with 43 goals. There were other fabulous players, like Otto Stanaitis, Bruno Nemickis, Reinhold Theiss and goalkeeper Walter Sprance but they were all graduating the following Spring, and it was going to be up to us JV guys to fill their shoes and keep the Tech legacy alive the following fall.

In any event, the JV season of 1958 with Mr. Norman as our coach must have been successful enough to keep me in the soccer team homeroom for the next year. Certainly, my grades still needed help. Fortunately, my friends Shep and his pal Jarapolk "Jerry" Kalyna (aka "Whitey") and friend and teammate John Nussbaumer would come to our apartment in Greenpoint, and they would tutor me and help me with my studies. I just did not get it. I did not have that math aptitude. I barely made it to be eligible for the varsity my senior year.

I don't remember any of those JV games and the records may not have even been kept. But my performance in goal, my "kamikaze style" as it was described, was sufficient for Shep to bring me to his club team to play in their junior soccer system and that team was the NY Ukrainians! How ironic!

My senior year at Tech as a member of the Varsity was quite eventful. I started as the back-up goalkeeper and later won the starting job. The team finished with a record of 12 wins from 14 games. We made the PSAL playoffs, won a few games and then came up against eventual champions Grover Cleveland High School. The semi-final game was played on Saturday afternoon at Pratt Institute Field a mile or so up DeKalb Ave. from Brooklyn Tech.

Grover Cleveland was located across the street from Metropolitan Oval, the home of three stalwart soccer clubs in the powerful German American Soccer League: Blau-Weiss Gottschee, NY German-Hungarians and DSC Brooklyn. Among the future famous Grover Cleveland players coming out of that area at the time were Sigi Stritzl, Gunther Haug, and most notably, Walter Loske, whose last club was Austrian side SK Sturm Graz.

In the game, I remember Loske breaking down on my right side, getting free for a shot that was so quick and powerful that it knocked me over. I recovered to pounce on the ball before he could get there and to this day remember hearing my first applause for making a save! We lost the game 3-0 and, with it, the City Championship dream. Mr. Peck consoled me in the locker room after the game and said that he had "never seen a goalkeeper play better".

A week after our elimination, the team was treated to a post-season dinner at the nearby Norwegian Seamen's Home. It was my very first experience with a true smorgasbord of raw fish, clams and oysters, a treat that I will long remember.

Fortunately, there were a lot of people at that game that were of the same opinion as Mr. Peck. Long Island University's (LIU) coach Gary Rosenthal was mandated to start building a soccer program at its Brooklyn Campus just two blocks from Tech. He wanted Ray Klivecka to lead his attack and Mr. Peck convinced him to take a chance on me as goalkeeper. LIU had not won a game the two seasons before, what did they have to lose?!

Notably, that PSAL Tournament game was the only match played that my mother came to watch. She just could not stand the pressure and the play in front of the goal. She said it was too dangerous. "And how could they hit the ball with their heads?" But my father, after asking "What do you know about soccer?", when I told him that I had made the Brooklyn Tech team, he became a huge fan!

One Saturday, while working part-time in the local "A&P" supermarket, I learned that TVs *ABC's Wide World of Sports* was going to air its first-ever live soccer game, the English FA Cup final between Tottenham Hotspur and Leicester City. I asked my manager to give me two hours off from work to be able to watch the game. He realized how important that was for me and agreed to my request.

The game was most memorable for Leicester's full-back injuring his leg after five minutes of play. Because there were no substitutions back then, he had to finish the game as a "walking player" on the wing. It was later learned that he had a broken bone in his leg. He finally left the field with ten minutes to play with Tottenham leading 2-0, which was how the game ended.

Back at the supermarket, after closing, I would sweep the floors of saw dust and mop up using the same industrial cleaner that we used at St. Anthony's to mop the aisles and vestibule.

I graduated from Brooklyn Tech and am very proud of that fact. I learned one of the most important lessons of my life that I sometimes joke about: No way was I prepared, and no way did I want to ever become an engineer.

But the best memory was graduation night as me, Shep, Whitey, John Nussbaumer and teammates Jurgen Broner and Ewald Karbiner (Mr. Peck called Nussbaumer and Karbiner the "best two crisscrossing wings in the city" which we often teased them about) went to a bar in Ridgewood where Broner and Karbiner were known and we drank beer all night long, revisiting our memories, telling stories and listening to the Tokens sing *The Lion Sleeps Tonight* on the jukebox. Years later when Disney's *The Lion King* debuted and used the song, my granddaughter, Olivia, was incredulous that I would know every word. She thought it was a new song.

"A Wimoweh!"

Shep left the New York area to raise a family in Cleveland. He remained actively involved in the local Ukrainian club and became recognized for his contributions to soccer there. He has a field named after him and in 2023 was inducted into the Ukrainian Sports Hall of Fame. He also became a referee and worked in the Major Indoor Soccer League.

We stayed in touch over the years, Shep and his family visiting us in Connecticut and during the time that I was studying at the University of Utah. Shep's oldest son, Michael, became a goalkeeper of some renown and was a principal staff member of the early No.1 Goalkeeper's Camp that I later founded in 1977.

Without Tech, I would have never met my friends Shep, Whitey and John. Never played soccer at any level. Never would have been accepted to play at Long Island University and never had the opportunity to know, love and play for the New York Ukrainians! Never had the honor and privilege of meeting Walter Chyzowych, watching him play and coach and working with and for him at so many different levels.

Thank you, Brooklyn Tech!

Brooklyn Tech's varsity team in 1959. Kneeling third from the left with the ball. Teammate John Nussbaumer is standing third from the left and Andrew ("Shep") Sheparovich who brought me to the team is standing fifth from the left.

The Machnik Family in 1959; parents Joe and Viola and sisters Madelyn (14) and Debra (6).

Chapter 3

The New York Ukrainians Sports Club
"TEMPO YCK"

I was introduced to the New York Ukrainians with my friend Shep's invitation to play in their junior team system. The NY Ukrainian team was nicknamed "YCK!" (pronounced "Oosk"), which is short for Ukrayinskyi Sportovyi Klub, or Ukrainian Sports Club. And when their many fans wanted to inspire the team from the sidelines, they screamed "TEMPO YCK".

Shep was to play for the Ukrainian Junior B team that season and they needed a shot-stopper. So, on a Wednesday afternoon I boarded the GG at the Nassau Avenue station for one stop and transferred to the 14th St. BMT line to ride into Manhattan. Exiting at 14th St., there was a short six-block walk south on the east side of Third Avenue to Eighth Street which for three blocks between Cooper Square, the home of Cooper Union University and Tompkins Square Park, is named St. Mark's Place.

The reason I had to be there was to sign a registration form and present two photos for my player pass in the German American Soccer League (GASL) which, along with the rival American Soccer League (ASL), was arguably considered among the two top leagues in the Greater NY area, if not the country.

The address of the YCK headquarters was 12 St. Mark's Place, considered today to be a historic landmark in the East Village. Built in 1885, it had previously been home to the German American Shooting Club. There was a non-affiliated bar/restaurant on the street level floor, the Ukrainian Club occupied the second and third floors. The third floor was mostly for storage of equipment, uniforms and the like while the second floor was a large room with tables and chairs, a ping-pong table, a TV in the corner and a small bar area with a refrigerator where beer/soda etc. could be served. Here I met my new coach, Mr. Popovich, signed the paperwork and received a black goalkeeper jersey with padded elbows, padded shorts and black socks. Our team jersey was red and black striped, the same uniform I saw approximately ten years earlier in McCarren Park.

Without a practice of any sort or meeting other teammates, I learned that our first game was the following Sunday against Sport Club (SC) New York at their field known as Throggs Neck Stadium, and that I had to be at the clubhouse at 8:30am so we could meet and travel on the subway for the 11am kick-off in the Bronx.

Throggs Neck Stadium was no stadium at all. It was a sandlot field behind a German restaurant/bar that SC New York called home. The field was surrounded by fencing and was right on the water in the shadow of the Throggs Neck Bridge which was under construction. As a Tech graduate, I marvelled at being able to play beneath a second bridge as I previously watched the Verrazano-Narrows Bridge being built within view of our high school field in Ft. Hamilton.

There was not a blade of grass to be found. I once joked when speaking about the development of youth soccer in America that there was no "grassroots youth soccer" because there was no grass. I found the conditions to be the same regardless of where we played, home or away. It was truly "sandlot" soccer.

We were thoroughly outplayed that day, but we lost by the slightest of margins, 1-0, and I realized why they gave me padded shorts and a jersey with padded elbows.

That night my pajamas stuck to the "raspberries" on the outside of each of my thighs and my left elbow hurt like hell, but I felt good about my game. So did my teammates. And Mr. Popovich was already telling all those back at YCK that they had found a goalkeeper!

After the game I was told that there would be training every Thursday night at the Chelsea High School Gym. The juniors would train early, starting at 6:30pm. The seniors would come in after that, and we were permitted to watch them train.

One night after the obligatory running of laps around the gym, with the last person needing to sprint to the front on the trainer's whistle and similar tasks and commands, the goalposts were set up and the mats put down as it was time to scrimmage. Trying to impress as always on one shot to my left, I dove past the mat and hit my head on the wooden floor, opening a sizable gash above my left eye. It was now about 9pm at night and going to the emergency room for stitches did not seem an option. I was told the official team physician was Dr. Voyevidka and that I should go to see him after school the next day. By this time, the good doctor determined that it was too late to stitch the wound, so butterfly band aids became the order of the day. I do not remember if a tetanus shot was given, or antibiotics were prescribed.

The Ukrainian community in NY was flourishing at the time and there were significant numbers of players to support two junior teams (A&B), two reserve teams (the "B" reserves had the nickname "Sluggers") and the first team. Typically, on Sunday, the Sluggers would have a 9am kick-off, one of the junior teams would play at 11, the main reserve team would play at 1pm and the first or senior team would start their game at 2:30 or 3pm.

While Shep and I played for the junior B team, Whitey had made the junior A team along with another Tech alumnus, Wasyl Panczak, who was known as "Pancho". Nicknames were popular among the Ukrainians, and I later came to know "Cool Baby" Kulba, "Junior" Walter Schmotolocha, and many others by their pet names only. One player had the nickname "Kangaroo" and there was also "Kangaroo's brother".

Our second game was to be a home game, and our home field was New Farmer's Oval on Metropolitan Avenue, the current site of Christ the King High School. This was the same New Farmer's Oval where I played baseball that one night for St. Anthony's, now laid out with two separate soccer fields. The Ukrainians' designated field was the one furthest from the road parallel to a stone wall which separated it from a cemetery. Again, there was no grass to be found. A true sandlot!

Cossie and I remained close, and he came with me to the game and several more that year and the next. But we had begun to live separate lives. He went to Chelsea High School and studied to be an electrician, while I was at Brooklyn Tech and soccer and my new friends and teammates consumed me!

We had a decent record that year 1958-59, winning more than losing and never embarrassing ourselves until we were paired up against an A-level team in the McGuire Cup National Junior Championship Tournament. That was our first visit to historic Eintracht Oval near the foot of Steinway Street in Astoria, Queens, home of Eintracht SC, and the team of my Tech friend, John Nussbaumer.

Eintracht Oval was unique, fully enclosed with a covered grandstand on one side and a picnic area behind the goal at one end. The field was several feet below street level, which gave it a real stadium feel. The playing surface was crushed cinder and coke and was mostly black in color. I loved it and it would become my favorite field. Unfortunately, Eintracht sold the field in 1967, and the location is now the site of a shopping center and its parking lot!

I watched many games at Eintracht Oval. One night, my soccer friends and I saw the West Berlin All Stars play the NY Hungarians, the best team in New York at the time as many players had come from Hungary after the revolution in 1956. Eintracht Oval was also the venue for my first experience watching the fabulous Philadelphia Ukrainian Nationals with Mike Noha and Alex Ely playing in the Open Cup. The Philadelphia Ukrainians were known as "Tryzub", meaning three teeth, which is their national logo and appears on so much of Ukrainian lore.

The German American Soccer League (GASL) had three Senior Divisions, the highest named the Oberliga. To be recognized as a soccer power and to regularly play at the better fields such as Eintracht and Metropolitan Ovals, Schuetzen Park and Farcher's Grove in New Jersey, a team aspired to be in the Oberliga. There were ten teams in each division. With the process of promotion and relegation, a team could start in the bottom division and make it all the way to the top.

I watched one Saturday afternoon as YCK failed to get promoted into the Oberliga after losing to DSC Brooklyn at Eintracht Oval.

There was some hope for the following season, however, as the NY Ukrainians had purchased land in the College Point section of Queens and had built their own field, "Ukrainian Field", where they could control and charge admission (usually two bucks) and not have to pay rent elsewhere.

YCK finally made it into the Oberliga with the help of new players Walter and Gene Chyzowych, Zenon Snylyk and others.

The Junior A team to which I was promoted for the 1959-60 season captured The GASL Junior Division "White Division" Championship for which I received my first plaque — and it had my name on it!

During my time with both junior teams, I continued the practice of staying after my 11am game to watch the reserve team play but more specifically to stand behind the goal during first-team games. I wanted to continue to learn as much as possible about the goalkeeping position. There were terrific goalkeepers at several clubs which I focused on: Geza

Henni of the NY Hungarians, Hungary's former Olympic goalkeeper with 16 international appearances (caps); Uwe Schwart of Eintracht and Sandor Baranyi, who had a brief stint with DSC Brooklyn. When Bill Cox started the International Soccer League (ISL) with double-headers every Sunday at Randall's Island Stadium, the Polo Grounds and elsewhere, I had a host of top-level goalkeepers to imitate and emulate.

I learned that there was a goalkeeper in Poland named Jozef Machnik who had two games with the national team and careers with Gornik Zabrze and Zaglebie Sosnowiec. He unfortunately broke his leg in an ISL game in Chicago. I got phone calls from friends inquiring about my injury because, after all, how many Jozef (Joseph) Machniks are out there? I felt honored for some to think I could play at that level.

After graduating from the juniors, I was promoted to the first reserve team and continued the practice of watching first-team games from behind the goal.

It wasn't enough for the NY Ukrainians to just be in the Oberliga, they wanted to win it all including the National Open Cup (a open knockout competition started in 1914 now known as the Lamar Hunt Open Cup) which their sister club in Philadelphia had already won several times.

To further improve their team, YCK had contact with the Toronto Ukrainians as well as Toronto Italia, Toronto Roma and Toronto City to bring players down from Canada each Sunday. Among those were John Young, later to play for the original Cosmos, Gordon Bradley, the first Cosmos coach, former Sunderland legend Ted Purdon, Anders Yrfeldt, and goal scorer Peter Smethurst. Additionally, Mario Paz of Belenenses, Portugal, stayed in the US after his team's appearance in the ISL and became, along with Bradley, the team's trainers. Bradley, Purdon and Smethurst would become stalwarts on the team for several years. Walter Chyzowych led the team and the league in scoring that year.

Clearly, the NY Ukrainians were no longer an amateur team. As I was now enrolled in Long Island University, there was a chance I could jeopardize my college soccer eligibility by being associated with a professional club. NCAA rules prohibited practice or playing with a professional team or players.

I was fortunate to secure my release from the Ukrainians and play for a GASL Third Division (1. Liga) team College Point FC. At College Point, I was joined by two teammates from LIU, Paul Bertrand and Norbert Reich, and two former Brooklyn Tech players, Johnny and Walter Schneider. College Point had a great clubhouse, the Village Grove on 14th Ave. It was a German restaurant with a full bar and a shuffleboard table. Their home field was at the former Flushing Airport, a huge expanse of property that was still big enough to land a small plane.

I had two terrific seasons playing for College Point, the second of which I made the 1. Liga All Stars team which would play against the Second Division (Liga) All Stars in a preliminary match to the Oberliga (first division) All Stars playing a team from Germany in the GASL's annual Soccer Festival at Randalls Island. Unfortunately, I made a huge error mishandling a low cross at the near post which resulted in an own goal, or as reported in the German newspaper Staats Zeitung und Herald, an "eigen Tor". My side lost the game 2-1 to goalkeeper Yuri Kulishenko, a Ukrainian legend, representing the second division.

In addition, the GASL published a listing of the Most Valuable Players in each division, and that year I finished second in the MVP race to Art Lavery of Stamford. I was the only College Point Player of the twenty-two players chosen. My friend, John Nussbaumer, also received votes playing for Eintracht, now in the second division, which tied him with three others as the fifth most valuable player. The overall top vote-getter in the Oberliga was NY Hungarian's Andrew Mate, their leading goal scorer, with Gordon Bradley placing sixth. Mate would go on to have a noteworthy career in Europe with Hamburger SV.

Probably, my best and favorite game playing for College Point was a 2-1 win over the Lithuanians played at Bushwick High School Field. The Lithuanians featured my LIU teammates Ray Klivecka and Steve Nagy, and the game had lots of meaning on campus. I did not know it at the time but my play in goal at College Point was being tracked by my former club, New York Ukrainians.

With my three seasons of college eligibility at LIU over in 1963, I was contacted to return to the NY Ukrainians, this time for a contract to be the back-up goalkeeper for the first team while playing every Sunday for the reserves. I was paid $35 per game. By this time the Ukrainians were being sponsored by K&B meat market and its owner Jaroslaw (Jerry) Kurowycky, who could be seen in many of the team photos of that time. The team's maroon sweatsuits were lettered on the back with a 12-inch "K&B".

One of the highlights of my soccer-playing life occurred on a particular

Sunday when the fog was so deep around the NY area, due to melting snow and an unusually warm early spring day, that the players who were to fly in from Toronto could not make it as all flights were cancelled.

I helped the reserves win 4-2 in the preliminary reserve team game before being called upon to suit up as an outfield player for the first team in the second match. Our first-team goalkeeper Nelson Yebleski was excellent and available. Without the players from Canada, however, we would start the game with only nine players. I asked for Peter Smethurst's number nine jersey — perhaps I could fool the opponents for a while when chasing balls up front!

Walter Chyzowych was now playing for Giuliana (our opponent in both games) and had signed with a record bonus of $2,000. I took some pride in defending against him on corner kicks!

Late in the game we had a free kick just outside the top of the penalty area on the left side of the field. Walter Schmotolocha hit a low drive wide of the goal and I stayed onside long enough to try to slide the ball past Giuliana's goalkeeper Favellato. Unfortunately, I was a fraction late and did not contact the ball. There was a huge roar from the Eintracht Oval crowd about the missed chance.

The game finished 0-0.

Ukrainian Field was wide open, and there was a parking area for cars behind the nearest goal as one walked past the ticket booth. During extreme cold weather, spectators could stay in their cars and still see most of the field. Whenever YCK scored a goal, they would blare their car horns. Typically, when I was defending that goal, spectators just walking in would come behind the goal and ask me in Ukrainian for the score. I got used to the question and was able to answer mostly in English, but I also knew Ukrainian for low numbers. And of course, if I hadn't yet let in a goal; I was always proud to answer; "Zero!". I was now fully adopted into the Ukrainian community. One Ukrainian gentleman explained to me that the word "Mach" had something to do with the poppy seed used in Christmas and Easter cakes and that the Machnik's must have been bakers or farmers. Of course, in German, Machnik (Macht Nicht) can be translated into "it doesn't matter", which was hardly my case, at least I believed.

At the other end of Ukrainian Field, up against Flushing Bay, we could watch Shea Stadium being built and would lament why we were playing on a sandlot.

One winter, the GASL sponsored an indoor tournament at the 34th Street Armory in Manhattan. The Ukrainians entered the competition and brought down Ted Purdon and others from Canada as a sign that they were going after the championship. The playing surface was splintered and creaky from the heavy armored vehicles that ran there and that might have been the reason I was given the start. I was a good shot-stopper, not so strong in the air; but the indoor game did not feature the aerial crosses which often gave me difficulty. I don't remember if the goals were full size or not, but it didn't matter to me, I was going to save everything.

In the middle of the game with the Ukrainians leading, a fire alarm went off! The game continued for a while as the alarm continued to blare until the PA announcer in both German and English called for a mandatory evacuation. Yes, there was a real fire and now it was a rush to the emergency exits. The balance of that night's play was cancelled, and the indoor tournament was not rescheduled.

During Easter Week of 1965 an international tournament was scheduled for Randalls Island Downing Stadium, a 22,000-seat concrete edifice with lights that were rumored to have been taken from Ebbets Field in Brooklyn after the Dodgers left for Los Angeles. The tournament was to feature the GASL's best team at the time, the NY Ukrainians, with its huge crowd following and three international opponents: Aris Thessaloniki of Greece (sure to bring several thousand spectators that followed the NY Greek Americans each Sunday), Fiorentina of Italy and Eintracht Frankfurt of Germany. The tournament was to be played as a Sunday afternoon, Wednesday night, Sunday afternoon affair.

The GASL hired a public relations firm to promote the tournament and arranged for players to be interviewed on local television. Since many of YCK's players were in Canada and few of the others spoke broken English, I was selected to be spokesperson for the team. The first show was ABC's *Nightlife*. The program was hosted by comedian Jack Carter. The plan was to knock the ball around, get Carter involved and answer questions about soccer in general and specifically the tournament. I did all the talking!

The second opportunity was on Joe Franklin's *Memory Lane*, a daily afternoon program with guests on WOR Channel 9. This was a live show without an audience broadcast from a small studio somewhere in NY. For some reason, I was not nervous in front of the camera and was told the interview went well. There was no juggling exhibition or demonstration, and I was happy about that!

I showed up to the locker room before our first Easter Tournament game with my full bag of equipment, expecting to once again be on the bench as Nelson Yebleski's back-up. Upon entering the room I saw Uwe Schwart, arguably the best goalkeeper in the league at the time, dressing as if getting ready to play. Yebleski was there as well.

I was then taken aside and explained that I would not be dressing for these games. I must have shown obvious disappointment, but I did not immediately leave the locker room or pull an attitude. Then I saw a conversation take place between Gordon Bradley, our coach and leader at the time, which I later understood to have gone like this: Bradley: "We are going to need Joe as back-up down the stretch of the regular season." Management: "But if we allow him to dress, we will have three goalkeepers and we will have to pay him." Bradley: "If that's what it takes, that is what must be done."

Bradley stuck up for me and it was an important moment. Years later, when I saw Gordon in Washington DC at a NASL party before the Soccer Bowl Championship Game between the NY Cosmos and Ft. Lauderdale Strikers, he reminded me of the incident. Somehow, it must have been important to him as well!

In any event, the Ukrainians lost the first game 5-1 to Fiorentina. Ted Purdon scored the lone goal for YCK. He wore the number 9 for the game as Peter Smethurst did not make the trip. Purdon usually wore the number 10. He explained to me after the game: "When you wear number 9 you have to score!"

It was the only goal of the three-game tournament for the Ukrainians, who lost 2-0 to Eintracht Frankfurt but came away with a satisfying 0-0 tie in the last game against Aris!

We were at the top of the Oberliga table and making a good run at the National Challenge Cup. The pressure to win an Open Cup was huge as sister club Tryzub in Philadelphia had won it three times between 1959 and 1963. After defeating the NY German Hungarians in the quarter-final 2-1, YCK had to overcome the Philadelphia Ukrainians and did so with a

4-3 aggregate win over two games.

Now it all came down to a home and away playoff series against Chicago Hansa with star striker Willy Roy. Hansa had gotten to the final by defeating St. Louis Kutis and the Los Angeles Kickers. (An excellent article: *Open Cup Rewind: When the Ukrainians Ruled America* by Jonah Fontella, written for US Soccer on April 27, 2017, accurately describes the time, the tension and the environment.)

The first game of the home and away series was played on June 27th and finished in a disappointing 1-1 draw for the Ukrainian home side. All the marbles would be on the line for the final winner-takes-all rematch in Chicago. The date for the final in Chicago was set for July 4th.

I was not able to be with my team the NY Ukrainians for this historic game in Chicago and celebrate the accomplishment of their winning the Open Cup. Obviously, after spending more than ten years rising through the club's ranks and becoming the back-up goalkeeper, this was a huge personal disappointment! The Ukrainians were disappointed in my decision as well and later informed me that I would not be a member of the team the following season.

Fortunately, I was able to secure a try-out with the Newark Ukrainians (known as Chornomorska Sitch or Sitch), which was being coached by Gene Chyzowych, and which featured his brother Walter finishing up his illustrious career up front along with other Ukrainian notables Zenon Snylyk and my friend from the Ukrainian junior A team, Anatol Popovich. Sitch was playing in the American Soccer League in 1966-67 a whole new and different set of opponents for me. There was no reserve team, so I started as back-up goalkeeper and our first game was on the road in Connecticut against New Britain.

We were joined by a group of fans on the bus, and it was packed. One of the supporters started a pool which for a $2 entry fee the participant could pick a blind score out of a hat. If the game ended with that score, the winner would be paid the full prize which amounted to $88.

I did not start the game, but with Sitch leading 3-0 at half-time, coach Gene Chyzowych decided there could be little harm putting me in goal for the second half.

Early in the second half, Popovich played the ball back to me on my left-hand side of the goal. Either the pass was too soft, or I was too slow coming off the line, and the attacking player beat me to the ball, went around me and scored, making it 3-1. Shortly thereafter, there was confusion between me and my central defender (sweeper back then) and his back header went over me for a goal. It was now 3-2 and panic was setting in, not only my own but for those in front of me and on the bench.

Then late in the game, with New Britain in full force pressing for the equalizer, I was able to make a save in the upper right-hand corner of the goal, diving at full reach to catch and hold the ball. The save was so good that it made the two goals scored against me look suspect.

When we got back to the bus, everyone was shocked when I revealed I had the result as 3-2 for Sitch in the bettor's pool. It looked like I manipulated the game for $88! Trust me, I did not! However, Walter Chyzowych thought it was the coolest thing!

Sitch played its home matches at Ironbound Field in Newark, which was also shared by the ASL's Newark Portuguese. Later, games were played at Ironbound Stadium, a field which was closed in 1987 when toxic levels of PCBs and other chemicals were discovered. It was declared an EPA Superfund site and has been totally rehabilitated. But at $35 dollars for a win and $15 for a tie, was it worth the risk playing there?

Remarkably, Michael Lewis, in his book *Alive and Kicking —The Incredible but True Story of the Rochester Lancers*, cites that goalkeeper Joe Machnyk denied Lancer player Nelson Bergamo on a 1v1 opportunity in a Lancer 2-0 loss to Newark Ukrainians Sitch. The Ukrainians often spelled my last name with a "nyk" instead of an "nik" to make it look more Ukrainian (see page 36 in Lewis' book).

After moving to Connecticut in 1969, I played two seasons for New Haven City in the Connecticut State League. Our side was made up of mostly college coaches: Jim Kullman of Fairfield U, Hubert Vogelsinger of Yale, Don Wynschenk of New Haven College, Efrain "Chico" Chacurian, an assistant at Southern Connecticut State. On occasion Brown University All-American Ben Brewster would be in the line-up. Local soccer legend Gigi Garafano scored most of our goals.

The most memorable match that I played for New Haven City was an early spring contest against Bridgeport Vasco de Gama in Bridgeport's Seaside Park. It was a beautiful day, but the field was muddy from the defrosting of winter.

Because of the beautiful weather, the field was surrounded by spectators including members of a motorcycle group that called

Bridgeport their home and Vasco their team. I had a strong game (I always played well in the mud).

A penalty kick was awarded against us in the first half. I was defending the far goal which borders on the Long Island Sound, hence the name Seaside Park. I challenged the shooter, as was common practice back then, by coming out to the penalty spot as he placed the ball, and I participated in other gesticulations and actions which by today's rules would be clearly worthy of a yellow card.

Sure enough, the shot wound up over the goal into the water. A retake was called by the referee because I had come well off the line prior to the shot (also a common practice, even in big-time soccer until the development of VAR – Video Assistant Referee). And then I saved the second attempt…thoroughly upsetting the home crowd.

With the score 1-0 in our favor and with some six minutes left to play the referee blew the final whistle and ran to his nearby car with most players from both teams situated at the LI Sound end of the field and with me isolated at the near end which was close to the road. Immediately afterwards, there was a field invasion and since the invaders could not get to the referee, I was the easiest available target. Sensing the danger, I began to run, being chased by at least ten members of the motorcycle group just behind the goal.

After being punched a few times, kicked at and otherwise pulled and pushed; I found refuge under an ice-cream truck until rescuers were able to disperse the crowd.

My wife, Barbara, was at the game with our two daughters, Colette and Janine. She remembers running to the ice cream truck to try to stop the assault. She remembers to this day; a fist being stopped right in front of her face when the potential assailant realized she was a woman.

I had a few broken ribs, some hair pulled out, a lost chain and medal; I got away lucky.

However, a week later we went to see "Clockwork Orange", an ultraviolent film, which we had to walk out on as the memory of my being attacked was still vivid.

I returned to play a few more games after a month out! That spring I was selected to the Connecticut State All Stars team for a game scheduled against the New Jersey All-Stars at Farcher's Grove. The other goalkeeper selected was Tony DiCicco. Also on the team were Hubert Vogelsinger and

Peter Gooding, the coach at Amherst College. I played the first half of the game and Tony the second. Neither of us surrendered a goal and we won the game 1-0. That pretty much was the end of my playing days.

I never played in the NASL, MISL or any major professional league. But an argument can be made that I had playing experiences of a lifetime during an era of soccer that is now mostly forgotten. It helped in my development of real "football understanding".

Ukrainians Junior Team (1959-60) at Eintracht Oval. Divisional Champions. I am once again kneeling with the ball fourth from the left. "Shep" is standing second from the left.

German American Junior League 1959–60 Divisional Championship Plaque, my first soccer award.

NY Ukrainians Senior team 1965-66, US Open Cup Champions. Notable players: Gordon Bradley is standing fourth from the right and Ted Purdon and Peter Smethurst standing immediately to Bradley's right. Captain Walter Schmotolocha is next to me on my right. I played back-up goalkeeper to Nelson Yebleski, kneeling first on the left.

At Ukrainian Field in College Point, Queens, NY. I am standing second from the right. Notable players: John Young is standing fourth from the right and Mario Paz is kneeling first on the left.

The YCK crest: team colors were red and black, the blue and yellow are from the Ukrainian flag, blue for the sky and yellow for the wheat fields.

As a member of the Open Cup Championship team, I was inducted into the Ukrainian Sports Hall of Fame.

Action at Eintracht Oval as former Tech teammate John Nussbaumer attempts to block a cross from Peter Schaefers with Ted Purdon in the background. We drew great crowds to the sandlots.

Chapter 4

Long Island University
"I Want the Job"

Long Island University (LIU) was a basketball powerhouse in the years after the Second World War but, in 1950, it was one of seven schools nationally (four of which were in New York) involved in a scandal commonly referred to as the "CCNY Point Shaving Scandal".

As such, LIU shut down its athletic program in 1951 and it stayed mostly dormant for six years until it hired William T "Buck" Lai as Athletic Director to lead a rebirth. The school was located at the corners of Fulton Street and Dekalb Avenue in Downtown Brooklyn within a short walking distance from Brooklyn Tech and only one stop further on the infamous GG subway line from Greenpoint.

LIU's main building also housed the still operational Brooklyn Paramount Theater, a 4,084-seat ornate palace in the traditional theater sense. Additional adjacent land was secured between Willoughby Street and Ashland Place through urban redevelopment and the removal of a block of derelict housing upon which a baseball and soccer field were to be laid out.

The field sloped down at one end toward Ashland Place, where across the street Brooklyn Hospital existed and a medieval castle-like structure which was the Raymond Street Jail. Because of the slope, the soccer field was not able to be laid out in full length and therefore was undersized, shorter than 100 yards. In addition, the "skin" part of the baseball infield between second and first base protruded on to the soccer field which was often a sloppy mess or when dry, gave the attacking right side player firm footing and a true bounce.

There was no gymnasium on site and LIU's emerging Physical Education Program used the Brooklyn YMCA facility for its classes until the Brooklyn Paramount Theater, with its Wurlitzer organ, was converted into a gymnasium in 1962 by removing enough seats to build a basketball court and using the stage area for gymnastics. Much of the rococo design remained, however, and the theater is once again being used as an entertainment complex as LIU has since built a standalone gymnasium. Interestingly, the original offices for "Buck" Lai and the coaches he hired were in the dressing rooms of the vaudeville and other stars who played at the theater since its opening in 1928.

Throughout the dormant period, LIU maintained a rudimentary soccer program coached by SJ Picariello, who stayed on the staff through the shutdown. The combined four-year record from 1953 was 5 wins, 26 losses and 2 draws. In 1957, Gary Rosenthal, a former goalkeeper on the team, took over as Head Coach and recorded a 4-7-1 season. After a year's absence, during which the team had a 4-5-1 record, Rosenthal returned to the coaching ranks for his second stint at LIU.

In 1959, a decision was made to invest further in the soccer program and Rosenthal began its first recruiting class. Prior to that, the combined record for the LIU team (1959-60), made up of mostly of physical education students studying to be teachers in the New York City School System and Korean War veterans attending on the GI Bill, was zero wins, 17 losses and a tie.

With Brooklyn Tech having won the PSAL Championship in 1958 and being a competitive semi-finalist in 1959, Tech players became LIU's target.

Rosenthal recruited Ray Klivecka to score goals and me to keep the ball out of the net!

I reported to LIU several days after the semester began. Back then, freshmen were not eligible to play varsity NCAA sports, so Ray and I practiced with but could only watch, painfully, as the 1960 team went winless.

Just like at Brooklyn Tech, I struggled academically that first year. Perhaps it was freedom? Professors didn't even take attendance. Perhaps it was the course load? Dissecting a fetal pig didn't seem to have any relevance for me. Philosophy 101 was a bore. And the physical education classes for freshmen included Modern Dance. Not my thing!

The result: a grade of "F" in both Biology and Philosophy and a Grade Point Average (GPA) of less than 2.00, which meant being ineligible to play as a sophomore and forfeiture of my financial aid. Unless, of course, I went to summer school at my own expense and took those failing courses over!

I had danced with Barbara Otlowski a few times at Saint Anthony's, so

I felt comfortable one night asking her if I could accompany her home as she now lived nearly a mile away on Kingsland Avenue.

With Barbara's help, encouragement and forced study time I changed those two "Fs" to two "As", much to the disbelief of all observers, parents, teammates, coaches and others, I was now eligible to play for LIU as a sophomore during the Fall season of 1961.

My grades improved substantially after that to the point that I received an Eastern College Athletic Conference (ECAC) Award in 1964 for "Scholarship and Athletic Prowess". "Prowess" was a new word for me.

College soccer was very different to the game I had been used to playing in several ways. It seems the governing body NCAA wanted to "Americanize" the sport. Kick-ins replaced throw-ins, which put the goalkeeper under a lot more pressure. There were two referees and they both had whistles and were dressed in striped shirts and white knickers and wore white hats. The penalty area was semi-circular rather than a rectangle, and the game was played in 22-minute quarters or periods which provided additional substitution opportunities, as well as the option to change tactics though a sideline team meeting with the coaching staff. There was "free" substitution and re-entry. The official time was kept on a handheld clock at the mid-field scorer's table which was most often manned by a student manager. That person would yell out "one minute" and then countdown the final ten seconds of each period. There was ample opportunity for local gamesmanship and chicanery!

This factor came into play in my senior year when, at City College of New York (CCNY) in a tight game, their timer yelled out "one minute" to play in the half and then sounded the horn to end the period just as Ray Klivecka scored a goal seemingly within much less than a minute. As captain, I charged out of the goal to the table at mid-field, inadvertently knocking the clock off the table. When referee Tom Callahan picked up the clock, he saw that there were 40 more seconds to play and reversed his previous decision, awarding the goal. In the second half, I saved a penalty, but it was called back because I moved too soon off the line. The CCNY player, Cliff Soas, was awarded a second attempt but his shot hit the crossbar. We won the game 2-0.

Our first game in 1961 was on the road at Hunter College. We evidently surprised the home team, coming off two seasons where LIU hadn't won a game, by scoring four first half goals. The final score was 5-2. Ray Klivecka scored four goals and assisted on the fifth, and I saved a penalty in the second half. Our five goals equaled the sum of all the goals scored by LIU the previous season.

We must have been scouted by our second opponent, Adelphi University, as they were able to bottle-up Klivecka with double man-marking and we lost the game 2-0 in Garden City!

Our third game was against powerhouse CCNY, played at Lewisohn Stadium, a combined amphitheater and athletic facility with a capacity of 8,000 that opened in 1915. There was not a single blade of grass inside a field surrounded by a track and concrete Greco-Roman style seating, on three sides and on the fourth, a huge stage. To make the field look regulation size in width, they made the penalty area a yard shorter on each side (at least). It was another sandlot!

The stadium appears in the movie *Serpico*.

A *New York Times* photographer, Roland Thau, who lived across the street from the LIU field, began to follow the team. He captured one of the saves I made, and the photo appeared the following morning in the *Sunday Times*. The caption under the 7x5 photo reads: "OLD COLLEGE TRY: Joe Machnik, Long Island University goalkeeper, leaps to forestall a scoring attempt by City College during the soccer game played at Lewisohn Stadium. City College took the visitors by a 4-2 score."

We finished the 1961 season with a relatively satisfying record of five wins and five defeats, finishing fourth in the Metropolitan Conference. Brooklyn College won the Championship. We lost to them 2-1 on a late penalty kick. Ray Klivecka scored 17 of our 33 goals; I recorded three shutouts. Most personally disappointing was a 6-5 loss to my high school teammates Shep and Whitey, who were both now playing at Pratt Institute. We had hoped to finish above 500.

Several new German-born players, including two pre-med students Paul Bertrand and Norbert Reich, and Dieter Ficken (who went on to a professional career and had great success as a college coach at LIU and Columbia), added depth and soccer expertise to our team in 1962. Another Tech graduate, Bob Feger, sacrificed to play center back even though goalkeeper was his favorite position. That year was LIU's first winning season at 8-2-1. We missed out on winning the Conference Championship with a 2-2 tie vs. Pratt Institute. My (our) nemesis!

Ray Klivecka scored 15 goals, and we recorded five clean sheets.

Both Ray and I were named to the College All-American Soccer Team by the National Soccer Coaches Association of America (NSCAA) and were invited to a luncheon at their National Convention held in the Hotel Manhattan on Eighth Avenue in New York City. There were perhaps several hundred coaches and a few other local players there, and Walter Chyzowych sat on the dais in some sort of official capacity. Dieter Ficken, Bob Feger and defender Steve Nagy were also named in the All-Metropolitan Conference Team in addition to Ray and me.

There were two exhibitors (vendors) at the Convention: Max Doss and his Soccer Sport Supply, which is where almost everyone purchased their uniforms, shoes, soccer balls and all other soccer equipment; and Peter Green Limited, a company out of Pennsylvania which represented the Admiral brand.

All eyes began to focus on the 1963 season, our senior year. I was named team captain, which was rare for a goalkeeper at the time and we finished with a regular season record of 10-3-1, the tie coming in a 2-2 draw against, you guessed it, Pratt Institute.

Our strongest game was a 2-1 win over Hartwick in upstate NY, reversing a loss by the same score the year before. Hartwick had just beaten NYU, played in the 1962 NCAA Tournament, and had never lost a game on their home field, where traditionally several thousand students and local town folks came out to watch them play. Oneonta, where Hartwick is located, was beginning to be called "Soccer City USA", so much so that it housed the first Soccer Hall of Fame not only for US Soccer, but also for the NSCAA and NISOA, the organization of college and high school soccer referees.

Hartwick peppered us throughout the match but goals by Ray Klivecka and his younger brother Giedris (Gerry), also a Tech graduate, sealed the victory. I had my best game ever! That win alone may have been the difference that got us into the NCAA Soccer Tournament, LIU's maiden appearance and the first NCAA recognition in any sport in 13 years since the point-shaving scandal of 1950.

Our NCAA Playoff game was scheduled for Saturday, November 23rd against legendary coach John McKeon's University of Bridgeport. The NCAAs were no stranger to Bridgeport as they had competed in the very first tournament in 1959 as runners-up to champions St. Louis University and also appeared in the 1961 competition. Bridgeport's home field was Seaside Park, which was not enclosed and did not meet NCAA standards. Neither did LIU's field as it was legally too short. So, the game was scheduled at the Pratt Institute field, which was mostly grass, full size and enclosed enabling the $1 mandatory admission fee to be collected.

It gets dark early in late November on the East Coast, hence the 1pm start time. LIU scheduled an early practice on Friday in anticipation of the game. The practice went extremely well, and we were pumped for our first-ever NCAA appearance the next day.

At approximately 1:30pm in the middle of our practice, the news came that President John F. Kennedy had been shot in Dallas and shortly later it was confirmed that he had lost his life. Obviously, the country was in shock and all activity except the NFL came to a halt. Our NCAA Tournament game was postponed to the following Wednesday, played at 1pm in front of very few spectators.

Bridgeport was loaded with star striker Sammy Slagle (15 goals) leading the way to their 10-2-1 regular season record. The game was scoreless through the first quarter and LIU scored first in the second period with half-back Vincent Cannuscio breaking in and converting his own rebound. It took almost until the last minute before half-time for Bridgeport to tie the score. Slagle went to work in period three, scoring two goals within 30 seconds and the final score of 3-1 for Bridgeport was in the books.

Interestingly, the other Metropolitan Conference entry in the tournament, Adelphi University, which won the Met title by a single point over LIU because of our (once again) tie with Pratt, lost their game to Army 4-2. Army and Navy had strong soccer teams in the '60s and it seemed that if LIU were to continue its soccer development and progress it would need stronger players, more depth and the wherewithal to get past service academy teams.

My association with Long Island University did not end with the 1963 soccer season or with graduation in 1964. I was offered the opportunity to be Gary Rosenthal's Assistant Coach while working on a Graduate Assistantship for a master's degree. LIU had a strong postgraduate program in Guidance and Counseling, where many current and future teachers were enrolled, either to become school guidance counselors or to enable qualification for an increase in salary that came with a master's degree.

The Guidance and Counseling Department had several professors who were disciples of the Carl Rogers Humanistic Psychology approach which was very person-centered on four key concepts: self-actualization, the need for positive regard, individual congruence and empathetic understanding. The principles are easily applied to everyday life, dealing with people and relationships and in many ways molded my future approach to coaching, family and life in general.

By now, Barbara and I were inseparable and did most everything together. Sometimes on a date, we would take my youngest sister Debra to places like the Bronx Zoo, the Ice-Capades or Follies, Ringling Bros Circus and Radio City Music Hall.

Gary Rosenthal's strength was that he was a great motivator, but he also recognized that there was another whole world of soccer out there and he adapted on the fly to the experiences of others who had played in the Sunday ethnic league environment. And his personality and sense of humor made him fun to be around whether on the field or at his office which was always crowded. Gary was in his early thirties during this time and his energy for the game was beyond insatiable. He often accompanied his players to Randalls Island for International Soccer League double-headers on Sunday. The success of the LIU teams of the middle to late '60s brought him some notoriety and he became friends with British journalist Brian Glanville. He traveled to Wembley to watch England play and authored three soccer books: *Soccer: The Game and How to Play It; Soccer Skills and Drills* and *Everybody's Soccer Book*. In 1969, Gary Rosenthal was named Coach of the USA Maccabiah Team for the games held that year.

During my playing days at LIU, Rosenthal's assistant coach was his friend, Ira Weiss. Both attended LIU and played on the early soccer teams. The two coaches together set a most enjoyable playing and practice environment. Both had a fabulous sense of humor and the bus rides to and from games were often hilarious, sometimes ridiculous, especially when we won. Some of their "one-liners" I remember to this day and recall using them with my own teams. Like on the way to a game we knew that if we saw "two nuns in a Cadillac" then victory was guaranteed. We never did see those two nuns!

Weiss would later go on to become head coach at New York City Community College, where he would recommend his top talent like Otto Leitner, Paul Leite and Rupert Brown to continue their education and playing careers at LIU. And later, that practice would continue when I began coaching at the University of New Haven.

In the summer of 1962, LIU Assistant Basketball Coach Ken Hunter asked Gary to recommend two soccer players to work at a sleep-away camp in the Pocono Mountains in Greeley, PA. Ray Klivecka and I were selected, and we traveled to Philadelphia for interviews with Marvin Black, the owner of Pine Forest Camp. We were offered the job as bunk counselors but also as soccer instructors. This provided an opportunity for Ray and I to train during our off periods or when the camp was on a field trip which we chose not to attend. We even got up early to do roadwork, which I hated.

The 1964 LIU soccer season was my first as an assistant coach. Also, Bob Hess, who was newly hired to coach gymnastics but had a soccer background, was hired to serve as freshman/JV Coach. The team finished with winning the elusive Met Conference Championship and a record of 10-3-1, but no invite to the NCAA Tournament.

Gary Rosenthal was named Met "Coach of the Year" and Gerry Klivecka was named First Team All-American. Bob Feger got his chance to play in the goal and was named to the All-State team. Ten players received All-Met honors. It was the beginning of a dynasty with players Carlo Tramontozzi, Marcello Launi, Alix Perrault joining Gerry Klivecka, who still had another year of eligibility.

Serving as Gary's assistant coach provided us with opportunities to become much closer. We shared the same locker room, prepared practices together and Barbara and I socialized with Gary and his wife Lynne. We became the best of friends.

So much so that when Gary was offered the head counselor's job for the summer of 1964 at Silver Birch Camp (SBC), he offered Barbara and I the opportunity to be away for the summer. I would become a bunk counselor and soccer coach while Barbara was offered a position as Gary and Lynne's babysitter for their two young boys, Robert and Allen.

SBC was quite cozy compared to Pine Forest, with a capacity of only 200 youngsters, split evenly between the Girls and Boy's Hills of ten bunks each. It had a small spring and stream fed lake, a softball field, gymnasium/social hall and a recreational field surrounded by a track, but no swimming pool. The field was not big enough to host a full-size soccer field and the goalposts at each end were not anchored into the ground but instead were held up by support legs at the bottom which protruded into the field and goal. Gary warned me about the goal and that I also needed to bring the nets from LIU.

Creating a soccer team out of the senior boys' campers, aged 12-16, most of whom had never played before, was a challenge to be sure. And the camp had scheduled weekly games against the other camps around, of which there were many. In our first away game, we lost 10-0 to an experienced team with a coach from Germany who had been at the camp for several years. Fortunately, we did not have to play them again for a while as the return match was scheduled for later in the summer.

When that team showed up and saw our irregular field and strange goalposts, they had smirks on their faces and the look of over-confidence. Somehow, with an organized defense we managed to defeat them even though Gary's brother, Ira, called a penalty against us. It was my first sense that I might be able to be a coach.

We had such a good time that summer at SBC that Barbara and I decided that we would like to go back. But we wanted to spend more time together at camp. With Gary's guidance and support, Barbara and I were married May 1, 1965. Gary served as my best man and Lynne was one of Barbara's bridesmaids!

After Barbara and I were married, I was offered the Senior Boys bunk (an honor) and the assistant head counsellor position to Gary, and Barbara became a counselor and had a bunk of her own with the youngest girls.

We had just gotten to camp when the US Open Cup final (NY Ukrainians vs Chicago Hansa) second leg was scheduled for July 4th in Chicago. I discussed with Gary the possibility of leaving camp for what would have amounted to at least four days with travel. It was too much to ask.

This was one of the most difficult decisions in my life. I was looking at a future in teaching and coaching, even perhaps, one day, being head counselor at Silver Birch. Should I risk that future or was my future being a part-time Sunday goalkeeper? I stayed at camp and was so happy to learn that my beloved NY Ukrainians survived without me and were US Open Cup champions. I was told that I missed a celebration of the century. The decision cost me my position at YCK, however!

Because we regularly attended Friday night religious services in the social hall at SBC, Barbara and I and several other LIU staff were allowed to drive into town on Sunday to attend church. One Sunday, now driving a '53 Chevy Bel-Aire which my uncle Mike Cunningham gave me, I had the car loaded with our Sunday regulars: Barbara and I, Carlo Tramontozzi, Danny Sullivan and Jon Levy (Lynne Rosenthal's brother who just wanted to get out of camp). Carlo was dressed in his Sunday best.

Instead of taking the normal three-mile route down the mountain from camp, I decided to take an alternate dirt road over the top. The grade was too steep for the bald tires on the car to hold the road and we started to slide, especially when I pumped the brakes. There was no stopping the car.

There was a shallow ditch on the driver's side of the road, and I decided that pulling into the ditch might be the only way we were going to stop. I underestimated the result as the car flipped over and we were now upside down but stationary. Immediately some kind of oil, maybe power-steering fluid, began to drop out of the steering column all over Carlo's suit. We all climbed out of the car and inquired about each other's wellbeing. There were no injuries, and we all started to laugh instead!

Danny Sullivan was a six-foot five basketball player and with his immense help, we were able to right the car up on its wheels. There was heavy damage to the roof and driver's side but no broken glass. We all got back into the car. We missed church but had a solid breakfast in town.

It would not be my last roll-over!

After that summer Barbara and I were able to move into our "newlywed apartment" in the basement of a single-family home on Crescent Street in the East New York section of Brooklyn. The following March we welcomed daughter Colette into our family.

At Silver Birch the next summer, with our newborn baby, we were given our own private quarters in a room next door to the Nature Shack. We became good friends with Milt and Harriet Kopelman. Milt was the Principal of the Bronx High School of Science, and I loved going on nature walks with him each Sunday when he took a group of campers along the various trails which surrounded Silver Birch.

I was offered a full-time position in the Department of Athletics and Physical Education as Director of Intramurals and Lecturer, with the expectation that I would teach three hours per week in the Fall and Spring. The appointment letter dated July 12, 1965, called for a salary of $5,500. And, of course, I would continue to serve as Gary's assistant coach.

I loved the additional responsibility of directing the Intramural program. I organized tournaments in flag football, volleyball, basketball, softball and the like. And, as there was no budget to hire referees, I officiated most of the games. It was the beginning of my officiating career, and I was good at it because of the referees that I watched in the NHL (John Ashley, Frank Udvari, Bruce Hood, Art Skov and later Andy Van Hellemond) and also the soccer referees I watched while playing for the NY Ukrainians. We did have an equipment budget, however, which allowed the purchase of 25 pairs of real roller-skates with full boots, a couple dozen hockey sticks and hockey-style goals with nets.

Every Saturday morning after the soccer season and throughout the winter, we played roller hockey on the tennis courts, with LIU students and several of my friends, Anatol Popovich, "Whitey" Kalyna, Steve Leoniak, John Nussbaumer and others.

During my time playing at LIU, I had only three injuries. I was concussed after being kicked in the head by one of my own defenders, although I still finished the game after our trainer, Ted Childs, certified that I was ok to continue. Then I tore my left rotator cuff in my senior year, during a training exercise that I was leading as captain. But the most serious injury came while teaching a physical education softball class which was held on the tennis courts because our field was underwater. To facilitate everyone being able to have success at bat, I served as pitcher for both teams. Then, I made the mistake of covering home plate as a runner was attempting to score. He determined that he was going to slide, even on the tarmac court. He took me out through my standing right leg, doing severe damage. I cancelled the rest of the class. Over the years I had several operations and injections in that knee, which because of my favoring it throughout the rest of my life, resulted in having to replace my left knee.

The 1965 soccer season was to be very special. Gary Rosenthal's team, enhanced by the presence of a very special player, Dov Markus, started the season with four straight wins including a 6-1 trouncing of Bridgeport and a 5-0 defeat of Hartwick played under the lights in a downtown Oneonta baseball facility. Markus scored 35 goals in 14 games. He was complimented that extraordinary season by senior All-American Gerry Klivecka and sophomores Marcello Launi, Carlo Tramontozzi up front and a defense led by Sam Farrell, Ron Jabusch, Louis Gallaro, Alix Perrault and John Limberis. Even the nemesis, Pratt Institute, fell victim by a 6-0 score.

For the second consecutive year, LIU won the Met Conference, finishing the regular season with only a single loss to Rutgers and had a regular season record of 11-1-1.

The NCAA Tournament was on the horizon and LIU drew Army away in the first round. Army still had one game to play on their regular season schedule and that was against Navy in Annapolis. Gary and I went down to scout Joe Palone's Army team. Army had several successful seasons prior to this match-up, making it to the NCAA semi-finals in 1963 and 1964 (losses to Navy and Michigan State) and continuing to make the national tournament for a total of six straight campaigns.

What we witnessed in a stadium full of Cadets and Mid-Shipmen in Annapolis unfortunately could not be described as a soccer game. Inspired by the mostly uniformed crowd, each team brought their physical best to the match and the referees had a difficult time controlling the level of intensity and number of fouls (this was before the yellow and red card system started by FIFA for the 1970 World Cup).

Perhaps it was our naivety or lack of experience with the Army/Navy rivalry, but Gary and I came away with the wrong impression of Army's soccer prowess (that word again) and gave a scouting report to our LIU team that did not serve them well. The Army team possessed a skillful side with many talented players but that was not on display in their 2-2 tie with Navy, or at least we failed to recognize it.

Soccer had become a big sport at LIU during this time and the Student Council arranged for several buses to provide transportation for the faithful. More than 300 fans showed up for the 3pm start at West Point that Tuesday. And there was not a Cadet in sight until shortly before kick-off when what seemed like the entire West Point Military Academy came marching in file to cheer their squad.

Disarmed with a strategy to play the ball quickly and minimize dribbling because of the perceived physicality of the Army team, LIU could not get going, could not stream together consecutive passes and was unable to demonstrate the skill and finesse that led to their most productive season. Army scored two goals in the first half and led 3-0 early in the second half before LIU, now playing without fear, got two goals back to make the score respectable, although this was of little consolation. There was immense disappointment, and the coaching staff had played a major role, for it was generally felt and believed that if our players were encouraged to play their skillful game from the start, this match would have ended with a positive result. Among the most disappointed, and rightfully so, was Gerry Klivecka who had played his last LIU game.

Despite the loss, Gary and I, Barbara and Lynne were invited as guests of honor to the Intra-Fraternity Council Ball held at a fancy facility in Brooklyn. The entertainment for the night was the local singing group *Jay and the Americans*. We became huge fans! They appeared at the Brooklyn Paramount to celebrate the opening of the LIU gym, and we later saw lead singer Jay Black in his elder years at Foxwoods in Connecticut and at Eisenhower Park on Long Island. We still listen to his music regularly.

"Cara Mia"!

An annual highlight of the end of the spring semester was the Varsity Club Dinner, where all the athletes were gathered and treated to a fine dinner, entertainment and a night of awards. One of the best memories of those evenings was when a gentleman sitting on the dais, was introduced as an Italian General visiting from the UN. "The General" turned out to be August DiFlorio, an entertainer who then delivered one of the funniest speeches ever heard by the young athletes, mispronouncing nearly every name, place and athletic accomplishment. I compared his performance to that of Charlie Callas, who became famous for his appearances on *Dean Martin's Celebrity Roasts*. I vowed that if I was ever able to facilitate another appearance by DiFlorio, I would not hesitate!

After nine months living at our "newlywed" apartment in East New York, Gary Rosenthal arranged for us to move into University Towers, one of three 16-story apartment buildings newly purchased by LIU. Our apartment was on the 16th floor and Gary and Lynne lived one floor below. From our kitchen window I could see half of the LIU field and most of the campus. Our rent was $112 per month (a little over $1,000 in today's money). A similar apartment in that building today would rent for up to $3,000 per month!

I did not know at the time that Provost William Birenbaum had asked Gary to become full-time Dean of Students and that he would have to give up coaching his beloved soccer team at the height of its strength and popularity on campus. Birenbaum even hosted a farewell party for Gary and the team at his home in Brooklyn Heights.

That year LIU started a project to improve the athletic field, building a cradle at the Ashland Place end and filling it in to eliminate the slope.

Then the field was to be sodded to be ready for the 1966 soccer season. The increased field length, however, would still not meet NCAA regulations.

In addition, William T. "Buck" Lai was charged with overseeing the overall athletics program at LIU's sister institutions C.W. Post and Southampton, as well as at the Brooklyn Center. His office would now be in Brookville, Long Island on the Post campus. Basketball coach Roy Rubin was named Athletic Director under Lai's direction at LIU Brooklyn.

Gary's resignation came as a shock to everyone on campus, especially the players he recruited and, of course, yours truly. The LIU soccer job, a full-time role while many soccer coaching positions were still part-time, was coveted in the New York area as well as the entire country.

Soon, I was able to witness coaching candidate after candidate interview with Roy Rubin, whose office was down a short hall from mine. Gary's office was no longer in the Brooklyn Paramount building but on the second floor of the newly constructed LIU dormitory. Gary's players would come to me to ask who was going to be their next coach.

Finally, I went to Gary's office and said, "I want the job!" He immediately took me over to Roy Rubin's office and together, almost simultaneously they stated: "That's what we have been waiting for you to say; what took you so long?"

I was now head coach of Gary Rosenthal's soccer team. I was offered a new contract with a new salary of $7,150.

There was little opportunity left to recruit additional players, as summer was nearly upon us. Ira Weiss provided two community college players, Kalman Magyar and Eddy Perodin.

I decided to take a little used field player, Mickey Cohen, who was also a catcher on the baseball team, to Silver Birch Camp to work him out as a goalkeeper. Anatol Popovich was hired as swimming director at SBC and every day during lunch break, we hammered Micky with shots while providing helpful hints.

The 1966 LIU team, listed in alphabetical order with their numbers, contained only 17 players: (16) Jerry Babij, (1) Mickey Cohen, (4) Sam Farrel, (5) Louis Gallaro, (7) Mike Hogan, (2) Ronnie Jabusch, (8) Marcello Launi, (6) John Limberis, (18) Kalman Magyar, (9) Dov Markus, (19) Tom O'Leary, (11) Eddy Perodin, (3) Alix Perrault, (12) Hugh Reid, (17) Steve Reinhardt, (14) Albert Soria, (10) Carlo Tramontozzi.

Cohen won the starting goalkeeper job. O'Leary, a transfer student from

Nassau Community College, was to be his back-up. Reid, Hogan and Soria were valuable holdovers from Gary's squad and Reinhardt was a Physical Education major who had high school playing experience. Babij was a so-called "walk on".

I appointed Carlo Tramontozzi as our captain. Carlo had a unique soccer background and experience. I embraced Carlo's soccer knowledge just as Gary Rosenthal embraced Ray Klivecka's and mine. Carlo was like having an assistant coach on the field. He often slid proposed line-up changes and formations on a piece of paper under the coach's locker door prior to practice and even games.

We opened the regular season on the road with a convincing win over C.W. Post and were scheduled to open at home the following Saturday, October 1st. It rained all day Friday and throughout the night, continuing into Saturday morning in advance of the scheduled 2pm start against powerhouse, NYU. LIU had just sodded the field, and I could see standing water on the field from my kitchen window.

As it was a Saturday, there was little opportunity to contact anyone on campus and it was going to be my decision whether to play or not in this weather, with the potential of ruining the brand-new field being used for the first time. I knew our team was primed and that rescheduling the match if postponed was unlikely. And we needed a win over a strong NYU team to establish ourselves — and mostly for the new coach to win over the confidence of his squad.

I decided to play the game, which we won 2-0 with Mickey Cohen making several key saves as he established himself between the posts. The next day, with beautiful sunshine, I spent the day on the field replacing patches of grass and stamping down the turf that had been uprooted. I was nervous about what Monday would bring with criticism, if not more, of my decision. The win helped. I didn't get fired!

Our fourth game was at the University of Bridgeport at Seaside Park. Goalkeeper Cohen received a concussion in the 2-1 win and was ruled out of our next match, a home contest against Temple University. It was the only game we lost that season, finishing with a 12-1 record and another Met Conference title.

Wearing one of several helmets that trainer Ted Childs had concocted, Cohen was able to play the next games. And we prepared for the NCAA Tournament.

The first tournament game was played at Cortland State in upstate NY. The 6-1 result does not indicate how close the game was as LIU scored four fourth-period goals. Dov Markus scored late in the first half to give LIU a 1-0 half-time lead. He scored again early in the second half and Sam Farrel had two goals in the fourth period to sandwich goals by Carlo Tramontozzi and Mike Hogan.

The next game was to be against the University of Bridgeport, who defeated Colgate. Since neither team had a field which met NCAA standards, the beautiful grass field at C.W. Post was chosen to host the match. Each team was permitted to nominate a referee from their area. I chose Tom Callahan, who had officiated several of our regular season games and had a wealth of experience. Bridgeport's coach, Joe Bean, selected Paul Bourdeau, who along with his regular partner Brian Kelly, worked most of the big games in New England. Bourdeau was famous for writing the book on how to officiate soccer with a two-man system called the "dual system of control". Bridgeport had an outstanding striker, John Verfaille, who gave us fits during our regular season meeting.

I had often asked our defender, John Limberis, to mark players 1v1, taking them out of their regular rhythm, preventing them from receiving the ball or interfering with their first touch. John Verfaille and Limberis went at it throughout the match to the point where Verfaille lashed out at Limberis, who retaliated. Bourdeau, seeing only the latter incident, came running in to eject Limberis from the match. Fortunately, Callahan saw the entire fracas and gave Verfaille his marching papers as well (no yellow or red cards yet back then). We were now playing 10v10. I thought it was an even trade!

With the extra space on the field, defender Ronnie Jabusch was able to dribble nearly the length of the field to score his first collegiate goal, a low shot to the far post.

The game ended 1-0 for LIU!

LIU was going to the NCAA finals. Who would have dreamed? And the games were to be hosted by the University of California, Berkeley. California, here we come!

As the team celebrated on the field at the final whistle, I remember seeing tears in my father's eyes.

The final four teams at the NCAA Tournament were the mighty Michigan State (MSU), which had beaten Akron and Temple and had been in the

Championship Game the last two years; Army, which had beaten U Conn, Navy, and San Francisco (USF) qualified by beating Colorado College and St. Louis University.

In terms of goals, each team had their superstar. Dov Markus had scored 26 of LIU's 81 goals, Guy Busch and Tony Keyes with 26 apiece had 52 of Michigan State's 63 goals, Joe Casey had 16 of Army's 70 goals and Eduardo Rangel had 21 of San Francisco's 41 goals.

The games were to be played in the 75,000-seat Memorial Stadium built in 1923 on Berkeley's campus. A double-header was scheduled for noon, Thursday, December 1st with LIU vs. MSU in the first match followed by Army vs. USF at 2:30pm. The final was scheduled for a 1:30pm start on Saturday, December 3rd.

I had asked and really wanted Gary Rosenthal to join us in California, but he refused saying that it was not his team anymore and he "didn't want to get in the way".

The Student Council arranged to have the play-by-play commentary of the game piped into the Brooklyn Paramount gymnasium via a telephone hook-up placed close to a microphone. We were told that the gym was packed. The team received more than 50 telegrams that day, the equivalent of modern-day email or text messages.

Unfortunately, several days of rain created a muddy playing surface as much of the grass had been worn thin during the college football season. Fewer than a thousand spectators were in the stadium despite the fact the legendary broadcaster Heyward Hale Broun did a CBSTV feature on the teams and tournament locally.

Michigan State's football team must have played in the stadium numerous times as the scoreboard had a huge display of their school's name while LIU was written in the smallest of hastily prepared letters. I used the slight as a motivator for our team, stating that no one expected us to win, and they did not respect us enough to give us equality on the scoreboard.

Carlo Tramontozzi opened the scoring in the first period and Dov Markus scored his 27th goal of the season in the second. However, the game was tied at two-all when Tony Keyes assisted on goals by Guy Busch and Barry Tieman. After 88 minutes of regulation play, two five minute "sudden death" overtime periods were played. Still no goal, an additional ten minutes of sudden death play took place. Incredibly, as it might now seem, the remaining tiebreaker was to go to the team leading in corner kicks if no goals were scored. Corner kicks were tied at 5-5 through the first two OT periods. During the third OT period, with this knowledge coming into play, players seemed to be trying to win corners rather than attack the goal. Marcello Launi earned LIU's sixth corner kick, and it was enough to eliminate the previously unbeaten Michigan State soccer team after a fourth OT period 6 corners to 5. I saw "Buck" Lai in tears. As the institution he had led in the rebound from the 1950s basketball scandal was now back in the NCAAs with a chance to win a National Championship.

Holy Cinderella!

In the second game, San Francisco easily handled Army 2-0 with goals by Sandor Hites and Luis Sagastume. Goalkeeper Mike Ivanow had the shutout and was to go on to play eight seasons in the NASL and earn ten caps for the US national team.

Back at the Durant Hotel, now the Graduate Berkeley (for some reason, all three out-of-town teams stayed at the same hotel), I had a room at the end of the hall directly across from Michigan State's athletic director, "Biggie" Munn. I was able to hear a conversation which started in the hallway between Munn and his coach, Gene Kenny. It was not a pleasant conversation as Munn expressed his disappointment with the loss and Kenny criticized a "crazy rule" referring to the decision to end a tie game with a corner kick advantage.

San Francisco was loaded with talent all over the field with players who would make their mark in soccer later in life. The previously mentioned Sagastume played for three years in NASL and went on to enjoy a 28-year coaching career at the Air Force Academy. He was elected into the United Soccer Coaches Hall of Fame. Hidden in their line-up was future United States Olympic and national team coach Lothar Osiander.

While rain was predicted for Friday, it turned out to be a relatively clear day. But the damage done to the field with two semi-finals (one with overtime) on top of a regular gridiron football season was irreversible. An argument could be made that the field conditions for the Championship Game were worse than on Thursday.

To prepare, San Francisco held a practice session on the beach. I thought it best that our players rest and recover from the lengthy overtime game in the mud.

And while all eyes were on USF's Eduardo Rangel, the scorer of 21 regular season goals, it was Sandor Hites, who had only eight regular season goals, who stole the show in the final.

Hites (pronounced Hit-tesh) opened the scoring after 12 minutes, assisted on a goal in the second frame and scored another before Marcello Launi got one back for LIU. We went into the locker room trailing by that 3-1 score but were confident that we could get back in the game.

Early in the second half, Ivanow slipped in the mud trying to reach a cross and Launi made it 3-2.

Here we go!

Unfortunately, Hites scored again making it 4-2 and then Osiander added a fifth.

The bubble burst! Obvious disappointment!

After accepting the NCAA plaque for second place, the realization that we were not champions began to hit home. The locker room was quiet, some were in tears. I had to leave the room to be by myself before addressing the team. Several players came up to say they were "sorry".

There was no game for third place!

It was no consolation that I was told that, at age 23, I was the youngest coach to coach in an NCAA National Championship Game.

Overconfident? I don't think so. Afraid? Definitely not! Overmatched? Not that either.

Would we have changed anything? Never gave it a second thought.

Would we get another chance? Only time would tell.

The December 12, 1966 issue of *Sports Illustrated* has a nice summary of the match in an article by Joe Jares entitled: "USF Wins One for the UN."

There was some consolation that we had won a third consecutive Met Conference title and many of our players were honored. Dov Markus scored 27 goals, bringing his two-year total to 62! I was named Met Conference "Coach of the Year", but it was of little consolation. As a reward, Chancellor R. Gordon Hoxie offered to host the team at a special dinner. I recommended the Norwegian Seamen's Home, site of the Brooklyn Tech celebration some seven years earlier. The smorgasbord did not disappoint! Not only was it a celebration of LIU soccer but also of the much-needed national publicity the emerging university received!

Chancellor Hoxie wrote a personal letter of thanks, writing: "We are so very proud of you and the Soccer Team: the spirit is great, and you--all---are great!"

I joined the National Soccer Coaches Association of America (NSCAA) as Gary Rosenthal's assistant coach in 1964. The annual convention was being held in NY first at the Hotel Manhattan and later at the Commodore on 42nd Street. The 1967 convention was noteworthy for the number of young coaches with playing experience that were becoming members and looking to have an impact on the growth and development of the game. Changes had already been made with the throw-in replacing the kick-in and field markings representing the international game. The game was still being officiated by the dual system of control, which had many proponents believing that two whistles on the field were better than one.

The NCAA provided each team in the tournament with a 16mm film of the Championship Game. After repeatedly watching the match, I began to see the inadequacies of the dual system as officials were never in a position where they could accurately judge offside, due to the need to also keep an eye out for fouls and misconduct at both ends of the field and judge balls out over the touch line. The importance of accurate offside decision-making has come into focus in modern times with the development of Semi-Automatic Offside Technology (SAOT).

With the score 3-2, a LIU counterattack was inaccurately judged to be offside. The possibility of tying the score at 3 was aborted before even a shot at goal. This is not written as sour grapes! But I did sour on the dual system of control and began a campaign to require games to be officiated with three officials in the international diagonal system of control. It would take years for the NCAA to finally get there!

In the summer of 1966, Walt Chyzowych and his brother Gene, along with Lenny Lucenko, an assistant coach at Pratt Institute, and the college's head coach and athletic director Wayne Sunderland started the All-American Soccer Camp and School, which was held at the Ukrainian Workers' Association (UWA) resort in Glen Spey, New York. "All-American" wasn't the first such soccer camp in the States but it became one of the most successful and important as Walt was able to attract staff from the emerging professional leagues as well as top college and high school coaches. I often traveled to Glen Spey and worked specifically with the goalkeepers in camp. Later, the camp moved to the NY Military Academy in Cornwall, 60 miles north of New York City.

As a result of the "success" of the 1966 LIU soccer team, I was invited to appear at many other emerging soccer camps and to present "goalkeeping clinics" across the country, but I always returned to All-American Soccer Camps whenever possible.

In addition, LIU was contacted by the United States Information Agency to appear in a 15-minute color documentary film being produced by Hearst Metrotone News, Inc. which would be shown abroad to "tell something of American sports life and education at a large metropolitan college" according to J. Walter de Hoog, the producer-writer as quoted in a five-column article in the October 1, 1967 *New York Times*. The film featured two LIU student athletes from Africa, Alieu Sallah and Tejan N'Jie, both of whom walked onto the team when they arrived at the Brooklyn campus.

Upon completion, the film was presented at the NSCAA Convention to positive reviews. Unfortunately, LIU was not provided with a copy, nor do I have one personally, and I have not been able to find it on YouTube or elsewhere!

Several outstanding players would not be available to the 1967 LIU soccer team due to graduation. Gone were Carlo Tramontozzi, Marcello Launi and Mike Hogan. But we still had Dov Markus, Ronnie Jabusch, John Limberis, Louis Gallaro and Sam Farrell. Also, newcomer Paul Engl, who I had first met while playing with College Point, was added to Otto Leitner and Paul Leite from Ira Weiss' junior college team.

The season started with a 4-2 home victory over Vermont, during which Dov Markus missed a penalty kick. He decided thereafter that his close friend, John Limberis, would take any future penalties. Limberis finished the season with 16 goals, 11 of which were spot kicks. Had Markus taken those penalties, and with the assumption that he would have scored those attempts, Markus would have finished his career with 89 goals in three years instead of 78. Markus was the first player honored with the Robert R. Herman Award (soccer's Heisman Trophy) in a poll conducted by the *Sporting News* for the National Professional Soccer League (NPSL). He was also drafted by the NY Generals in that league's College Draft.

LIU finished the season with a 12-1-1 record and another Met Conference crown. A loss to NYU and a tie away to Temple tarnished the record. Goalkeeper Mickey Cohen recorded eight shutouts.

The NCAA invited the team to the national tournament and LIU opened with another victory over Bridgeport, played at C.W. Post, this time 2-0 after goals by Leite and Markus. Following the game, we learned that our next opponent would be Trinity College of Hartford, Connecticut, who had defeated Army, remarkably, 6-1.

A win over Trinity would mean another trip to the national finals, this time hosted in Saint Louis. The tournament began with 16 teams and the final four came down to Michigan State (again), who defeated Maryland and Akron; Navy, which defeated West Chester State and Buffalo State, and Saint Louis, which got through via wins over Colorado College and San Jose State. Defending champion San Francisco lost their opening game on penalty kicks after a 3-3 tie with San Jose. It had not taken long for the NCAA to eliminate corner kicks as a tiebreaker.

Prior to our Friday bus ride up to Hartford, where the game would be played, I went to a local travel agency and asked for 20 airline ticket envelopes which I filled with blank sheets of paper so that they would look like plane tickets purchased with confidence for our hopeful trip to Saint Louis.

The game in Hartford was played in muddy conditions and LIU was thoroughly outplayed in the first half, going into the locker room losing 1-0. I thought that we needed to raise our intensity level, and to motivate the team, I took the bogus airline tickets out of my vest pocket and waved them in the air. "You want these, or will they be thrown in the garbage after the game? Along with your 'garbage' of the first half."

Additionally, I replaced one of the midfielders with little-used back-up goalkeeper Marcel Le Bec, who had decent field playing skills in addition to a high energy level. Second half goals by Markus and Leite (2) finalized the scoring with a positive 3-1 result.

Lo and behold, we were to face Michigan State again. The Spartans came into the tournament with an 11-0-1 record, a tie with St. Louis being the only blemish, and they outscored opponents 68-11.

Even though State's star forward Tony Keyes was out with a recent appendectomy, LIU was not a match for Michigan State this time. It was close at the halfway point (1-0) but three second half goals rendered the game a blowout. Michigan State had gotten their revenge.

In the second game, Saint Louis defeated Navy 1-0. The Championship Game was again played on a muddy field which began to freeze over as the game progressed. I remember a Michigan State player being involved in a challenge just outside of the barely visible penalty area and sliding on the frozen mud until stopped by contact with the goalpost. The officials got together and suspended the match.

It was not replayed, and co-champions were named after a scoreless slip and slide. For many years now, there has been a movement that intercollegiate soccer be played as a split season Fall/Spring sport with a Championship played in late Spring under desirable conditions for players and fans. LIU's 1966 and 1967 experience would certainly attest to the need for that effort!

In attendance at the game versus Trinity in Hartford were my Connecticut relatives from Old Lyme, Leon and Ellie Machnik. My father took me to their country home as a ten-year-old and we visited there on several occasions, including in the summer just prior to my first season at Brooklyn Tech.

Among the properties owned by the Connecticut Machnik family was a 200-acre wooded site with a 30-acre lake on Witch Meadow Road in Salem, Connecticut, just off Rt. 85 and just a few miles north of the Waterford Speedbowl, where I watched my first stock car race in 1953. Leon and Ellie had plans to build a campsite on the property as the camping industry (small tent campers, tents and trailers) was beginning to become a popular summertime activity in Connecticut.

They asked Barbara and I to visit with them over Christmas to discuss the possibility of our being involved as a potential summer employment opportunity at the campsite. It sounded like an interesting proposition and something we would consider. Raising a family in the Connecticut countryside as opposed to the 16th floor of a major apartment complex was attractive to be sure. As soon as Spring arrived, I spent nearly every weekend at the Salem site, clearing land, building picnic tables and fireplaces. When our second daughter Janine was born, on June 18th, we rushed her baptismal celebration and eight days later moved up to Salem for the summer. Debra, my sister, accompanied us to help Barbara with our newborn and Colette, our daughter, who was two years, three months older than Janine.

Leon Machnik was the surviving owner of Machnik Bros. Construction Company of Old Lyme, and he moved a mobile home on site which was to be our home. When we arrived, there still was no running water or electricity to the trailer and there were earth moving machines all over the place.

Although I did my best to describe the situation to Barbara before we made the move, I probably over-exaggerated the amenities in my excitement about having a place for the summer. Barbara broke down in tears getting out of the car with a nine-day-old baby in her arms and toddler Colette by her side. She had no idea she was going to live at a construction site.

In time, a well was dug, we had water and electricity, and the summer moved along nicely!

At the end of the summer, Leon and Ellie proposed that they would build a house on the property, which would be ours if we decided to accept the full-time summer job of running the campsite which was to open for business the following Spring. It would become necessary, then, to find employment in Connecticut for the fall and winter months.

That September, I received a letter from Melvin R. Schmid, Second Vice-President and Program Chairman for the NSCAA. It was an invitation to serve on a panel/debate with Walter Chyzowych, addressing the topic "Adjusting Offense to Defense and Vice Versa" at the Convention the following January in the Hotel Commodore. A Q&A session was scheduled afterward.

The 1968 soccer season at LIU did not go as planned. As reported in the 1969 issue of the LIU Yearbook *Sound*, "The Long Island University Soccer Team's domination of the Metropolitan Collegiate Soccer Conference ended last season (1968) when the squad finished with a 4-2 record, good for second place in the League. Overall, the Birds (we were known as the "Blackbirds") were 8-4-1. Seeking an unprecedented fifth consecutive title and 35th straight Met Conference win, the Blackbirds were unceremoniously dumped on their tail feathers, so to speak, by the Knights of Fairleigh Dickinson, 3-1. This season marked the first time in the three-year reign of Coach Joe Machnik that the soccer team failed to receive a post-season tourney bid. No small wonder, when one considers that no fewer than 12 seniors left the squad, including the great Dov Markus and All Met choices Louis Gallaro, Ronnie Jabusch and Sam Farrell. Coach Machnik's record over the three years that he has been coaching the varsity is a cool 36-8-3, for a scorching .818 winning percentage."

There were many lessons to be learned over that three-year period. Certainly, it is seemingly easier to get to the top unexpectedly than to stay there when opponents are primed to upset you as the biggest game on their schedule. Additionally, young players participating in their first varsity games are no match for the other team's seniors, especially when they are under such pressure to maintain a program's legacy of success. This is not meant to disparage the work, skill or level of commitment of the new team members. Co-captains Arnie Ramirez and Paul Engl did all they could to provide leadership on and off the field. The chemistry was just not there. And the two-time Met Conference "Coach of the Year" did not have the answers.

At the Coaches Convention, Walter Chyzowych and I conducted our debate in front of a packed room. Walter had already been successful coaching at Philadelphia Textile and despite the 1968 season, I was still considered a coach to be heard from. During the discussion, I shared a methodology defending free kicks. It was common practice to line up a defensive wall for less than the required ten yards, thus winning some time to get more players back in defensive positions as the attacking team protested and the referee was required to step the yards off.

Several in the audience believed this practice was unsporting and had no place in the intercollegiate game. Later that year, I received a letter from the NSCAA criticizing my role in the presentation.

After the debate, I was approached by Don Wynschenk, a part-time soccer coach at New Haven College in Connecticut, who was charged with finding a new coach, as he was to become chairman of the Department of Physical Education and supervisor of a new gymnasium building on newly acquired land known as the North Campus. Wynschenk inquired as to my possible interest in moving, having no idea that I had relatives in Connecticut and was planning to spend summers operating a campsite, especially if I could find a full-time job teaching/coaching during the academic year.

Early in February, I drove to West Haven, Connecticut to meet with New Haven's athletic director, Don Ormrod. Ormrod and Wynschenk gave me a tour of the facilities, especially the North Campus, which would also house the baseball and soccer fields. Baseball games were at the time being played at Quigley Stadium, a minor league park in West Haven, and soccer games were played at Quigley and in New Haven's Edgewood Park. Basically, in 1969, New Haven College had no athletic facilities of its own. And it was a member of the NAIA, not yet of the NCAA. But most important to me, it was located in Connecticut.

At the interview, I was asked what else I could do, in addition to coaching soccer and teaching physical education service classes, to justify the creation of a full-time job. Although I had never coached hockey, and could hardly ice skate, I mentioned my love for the game. Ormrod immediately informed me that New Haven did have a hockey team and that the coach, Jim Fanning, was stepping down.

I accepted the position of soccer and hockey coach and a faculty position in the Department of Physical Education. The salary was $10,000! And we would be living rent free at the campsite in Salem, albeit temporarily in a construction trailer.

Instead of recruiting for LIU, I was now hopeful of bringing players to Connecticut. Two of the students we played roller hockey with on Saturdays, Joe DiCostanzo and Henry Avelon, accompanied me to Choate School to see a New Haven College ice hockey game. As they both also played in the NY junior league, they informed me that they thought they could compete at the level they were watching that evening at Choate. They had never thought about playing college ice hockey in NY, so this opportunity was "real", and it was suggested that many NY area players would also be interested. I also thought that many New York City high school and junior college soccer players would love the opportunity to play in Connecticut.

Witch Meadow Lake Campsites opened with 40 campsites on May 1, 1969, and the season was to run until October 31st. We moved to the trailer earlier that spring, putting most of our New York furniture in storage. Barbara drew the camp logo, and we created a brochure, decals and bumper stickers. A separate building was constructed to house toilet facilities, showers etc., an office and a camp store. My A&P experience served me well in ordering the various camping staples, groceries and almost everything the campers forgot to bring for their weekend or week camping with us on site. The first summer was a huge success. The forty camp sites were sold out every weekend and most weekdays. Wherever possible new sites were being constructed. Playground equipment was installed. A beach was created bringing clean sand in for one end of the lake. The fishing was fantastic! And it was less than 20 miles into downtown New London. And no one could predict at the time that some 30 years later, with 150 campsites, that two large casinos would open just miles away! A gold mine!

I commuted back and forth to LIU to finish up my teaching responsibilities that spring. Shortly after I left LIU, there began a very public dispute between LIU Provost Birenbaum and Chancellor Hoxie. The result being that Birenbaum left to become the President of Staten Island Community College, later to be known as the College of Staten Island.

Gary Rosenthal also left thereafter to become Chair of that institution's Physical Education Department. Birenbaum left Staten Island in 1976 to become President of Antioch University.

Gary Rosenthal's legacy at LIU is huge. In addition to earning two Met Conference Championships, he coached five All-Americans and led the team into two NCAA playoffs. He encouraged Ray Klivecka and I to continue our careers after playing.

Ray Klivecka had a stint as head coach of CCNY and as assistant to the US national youth team before becoming an assistant to the NY Cosmos under Eddie Firmani and then becoming the Cosmos' head coach. Klivecka later coached in the MISL with Buffalo and New York Express.

Dieter Ficken returned to his Alma Mater first as an assistant coach but then as head coach during the 1976-79 campaigns. He then coached Columbia University for 27 seasons, leading them on one occasion to the NCAA National Championship Game.

Carlo Tramontozzi went on to be head coach at Saint Francis College and Athletic Director. He had a 21-year coaching career, winning 190 games with five NCAA appearances, making the quarterfinals in 1978.

Indirectly through Gary, Arnie Ramirez garnered 214 LIU wins between 1979 and 1998, developing nine All-Americans and earning four NCAA appearances.

LIU remained a strong soccer powerhouse. Finally, after many years, the field was set with artificial turf and was laid out in the opposite direction which enabled it to be classified as full sized. The soccer office was moved from the Brooklyn Paramount building into a new athletic facility with windows overlooking the soccer field.

Gary Rosenthal passed away unexpectedly in 2010 at the age of 75.

With the help of the then current soccer coach, TJ Kostecki, who also had a 20-year coaching career at LIU, I was asked to lead a fund-raising drive which upon reaching its goal, would enable the LIU soccer office to be permanently named The Gary Rosenthal Soccer Office.

It was an easy task as many of his former players were quick to contribute. There was a thoughtful and heartfelt ceremony attended by Gary's wife Lynne, Carlo Tramontozzi, Gerry Klivecka and many others.

Unfortunately, in 2018-19, a decision was made to terminate LIU's outdoor sport programs and to combine them with C.W. Post's on Long Island, even changing the historic "Blackbirds" name to "Sharks". More than 60 years of positive soccer tradition in Brooklyn would soon evaporate into memories.

Gary Rosenthal's office no longer looks out onto the Brooklyn campus field where legends were made as the field no longer exists.

Hopefully though, Gary's memory and legacy will exist, forever!

Bye Bye Blackbirds!

My earliest photo for the University's weekly publication "Seawanhaka". Note the stitched ball (you can't see the laces) and the lack of goalkeeper gloves.

With Head Coach Gary Rosenthal and Ray Klivecka (center).
Ray was recruited to score goals, and I was recruited to save them.

Ray Klivecka and I were both named to the
All-American team for our efforts in 1962.

1962 LIU team photo with Ray Klivecka kneeling third from the left. Bob Feger and Dieter Ficken are kneeling to my right.

Starting line-up in a 1963 game at LIU Field. Note the 16 story apartment buildings in the background, our home while later coaching at LIU.

NEW BLACKBIRD CAPTAIN Joe Machnik is seen here making making a save against Brooklyn College last year. Machnik turned in another shutout Saturday as the booters blanked Drew, 4-0.

Managed to get this one over the top.

Saved this long range shot from Pratt Institute's Walt Schmotolocha; ball can be seen after I deflected it at the top right-hand side of the photo.

IN AND OUT: Goalie Joe Machnik grimaces (photo right) as one of Bridgeport's three goals eludes his outstretched hands. Machnik made many spectacular saves (photo left) but he couldn't do the job alone as the Knights' offense overwhelmed the Bird defense.

COLLEGE TRY: Joe Machnik, Long Island University goal keeper, leaps to forestall a scoring attempt by City College during the soccer game played at Lewisohn Stadium. City College took the visitors by a 4-2 score.

Early game photo vs. CCNY at historic Lewisohn Stadium. The action was captured by Roland Thau and appeared in the Sunday New York Times.

Saved this one with my face. (Roland Thau photo)

Being carried off the field on the shoulders of reserve players and fans after clinching the Met Conference Championship and gaining a NCAA Tournament berth in 1967.

LONG ISLAND UNIVERSITY

LIU: (Back Row, left to right) Coach Joe Machnik, Carlo Tramontozzi, Samuel Farrell, Kalman Magyar, Eddy Perodin, Steve Reinhardt, Hugh Reid, Dov Markus, John Limberis. (Front Row) Reinhold Jabusch, Louis Gallaro, Jerry Babij, Michael Cohen, Thomas O'Leary, Albert Soria, Alix Perrault, Michael Hogan, Marcello Launi.

LIU ROSTER

No.	Name	Pos.	Ht.	Wt.	Class	Home Town
16	Jerry Babij	F	5-9	145	Sr.	Bridgeport, Connecticut
1	Michael Cohen	G	5-11	165	Jr.	Brooklyn
4	Samuel Farrell	HB	5-8	160	Jr.	Brooklyn
5	Louis Gallaro	HB	5-9	165	Jr.	Manhattan
7	Michael Hogan	F	5-10	155	Jr.	Brooklyn
2	Reinhold Jabusch	FB	5-9	160	Sr.	Brooklyn
8	Marcello Launi	F	5-8	150	Jr.	Queens
6	John Limberis	HB	5-8	155	Jr.	Bronx
18	Kalman Magyar	FB	5-6	165	Jr.	Queens
9	Dov Markus	F	5-6	180	Jr.	Manhattan
19	Thomas O'Leary	G	5-10	160	Jr.	Bronx
11	Eddy Perodin	F	5-8	150	Jr.	Levittown
3	*Alix Perrault	FB	5-7	160	Sr.	Brooklyn
12	Hugh Reid	F	5-9	165	Sr.	Queens
17	Steve Reinhardt	F	5-8	150	Soph	Bronx
14	Albert Soria	HB	6-0	165	Sr.	Queens
10	Carlo Tramontozzi	F	5-8	160	Sr.	Brooklyn

* Captain

JOE MACHNIK
LIU Coach

1966 RECORD

LIU		Opponent
12	C. W. Post College	0
2	New York University	0
7	Seton Hall University	0
2	University of Bridgeport	1
3	Temple University	4
5	Brooklyn College	0
3	Pratt Institute	0
6	Adelphi University	1
5	Fairleigh Dickinson	4
8	Queens College	1
10	Hofstra	0
6	Rutgers	0
6	*Cortland State	1
1	*University of Bridgeport	0

* NCAA Playoffs

1966 SCORING

Dov Markus	26
Marcello Launi	15
Carlo Tramontozzi	14
Hugh Reid	7
Sam Farrell	6
John Limberis	4
Mike Hogan	4
Albert Soria	3
Lou Gallaro	1
Reinhold Jabusch	1
TEAM'S TOTALS	81
OPPONENTS' TOTALS	12

Record: Won 14, Lost 1
Colors: Blue and White

The 1966 LIU team, my first as Head Coach appearing in the NCAA Soccer Championships Game Program.

With team Captain Carlo Tramontozzi discussing strategy at half time.

I started dating Barbara Otlowski while attending LIU. Here we are together on Easter Sunday at Ukrainian Field prior to a game in 1961.

Receiving the 1966 second place NCAA Championship plaque with LIU Captain Alix Perrault in Berkeley, CA.

Being hugged by LIU striker Dov Markus, the first Hermann Trophy winner after coming from behind at Trinity College in Hartford CT and qualifying for the 1967 NCAA National Tournament Finals in St. Louis.

Chapter 5

New Haven College/ University of New Haven
"Becoming Dr. Joe"

The University of New Haven was founded in 1920 as the New Haven YMCA Junior College. It received a state charter as New Haven College in 1926 and in 1960 moved to the site of a former county orphanage on top of a hill on the Boston Post Road in West Haven, Connecticut.

When I arrived for that first interview in the spring of 1969, the North Campus Athletic Complex on the other side of the Post Road, was still in the construction phase. My interview occurred in Athletic Director Don Ormrod's office at the end of the ornate orphanage building which also housed a small gymnasium, less than the size of a regulation basketball court, certainly in width. In the basement were a few lockers and shower areas in a room of peeling paint, exposed plumbing and asbestos wrapped pipes supporting the building's heating system. There was no air conditioning.

The soccer program was started in 1962 with coach Richard Curren and then with Paul "Topsy" DelGobbo taking over for the next four years. The team had a winning record through 1967 when Don Wynschenk took over but fell to 5-6-1 in his second year. Wynschenk's two-year coaching record was a healthy 13-8-3.

The ice hockey program under Jim Fanning started in 1967 and was in its third year when I arrived.

The city of New Haven has had a long hockey history with its first arena opening in 1914, reconstructed after a fire in 1927 and owned and operated by the Podoloff family, famous for founding the NBA. The Eastern Hockey League's New Haven Blades were the hottest ticket in town and the 4,400-seat New Haven Arena was always full for hockey. New Haven College often practiced and played in the Arena but also used the rink at Choate School as it waited for a rink to be built at West Haven High School. High school hockey was a huge sport in Connecticut, with nearby Hamden High School possessing their own rink, often challenging for the State title.

After accepting the combined soccer-hockey job at New Haven, I went to several Rangers practices at New Hyde Park's Skateland to see what an actual hockey practice looked like. I was very fortunate to learn that Artie Crouse, the high school coach at West Haven, would stay on to be my assistant. Artie was a local hockey legend, who played pro, officiated big time college hockey and was generally regarded as "Mr. Hockey" in West Haven.

As far as hockey was concerned, every game would be my first. And the schedule contained powerhouses Boston State, Salem State (the future coaching home of NHL coach John Tortorella) and other teams from the hockey hotbeds of Boston and Worcester, Massachusetts.

As far as soccer was concerned, I was fortunate to recruit several soccer players from Francis Lewis High School in New York, where coach Martin Kaplan had previously directed players to LIU. Brothers Tom and John Kowalski had arrived from Poland as recently as 1965 and were playing for the NY-based German Hungarian club junior teams. They would become the backbone of the New Haven defense. There was a full complement of returning players led by Delfim Pereira, who would be named captain, Greg Smith, the Meskill brothers Mike and Tom, and a fine collection of incoming freshmen. Back then, transfer students had to sit out a year and could not play varsity. Fortunately, the National Collegiate Athletic Association had recently changed its eligibility rules and freshmen were now able to suit up. Don Wynschenk was to be my assistant whenever he could get away from his administrative duties.

During the summer prior to my first year at New Haven, Barbara and I continued to work at Witch Meadow Lake Campsites. I took a day off from camp to travel to the college to get some administrative work done. Around 3pm, legendary baseball coach Frank Vieira, Sports Information Director (SID) Bob Cornell, himself a former goalie on the soccer team and other coaches who wanted to get to know me went out to a nearby watering hole, The House of Zodiac. We obviously had a good time as when six o'clock came around, I realized that I was not in sufficient condition to drive home safely. I had to call Barbara in Salem at the campground to come and pick me up. At this time, I think, we realized just how far the college campus was from our new home. More than an hour!

Even though the camping season at the Witch Meadow Lake Campsites that first year was advertised as May 1st to October 31st, it was clear that after the sold-out Labor Day weekend, business would seriously decline. In fact, when I left for work on Tuesday, September 2nd to meet with the soccer team for the first time, the campground was completely void of campers, tents and trailers. When I returned later that evening, Barbara and I discussed the situation at length and decided as two kids who had grown up in the largest city in America and had last lived on the 16th floor of a three-building apartment complex, that we were not going to be able to make it through the fall much less the winter living in a trailer in the woods absent any neighbors.

The next day, after practice, I discovered an almost brand-new, all-electric apartment complex at the foot of Campbell Avenue in West Haven. It had a huge swimming pool built on West Haven beach, a playground, and a nearby shopping center with restaurants. The site was previously part of the Savin Rock Amusement Park. It was going to be a great place for Colette and Janine to grow up and was less than two miles from the campus, meaning my family could become part of the greater university community. We moved in later that week, forsaking what our dream opportunity had been of working at a family campground for the summer and living in a house built just for us by my Machnik relatives in Old Lyme. Obviously, there was surprise, disappointment and disbelief with our decision in Old Lyme and no doubt we felt bad as well, but in retrospect the decision was a matter of survival. The question was, would we ever own a house?

The 1969 soccer season at New Haven was a disaster. We lost four games by one goal and three others in overtime. We were shut out five times and scored a single goal on five other occasions, our goal total being only 15 for the season — and four of those were in a 4-6 overtime loss to my nemesis, again, Pratt Institute. Chyzowych took it easy on us in Philadelphia, beating us 3-0. The final record: 2-10-1. That's ten losses!

So much for "Coach of the Year!" It was the worst season in New Haven College soccer history!

The 1969-70 New Haven hockey squad had an excellent "starting five" in forwards Jeff Andrews, Paul Kane and Bobby Daft, bolstered by defensemen Kirk Roberts and Rick DellaRocco. Regardless, we opened the season 0-2 before our first game at Salem State which we lost 17-0. With two wins in our next three games, we faced Salem State again, this time at home. The Salem coach, Barry Urbanski, called ahead, suggesting we play our transfer players to provide the Salem State Vikings with better opposition.

During the game, I lamented that I should have gotten his request in writing because we were ahead when he called a timeout and laid into his team. We finally lost the contest 6-3 and I was relieved in a way because had we won, Salem had the right to protest our use of ineligible players.

The hockey season finished a respectable 7-10-1 thanks to the incredible contribution of Artie Crouse, who conducted the practices and prepared the team for each game, as I learned to run the bench and appreciate how much I didn't know about hockey.

I received a call from Lenny Lucenko telling me that Phil Woosnam, Commissioner of the NASL, had secured the TV rights to the 1970 World Cup and that he wanted to sell the rights to individual entrepreneurs who would then show the games in local cinemas and arenas on Closed Circuit Pay-Per-View Satellite, a new system. I told Lenny that the 4,000-seat New Haven Arena would be a perfect setting and since the greater New Haven area had a large Italian population, we should buy one game involving Italy and, of course, the final. Lenny also contacted Bob McNulty, coach of Jersey City State and the three of us partnered in the endeavor. Italy was also one of the favorites to win the competition. We were fortunate that Italy got out of their group, as we had the date booked during which they would play in the quarter-final against México, the host country.

I met with Nate Podoloff, owner and operator of the Arena, and booked the dates: Sunday, June 14th and the final, a week later, on June 21st. Podoloff advised that we were taking a financial long shot and turned down an offer to co-promote which would have minimized our risk. Podoloff also informed us that in addition to the cost of renting the Arena, we would have to pay stagehands and a mandatory union spotlight operator at $70 for the day. Somehow, I convinced him to allow the use of our own ticket window staff and ticket takers. Podoloff would keep all the concession receipts. There was no advance sale, Ticket Master, Stub Hub or Seat Geeks to help us out! While the 1966 World Cup Final between England and Germany was televised same-day-tape-delay on NBC, the 1970 arrangement would permit only Closed Circuit Pay-Per-View.

Not thinking anything of it, I began to send mailers out to all the local Italian establishments, restaurants, barber shops, pizza parlors etc. on college stationary using the school's postage machine. We formed a company, Soccer Enterprises LTD, listing my home as its business address. General Admission tickets were $6.00 and Reserved Seats (up front) were $8 and $10.

On game day the Arena was set up beautifully with theater-style seating on the main floor, the screen and projector in place. We opened the doors and waited for the crowd.

The first cars showed up full of fans and the excitement grew. "How many games are you showing?" asked a driver. "One, Italy v Mexico," we replied.

"Madison Square Garden (MSG) is showing two!" They replied and kept on driving. We had no idea that the Garden had undermined us by purchasing two games that day. The same happened to Walter Chyzowych who promoted the game in the Philadelphia area, almost equidistant to NY as New Haven. They just kept on driving.

The final attendance for the quarter-final in New Haven was 1,020 and we had expected at least twice as many. At that number, we barely broke even.

Italy won the match 4-1 after an own goal from Javier Guzman, a Gigi Riva brace and a further strike by Gianni Rivera. And they won their semi-final 4-3 in extra time with Rivera's 111th-minute goal breaking West Germany's hearts after Gerd Muller had briefly leveled the score a minute earlier.

Several local coaches traveled down to Madison Square Garden for the semi-finals, which was a double-header, with Brazil beating Uruguay 3-1 to advance to the final versus Italy. A dream final for those owning the closed-circuit TV rights! The semi-final games still stick in my mind with a fabulous performance by the Uruguay goalkeeper Ladislao Mazurkiewicz and the memory of Franz Beckenbauer playing in a sling to protect his broken collar bone and dislocated shoulder.

With no MSG double-header to thwart us and with a glorious final to promote in New Haven, Brazil with Pele and Italy with their fantastic following, 3,000-plus showed up at the Arena, completely filling the seats on the main floor and spilling over to the end zone and sidelines.

I watched the game from the press box where New Haven Register reporter Tom McCormick came not only to report on the game but on the phenomenon of thousands of people showing up to watch it on the new phenomenon, Closed Circuit TV.

Several weeks later, as a participant at the very first US Soccer Federation Coaching School in Providence, Rhode Island, while talking on the hall pay phone in the dormitory, Barbara informed me that I had to come back to New Haven for an emergency meeting with the New Haven College President, Dr. Marvin Peterson.

Evidently, many of the brochures and fliers that I had mailed out using the college postage machine were coming back as undeliverable: "Address Unknown — Return to Sender." I tried to explain that I was trying to promote the sport locally, but it fell on deaf ears. While I could have been fired for the lack of judgement I had shown in using the college postage machine, Peterson instead suggested an alternative. If I paid for the postage of all the diplomas that had yet to be sent out, all would be forgiven. Having no choice, I accepted the compromise.

At the end of the day, after splitting the "profits" with McNulty and Lucenko and paying for the diplomas to be mailed, I wound up losing money on the deal. But, at least, I still had a job.

The 1970 soccer season witnessed a complete turnaround. Even though we opened with a disappointing 1-1 draw with Quinnipiac; we managed to win the next six games before falling to CCNY at Randalls Island. At the end of the regular season, we were 10-3-1, even beating Pratt Institute 1-0, and both Southern and Central Connecticut State by scores of 3-0 and 2-1 respectfully.

And we qualified for the NAIA Regional Tournament.

The team was bolstered by several transfer students from Ira Weiss' NY City CC. Namely a speedy front runner named Kelvin Hazzard and winger Perry Laventure, plus the return to New Haven of a gritty forward Glen Banks, who had completed his military service. Add the defender Ike Lieberman, and the maturation of the Kowalski brothers and other returning veterans such as Ray Connolly and Captain Del Pereira, plus converted hockey player Joe DiCostanzo in goal. We also had Reinhold Steinsdoerfer, Stanley Dziurzynski, George Rand and back-up goalkeeper Steve Benko who could also, if needed, spell a player on the field.

And from Kingston College in Jamaica, with the assistance of two Jamaican players from LIU, Denis Johnson and Noel Miller, I recruited unseen defender Neville Brown. The problem was we were now stacked with defenders and Neville had to play out of position, on the wing. It didn't matter which wing Neville played on. During home games Neville liked playing in front of the crowd which gathered on a hill overlooking the field. So, he played right wing when we attacked the north goal in the direction of the gymnasium site and left wing when we attacked in the direction of

Frank Vieira's baseball field.

A 1970 team picture taken in front of the north goal shows the still incomplete construction of the new gymnasium with scaffolding and even a crane in the background and of course not a single blade of grass. Now coaching on sandlots!

In fact, North Campus maintenance director Don Wright and Augie, his assistant, would collect pails full of stones and rocks off the field prior to every game. They seemed to come out of nowhere.

The NAIA Area Eight Regional Tournament was held at Eastern Connecticut State in Willimantic. We barely survived a 3-2 win over Ricker College and then managed a 1-0 win over the hosts on a goal scored directly from a corner kick by Neville Brown. Such a goal is now called an "Olimpico". The name is derived from the alleged first such goal scored in 1924 by Argentine Cesareo Onzari against Uruguay which had just won the Olympic title that year!

So, in the year following a 2-10-1 season, New Haven was going to the NAIA Final Eight which was to be played in Dunn, North Carolina. Athletic Director Don Ormrod arranged for two nine-passenger vans as transportation. Don Wynschenk drove one van and I drove the other. There must have been at least another car following with equipment and luggage because we were a party of 20 — 18 players and two coaches.

The plan was to make the 597-mile trip in one day. Normally that would take just under 10 hours, but there was no GPS at the time and somehow our navigator had us drive around the Washington DC loop twice. We did finally get to our hotel, the Dutch Inn, about 11pm that night. Once we crossed over the North Carolina border the conversation mostly turned to the signs we saw on the roadside, "The Ku Klux Clan Welcomes You," and of the concerns of our three players of color.

Four matches were to be played on the first day in the tournament's first round and we were fortunate in one way to get the late game under the lights, as the daytime temperature was much higher than what we were used to playing in middle November in New England. On the other hand, we drew tournament favorite Davis & Elkins (D&E) in our first match.

D&E had won the NAIA Championship two years earlier but had lost in the 1969 final to Eastern Illinois 1-0 after two overtime periods. The team was coached by Greg Myers, who went on to a career in the NASL and had star goalkeeper Bill Nuttall, playing behind a future legend in the history of soccer in America, the future Federation Secretary General Hank Steinbrecher.

Playing defense like never before, the score of our first game finished 0-0. Overtime periods would be five minutes each. But after two overtime periods the game was still scoreless. And there had to be a winner!

Prior to the seventh overtime period (after 120 minutes of play), I approached referee Pat Smith about the possibility of flipping a coin (a method sometimes used in knockout competitions with the score tied and no goal in sight). He laughed, and we continued to play. D&E finally scored in the eighth overtime period (40 minutes of extra play) against the exhausted New Haven team still struggling with its 12-hour van excursion and tour of Washington. It was the longest game in NAIA history. It was well after 10PM when we finished.

Still recovering from the travel and the equivalent of playing a game and a half the night before, New Haven struggled against its next opponent, Ottawa of Kansas, losing 3-0. With a day's rest, we were drawn in the seventh-place match against Earlham, and with pride on the line, managed a 4-2 win.

After completing my master's degree in 1966, I amassed 26 credits toward a Ph.D. over the next three years. It was difficult work, expensive, and there was no guarantee that after achieving 60 credits that a dissertation outline or even the dissertation itself would be approved. There was always the possibility of achieving a worthless "Ab.D." — "All but Degree!"

Lenny Lucenko called again. He was now head coach and a faculty member at Montclair State in New Jersey and in a similar career position. A colleague of his, James Santomier, had gone to the University of Utah, transferred his post-master's credits, received a warm welcome, had a great experience and was primed to receive his doctoral degree in Salt Lake City. Lenny asked if Barbara and I would consider going out with him and his family to Salt Lake City in Utah for the summer.

When I took the job in New Haven it came with the rank of Assistant Professor and the next step was Associate Professor with all the benefits, increased pay, preferential teaching load and the possibility of being placed on the tenure track, tantamount to a lifetime contract. A Ph.D. would almost guarantee tenure. It was worth a try, and we decided to make the journey to Utah mostly on a lark.

We hitched a U-Haul trailer to our Chevy station wagon and made the trip in four days, driving on average 600 miles per day. We met the Lucenkos in a downtown motel and waited the five days we needed before our rental house in the foothills would become available.

We got to the university in time to register for pre-summer semester courses where two credits could be attained in one week attending class all day from nine to five. I had come into possession of a small 125cc motorcycle which Lenny and I used to commute back and forth. At the end of the summer, I accumulated 19 straight A credits and loved every minute of it. On weekends we would travel to the four corners of the State and even into Idaho. It was like living on another planet. There was even stock car racing at the State Fairgrounds and at a small track on the Nevada state line near Elko called Bonneville Speedway. We decided that we would go back the following summer, and we applied for "Married Student Housing" on campus.

I would coach ice hockey for only two more seasons as it was becoming more obvious that despite some good results and a full roster of players, the program needed someone more dedicated to the sport, not a coach whose mind was on soccer primarily.

But my love of hockey and knowledge of its rules would pay dividends some years later with the introduction of the Major Indoor Soccer League (MISL).

It would be another year competing in NAIA soccer in 1971, and the season got off to a great start with six straight wins and five shutouts, including a 5-0 win over Central Connecticut. But the Chyzowych Textile team beat us 2-1 in Philadelphia. We finished the regular season 12-3-1 and qualified for the regional tournament, even getting to host two first-round games, a 1-0 win over Babson and a three-overtime victory, 2-1, against Barrington. However, we were upset at a neutral site encounter in Willimantic with a 2-3 loss to Keene State. A return to the Nationals was not in the cards. Kelvin Hazzard would lead the team with 22 goals, Neville Brown had 16 and newcomer Reuben Salas had seven. Eight shutouts were recorded over the 18-game schedule by Joe DiCostanzo, bringing his career total to 13.

It would be back to the University of Utah for the summer of 1972. I had accumulated an additional eight credits during the academic year with two independent study courses.

If I was going to be serious about the possibilities of achieving a Ph.D., I would have to register for a minimum nine-month residency in Utah. I applied for sabbatical leave from New Haven for the Spring semester 1973 and it was granted with the caveat that I return to the university for a minimum of one year. I had only been at the now "University" of New Haven for three and a half years, so the granting of the leave was extraordinary, and I had to be especially thankful to the Chair of the Promotion and Tenure Committee, Dr. Gwen Jensen, one of the very few female faculty members at the male dominated institution for championing my cause.

Certainly, with the reality that I would not be on campus for the Spring semester, along with my previously identified shortcomings in the sport, it was important that the hockey team had new leadership. Hence my decision to step down from that coaching position was made personally easier and generally welcomed on campus. I introduced the new coach, Steve Lane, to his players during a meeting conducted at our apartment in West Haven.

The soccer team was invited to a pre-season "Jamboree" at which multiple teams would play against each other in shortened games. During a break, one of the referees, Keith Johnson, approached a group of coaches having lunch stating that the Connecticut State Soccer Association season was starting the next day, and the games were short of referees. Having had some experience as a high school and junior soccer referee while at LIU, I raised my hand. And without a rule book, an exam, or a fitness test, I found myself in the middle of a game without linesmen at a park somewhere in Waterbury. I loved it.

This began a regular practice of officiating every Sunday, advancing to the first division with games with teams like Hartford Hellenic, New Britain Falcons, Hartford Italian American-Stars in Colt Park, Dillon Stadium, Polish Falcons Field and other sandlots.

Barbara and I became friendly with faculty member Dr. Allen Sack and his wife Gina. Allen was a former high school football star quarterback in eastern Pennsylvania who was recruited by Ara Parseghian at Notre Dame. He played defensive end on the 1966 Championship team and was drafted by the Los Angeles Rams. He became a "hard hitting critic of college sports" according to Notre Dame Magazine, fighting for the rights of college athletes.

We often had contentious discussions about the athletic program at the University of New Haven, as I tried to explain the differences between big time NCAA Division I football and basketball and what was taking place at our Division II school. Allen taught in the Sociology Department and had a long-term vision about Sociology of Sport, a course I took and loved at the University of Utah with Professor Merrill Melnick, a legend in the field.

One of my closest friends during these days was John Benevento. John started his career at the university as an assistant financial aid officer and performed a similar role in the Admissions Office before becoming Director of Admissions. As a coach, it was good to have a friend in the Admissions Office. John also dabbled in real estate and classic cars, helping us buy our first house and a Benz or two, but most importantly he became a Vice President and confidant to President Philip Kaplan which facilitated a close bond for me with the university's top executives.

The 1972 soccer season, our first as a NCAA DII team, saw the side finish with a 9-1-2 record. The highlights were a hard-fought 1-0 win over Southern Connecticut and a home 2-2 tie with Philadelphia Textile, which scored a late penalty kick. We received an invitation to the inaugural NCAA Division II Tournament following the separation of Division I and II programs for national competitions. The Division III Tournament did not start until 1974.

Our NCAA Tournament game was a disappointing 1-0 loss to the University of Bridgeport, played at New Haven because Bridgeport was still using Seaside Park as their home ground. As a knockout game, we were "one and done". Bridgeport then went on to lose to Springfield 1-0, and Springfield then lost to Oneonta State.

Of course, being on sabbatical and over 2,000 miles away did nothing for my ability to recruit replacements for the departing seniors. I had learned about a player at South Central Community College in New Haven who was also playing amateur ball in the Sunday League. Roberto Taylor led all scorers on the 1973 team with 14 goals and five assists, and Neville Brown finished his career being named to the New England Intercollegiate Soccer League (NEISL) All-Star team as well as being named "All-New England". It was John Kowalski's first season as assistant coach — his coaching career led John to the very top of soccer in America. Overall, the team finished 9-4-3 with an invitation to the Eastern College Athletic Conference (ECAC) tournament in New Jersey, in which we defeated Kean College 4-1 before losing to Hunter College 1-0.

The day after Christmas 1972, we loaded the family and the gear into the station wagon for our third trip to Salt Lake City. Colette and Janine sat in the back and for much of the journey we entertained each other with board games such as Candy Land.

It was a spring semester course Recreation for the Elderly which set me on my dissertation path. My dissertation, entitled "Recreation in Planned Retirement Villages", successfully endeavored to survey, evaluate and make recommendations pertaining to the recreational opportunities offered in planned retirement villages. Ten such retirement villages would be contacted and visited in the Southwest and on the Pacific Coast during a three-week journey via station wagon and pulled tent camper. We would live primarily on canned beef stew, deviled ham and Spam.

A survey instrument was developed, and recreational activities classified as being either sensory-motor, affective or cognitive with participation in these activities compared to elements of "successful aging" as defined primarily as the retardation of senility, using Dr. Thomas J DeCarlo's research in a Twin Study, *Recreation Participation Patterns and Successful Aging*.

The fact I brought daughters Colette and Janine (aged five and three) with me to the retirement villages was key to being accepted by the residents and their willingness to participate in my research. At one such establishment, we were asked if we wanted complimentary VIP tickets to nearby Disneyland, which we would not have been able to afford otherwise.

In my dissertation acknowledgements, I wrote : "Finally, this survey is dedicated to my wife, Barbara, who provided understanding, confidence, encouragement and patience, but more importantly, has provided friendship and love and to our two daughters Colette and Janine who have been the motivation."

The 182-page dissertation was very well received, even to the point of my being asked to write an article for *Retirement Living* magazine and to participate on a panel. "The Opportunities and Problems of the Aging in Urban Recreation", being held jointly by Southern Connecticut State and the Connecticut Recreation and Park Association.

When I returned to the University of New Haven with a Ph.D., baseball coach Frank Vieira was the first to call me "Doctor Joe". Frank was also a college basketball referee of distinction and was familiar with the already legendary "Doctor J", Julius Erving, who had played locally at the University of Massachusetts, Amherst and professionally for Earl Foreman's Virginia Squires of the American Basketball Association.

The final trip home from Utah was eventful indeed. Just days before the start of our trip, something broke in the Chevy wagon's engine and there was no time to get it repaired, as no one had the parts. So, we rented a U-Haul cargo van with a hitch and towed the station wagon behind. We made it all the way to the Delaware Water Gap in New Jersey when a detour directed us off the highway.

On a side road, going down a steep hill, it started to rain, and the water mixed with the oil and grease on the heavily traveled detour made it extremely slippery. When I hit the brakes to slow down, the towed station wagon started to fishtail behind us, and I struggled to regain control as we swerved into the oncoming lane. We swiped one oncoming car, taking off its side view mirror, before somehow lodging a telephone pole on the passenger side in the space between the cargo van and the towed vehicle. The station wagon was destroyed. I checked that Colette and Janine, who were sleeping in the van, were okay and ran up the hill to check on the car we swiped. Miraculously, they were fine and just wanted to keep going on their way. I never heard from them again. When the police came, they were very sympathetic and offered to have the car towed to a nearby garage. We left the "totaled" station wagon in New Jersey and continued our way home. We were now without a car!

Fortunately, with the insurance settlement, we were able to buy one of the first Hondas in America, a tiny vehicle with an asking price of $2,500. And Frank Vieira sold us one of his older cars so that Barbara would have a vehicle as well.

With the Ph.D., Allen Sack asked if I would teach a course in the Sociology Department, so I developed a curriculum for the "Sociology of Aging" which I taught for several years in UNH's Graduate School.

When I returned to the university after nine months in Utah, it was notably different. The cordial atmosphere in the Athletic Department had changed. Tension filled the air. A feud of sorts developed between Don Ormrod and Frank Vieira over the use of one or more players in the fall baseball program who may not have been full time students. It was Vieira's contention that fall baseball was an informal, recreational sport, and Ormrod differed, taking the situation to President Kaplan who then issued that all the players must be full-time students.

With my recently earned Ph.D. I began to think about other opportunities where I might continue coaching but also make use of my degree in a bona-fide physical education or recreation majors' program after my obligatory one year in New Haven. I was one of three finalists for the soccer job at Penn State and was flown there for an interview. I thought I had a good shot having been an NCAA runner-up in 1966 and semi-finalist in 1967 with LIU and the early NAIA success at New Haven.

Tensions continued to boil at New Haven and on October 8, 1974, Don Ormrod resigned as Athletic Director. Because of my Ph.D. I was asked by President Kaplan, perhaps with John Benevento and Gwen Jensen's influence, to serve as Acting Athletic Director while a national search was conducted. I was expected to apply!

In the *University Student News*, answering a question as to what my plans for the Athletic Department were, I replied: "I would like to rearrange the Athletic Control Board to enable more students to be on it." I talked about the formation of a Captain's Council, asking coaches for their short and long-term plans for their respective sports, increasing athletic financial aid and developing plans to attract more students to the North Campus. I also, in separate conversations with the Student Council, addressed the desire to make football a varsity sport rather than a club sport and to develop additional property in the woods behind the baseball field as a separate field for football. Lastly, I began to think about the lack of sports for the increasing number of female students who have been attracted to the university by several of its new academic offerings.

Dr. Kaplan formed a Search Committee which recommended five candidates from the 93 that applied, and despite strong letters of recommendation from William Birenbaum, President of Staten Island Community College and Gary Rosenthal, its Chairman of the Physical Education Department, I placed fifth. The fourth person withdrew, and the group was narrowed to three. I did not make the cut!

New Haven Register reporter Jon Stein wrote in his *College Corner* column an article entitled "Dr. Joe Left Out in the Cold". It described the support I had on campus, from coaches led by Frank Vieira who personally appealed to Kaplan and a student petition led by the President of the Day Student Council, Dave Buffallini. Also, there was a powerful letter written to Dr. Kaplan by Gary Alexander, sports director of the university radio station *WNHU* and sports editor of the school newspaper *The News*, that became public.

In the meantime, the phone rang in our office, and it was announced that Penn State was on the line for me. Sudden panic!

Here I am being considered for the Athletic Director job at New Haven and Penn State is going to offer me their open soccer position. The caller said, "We thank you for your application. We want to inform you that we have offered the job to Walter Bahr, and he has accepted"!

Relief!

On March 27, 1975, Dr. Kaplan recognized the support I had earned with the Student Council, and I was appointed Athletic Director. The student newspaper headline read *Machnik Athletic Director – Student's Voice Heard*. Kaplan issued the following statement for the press: "Dr. Machnik is a talented and dedicated teacher and coach. He is innovative, imaginative and deeply committed to the best interests of the university. He is professional in every respect and enjoys the respect of other professionals in the field. I think the University of New Haven is fortunate to have Dr. Machnik as its Athletic Director."

The next day, George Wadley wrote in the *New Haven Register* article *Dr. Joe – Revisionist* that "Dr. Joe is a shrewd and crafty infighter with an instinct for survival and a conviction that UNH's athletic program needs drastic revision. Dr. Joe is convinced that the job has been turned over to the right man."

The turmoil around the Athletic Department, my impending role as Acting Athletic Director and the focus on all that it entailed took its toll on the 1974 UNH soccer team. We started by waiting over two hours for a team representing the University of Mexico to arrive at the North Campus. We had a huge crowd for a 3pm kick-off, but hardly anyone was still there at 5pm. We lost the game 1-0 and that was a harbinger of things to come, being shut out five more times, scoring a single goal in two other contests and finishing the season with only five wins. It ended the two-year career of Roberto Taylor, who proved himself to arguably be UNH's most skillful player. Taylor scored 25 goals in 26 games, made the All-New England Team and was drafted by the Connecticut Yankees of the American Soccer League for which he scored 14 goals in his Rookie Year. He then moved to the NASL's Hartford Bicentennials and was declared "Player of the Match" in a game vs. the NY Cosmos which included Pele. His career was cut short by a 1977 automobile accident which left him unable to continue playing.

One of the first projects I insisted upon as Athletic Director was to institute an All-Sports Awards Banquet like the Varsity Club Dinner at LIU. Held at scenic Amarante's Seacliff Inn in East Haven, I invited the "Italian General", August DiFlorio, to be guest speaker. His impersonation fooled everyone present. He hadn't lost his touch since the night I first saw him at LIU years earlier.

Roberto Taylor was named "Athlete of the Year" at that very first affair. Roberto and I remained friends over the years, he became a huge supporter of UNH athletics and my racquetball opponent every Monday night. Later, he went on to own a successful insurance company while coaching at Sheehan High School in Wallingford, CT. He was voted into the UNH Hall of Fame in 1984 and the Connecticut Soccer Hall of Fame in 2008.

As Athletic Director, I was able to negotiate an increase in the department's athletic financial aid structure and negotiate where possible for academic financial aid. As such, all teams seemed to benefit. At an NCAA Athletic Directors' meeting, I learned that there were only three Athletic Directors in the country who were soccer coaches.

With an increase in financial aid and a recruiting budget, Steve Lane's hockey team, for example, with Artie Crouse remaining as assistant coach, finished their season with a respectable 13-8-1 record.

We were able to rejuvenate the soccer team with a good incoming class of Peter Zimmerman, goalie Rick Kessel, Carl Babb, Krys Furman, Glen Joseph, Carlos Palencia, Alvaro Barrios, Dimas Couto, Kevin Scully, Keith Van Ness, Dan Gourash and others.

Zimmerman was a unique prospect as he was recruited sight unseen as an American living in Germany. His father had played in the German American Soccer League. I took a chance on his pedigree and was not disappointed. Kessel's father played as a goalkeeper at Temple University on the same team as Walter Chyzowych. So, he sent Rick to Walt's All-American Camp, and I worked with him there as a camper and recruited him in the process. The 1975 team finished with a strong 10-4-2 season and five shutouts, gaining a bid into the NCAA DII Tournament.

Inexplicably, we came out flat in the competition, losing at home to

Le Moyne, which went out in their next game losing to Adelphi 6-0. The tournament was won by the University of Baltimore over the finals host, Seattle Pacific.

Although the landmark civil rights case known as Title IX was passed in 1972, the University of New Haven, like so many other institutions of higher education, was slow to react to its statutes until there was further federal guidance on its interpretation and enforcement. Regardless, during the 1974-75 academic year, Carole Aiken, Director of Women's Affairs at the University of New Haven, spearheaded a campaign to be ahead of the game through the hiring of a full-time Coordinator of Women's Athletics.

Debbie Chin began her career at the University of New Haven coaching four sports: volleyball, basketball, tennis and softball. She had been a pioneer in the support for Title IX while working in New Haven's public school system, suing the city for funding for the girls' sports program she and two others were financially supporting on their own.

In the interview process at New Haven, Chin inquired: "How far do you want me to take the program?" I answered with a further question: "How far can you take it?" It was one of the reasons she later cited for accepting the position.

Chin had unparalleled success in volleyball, her principal sport, and over time hired replacements in the three other sports as she assumed the role of Associate Director of Athletics. Under her leadership, the women's sports teams continued to develop and in fact, UNH's first NCAA National Championship came in the sport of women's basketball.

Chin would eventually have a four-decade career leading UNH's 16 sports programs with more than 70 NCAA tournament appearances: retiring as Associate Vice President and Director of Athletics and Recreation.

It was a banner year for the 1976 UNH soccer team. The addition of Mario Olivia, Paul Walker, Keith Van Ness, Oscar Rendon and Darko Mrakovic, and the soccer maturation of Kevin Scully, Jako Nikaci, Charles Smith, John Jedrelinic and others with the leadership of Zimmerman, Kessel and Furman created magical chemistry which carried the team to a 9-5-2 regular season record with its first win over Philadelphia Textile, but more importantly, an incredible run in the NCAA DII Tournament. A key moment during the season was the switching of Carlos Palencia from midfield to the "stopper" position. Each of these players experienced different routes to the University of New Haven. Barrios, for instance, was recruited by John

Kowalski, as was Krys Furman.

My high school friend Shep brought his youth team from Cleveland for two games in the New Haven area. I recruited Danny Gourash from that team and named him "Rocky" as he came from Rocky River, Ohio, and the Stallone movie was popular at the time. Rocky played three seasons at New Haven, deciding not to play his senior year to bone up on his studies with Law School on his mind post-graduation. He became a highly successful Cleveland area-based attorney, a partner in the firm of Seeley, Savidge, Ebert and Gourash.

With a 4-0 win over C.W. Post in the tournament's first game, UNH now had to play Southern Connecticut a second time, having barely beaten Bob Dikranian's team 1-0 a fortnight earlier thanks to a goal by Krys Furman. Now, UNH would be playing Southern for the right to go to the finals, which were again to be hosted by Seattle Pacific. Southern had advanced to the regional semi-final with a 4-1 win over Hartford.

A huge crowd of over 1,200 spectators representing both schools attended the match. The game lasted four overtimes and was decided on a goal by Peter Zimmerman.

The winning goal was created by four players, starting with Kessel, in goal, who played the ball to Glen Joseph, who played it to Oscar Rendon, who gave a bouncing pass that Zimmerman ran on to. He split two Southern defenders Adolphus (Doc) Lawson and Mario Flanders to slot a low shot to the goalkeeper's right which tucked neatly into the far corner.

In an article in the *New Haven Register* the next day, Frank Vieira, who I had now appointed as Director of Public Relations for the entire Athletic Department, stated: "I would say that this was the all-time great scene we've had up at the North Campus." The article was entitled, "UNH Campus Aflame with Soccer Spirit".

I almost missed seeing the winning goal as I had looked away to talk with John Kowalski about the list of players we would need to prepare to send out for tie-breaking penalty kicks (called "Kicks from the Mark" back then).

The national semi-finals were to be played on Thanksgiving Day with the final the following Saturday. Our flight took off from Hartford/Springfield airport on Tuesday for the Thursday match. Our opponent was to be the University of Missouri at St. Louis (UMSL) which had defeated Oakland 5-1 and Western Illinois 2-1 in overtime. The other semi-final paired Loyola of Maryland and Chico State. The games were to be played in the huge Memorial Stadium in Seattle.

The semi-final against UMSL was a back-and-forth affair with each team scoring and missing chances for the winner. With time running out, I asked assistant coach John Kowalski to "do something". And unbelievably, he improvised a throw-in play involving two non-starters that led to the winning goal in the second overtime period. Alvaro Barrios, who had a long throw-in, threw the ball in to Scott Humphrey at the near post. It was supposed to go to Humphrey's head for a flick-on but fell short. It landed at his feet and when he was about to attempt to turn and shoot at goal, Jako Nikaci called him off and stuffed the ball in at the near post.

An overtime win!

Cinderella, again? We would be playing Loyola in the final.

I had always relied on John Kowalski as an assistant coach. Even as a player, he came to New Haven with books on coaching, written in Polish. John and I would often meet at a local establishment for clams on a half shell and discuss strategy for our next game. The records will show that these meetings often resulted in wins! Over the years, John and I collaborated on a great many soccer-related activities, and shared wonderful experiences on and off the field!

In Seattle, we had a great day off on Friday, going up to the mountains in our vans and celebrating Thanksgiving a day late with a great dinner, but with the knowledge that we were playing in the Championship Game. It would be my second NCAA Championship Game appearance as a head coach.

And once again, no title! Loyola goals by Ian Reid just before half-time and one by Pete Notaro in the 73rd minute put an end to another dream! We finished the season 12-6-2. Did we eat too much?

The 1977 season had an even better start. We went 14 games without a loss, and finished the regular season 14-1-2, losing only to my Alma Mater, LIU 2-3.

Once again, we beat Southern Connecticut in the regular season 1-0. And we knew that most likely we would have to meet up with our crosstown rivals again in the regionals.

The NCAA DII Tournament was scheduled to be played in Miami, a nice incentive for teams from the Northeast who would be playing in the early rounds in winter-like environments.

Our first NCAA playoff game was against the University of Hartford with Dan Gaspar in goal. Gaspar would go on to a fabulous coaching career, mostly as an assistant to Carlos Queiroz and would become an internationally recognized goalkeeping coach, clinician and instructor.

Hartford was defeated 3-0. And again, Southern Connecticut was defeated by the same 1-0 scoreline.

At the nationals in Florida, we got beat by Alabama A&M 2-0 in the semi-final, but bounced back proudly to beat Wisconsin Green Bay on penalties 3-2 in the third-place game.

I am saddened to reflect on the fact that five members of that very special group of players have passed away. Philip Gardner, a back-up goalkeeper, Krys Furman, Keith Van Ness, Dimas Couto and most recently Alvaro Barrios have all moved on to the soccer field in the sky!

Looking back at that season, I still remember the 1-1 tie at Eastern Connecticut State and speaking with their goalkeeper, Greg Andrulis, after the match. He played a terrific game, keeping Eastern in the match until the final whistle. The tie against powerful New Haven was considered a win by Eastern. I offered Greg a job the following summer in what was to be the second year of the No.1 Goalkeeper's Camp. He became a fixture at the camp over many years and our families have remained close. The Andrulis family now manages the camp which was still running strong as it approaches its 50th year.

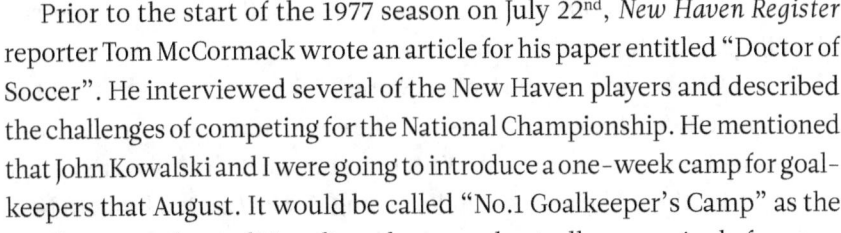

Prior to the start of the 1977 season on July 22nd, *New Haven Register* reporter Tom McCormack wrote an article for his paper entitled "Doctor of Soccer". He interviewed several of the New Haven players and described the challenges of competing for the National Championship. He mentioned that John Kowalski and I were going to introduce a one-week camp for goalkeepers that August. It would be called "No.1 Goalkeeper's Camp" as the number 1 was the traditional number worn by goalkeepers. And of course, the number 1 was meant to signify coming in first and being the best.

To finance the application to be incorporated as a business in the State of Connecticut, Kowalski and I ran an indoor tournament in the University of New Haven Charger gym. We had Don Wright, maintenance supervisor, construct goals appropriate for the size of the basketball court we were going to play on. We decided on a width of 12 feet and a height of six feet, six inches.

Indoor tournaments were a popular activity for college soccer teams in the winter. The University of Connecticut had a huge tournament using two fields in their Fieldhouse. Hartwick College had a good one as well. One Sunday night, coming home in a van from Hartwick, the radio had CBS FM's "Doo Wop Shop" and the players could not believe that I knew the words of every song played, most of which they had never heard before. Even Clyde McPhatter's *It's a Lover's Question*!

During our indoor tournament, at which participating schools paid an entrance fee and John ran a very successful concession stand of Polish delicacies, Walter Chyzowych surprised us when he walked in the door. We had a wonderful conversation, but he never really explained the reason for his visit. While he was there, Carl Babb scored a goal from "half court" that was hit with pace and dip against the pro team Connecticut Yankees, eliminating them from the competition. Carl stayed in the New Haven area like so many others that came to the university and had a great career in the New Haven Public Schools system.

Of course, by now, Walter and I had developed a relationship of trust, whereby, ever since the attainment of my "A" Coaching License in 1974, he had included me in many clinics and other appearances. And for the most part, I became the goalkeeping specialist at the United States Soccer Federation's National Coaching Schools.

Walt's two older brothers, Gene and Ihor, visited the North Campus for our home game against Philadelphia Textile, checking New Haven out to get a sense if it was an appropriate place for Ihor's son, Ihor (Junior) to pursue his college education and playing career.

When Walter brought the United States U16 team to a tournament in Montaigu, France, the organizer asked if he could find a place for his son to go to school and play in America. Walter was not sure of the player's ability to play at Textile, so he recommended young Denis Van Den Brink to New Haven. Denis proved to be a very worthwhile player and more so, his father invited the college team to play six games in France the following summer. He would pay for half the plane tickets and all the accommodations, local transportation, referees, security, field rentals, etc.

My good friend John Benevento and wife Joan accompanied us on the trip and, of course, Barbara was with us as well. Barbara had begun to matriculate at the University of New Haven, was in class with many of the soccer players and, as such, socialized with many of her professors at university functions. She graduated magna cum laude with a Bachelor of Arts in 1983.

John had recently helped us buy our first house through his realty firm, Carmel Realty, named after his mother. We now lived in Guilford, another shoreline community in a ranch type house on nearly an acre of land. We often hosted the team for "leaf raking parties" in the Fall and Barbara would cook a huge meal for the players, many of whom were not on the dorm's weekend meal plan. Our home also became the place where injured players could recover, being taken care of by the coach's wife, who was also their classmate.

On our way to France, we boarded the bus for JFK airport with the tickets we had purchased in hand ready to grab our World Airlines flight to Paris. When we arrived at the terminal, we were informed there were no extra tickets for us at the counter. We were given a choice of sending half the team on to Europe with the hope that the other tickets would arrive in the morning. I could not take that chance leaving unsupervised players in France. And of course, we were suspicious as to whether the other tickets, purchased in France, would ever arrive.

John Benevento, the businessman that he was, somehow was able to get the President of World Airlines on the telephone. The airline agreed to put us up at the International Hotel at JFK and fly the team Business Class the next day to Brussels. We then took a bus to Paris and took it as a bonus. We won five of six games in France, much to the shock of our hosts and adversaries. I think we could have won the sixth game as well if we started our reserve players who, when substituted, won the second half. The first-team players were exhausted by the games, the food and the travel.

Some of the players had difficulty with the diet of goose liver pate and tongue and couldn't wait to get to a McDonald's in the airport.

Before leaving France, Andre Van Den Brink, Denis' father, asked me and John Benevento if we could purchase a new Cadillac for him and ship it to France. It was model and color specific, the details of which I cannot remember. Once home, John and I went to the Cadillac dealer on Whalley Avenue whom John knew personally and drove the new car to the shipyard in New York for shipping that had been previously arranged. This was at a time before locked shipping containers. The Cadillac was driven onto the ship and placed somewhere naked in the hull. When it arrived in France, it had been stripped of its hub caps, grill and most of the chrome. But Mr.

Van Den Brink didn't care, he was able to have replacement parts shipped some six months later.

Our success in France created a problem as we came away thinking we were better than we were as a team, overconfident, big-headed and went into the college season ill-prepared mentally.

Regardless, we opened the season at the Villanova Tournament with a somewhat revengeful 0-0 tie with Davis & Elkins before dispensing with the hosts 7-0. Then there was a period of seven wins in a row after an alarming 0-3 loss to Southern Connecticut which had vastly improved their team with the realization that they would have to get by UNH to make it to the NCAA national finals.

We hosted the first NCAA tournament game of 1978, beating Hartford 3-1, improving on a 1-1 regular season result. And then we were notified by the NCAA that our tournament game against Southern would be played at their campus field, even though we had a better regular season record. But then again, they had that big win against us in the regular season.

Bernard Zimmerman, Peter's brother, opened the scoring following an assist from Krys Furman, but that was all we could muster, handicapped somewhat by a second yellow card to Ihor Chyzowych. The season finished with a 13-2-4 record, but no trip to the nationals. Southern Connecticut now owned the city of New Haven from a soccer point of view.

After our loss to Southern, the very next day, John Kowalski left with his friend and former Quinnipiac coach Len Bilous for Cincinnati, where they would become coaches for the new Major Indoor Soccer League (MISL) team, Cincinnati Kids. I too had been approached by MISL and took a part-time position in charge of their officiating program.

The headline in the *New Haven Register* on December 16, 1979, read *UNH's Machnik Gives Up Soccer to Concentrate on Being AD*. The reporter, Pete Zanardi, highlighted the 11 seasons that I had coached soccer and the 110-54-21 record. "Being an athletic director," I am quoted as saying "is being head coach of the entire athletic department. Getting unity within the department is coaching and I am challenged by that skill," I continued. I liked having more than one job, but something had to go when the MISL took off and I did not believe that I gave my 1979 team my very best.

A year later, Dr. Kaplan offered me a leave of absence from the university, which I had requested so that I could concentrate on the challenges of the indoor pro league.

Debbie Chin had been administering UNH's women's sports since her hiring in 1975. Chin already had the title of Associate Director of Athletics and Coordinator of Women's Sports. She would be asked to manage the department with Frank Vieira's assistance during my leave of absence.

My part-time role as Referee-in-Chief of the Major Indoor Soccer League was increased to a full-time position, which included being named Director of Operations. I received a second year's leave for the 1981-82 academic year, but Dr. Kaplan, rightfully so, prior to the 1982-83 academic year, asked me to decide: "The Major Indoor Soccer League or the University of New Haven?"

The risk taker that I have always been, I forfeited tenure as an Associate Professor and relinquished the Athletic Department Directorship and chose the Major Indoor Soccer League.

1970 NAIA Regional Championship team prior to going to the NAIA Final Eight Tournament in Dunn, North Carolina.

New Haven College Ice Hockey team 1970. (I should have worn my skates)

My first New Haven College soccer team photo (1969) taken on the Main Campus prior to the completion of any athletic facilities. Standing in the back row left next to Captain Del Pereira with freshman John Kowalski next to him.

With assistant coach Artie Crouse in the New Haven Ice hockey dressing room.

1976 NCAA Division 2 National Championship Runners-Up (second Place) Team.

I am named "Athletic Director".

104   Joseph A. Machnik

1977 NCAA Division 2 National Championship Third Place Team.

While on Sabbatical Leave from New Haven I earned a Ph.D. from the University of Utah and the nickname "Dr. Joe".

Chapter 6

USSF/US Soccer Coaching Schools
"Where It All Began"

Shortly after the excitement of promoting the closed-circuit TV broadcasts of the 1970 World Cup final from Azteca Stadium in Mexico in the New Haven Arena, I received a phone call from the Yale soccer coach Hubert Vogelsinger. He asked: "Are you going to the coaching school next week in Providence?"

Hubert explained the details and that the course would start the following Sunday at Moses Brown School. The way it was described, it would be a "can't miss" opportunity.

With a little research and a few phone calls, I learned that the course was being organized by the Southern New York State Soccer Association (SNYSSA) and the United States Soccer Federation (USSF) and would be conducted by FIFA coach Dettmar Cramer.

I had not heard of Cramer but learned he was coming directly from the World Cup in Mexico, where he was a member of the Technical Committee studying the games and trends and, of course, the new yellow and red card system.

The card system was put into place as a possible solution to the communication issues which existed between the on-field officials and players and coaches who did not speak the same language. The movie *Goal!* recalled a colorful example of this when the Argentine player Antonio Rattin was sent off in the 1966 World Cup game against England by German referee Rudolf Kreitlein and refused to leave the field, allegedly not understanding the referee's instructions.

I called Lenny Lucenko, who also had just learned about the course, and he informed me that both he and Bob McNulty would also attend. It was less than a two-hour drive to Providence from New Haven, so it was convenient.

When I got there and first saw Dettmar Cramer, I immediately recognized him from the movie *Goal!* sitting on the bench next to Germany's head coach Helmut Schoen during the 1966 World Cup final, which was decided by a goal that only today's goal-line technology could prove one way or the other.

There were 15 candidates signed up for the one-week course. There would also be two additional courses with separate groups of candidates.

As it was raining that afternoon, the first session was to be conducted in the Moses Brown School Fieldhouse. Each of us received a ball and were told to warm up. Lenny and I were knocking the ball about and when I was chasing a loose ball, I stepped off the indoor track which surrounded the fieldhouse playing surface — not realizing there was a drop of more than a foot into the gymnastics area — and twisted my knee, the same one that was injured teaching softball at LIU.

No way was I going to let this ruin my week. I continued to knock the ball around, concealing the pain and discomfort.

After the session, dinner was served in the school cafeteria, and we headed to the classroom to formally meet Cramer, who was introduced by the very distinguished Harry Saunders, President of the SNYSSA.

Cramer appeared in his traditional blue warm-up suit with a FIFA badge. He meticulously removed the jacket and precisely folded it in such a way that it could be hung up on a nearby hook to the left of the blackboards. Saunders' introduction included Cramer's background and experience, especially his work in Japan, leading their team to a victory over Argentina in the Tokyo Olympics of 1964.

Cramer's first lecture set the tone for the rest of the week as he introduced the concept of four elements of the game: physical, technical, tactical and psychological. For most of us, it was eye opening! It was so simple and made so much sense.

We were then told that each of us was eligible for either the "A" or "B" coaching license, depending on how we did in our classroom presentation, our on-field coaching presentation, our playing performance in a game and our technical ability with the ball. Cramer was of the belief that "a picture was worth a thousand words" and that to be a successful coach, one needed to demonstrate, and ball juggling would be the key.

Knowing that I was a goalkeeper, Cramer tried to challenge me with a classroom topic he thought might be troublesome, "Midfield Play!" I was no stranger to being in front of a classroom.

I immediately went to the blackboard and wrote down the starting lineup of Dukla Prague used in the 1961 International Soccer League (ISL) Championship Final! I highlighted midfielder Josef Masopust and his role on the team and within five minutes, maybe less, Cramer asked me to sit down. He had seen enough, immediately recognizing "pedagogical talent", in his words not mine. Others had much longer sessions in front of the class. It was at the end of my presentation when Cramer jokingly asked: "Was Means Machnik?" Because in German "Macht Nich" means it doesn't matter. That was hardly my case!

As I was the only goalkeeper present at the course, Cramer asked me to do a field lesson on goalkeeping. I think I "blew his doors off" in racing terms. So much so that he asked whether I would be able to come back for weeks two and three to give the same lesson. Of course, I agreed.

And of course, I held my own in the game which was played against a pickup team of Brown University and local club players. I could still play a little bit!

I cannot say the same about my practical skill demonstration. I had never been asked to ball juggle before. Goalkeepers weren't asked to have field playing skills back then. The Laws of the Game permitted goalkeepers to handle (play by hand) "pass backs" and throw-ins from teammates. There was no "six second" rule, that limited how long a goalkeeper could hold the ball in their hands, either.

One of the unique aspects of Cramer's course was that he would announce the pass-fail status for each of the candidates in front of the entire group at the last classroom session. There was lots of nervousness about this potentially ego-threatening situation.

For the record, here are the names and results of that first class: James Bradley - B, Eugene Chyzowych - A, Leonard Lucenko - B, Joseph Machnik - B, Robert McNulty - B, Joseph Morrone - B, Wilbur Myers - B, Thomas Nevers - B, Steve Parli - B, Trevor Pugh - B, Dominic Rahn - B, Robert Ritcey - B, Manfred Schellscheidt - A, Layton Shoemaker - B, Hubert Vogelsinger - A.

While doing research, I found a faded faxed copy of a letter from Harry Saunders listing all the candidates from that first week. The letter is dated July 6, 1970, meaning it was written prior to the completion of the third week. The letter invited all candidates to a dinner and reception to be held on July 22, 1970, at Foresters Rendezvous on East 84th Street between Lexington and Third Avenues in New York City, at which the coaching certificates would be awarded by Mr. Erwin Single, the President of the USSF.

There are several photos from that course that I treasure: the first being the team of coaches getting ready to play our game, which included not only Cramer but Harry Saunders and George Donnely, at the time President of the National Soccer League of New York. And the second being of the four Connecticut-based coaches that took the course with Cramer, Joe Morrone (University of Connecticut), Hubert Vogelsinger (Yale), Tom Nevers (Eastern Conn State) and myself. And lastly the full group in front of a goal.

There was a pay telephone down the hall in the dormitory at Moses Brown. It was in constant use during the week with coaches calling their families etc., but more importantly with coaches getting the word out that Cramer's course was indeed meaningful and worthy. My room was near the phone so answering it became one of my chores. I specifically remember speaking with Walt Chyzowych, telling him that he needed to be at the course in week two or three. His attendance enabled Cramer to recognize Walter's teaching and coaching talent, as well as his ability to demonstrate, and his charismatic personality that he brought to almost everything he pursued. Walter received his "A" license. All of us had given Cramer the nickname "Chief". At the dinner in New York, an Indian Chief in full headdress came running into the room in the middle of presentations. Cramer was named an honorary "Chieftain" of the Mohican Tribe. What could be more fitting?

We were told that every effort was going to be made to secure Cramer's services as Director of Coaching and National Team Coach. Cramer was able, it seemed, to perform both tasks and overcome the current belief that there were differences between teaching coaches and coaching coaches, and that the talents required of each didn't mix well.

Everyone in the room had good feelings about the future direction of the state of soccer in the United States. We were all going to play a role in its growth and development. There was some disappointment, however, among those coaches who did not have the requisite playing background or skill set to advance in the system to the "A" license level.

The success of the first USSF Coaching Schools led to the Federation planning and conducting schools nationwide throughout the following three summers. As I was in Utah working toward a Ph.D., during that time, I was unable to apply for my "A" license until the summer of 1974.

During the time that I was in Utah, I wrote to Walter Chyzowych about the need for more and better goalkeeping instruction in the United States, even to the point of naming a national goalkeeping coach. I felt confident that I could fulfil that role based on being asked by Cramer to do the goalkeeping sessions in Providence. Walter had been assisting Cramer with some of the coaching school administration. He wrote back to me that the idea was worth considering but that first I must get the "A" license.

The "A" license course in the summer of 1974 was to be held at Hartwick College in Oneonta, and due to Cramer's unavailability at the time, it was to be conducted by Walt Chyzowych, assisted by Bill Muse, the newly appointed coach of Princeton University.

Just like in 1970, there was a warm-up knockabout. Two of the participants were my former players at LIU, Ronnie Jabusch and Arnie Ramirez. But for some reason, I found myself knocking the ball around with Bob Gansler.

I had spent much of the previous year working on my ball skills. There was a kickboard at Yale that I used, and I was able to juggle the ball, not comfortably but successfully at least 20 times before getting into trouble. The left foot was still a problem.

The USSF National Youth Team was also in attendance that week at Hartwick, coached by George Logan and Timo Liekoski. They were preparing for the CONCACAF Youth Tournament of 1974, their first such appearance since 1964 when they were winless.

They would be our opponents for the performance in a game segment of the course and two games were scheduled. There were some fine young players on that team with some still familiar names: Ty Keough, Neil Cohen, Tony Bellinger, Larry Hulcer and Tommy Mulroy to name a few.

Mulroy has recently chronicled the events of that camp in his book, *90 Minutes with the King*.

The "A" course coach's team had some players as well. Gansler had made 25 appearances with the United States and captained the 1964 and 1968 Olympic qualifying teams. George Vizvary had experience with the

Hungarian national team. Ronnie Jabusch was voted the "Outstanding Defensive Player" of the 1966 NCAA Tournament. Ramirez was a solid winger who had played for the US Army team and was my captain at LIU in 1968. And Timo Liekoski would play for the coaches, adding depth to the lineup which included Nick Zlatar, Roy Pfeil, Jim Lennox, Garth Stam and Alex Bernstein.

Our team may have had some skilled and competent players, but fitness was an issue as well as lack of organization and the youth team won the first game handily 5-0.

Walter Chyzowych came in for the second game and asked that I prepare the tactical plan. We obviously needed to do more defensively and protect the goalkeeper, yours truly!

We played much better and lost only narrowly, 1-0. The winning goal came from a corner kick, which I could and should have done more about. Youngster Tony Graham, standing at only five feet six inches, outjumped me and George Vizvary to head the winner. George and I argued over whose responsibility that goal was for the next 40-plus years.

I had made enough difficult saves in the game to feel good about myself. Afterwards, a gentleman came up to me and introduced himself as a local news reporter. He did not know my name but said that he had seen me play before. He asked if I had ever played against Hartwick? I told him about the time LIU beat them 2-1 in a game where both Gerry and Ray Klivecka scored goals, and which was the first loss for Hartwick on their "upper field". He now remembered where he had seen me play and wrote about it the next day in the local paper.

At the end of the coaching school, Chyzowych announced that I had achieved the "A". Then we both left to join the staff of presenters at a clinic sponsored by the NSCAA at SUNY Binghamton. The other presenters were Gordon Bradley and Graham Ramsey as well as the organizer, Tim Schum, who was also the editor of the NSCAA's periodical *Soccer Journal*.

After the completion of my goalkeeping session at the clinic, I showered and changed for what would be a four-hour-plus ride back to my home in Connecticut. Coming back onto the field to watch and listen to Walter's presentation on shooting and goal scoring, he asked me to assist even while I was now in street clothes, albeit shorts. He used me to demonstrate diving headers and then to go into the goal for his segment on penalty kicks.

With all the coaches standing behind the goal, I managed to dive to my right and knock out one of Walter's strongest shots, getting immediately up, facing the group of coaches and asking: "Are there any questions?" For years after, coaches who were in that group talked about their memory of that save. And of course, as time goes by, it just gets better and better.

Dettmar Cramer was officially offered the position of USA's National Team Coach and Director of Coaching as announced on July 17, 1974. After coaching in only two games, Cramer announced in January 1975 that he would leave USSF to take the head coaching position at Bayern Munich. While most everyone was suspicious of how Cramer could so easily get out of his USSF contract, it was revealed that a contract never existed. Cramer went on to coach Bayern Munich to two European Cups in 1975 and 1976.

Soccer in America now was without a leader!

Just before leaving, Cramer had a conversation with Ursula Melendi at the USSF Headquarters in the Empire State Building in New York City. Ms. Melendi was one of only three full-time employees of USSF and had multifarious duties and responsibilities at the Federation. When that conversation turned to the Coaching Schools, Cramer was reported to say to Ms. Melendi: "Walter is the one, he needs to be in charge!"

The Coaching Schools had expanded to national level "A", "B" and "C" licenses. Various states like New York were offering "D", "E" and "F" licenses which could be attained on a single weekend or over several weekends.

One of the largest and most popular coaching school sites was at Saint Andrew's School in Middletown, Delaware. It was here the conversation arose again that there should be a way to achieve a national coaching license without the physical and technical demands that Cramer had insisted upon. There were many hugely successful college coaches who had limited practical on-field playing experience and could not demonstrate the required skills. It was not deemed acceptable at the time to use a player or assistant coach to demonstrate while the head coach talked through the exercise.

So, while most participants were happy with their USSF Coaching School experience, there were always a few unhappy participants who did not accept that they failed to achieve the desired license based on their lack of playing experience or ability to demonstrate.

Walter thought it important that his coaches have a say in the future of the Coaching Schools and formed a committee of staff coaches on which somehow, I became the secretary and report writer. On February 10, 1978, a report back to Walter "generally recommended" that the first-ever "Non-Participation USSF Coaching Course" be offered that summer at St. Andrew's.

Eventually, this led to the NSCAA taking up that mantle and offering their own Coaching Academy courses which did not have the rigid physical and technical requirements.

Some of the best and biggest National Coaching Schools were held in the winter in Florida. To make these courses unique, Chyzowych would invite his entire coaching staff, and usually an international guest coach. These included Helmut Schoen, Jacek Gmoch, Assistant to the Polish national team in its glory days, Dettmar Cramer himself, Svetislav Glisovic, a former Serbian international player and coach who had success in the States, coaching the Philadelphia Ukrainians to several US Open Cup Championships, Yugoslavia's Ivan Toplak and Holland's Hans Ooft.

Also, these winter courses welcomed several NASL coaches and players who were able to go straight toward the "B" license because of their professional league experience. Whenever I see former Chicago Sting coach Willy Roy, he reminds me how I "broke his thumb" in the goalkeeping session at the course he attended.

One highlight of every Coaching School was the Thursday night staff dinner. With all the instructions having been done and with the testing of the candidates on the field and in the classroom scheduled for the next day, Walter arranged with the Federation to pick up the dinner tab at a nearby restaurant. Sometimes the camaraderie and goodwill got a little out of hand and there was suffering on the field in the hot sun the next day watching the candidates go through their paces and on-field teaching assignments.

One Friday morning, Walter caught me sitting on a ball while evaluating a candidate's work. He called me over and face to face, eye to eye, stated: "Don't you ever let me catch you sitting on a ball again in front of the candidates, or you will be history." It was a lesson learned and remembered! There was always the highest level of professionalism expected in front of the candidates.

The United States had not qualified for a World Cup since 1950, a tournament remembered for the improbable 1-0 win over England in

Brazil. That team was coached by Bill Jeffrey, who had a 26-year career coaching at Penn State University. Jeffrey coached in only three national team games. After that the US was coached by John Wood in 1952 for two matches, Erno Schwarz for six, and Jimmy Mills and Tim Reed for one game each. Between 1964 and 1975, the team had ten different coaches: John Herberger — one game (1964); Phil Woosnam — nine games (1968); Gordon Jago — two games (1969); Bob Kehoe — four games (1971-72); Max Wozniak — two games (1973); Gene Chyzowych — five games (1973); Gordon Bradley — five games (1973); Dettmar Cramer — two games (1974); Al Miller — two games (1975); Manfred Schellscheidt — three games (1975).

At the request of then USSF President Gene Edwards, a sub-committee of Federation Staff Coaches was formed to evaluate the current structure and staffing of coaching education and national teams coaching and to submit a report in time to make recommendations relative to the 1976 coaching schools and international competitions. Bill Killen and I were charged with the responsibility of surveying all the staff coaches, polling their leadership choices and submitting a report.

A 20-page report with separate budgets for the National Team for the year starting in July 1976 and for the National Youth Team, starting in January 1977, was submitted.

Twenty-five different coaches received votes in a polling point system that was set up. Walter Chyzowych received the most points at 86. Those also receiving votes included previous National Team coaches, those who were at the very first Coaching Schools in 1970, NASL coaches, college coaches, coaches from the German American Soccer League, foreign coaches and current "A" license holders.

As a result, Walter Chyzowych was appointed National Team coach and held that position from 1976 to 1980. However, despite the strong recommendations of the Committee, the positions of National Team Coach and Director of Coaching were not financially possible to be separated.

This was the time of soccer in America when the rise of the NASL, Pele and the Cosmos, George Best, Johan Cruyff, Gerd Muller etc. had soccer at the forefront on many sport pages, with national TV exposure on ABC and a resultant rise in youth participation levels countrywide. No longer were youth programs only offered by ethnic clubs in the cities, but they were now organized by towns and communities in suburban areas where there was space to build fields, and in some areas of the country play year-round.

Even the US Army got involved through the formation of The Army College Fund which, with the cooperation of the NSCAA, offered a program of soccer clinics, MVP Awards, soccer films and even a book *Basic Soccer Skills*, with an introduction by Walter Chyzowych. The Army clinics were massive, usually attended by several hundred players, and yes, even a few female players also attended the Army's "Be All You Can Be" program.

I typically would be involved in as many of these clinics as possible, as well as others that were set up by either the USSF or NSCAA. In addition to getting out there in front of countless youngsters and their coaches helping to "sell" the game, the opportunity provided personal exposure and enabled me to hone my presentation skills. And, indirectly, promote the No.1 Goalkeeper's Camp which started in 1977.

Walter invited me to do a clinic for Delco SC in suburban Philadelphia, after which we had dinner in his home. I had met Walter's wife Olga once before at the All-American Camp, but this was a more personal and private introduction. Olga prepared seafood crepes and with white wine, we had good conversation well into the night.

Sometime, after having been appointed National Team Coach, Walter asked if I could join him in Squaw Valley near Lake Tahoe, where he would be working with young Olympic team hopefuls.

We stayed in cabins used by the former Olympic ski team and had to take a bus down to the city, where the land was flat enough to have a soccer field. I worked with a young goalkeeper, David Brcic, who would go on to a career in the NASL with the Cosmos.

Olga came out to visit and one day during down time, Walter, Olga and I took a canoe out on the Truckee River. With limited paddling experience, we all got soaked!

Walter asked me to drive up to Mansfield, Connecticut to a tournament where UCONN Coach Joe Morrone's two sons, Joe Jr. and Bill, were playing. In essence, if I liked them, which I did, they would be added to the national youth team or Olympic team player pool.

Later that summer, I assisted Walter with the Olympic B team on a three-game trip to Puerto Rico. The side was loaded with future Olympic and National Team players. David Brcic was in goal and there was Njego

Pesa, Jimmy Stamatis, Joe Morrone Jr., Perry Van Der Beck among others.

We lost the first game in San Juan and felt victimized by several dubious home team officiating decisions. The second game was played in the mountains at the birthplace of baseball legend Roberto Clemente, who had died in a plane crash in Carolina, Puerto Rico a few years earlier.

Olga and Barbara arrived the night before and traveled with us up the mountainside. That game didn't go as planned either. After some rough play, we had to make our way to the bus being chased by the spectators. We made it to the vehicle safely before the angry fans began rocking the bus, and as we drove off, several rocks and stones were thrown at us.

Walter decided we were not going to play the third contracted game and demanded a meeting with officials from the Puerto Rican Soccer Federation, including its President, Dr. Monroig. When begged by the Federation to stay as they did not want the resultant negative publicity having only first become recognized by FIFA in 1960, Walter was asked, "What could be done to change your mind?"

Walter replied: "Bring in a neutral referee."

"How can we do that, there is no time, the game is tomorrow?" the hosts responded. Then Walter pointed to me.

Walter knew that I had done some refereeing in Connecticut, was teaching the Laws of the Game in the Coaching Schools etc. Of course, I agreed! I had to rush to a store to find a black shirt. I made yellow and red cards out of paper I bought in a stationery store. I would be working with two Puerto Rican linesmen whom I had never met and who most likely didn't trust me and resented me for replacing their comrade. We won the match, the only win on our three-game trip. Walter knew that I had the courage and conviction to get the job done. He knew that I never minded taking a risk.

The whole episode of my officiating the game in Puerto Rico is described in a full-page article in the MISL game program *MISSLE*, written by its editor and publisher, Don Ruck, with a heading: *Escape from the Bench-Listen Lester Patrick, Sir-Joe Machnik Tops Your Story.*

Lester Patrick was the New York Ranger Coach in 1928 who had to rush to the locker room to don equipment and finish a crucial Stanley Cup game when the starting goalie, Lorne Chabot, was injured. No back-ups on the bench in those early years. The Rangers won the game and the Stanley Cup that year. Patrick, at age 44 years and 90 days, remains the oldest player to play in the Stanley Cup finals.

Walter Chyzowych coached the USMNT for 32 full international games, winning eight and tying 10. His tenure was plagued by all the Federation inadequacies and lack of support that plagued the previous coaches over their much shorter careers.

In addition to lacking financial support for the players, which led to several "strikes" and another strike over footwear mandates, there was the added issue of the NASL not releasing its American players for national team duty. The NASL, while claiming to support the growth and development of American soccer, instead minimized the role of native players on their teams. Many NASL teams satisfied the required minimum number of Americans on the field by playing American players either in goal, in defense or as a defensive midfielder. Even bona-fide attacking players drafted out of college were subjugated to play defensive roles. As such, for the most part, the US national team was void of attacking midfielders and players comfortable going to goal! The lack of support from the NASL led to players having to fly across the country on national team game days and, in some instances, getting to the game just in time to dress on the sideline.

The lack of proper practice and training time, the inconsistencies in travel, meals and housing preparation, problems with compensation and per diem, the lack of proper equipment and training room supplies and even a shortage of uniforms were all issues that Chyzowych had to deal with over his tenure. Often the national team was prohibited from exchanging jerseys with their opponent post-match due to the short supply of uniforms.

At times, one would wonder who was in control of soccer in America, the USSF or the NASL. The NASL seemed to be calling all the shots.

While Tony Cirino's 1983 publication *"US Soccer vs. the World"* has a 30-page summary of the difficulties Chyzowych faced. It also includes the many successes US teams had under his leadership.

These include a third-place finish in CONCACAF qualifying for the 1976 Youth World Championship. Three American players (Ricky Davis, Gary Etherington and goalkeeper David Brcic) were named to that All-Tournament team.

A victory in the 1978 Festival of the Americas played at Randalls Island in New York City, overcoming club teams Universitaria of Ecuador,

Alianza of Peru and Millonarios of Columbia. It was the USA's first such tournament win.

The 1979 win over Hungary in Budapest! And the 1980 qualification for the Olympic Finals in Moscow, only to be denied participation by the boycott of the games issued by President Jimmy Carter over the Soviet Union's invasion of Afghanistan.

And, finally, the 1981 qualification for the Youth World Championship in Australia. During the five-year period that Chyzowych served as National Team Coach at several levels of competition, Chyzowych recorded an overall record of 65 wins, 44 losses and 21 ties. The 130 matches played by USA teams during this period were more than all the matches played in the previous 63-year history of the Federation. His record in full internationals including World Cup qualifiers was 8 wins, 14 losses and 10 ties.

During the games and tournaments listed above, Chyzowych introduced several new assistants to the program including Bill Muse from the Coaching Schools, Bob Gansler and Lothar Osiander. The latter two would play major roles in the future of the US National Team program.

Certainly, when Ed Tepper and Earl Foreman, the founders of the pioneering Major Indoor Soccer League, contacted Chyzowych regarding a possible role as "Consultant", Chyzowych saw its potential as providing useful playing time for American players. Walter was familiar with the indoor game in its various forms, having even dressed as a "guest player" in the match played in the Philadelphia Spectrum between Al Miller's Atoms and the Russian Red Army team. And when asked to recommend someone to organize a referee program for the new league, Walter recommended me. I became the MISL's Referee-in-Chief.

Of course, Walter's involvement in the creation of a rival league to the NASL did nothing to endear him further to that organization's hierarchy.

MISL Commissioner Earl Foreman had little use for the leadership of USSF and NASL, both of which placed obstacles in his path. As such, when it became time to have the MISL represented on various Federation and other committees, Foreman nominated his Referee-in-Chief to represent the league.

When Walter Chyzowych resigned after failing to qualify for the 1982 World Cup, I was appointed to represent the MISL on the Federation's Coaching Committee. There were several meetings in the Federation's

40th floor offices in the Empire State Building. I represented the indoor league and sat along with Phil Woosnam representing the NASL. Dr. Bob Contiguglia, a future Federation President, served as Chair.

There was strong sentiment among the American soccer coaching community that Walter Chyzowych should continue to serve as Director of Coaching. Finally, it seemed, the Federation was willing to have separate positions: Director of Coaching, who would take over the coaching schools and a National Team Coach, who would prepare the team for qualification for the 1986 World Cup. This same community was adamant that the hiring should be an American coach. I was unable to convince the other committee members of the importance of that factor.

As such, legendary German coach Karl-Heinz Heddergott, who had just published the English version of *New Football Manual* with the assistance of the California Youth Soccer Association, was hired to lead the Coaching Schools and Alketas (Alkis) Panagoulias, a former player and successful coach in Greece with Aris and Olympiakos, and who had led the NY Greek-Americans to several US Open Cups, was hired to lead the national team.

It would be a gross understatement to not recognize the criticism I was subjected to from the greater soccer coaching community at large for these appointments. Fortunately, at the next NSCAA Convention, I was able to clarify my position, as part of a panel discussion.

Neither Heddergott nor Panagoulia knew what was in store for them!

I tried to convey to Phil Woosnam, just prior to Heddergott's arrival at his first Coaching School assignment, that there already had been a meeting of the coaching school staff that degenerated into arguments as to who would support or undermine Heddergott. Woosnam suggested that I prepare Heddergott accordingly.

As a member of the Coaching Committee, it was my job to pick Heddergott up at the airport. I waited until we arrived at his hotel (he wasn't going to stay in the college dorm) to discuss this with him. Over a bite to eat, I gave him the news that there were some coaches in the group that hoped and wished that he would fail. Heddergott went totally ballistic! Slamming his fists on the table, screaming loud enough that the entire restaurant could hear. "The height of ingratitude," he exclaimed!

Panagoulias was a different story. Knowing that he would need some players from the now quite successful indoor league, he asked to attend a MISL Board meeting so that he could meet the owners and plead his case. No way were the owners interested in lending their players. At the meeting, realizing what he was up against for the first time, Panagoulias took a pair of "worry beads" out of his pocket and began to manipulate and massage them through his fingers. Later that evening, I sat with Panagoulias at the MISL All-Star game and pointed out to him which players were American.

In preparation for the 1978 World Cup, the NASL formed "Team America", which would compete in RFK Stadium in DC over a regular season NASL schedule. Team America had its problems as well and Panagoulias' side, playing as the US national team, lost the final qualification game for '78 at home to Costa Rica when they only needed a tie to advance. The game was played in Southern California in front of a crowd mostly in support of Costa Rica as the Federation still needed the financial gate to pay its expenses. There was never a thought of playing a game in Minnesota, for example.

It didn't take long for Heddergott to realize that he was not in Germany, and few respected his opinion or expertise despite previously idolizing the several books that he had written. One of Heddergott's first moves was to suggest that the coaching license process be a minimum of two weeks, not the one week that had been established prior. This idea fell on deaf ears as an American coach often did not have two weeks to spare, nor the finances to make it happen.

Discouraged with Heddergott's style and plans, many of the Federation coaches were now moving over to the NSCAA Academy programs with a curriculum written by Tom Fleck and Walter Chyzowych, which made more sense for the American coaching candidate.

And of course, Walter was still leading the NSCAA's Army College Fund program, which decided to organize the first national high school All-Star game. The fixture was going to be played at West Point and Walter and Ray Klivecka asked me to officiate the game.

In order to do this, I had to reapply to NISOA, the national governing body for college officials which had an agreement with the NSCAA. They wanted the game to be officiated in the three-person diagonal system of control which was just now finally being embraced by colleges across the country, and few northeast NISOA members were proficient in it.

After the game, the two linesmen, Bill Fortin and John Buckley, suggested I attend the NISOA camp prior to the start of the college season so that I might get assigned some college matches. It was a good suggestion!

Werner Fricker was finally elected President in 1984. He had refused to run against the incumbent Gene Edwards until such time that Edwards chose not to seek renomination.

After the debacle of not qualifying for the 1986 World Cup and the demise of the Coaching Schools under Heddergott's tutelage, Fricker turned to his Philadelphia friend, Walter Chyzowych, for guidance. Chyzowych asked for my help in writing plans and we collaborated on a *Five Year Plan: Proposal for Solution of Problems re: Soccer Coaching Instruction and National Team Programs in the United States*. Barbara typed the document in the No.1 Camp office. Dated June 18, 1984, the plan was submitted to Werner Fricker and mostly adopted by him over the years of his US Soccer leadership. The proposal called for the hiring of a Technical Director to unite all factions of US Soccer, and it included organizational charts, budgets and a re-evaluation of the direction of the Coaching Schools.

The Technical Director had to be Walter Chyzowych.

The contribution to the growth and development of soccer in the United States by the USSF/US Soccer Coaching Schools has often been minimized by those whose interest rested elsewhere. Hundreds, if not thousands of coaches who had achieved their national or state certification now felt empowered to spread the positive benefits of playing soccer across the country. It would take a while for small-sided games to replace 11v11 for youth players, but the philosophy of Cramer, espoused by Chyzowych and the USSF Coaching Staff, finally took hold.

Chyzowych also left several books as part of his legacy. Of course, the Federation's *Official Soccer Book*, first printed in 1978 with contributions by Bill Killen, Ray Klivecka, Leonard Lucenko, Bill Muse, Joel Rosenstein, Nick Zlatar and this author, is the most noteworthy. The Federation also published *One-on-One: Moves and Tricks of the Soccer Stars*, billed as the official skills book of the United States Soccer Federation. Written in conjunction with Ole Anderson, this book has drawings of domestic and international players illustrating a move or trick which helped make each famous. US stars Perry Van Der Beck, Ringo Cantillo, Mark Liveric, Louis Nanchoff, Ricky Davis and Ty Keough are highlighted.

There was also Chyzowych's *The World Cup*, published in 1982, which helped explain the world's biggest sporting event to a country that only 20 years earlier had to watch a 16mm film of the final between Brazil and Czechoslovakia if they were lucky enough to find an organization to sponsor a showing.

Walter was so embraced by the NSCAA that when they were offered to prepare a College All-Star team consisting of graduating seniors for an international tour, Walter was placed in charge. He nominated Bruce Arena to coach the team and Walter and I traveled to Turkey to finalize the details. The team was selected, and the Turkish Federation paid for the tickets of the players and coaches to get to New York's JFK airport. Then suddenly the Turkish national team players wanted more money for the games and the trip fell apart.

In the 20 years between 1970 and 1990, between US Soccer Coaching Schools, NSCAA Coaching Academies, US Army's soccer program, the All-American Soccer Camp and School, Walter Chyzowych coached, mentored, instructed, tutored and advised more than 20,000 coaches, including most of the 650 coaches who received their "A" licenses during this period.

The US soccer community was shocked when it learned of Chyzowych's sudden passing while playing tennis at Wake Forest University where he was coaching in 1994. He was only 57 years old. It was Labor Day weekend and the college/university soccer season was beginning to be in full swing. There was only the smallest of notes regarding his passing in local newspapers, no national TV coverage. The publication Soccer America featured his image on the front of its next issues as did most other soccer publications.

Walter Chyzowych was inducted into the National Soccer Hall of Fame posthumously, three years after his passing!

His family and friends started the Walt Chyzowych Fund (www.waltslegacy.com) in his honor which each year at the United Soccer Coaches Convention (formerly NSCAA) recognizes the achievements of leaders in the coaching and soccer playing community, while at the same time financially supporting aspiring young coaches and soccer organizations.

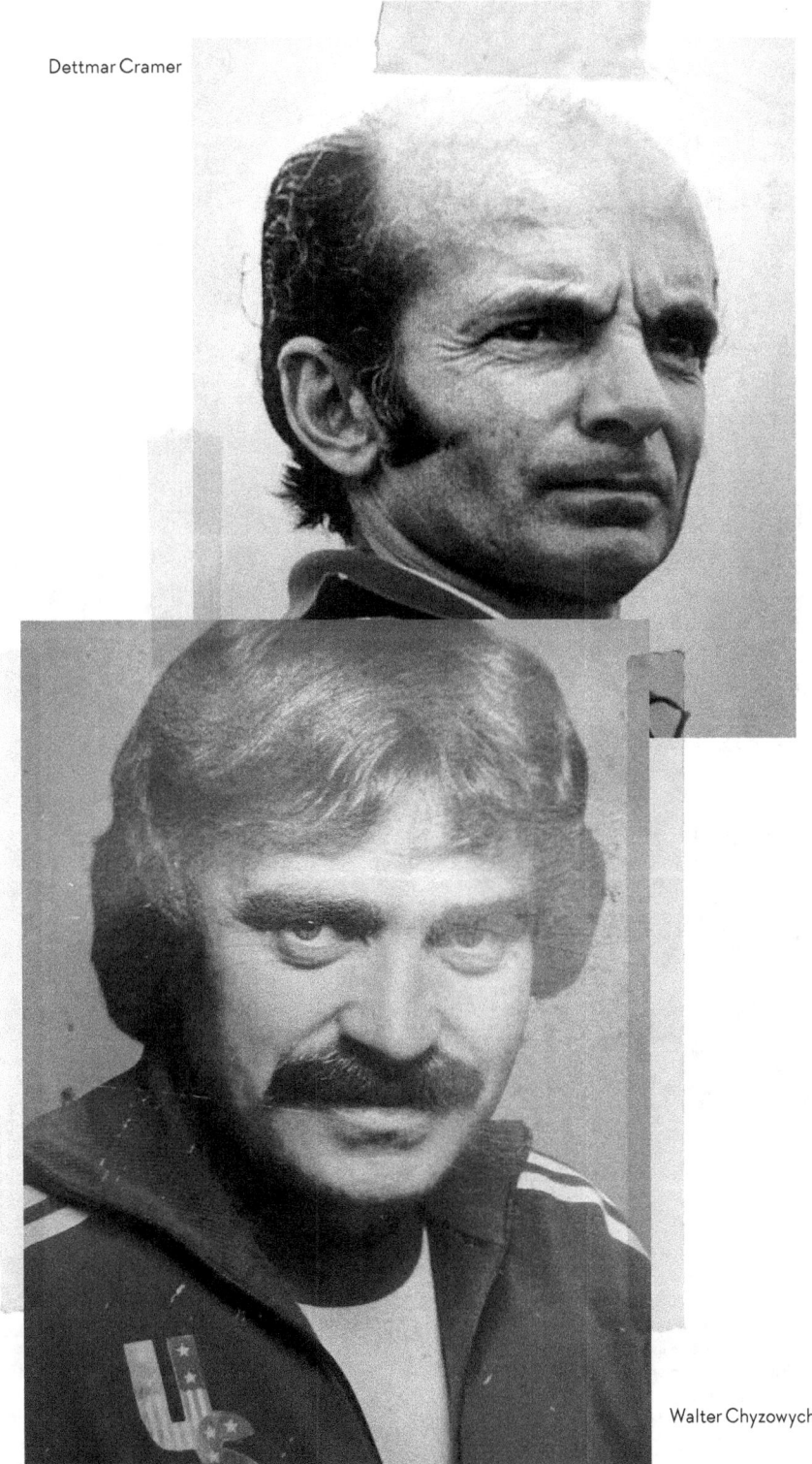

Dettmar Cramer

Walter Chyzowych

United States Soccer Federation

350 FIFTH AVENUE-SUITE 4010 • NEW YORK, NEW YORK 10001 • TELEPHONE: (212) 736-0915-6 • CABLE "SOCCER
Affiliated with the Federation Internationale de Football Association

presents USSF NATIONAL COACHING SCHOOLS 1976

The photo, from the 1975 winter coaching school in Orlando, Florida, shows (left to right), back row: Ray Klivecka, Timo Liekoski, Derek Lawther, Bill Killen, Bob Gansler, George Logan, front row: Lenny Lucenko, Bob McNulty, Director Walt Chyzowych, Guest Coach Jacek Gmoch from Poland, Joe Machnik, Bill Muse and Tom Lileodal.

USSF Coaching Staff

The school, under the direction of Walt Chyzow assistant to Dettmar Cramer, the founder, has the most successful and popular coaching d program in US sports.

The coaching staff has been carefully select growing pool of USSF 'A' licensed coaches. T ent the cream of the school's graduates. Ea combines knowledge of modern educational m extensive practical experience, coaching and p cer. Their background covers all levels of the g and girls, high school and college, amateur sional, national and international.

USSF National Coaching System

The United States Soccer Federation, the national governing body of soccer, decided, in 1970, to institute a national coaching system which has become a vital element in the growth of US soccer. Initially under the brilliant guidance of FIFA Coach Dettmar Cramer, and now under the direction of Walt Chyzowych, the USSF Coaching Schools have become extremely popular, and graduates of these schools have emerged as successful coaches and leaders in the sport.

By responding to the great need for soccer expertise in the explosively growing US soccer community, the coaching system has enormously accelerated our national development. The purpose of the coaching system is to provide instruction and practical experience in all aspects of

coaching and playing soccer. The system is ba modern methods of coaching soccer, the sam used world wide in all top level coaching represe than 50 years of international coaching exper

Particularly in the last 10 years, there has been in coaching methods. Developments in fitne technical and tactical training, applied psychol medicine, physiotherapy, and related fields p graduates with the most up to date know methods of coaching available.

In this, the seventh year of the coaching schoc phenomenal growth in youth, school, and p soccer. Our many graduates have been, and

1976 USSF Coaching School brochure with staff coaches which now included Bob Gansler, Bob McNulty and Ray Klivecka. Walter Chyzowych and I flank our guest coach Jacek Gmoch from Poland.

First USSF Coaching School–fifteen candidates in a one-week course with FIFA Coach Dettmar Cramer. Gene Chyzowych holding the ball, Manfred Schellscheidt kneeling first on the right. Hubert Vogelsinger, Lenny Lucenko flank Coach Cramer. I am kneeling second from the left.

FIRST COACHING SCHOOL
The men who took part in the historic first USSFA Coaching School. (Full story on following pages)

As we get ready to play against a local team as part of the Coaching School Curriculum.

The staff increases in size. This photo includes NASL coaches Ron Newman, Willy Roy, Al Miller and Timo Liekoski. Ralph Perez was there as well as Pat McBride. Our guest Coach was Helmut Schoen of the German National Team!

with Former German
National Team Coach
Helmut Schoen

COACHES LICENSED: Four Connecticut college coaches receive United State Soccer Football Association licenses after completing course during summer at Providence, R.I., conducted by internationally-known Federation coach Dettmar Cramer. Left to right: Joe Morrone, UConn; Hubert Vogelsinger, Yale; Cramer; Joe Machnik, New Haven College; and Tom Nevers, Eastern Connecticut.

Four Coaches from Connecticut were in attendance at the Moses Brown School, site of the very first US Coaching School.

1974 "A" License candidates at a USSF Coaching School at Hartwick College, Oneonta, NY. Bob Gansler sitting front row right with George Vizvary to his right. I can be found in the back row behind Nick Zlatar who is wearing a dark shirt. Two of my LIU players were in the course: Arnie Ramirez and Ronnie Jabusch.

Chapter 7

The Major Indoor Soccer League (MISL)
"You Can't Tell Smart People They're Stupid"

Almost anyone with a soccer background in the US is familiar with the story of the Philadelphia Atoms of the NASL hosting the Russian Red Army team in an indoor game played on an Astroturf carpet placed over the ice at the Philadelphia Spectrum (where the NHL Flyers played) on February 11, 1974.

The match took place at the height of the Cold War with the US still harboring resentment over how its basketball team lost to Russia in the 1972 Olympics.

The game was all square at 3-3 before the Russians prevailed 6-3 with three late goals. The Atoms' goalkeeper, Bobby Rigby, the first American soccer player to grace the cover of *Sports Illustrated* magazine, reportedly kept the game close.

In the stands that night, along with a paid crowd of 11,790, was Ed Tepper, a Philadelphia-based real estate investor and owner of the National Lacrosse League's Philadelphia Wings. The enthusiasm of the crowd convinced Tepper that professional indoor soccer had a future.

In fact, the following winter, the NASL ran a league-wide competition in the sport to keep their players fit in the so called "off season", and also to generate income year-round.

When one looks at photos of those games or any film or video recording, the strange size goals, four feet in height and 16 feet in length, stand out. The goals were not built into the end boards of the hockey rink but rather placed in front of them. Looked at as only a temporary rental for the arena at the time, there was a lack of willingness to restructure the hockey end boards to facilitate a few dates for indoor soccer.

The Philadelphia Spectrum was owned in part by Ed Snyder's Com-cast-Spectator company. Snyder was part-owner of the Philadelphia Eagles with Earl Foreman, who had married Snyder's sister, Phyliss. Foreman was a DC-based attorney with an extensive sports background (including early investment in soccer and ownership of the Virginia Squires featuring Julius Erving in the American Basketball Association) and was a natural for Tepper to speak with about the possible development of a professional indoor soccer league, with games, of course, being played at the Spectrum.

The arena was one of the last venues Elvis Presley performed in before his death in 1977.

There had to be other arenas across the country without an NHL, NBA or minor league sport franchise that were also looking for permanent tenants!

Tepper and Foreman founded the Major Indoor Soccer League in 1977 and opened offices at One Bala Cynwyd Plaza in Bala Cynwyd, PA, just north of Philadelphia. Of course, they would need a soccer consultant to assist with the development of a player pool and otherwise represent the League with the various soccer organizations such as USSF and FIFA, not to mention the local Eastern and Western Pennsylvania State Soccer Associations.

In 1977, Philadelphia based Walt Chyzowych was at the height of his involvement in US soccer, having been named National Team Coach and Director of Coaching. He was a Philadelphia legend of sorts, having been an All-American player at Temple University and having led the Philadelphia Ukrainian Nationals to an Open Cup Championship. And he also coached at Philadelphia College of Textiles and Sciences (Philadelphia Textile).

Chyzowych saw the indoor game as an extension of Dettmar Cramer's teaching as it was played small sided, five v five with goalkeepers, providing players many touches on the ball in close quarters. He also was constantly perplexed with the lack of playing time American players were receiving in the NASL and saw the MISL as an opportunity to give them experience in a professional league atmosphere.

The MISL would open its first season in December 1978 with six franchises: New York Arrows, which would play in the Nassau Coliseum, home to the NHL Islanders; Philadelphia Fever, to play in the Spectrum; Cleveland Force, playing in the Richfield Coliseum; Cincinnati Kids, playing in the Riverfront Coliseum; Pittsburgh Spirit, playing in the Civic Arena, and the Houston Summit, playing in an arena with the same name.

Chyzowych conducted several sessions of player tryouts where coaches and club staff could evaluate players for the first-ever MISL Draft. Where teams needed personnel help, he recommended coaches and staff that he was familiar with through the USSF Coaching Schools and All-American Soccer Camps. Len Bilous and John Kowalski took on the coaching reins of the Cincinnati franchise. The Fever hired Georgie O'Neill, a former Atoms player. Houston already had Timo Liekoski at the helm as he was the coach of the Houston Hurricane of the NASL, from which 15 players would transfer for the winter.

The MISL Board of Governors met on September 29, 1978, and approved a resolution that each team would contribute $10,000 to the signing of New York Cosmos star goalkeeper Shep Messing and that he would play in New York.

The following month, MISL applied to become a Regional League under Federation regulations and pay a fee of $12,500 per team. The League agreed to the established indoor playing rules except for the size of the goals. MISL was adamant that the goal be 12 feet by six feet six inches.

Commissioner Foreman and Deputy Commissioner Tepper devised a business plan whereby they would be in control of the League up to and including its 20th franchise. The initial franchise fee was rumored to be $51,000 per team, of which Forman and Tepper would split all but $1,000 between them, with the remaining money going into the League's operating budget. The arrangement would continue through to the application of the twentieth franchise. Of course, franchise fees would increase each year corresponding to the success of the league.

For the initial season, 1978-79, each team was required to submit an Irrevocable Letter of Credit of $150,000 and each agreed to a League Office operating budget for the year of $225,000 with each team paying $37,500. There was also a special assessment of $1,800 per club for the creation of the League magazine *Missile* by Don Ruck and Associates.

In addition, confirming that interest in competition between the Cold War rivals, United States and Soviet Union continued, an agreement was made with the Russian team, Spartak, Moskow (Moscow) for a six-game tour starting in February 1979. Each team was requested to fund the tour with an additional $19,200 and games were set to start February 2nd in

Pittsburgh and end on February 10th in Cleveland. The Russian team would feature the heir apparent to Lev Yashin in goal, Rinat Dasayev, who would go on to play in three World Cups from 1982 to 1990.

For the record: the scores of those matches with the MISL team listed first were Pittsburgh 2-8, New York 7-9, Houston 7-5, Philadelphia 4-11, Cincinnati 3-7 and Cleveland 2-20. The scores reflect the quality of the MISL teams and the final standings of that first year. The Houston win came the day after the Russians played their game in New York, the Russian team having to travel.

New York won the first MISL title, although Houston finished ahead of the Arrows in the regular season. Houston was upset in the playoffs, according to sources, because the Texas squad had already started practicing outdoors for the NASL season and couldn't make the transition back inside.

Chyzowych knew that the MISL would require game officials with specific talent to manage the indoor game with its unique field surrounded by NHL dasher boards providing for a fast-paced game with sudden "play on" advantages off the boards, rebounds, etc.

When Walter Chyzowych recommended that I interview for the position to lead MISL officiating, he did so with the confidence that I had already imagined what the game would look like and how it would be necessary to bring on some of the nuances of hockey such as time penalties, free substitutions while the ball was in play ("on the fly") and two minute time penalties for deliberately playing the ball over the boards and glass. And one of the things I knew for sure was that the goals would have to be built into the boards and be correlated with the size of the playing surface. Twelve feet wide and six feet six inches high would be perfect!

The USSF *Laws of the Game* for indoor soccer written in 1978 consisted of only eight pages and started with the sentence: "Inherent in this construct of rules is the understanding that the FIFA rules prevail with the following exceptions..." and then the indoor rules are spelled out. In other words, if something happens that is not covered in the eight pages, apply the outdoor rules. It's no wonder that, as Referee-in-Chief, once the games started, I would have to write bulletin after bulletin to address the issues that the original rule writers did not think of in advance. The last page of the rule book contained cartoonish drawings of referee signals.

The fact there was no signal for "boarding" was an indication that the rule book left a lot to be desired. And there was a signal tantamount to traveling in basketball for "goalkeeper carrying the ball" which was never a problem in the smaller indoor soccer penalty area. I adopted that signal for delay of game, as appropriate for kicking the ball over the boards from the defensive third of the field was a common occurrence, both deliberate and otherwise. A two-minute time penalty was established to deal with "clear and obvious" deliberate delays via this method.

In my interview with Earl Foreman and Ed Tepper in Bala Cynwyd, I indicated that not only did I want the job but that I also wanted to be one of the active officials on the floor. Foreman then came up with the title "Referee-in-Chief". I accepted the position, part-time, with a salary of $5,000 and another $100 per game officiated. I was still Director of Athletics and Soccer Coach at the University of New Haven.

One of the first responsibilities of the new position was to identify a cadre of officials who could "do" this game. At the time, USSF's Department of Officiating was deeply embedded within the NASL's officiating department to the point that some thought they were one in the same. I had some familiarity with the NASL referee corps through the many NY Cosmos and Connecticut Bicentennials games that I had attended in person over the years. Plus, I had risen to the rank of "National Referee" through the many "Sunday games" I had worked in the Connecticut State League.

While working at a USSF Coaching School field session at Manhattanville College, I saw a referee in charge of a youth game on an adjacent field and he officiated it with energy, enthusiasm, body language and charisma. I knew I needed him in the MISL. His name: Gino D'Ippolito!

The Cincinnati Kids had early access to their arena and were able to put down their carpet and conduct several intra-squad scrimmages. It was a perfect opportunity to assemble a group of officials for "tryouts" of their own. The first MISL referee clinic!

I selected and invited the officials to this first referee clinic. These included Gino D'Ippolito and Bill Maxwell from NY, Don Wynschenk, my colleague from the University of New Haven, Hans Schwink of Detroit, who Walter recommended having seen him officiate a Philadelphia Inter US Amateur Cup match in Detroit. Additionally, Guy Fraiture and Peter Johnson from the DC area, Gene Chyzowych, Walter's brother, local referee Nick Matavuli and Artie Wachter, whose NASL career had been shortened by a leg injury. There are some brief glimpses of the game action surrounding that clinic in a video still available on YouTube entitled: "Cincinnati Kids: New Kids in Town."

It didn't take long to recognize which officials were comfortable operating within the confines of the boards, and a very different set of stimuli. When the ball was live, there was no time to rest or lose concentration. Instead, the officials had to decide (make a decision) on average every four seconds. And they had better be comfortable talking with players and technical staff as there was no place to hide. And, on occasion, getting out of the way to avoid being hit by the ball or charging players by using the lips on the boards to boost oneself up as the ball or a player was coming in the same direction with speed.

In addition to training the on-floor officials, it was also important that I meet with the local State Referee Administrators (SRAs) to organize a group of officials that would serve as goal judges, penalty box attendants and the off-field referee (Alternate Referee) who would be uniformed and could whistle infractions from the sideline. The thought being, only the center referee would incur travel expenses.

The first MISL game was played on the Friday evening of December 22, 1978, in the Nassau Coliseum between the host NY Arrows and the visiting Kids from Cincinnati. Baseball superstar Pete Rose was a part-owner of the Kids and kicked out the first ball.

As Referee-in-Chief, I assigned myself to the first game as referee and Don Wynschenk as alternate. We drove down together from Connecticut for the 7:30pm start. Gino D'Ippolito came into the locker room at 5pm and could not believe that I was already in uniform and ready to go. He laughed at my level of nervousness. When Pete Rose kicked out that first ball, Foreman, Tepper, yours truly and Shep Messing were on the field. Messing handled Rose's kick!

A crowd of 10,386 watched that first game, which to the dismay of the fans and everyone else went scoreless in the first of four scheduled 15-minute periods. Messing and Kids goalkeeper Keith Van Eron put on a show in that quarter. And the Arrows even had the benefit of the League's first man-advantage two-minute penalty when I whistled the Kids' Buzz Demling, who was on loan from the NASL's San Jose Earthquakes, for a reckless challenge.

The final score, however, favored the Arrows 7-2. Steve Zungul scored four goals and Pat Ercoli, Mario Garcia and Jim Pollihan scored for New York. John Smile and Keith Tozer scored for the Kids. The game had a University of New Haven connection with Wynschenk, John Kowalski as assistant Kids coach and former New Haven players Krys Furman and goalkeeper Rick Kessel, who was a late sub for Van Eron. Kowalski was registered as a player for that game and 11 others that first season. He had continued his playing career after graduation from the University of New Haven with the New Britain Polish Falcons in the Connecticut State League. Unfortunately, the Cincinnati Kids folded after one year!

But in year two when the Pittsburgh Spirit won only five of their first 15 games under Alex Pringle, Walter Chyzowych recommended that Bilous and Kowalski rectify the situation. And rectify is what they did, winning 13 straight games, finishing 18-10, and making the playoffs.

The following year, Kowalski was hired to lead the Hartford Hellions and Bilous the Philadelphia Fever. Kowalski later returned as Head Coach of Pittsburgh. He kept that team at or near the top of the table throughout, leading to his appointment, again by Walter Chyzowych, to guide the USA's first Five-a-Side team. In 1989, that team went on to finish third at the Five-a-Side World Championship, which at that time was the highest showing by any team from the United States in a modern era FIFA tournament. And the first FIFA Medals awarded!

The initial MISL game was covered by soccer writer Alex Yannis for the *New York Times*, who reported that "the crowd was enthusiastic throughout the contest". When the Arrows were under pressure in the third quarter, having lost two players to the penalty box, keeping Shep Messing busy, Yannis quoted Shep's pregnant wife as saying: "I think I am going to have this baby sooner than I expect." Yannis also complimented my performance as referee: "The game was not as rough as might have been expected. Perhaps because it was officiated by the League's director of officials, Joe Machnick." (Machnik was misspelled).

The following day I drove to Philadelphia to referee their home opener against Pittsburgh. The game was a complete sellout, with 16,529 in attendance. Walter Chyzowych, who was present at both the first two matches, was later quoted by Gerald Eskenazi in a *NY Times* article that the indoor game was "a useful game suited for the American player and fan. You have to play in a smaller area, so you play faster and improve your skills". Chyzowych continued: "It's a good game for the American fan who doesn't understand the intricacies of soccer on a big field."

Chyzowych also advised Foreman and Tepper that the MISL had to do more than the NASL's rule of having just three Americans on a team's roster. As such, MISL teams were required to have 12 of 16 rostered players be North American. The overall first season was deemed a success. The average attendance that first year was 4,453 for the regular season and 4,766 for the playoffs. The following campaign opened with ten teams in two divisions. The Atlantic Division consisted of New York, Pittsburgh, Buffalo, Philadelphia and Hartford while the Central Division housed Houston, Wichita, Detroit, St. Louis and Cleveland.

By this time, I had developed a strong relationship with Commissioner Foreman. Since he lived in the Washington, DC area and I was still living in Guilford, Connecticut, the League rented an apartment within walking distance of the office which we would share. I learned that whenever Foreman was to be in the office, it was fortuitous for me to be there as well, not only while working 8am to 5pm but for the time we shared at dinner at a local deli and at the apartment. Foreman had difficulty sleeping and we would often spend long hours discussing not only the day-to-day operations of the MISL, but also the ins and outs of USSF, the NASL and other sport leagues of which he was familiar. Foreman once told me that I reminded him of his coach at the Virginia Squires, Al Bianchi. I felt in many ways that Foreman treated me like a son. I learned so much during those times. I consider Earl Foreman one of the three most important mentors in my life. Certainly Gary Rosenthal, my coach at LIU, Walter Chyzowych for everything he did for me, opening every possible door, and Foreman for his leadership and guidance which led to my becoming a knowledgeable sport administrator at many levels.

I refereed a game in Detroit in Cobo Hall where the home team "Lightning" defeated the New York Arrows. After the game, Foreman invited me to dinner at the London Chop House with Lightning owner, Jerry Perenchio, who was a partner with Norman Lear, the creator of TV shows *All in the Family*, *Maude* and *Sanford and Sons*. Their partnership also had the rights to a team in the San Francisco area. The discussion between Foreman and Perenchio was at times over the head of this kid from Greenpoint, but the fact I was included was taken as a level of trust and support by the Commissioner even on matters that were deemed confidential.

There were so many unique and fascinating things that happened on the field during those first two years in MISL. When the St. Louis Steamers came into the League with a mostly St. Louis based line-up, they regularly packed their iconic building, the St. Louis Arena, which was known as the Checkerdome when it was purchased by Ralston-Purina in 1977. Now the referees had the additional pressure of playing in front of standing-room only crowds. Not only were the Steamers locally based on the field, but they also were heavily sponsored by local brewery, Anheuser-Busch and their Budweiser brand, and had Saint Louis Cardinals baseball legend Stan Musial as an investor.

In setting up the local staff of officials that would service the Steamers' games, I met with Heinrich Schmidt, the Illinois State Referee Administrator, who was a brew-master for Anheuser-Busch, and he recommended a young local referee, Dr. Herb Silva, to be involved. I met Silva and we immediately hit it off both on and off the field.

Nothing was more unusual than the pre-season exhibition game played in Albuquerque, New Mexico, on November 25, 1979. The match was promoted by a local business person to interest the populace in bringing a MISL team to Albuquerque. What the promoter did not tell the League or the participating teams, Houston and St. Louis, in advance was that a horse show had taken place in the arena immediately preceding the proposed exhibition fixture and that the game would be played on dirt. I wrote a summary memo to Commissioner Foreman on November 28th which he responded to in a letter on December 5th, stating: "This matter was an absolute disgrace to the League. Appropriate action will be taken by me to prevent the re-occurrence of any similar type of situation. The less said about this matter the better. I therefore consider the case closed."

I was on the field in the Checkerdome as referee for a game between Detroit's Lightning and the Steamers. The home team Steamers were leading 6-1, with 10 minutes to play in the fourth quarter. The following account of what happens next is taken from the article *They Get Their Kicks on a Hockey Rink* by JD Reed that appeared in *Sports Illustrated* February 18, 1980 (the one with Mary Decker on the cover).

"The Steamers victory song, *Ain't No Stoppin Us Now* (by McFadden and Whitehead), was booming over the speakers when Lightning tough guy, Manny Hernandez, elbowed Ty Keough (Saint Louis native and local hero, his dad having played for the USA in their 1-0 victory over England in the 1950 World Cup) to the turf in front of the Steamers' goal.

"The crowd howled for Hernandez blood, and a bench-clearing semi-melee ensued with players pushing and threatening fisticuffs that never quite materialized. However, it was enough for referee Joseph Machnik. He sent Hernandez to the penalty box with a five-minute misconduct. Steve Pecher of the Steamers was also given five minutes for being the third man into the fight, and Steamer goalie Robert Robson was given a major penalty for chasing Hernandez to the Lightning bench.

"Playing with five men against St. Louis' four, Detroit scored a goal 26 seconds after the penalties had been assessed, bringing the score to 6-2.

"It then developed that no one in the Checkerdome that night knew what should happen next — except Machnik. Should stand-ins for the penalized Steamers now be allowed to enter the game — as the Saint Louis players argued — or should they be kept out of action until five minutes had expired, as is the rule in the NHL? The referee decreed that the penalties be served out. Detroit Coach Terry Fisher, one of three Americans guiding MISL teams, put a field player (Flemming Lund) in for his goalkeeper, and Detroit hammered the beleaguered Steamers (and a back-up goalkeeper) for five more goals before the penalties expired. This blitz occurred before an astonished, almost dead-quiet crowd of 15,125 seething Steamer fans.

"Ah, but this was indoor soccer. Trailing 7-6 when the penalties ended, the Steamers came back to tie the game in regulation time and win it 8-7 in sudden death overtime. The Checkerdome erupted in a shower of Busch Bavarian. Said a trembling security guard, wiping the perspiration — or was it suds — from inside his hat, 'whew, can you imagine anybody who bought a $3.50 ticket to this thing going home and saying they had a good time?'"

Truth be told, as a referee, I was terrified. After each Detroit goal the field was showered with debris from the local faithful.

The only thing that saved me was the Steamers turning around the score and the result. Herb Silva, who was not assigned to the game but was in the building, also made his way down to the hallway leading to the referee locker room just in case I needed some assistance.

The next day, while sitting at my desk at the University of New Haven, I received a phone call from Earl Foreman: "What happened?" Earl asked. He had received a phone call from the Saint Louis owners expressing concern for the safety of the spectators amid speculation as to what might have happened had the Steamers lost.

I immediately wrote a Referee Bulletin and instigated a rule change indicating that when there are dual five-minute penalties, one to each team, that the guilty players serve their time but are able to be replaced by substitutes on the field.

Coincidently, the NHL also made that switch so that teams did not have to play four v four with goalkeepers against this new superstar in Edmonton, Wayne Gretzky.

The excitement wasn't limited to St. Louis, however, as high-scoring games were commonplace throughout the League. So much so that the NASL started their own bona-fide indoor competition the following season.

I did have the pleasure of refereeing MISL's first All-Star game which was played in Saint Louis and the second such match which was played at Madison Square Garden, a particular thrill for me going back to my New York Rangers fandom. Amazingly, while sitting in the referee's room, the same one used by the NHL officials, I answered a knock on the door and it was the Rangers' two regular season goal judges, hoping to work the game. They were disappointed to learn that soccer referees had already been appointed.

It was during that fixture that Commissioner Foreman entertained his friend, Jim Foster, who was promotions director for the NFL. Foreman saw Foster as a potential investor, perhaps in partnership with the NFL. Perhaps to put a franchise in the Garden? During the game Foster is alleged to have taken out a manilla folder from his briefcase and used it to design an indoor football field, gridiron style within the confines of a hockey rink, that would become the blueprint for the Arena Football League.

We continued to officiate MISL soccer with one referee on the field and another with a whistle standing high over the boards between the penalty boxes. For the most part, this system would work with a referee who was able to read the game, was comfortable in the arena, understood the concept of time penalties, could keep up with the game, manage the players and coaches up close and personal, utilize the goal judges, sprint to catch up to play one end to the other and show the "illusion of hustle", one of my pet peeves.

There were also games where the alternate referee was required to assist, whistling fouls from the bench. As we now know, with VAR and multiple TV angles available to analyze every officiating decision, the referee's angle on a particular play may not be the best, regardless of whether he is in a good position or not.

At the end of the first season, I prepared a revision of the *USSF Indoor Soccer Law Book* which included many of the modifications that were needed to adjudicate situations which happened on the indoor field during that first year which were not apropos to outdoor soccer.

Specifically, the second MISL season would provide an alternate referee with "match control responsibilities off the ball and out of the Referee's view" in addition to the previously established duties and responsibilities of "the judgment of illegal substitutions, three-line passes, keeping a record of the game, and controlling the penalty box areas".

At the beginning of the season each coach was provided with a Referee Assessment Form, specifically for the indoor game, and a Directory of MISL Game Officials. A legitimate referee program was beginning to take shape.

There was often interesting feedback written by coaches as part of their referee evaluation. One of my favorites of all time was when Wichita coach Roy Turner criticized a referee for penalizing Glenn Myernick with a two-minute time penalty for playing the ball over the glass. Turner wrote: "This is Myernick, not Cruyff."

The MISL's first All-Star game was confirmed to be played in St. Louis' Checkerdome on February 27, 1980. Commissioner Foreman announced the hiring of Tracey Leiweke to serve as League Coordinator for the match. Tracy was the oldest of four Leiweke brothers who would leave their mark on the MISL and indoor soccer.

I had previously worked with Tracey's brother Terry in the production of an instructional video tape on the officiating of indoor soccer, using footage from the league's first one and a half seasons. That tape was used in referee training not only in the MISL but also at local indoor centers which were beginning to pop up all over the country, especially in colder weather environs.

It was the stated effort of the MISL to have its first All-Star Game outdraw the equivalent NBA and NHL matches. The game was also to be shown on tape delay on the Madison Square Garden TV Network. A crowd of 16,892 watched on as Pat Ercoli's hat-trick helped the Central Division to a 9-4 victory against the Atlantic Division. The crowd was nearly 3,000 stronger than the Steamers' regular attendance and cemented Tracy Leiweke's reputation as a marketeer and promoter of the sport. And it was the beginning of a personal relationship with the Leiweke family which facilitated my leaving the MISL office some four years later.

It was an honor and a privilege to officiate the first two MISL All-Star games. By year number three (1980-81), MISL was a serious league in terms of level of competition, evaluation of coaches' performance and scrutiny of the referee program. Twelve teams played in three four-team divisions: Atlantic, Central and Western. The quality of play was extremely high, and the level of intensity increased as the playoffs approached. Eight teams qualified for the playoffs and each round had tightly contested games. The quarterfinals were a best-of-three-games series, with the higher seed playing away for the first match and then at home for the following game and the decider if necessary.

Highest seed New York lost their first game in Phoenix 10-6 and were trailing in the second when a New York Arrows player struck the referee from a standing position in the penalty box. Several chaotic minutes followed. An announcement came over the public address system requesting that I report to the entrance of the locker room area. After a conversation with team owners, I immediately called Commissioner Foreman to report on the events. During that time, the referee decided to continue the game. The incident changed the momentum of the game and New York rallied to win. New York won the deciding fixture by a 6-5 score to advance to the next round.

Baltimore beat Cleveland thanks to an overtime goal in their first game, lost the second and won the third 6-5. Saint Louis won their series against Buffalo in two games, 6-4 and 6-5. Wichita lost their away game to Chicago 4-3 but won the remaining two 6-4 and 8-5. Now, the four remaining teams had to travel to Saint Louis for the Semi-Finals and Championship Games.

At the request of Commissioner Foreman, I did not officiate any of the playoff matches. He was trying to protect me!

By this time Gino D'Ippolito and Bill Maxwell, both NASL top-flight officials, had established themselves as being at the top of the class in the indoor circuit. D'Ippolito was the clear choice to officiate the final.

However, the NASL opened their outdoor season that same weekend and scheduled Gino to do a Saturday night game in Florida. As such, he had to catch an early flight Sunday morning to get to Saint Louis by kick-off. A police escort was arranged to ensure there would be no traffic tie-ups.

The semi-final doubleheader drew 16,236 and saw the NY Arrows easily defeat the Baltimore Blast 10-1. The game witnessed the alternate referee Anatol Popovich having to whistle multiple times in support of Bill Maxwell.

The second match saw Saint Louis come back from a 6-1 deficit to tie the game at 7-7 before the Steamers won in a shootout. The game pivoted on a play in which Steamers forward Don Ebert came together with Wichita Wings goalkeeper Mike Dowler outside of the penalty area, causing an injury which required Dowler to leave the game. Impartial observers opined that the contact should have been penalized for two minutes at a minimum.

To be fair to the officials, there had been season-long discussions on the use of time penalties, especially in meaningful situations near the end of closely contested games. Up until this point, officials had been following the NHL model of letting the players decide the contest, even to the point of "putting their whistle away" in the playoffs, especially in overtime.

When asked, prior to the start of the playoffs as to the use of time penalties, Commissioner Foreman suggested that a higher standard be adopted in the playoffs and that a time penalty should not be called under any circumstance unless the referee sees "smoke coming out of the gun". This message was delivered to the officials. As such, the intensity and physicality in this tournament was at the highest level yet!

And, of course, there was always the suspicion, founded or otherwise, that "MISL wanted St. Louis in the final".

On Saturday between the games, Herb Silva (an excellent sounding board) and I met to discuss the status of the officiating program. It was clear there would be push back from the owners and some coaches about the playoff's level of intensity and the role of the alternate referee. Silva and I had our own controversy during the season in a game between Detroit and Wichita where he whistled for a foul in midfield that I would not have called based on my angle. The restart gave the Wings the ball and they scored a goal which initiated a comeback and overtime win, thus eliminating Detroit from the playoffs. Our conversation continued in the hotel sauna where we decided it was time to bring the alternate referee on to the field and officiate the game with a dual referee system like that being used in most college and high school matches.

The Championship Game attracted 17,206 and saw the Arrows defeat the Steamers 6-5 with Steve Zungul scoring the winning goal with 30 seconds left in the match.

In addition to the criticism of "letting them play" there was also a complaint that most of the officials were based on the east coast.

Introducing the two-referee system to some of our officials who had only worked USSF games in the diagonal system of control received some push back but there was seemingly no other choice. The game needed more control. Interestingly, the NHL was also considering modifying their system by putting a second referee on the ice. One of the factors for consideration was the minimization of the referee's personality and its effect on the game. In addition, getting the officials to agree as to how the game should be called, by the book or bending the book? Or something in between?

In June of 1981, I had a career discussion with Commissioner Foreman. Prior to the start of the 1980-81 season, I was offered a leave of absence from my tenured position as a now Associate Professor at the University of New Haven and forfeited my role as Athletic Director as that was a staff position from which leaves were not granted.

I was able to secure a second year's leave thanks to the work of my friend John Benevento, who was now a Vice-President and trusted confidant to President Philip Kaplan. I was told by the university, however, that a third year's leave would set a precedent and therefore would not be possible. Plus, the university would need to decide on the hiring of a permanent replacement for me as Athletic Director. I strongly recommended that Debbie Chin, who had been performing the role in my absence, be named full-time Director of Athletics when I decided I was not returning.

I had to let the university know, one way or the other, by March of 1982. And I decided to go full-time with the Major Indoor Soccer League.

The identification of officials outside of the east coast was an obvious priority and I took the opportunity to assign two California-based referees, Heinz Wolmerath and Danny Goldman, both accomplished NASL officials who often worked as a pair, to a quarter-final playoff game in Saint Louis versus the Buffalo Stallions.

The game became famous in the history of MISL as Stallions player John Dolinsky and Steamers public address announcer Kevin Slaten exchanged words as Dolinsky entered the penalty box. Words turned into fisticuffs and Wolmerath showed Dolinsky and Slaten red cards.

I was at the game in my role as Referee-in-Chief and immediately found a pay phone to call Commissioner Foreman at his home to report the incident. "He did what?" the Commissioner asked as I described an unprecedented incident in Foreman's long sport-related history. The sending off of a public address announcer!

Foreman suspended Slaten for the remainder of the season and fined him an "undisclosed sum". The press release announcing the suspension included a quote from Steamer's owner Stan Musial. "I abhor the idea of violence connected with sports. I in no way condone the actions of Mr. Slaten and I certainly understand the position of the Commissioner on this and agree with him," Musial said.

By year two, in addition to writing the schedule, I also implemented changes in the way the game would be presented, hoping to put forward a more professional image. For instance, the league now required the coaches to dress in a suit rather than warm-up gear. Obviously, there was some pushback on this but in time the coaches became used to it and in fact often challenged each other for "best dressed". I also mandated that the players on the bench keep their arms and legs from hanging over the boards or from sitting on the boards. And we instituted a pre-game warm-up protocol in which players would do their stretching in the hallways prior to entering the field of play and then go through their warm-ups in a choreographic fashion set to music. We also limited the playing of music while the ball was in play. In instituting these standards, I was accused of trying to make the game presentation too much like hockey; after all, we were playing on a hockey rink, with substitutions on the fly, time penalties and a limitation of playing the ball on a fly over the center line like the restrictions known in hockey as "icing". We still called our game "indoor soccer" rather than "hocker" or "sockey" as it was sometimes referred to sarcastically by skeptical media.

After the adventure of having to arrange a police escort for Gino D'Ippolito to get to the Checkerdome for the Championship Game, due to the conflicting NASL schedule and the news that the NASL was contemplating "blackballing" officials who worked for the fledgling indoor soccer league, I authored a memo to Commissioner Foreman requesting an increase in pay for the MISL officials, bringing the game fee close to what was being paid for an NASL outdoor game. At the same time I floated an idea that as the MISL grew in size and stature, it would become necessary to professionalize a unique corps of officials who would officiate full-time in the new indoor sport. Specialists, if you will!

Indeed, after the conclusion of the 1980-81 season, Commissioner Foreman and the Board of Directors were convinced that a full-time referee program was going to be best for the League. Professional referees would add consistency to the overall interpretation of the playing rules, become familiar with all the players and coaches, playing styles, strategies and tactics, league standings, etc. Conversely, the players and coaches would become familiar with the referees and their personalities as they would be seeing officials they were genuinely familiar with, game in and game out.

As part of the interview process to determine which officials would be hired on a full-time basis, Commissioner Foreman arranged a lunch at his house in suburban Washington, DC and a dozen officials were flown in. I would retain my role as Referee-in-Chief and was part of the interviewing process. It was generally agreed that the starting salary would be $30,000 and the officials would receive a full benefit package including health insurance, etc. just like the other League employees. The program would not only be the first full-time soccer officiating program in the United States but arguably in the world.

Not all the officials were able to accept the position, however, as several had full-time jobs of their own and soccer officiating to them was more of a labor of love and a dedicated hobby. These officials would still be assigned the odd game when necessary or appropriate due to travel constraints, etc. They would be classified as "Senior Referees", second in rank to the Full-Time Referees and above those classified as simply "Referees", who would be assigned Alternate Official responsibilities as they worked their way up to Senior status and eventually full-time employment.

Six officials were hired full-time: Gino D'Ippolito, Jeff Mantel, Bill Maxwell, Herb Silva, Don Wynschenk from the University of New Haven and Anatol Popovich, my former teammate at both the NY and Newark

Ukrainians.

There were some top-flight officials in the Senior Referee group such as Julio Salas, Artie Wachter, Gus Constantine, Terry Campbell, Feliks Fuksman, Heinz Wolmerath, John Davies and Danny Goldman.

And in the Referee Group was the first appearance of an up-and-coming young official who started out as a goal judge in Saint Louis and Kansas City, Esse Baharmast. Also in that group were Don DeWeese, who would later be an owner of the Memphis team in the American Indoor Soccer Association; my high school friend, Andrew Sheparovich; the person who first introduced me to soccer, Alfred Kleinaitis (later to be employed by US Soccer's Referee Department) and Marty Templin who, like Baharmast, would gain full-time status in a few short years.

The following year, we added another distinguished FIFA referee to the full-time staff, Toros Kibritjian. And the roster of officials for the 1982-83 MISL season included Betty Ellis, among the very first female soccer referees in the country to work men's games at such a high level.

Of course, my own status within the MISL, having grown from the original part-time position, was in constant state of evaluation. There were some who questioned my leadership and ability to separate myself from the referees while still being one of them. There was also the question of my status at the University of New Haven and of my friendship and partnership with John Kowalski (Pittsburgh Spirit coach) in the No.1 Goalkeeper's Camp we started together in 1977. Some saw it as a conflict of interest!

When Ed Tepper exercised his right to a franchise (New Jersey Rockets) and left the League office, I was now second in seniority to Commissioner Foreman.

The Commissioner received a letter from the managing partner in Wichita requesting that I not be assigned to referee any game between Wichita and Pittsburgh (Kowalski's team) or be involved in adjudicating any protest involving a game between those clubs. In addition, he asked for written proof that I had resigned my position from the University of New Haven and terminated the partnership between Kowalski and myself in the Goalkeeper Camp.

I looked at this development as part of the growth and development of the League. Indoor soccer in the MISL was no longer an exhibition experiment but a bona fide competitive league with a TV contract (USA Network), growing crowds and with players, and coaches' and administrators' jobs on the line. And despite all the outward resemblance of success on the field, there was still money being lost.

A meeting was held on August 16, 1982 to discuss my future in the MISL and the reorganization of the front office. It was decided that I continue to be able to officiate as one of the full-time referees, but that Jim Budish would assist in some of the operational aspects of the League. I was offered a two-year contract at a salary of $55,000 for the first year with a 12 percent increase for year number two. It was also decided that I would have six weeks vacation during July and August, during which I would be allowed to continue to operate the soccer camp but that I "must sever my business relationship with John Kowalski" and "discontinue the practice of hiring MISL players or other employees as staff members at the camp."

Many MISL and NASL goalkeepers worked at the No.1 Goalkeeper's Camp in those first years. Richard But, Paul Coffee, Alan Mayer, Zoltan Toth and Krys Sobieski to name a few.

In a memo dated August 19, 1982 summarizing the meeting of three days earlier, the following was also documented: "Considerable discussion was had regarding the policy of avoiding where possible, the calling of time penalties in overtime or in regulation time in the closing minutes of a tie or one goal game. It was decided that this policy be discontinued and that a foul is a foul regardless of the time of such infraction." And it was at this meeting that the two-man refereeing system was given the go-ahead on an experimental basis for the first half of the ensuing season.

Of course, the single referee on the field system never returned and the changes as to how the game was officiated had a lasting impact on the quality of entertainment being offered. Value judgements can be mixed on the outcome of these two vital decisions and the ones soon to follow.

On August 30, 1982, I received a letter from Dr. Philip Kaplan, President of the University of New Haven, accepting my resignation with regret. I submitted that letter to Foreman the following week along with a notice that a meeting of the stockholders of the No.1 Goalkeeper's Camp was scheduled for September 30, 1982, in the office of Attorney James Nugent, at which time John Kowalski would submit his stock and resign as Vice

President, "terminating our partnership".

Strange things continued to happen on the MISL playing field. In a game played on the day after Christmas, 1981, Philadelphia beat Buffalo at the Stallions' "Aud" arena 6-3 despite having been called for seven (7) time penalties compared to only two against the home side. Philadelphia Fever coach Walt Chyzowych had to be restrained from referee Bill Maxwell after the match. Maxwell first displayed a yellow card, which he followed with a red. As a result, I had to inform Chyzowych that the Disciplinary Committee of which I was the Chairman was fining him $500.

Just over a year later, during a blizzard with a near empty "Aud" arena, Stallions coach Ray Klivecka and Rockets coach Timo Liekoski put the game into disrepute with an exercise now known as "Stall Ball". It started with Buffalo leading the game 3-1 and deciding not to attack further. Defender Denis Mepham and goalkeeper Paul Maxi passed the ball back and forth with no pressure from any Rocket player. At one point, a Stallion player sat on the ball.

This went on for the last four minutes of the half and into the third period, during which I received a phone call from the referee, Gus Constantine, asking what, indeed, he should do. With a follow-up call to Commissioner Foreman, I advised Constantine to caution the guilty players for game disrepute and inform both coaches of impending fines. The game finished 5-1 in Buffalo's favor.

Prior to the start of the 1982-83 campaign, the owners convinced Commissioner Foreman that the game was still "too rough" and despite my vigorous objection the season started with a "Six Foul Rule". In essence, the alternate referee would keep track of all fouls, regardless of their nature, and whistle the game dead, hold up a blue sign with the number six on it and the guilty team would receive a two-minute time penalty and play shorthanded for two minutes.

The result was devastating to the game. Coaches now instructed their players to play a zone low-pressure defense, falling back to defend as soon as the ball was lost. No risks were to be taken of potentially committing a foul in the attacking third of the field. So, the excitement of high-scoring games was now reduced to matches of 4-3, 2-1 and even 0-0 which had to be decided in overtime.

The "Run and Gun" fast-breaking game envisioned from the start of the League was now a thing of the past! Outdoor soccer was now being played indoors!

While Commissioner Foreman trusted my judgment as to how the game should be played, he was at the mercy of the owners. Every time an owner did not get his way, he threatened to pull out of the League the following season by simply not posting the annual Letter of Credit. And there is also the issue of constant re-location of teams trying to find the right market. It was difficult for Foreman to stand up to the owners when there was criticism of an officiating decision, whether it was justified or not. One owner would constantly be on the phone with Foreman complaining that the referees "did not know the rules". In fact, the owner did not know the rules. And when I suggested that Foreman point that out to the owner he said, often in fact, that: "You can't tell smart people they're stupid." I have remembered that quote throughout my entire career and it has guided me in certain situations. After all, I was just a "soccer guy".

There had already been significant turnover in owners and teams, starting at the end of the first season with Cincinnati Kids folding. Over the first five years, Pittsburgh Spirit took a year off, Houston Summit became Baltimore Blast, Hartford Hellions became Memphis Americans, which later played in Las Vegas, and Detroit Lightning became San Francisco Fog, which later became Kansas City Comets. In addition, Chicago Horizon and NJ Rockets lasted only one year, three teams from the NASL (Chicago Sting, San Diego Sockers and Golden Bay Earthquakes) played only one season (1982-83) before rejoining the NASL's indoor program.

An interesting ownership situation existed in Denver where the Avalanche, owned by sport entrepreneur Ron Maierhofer, is best described in his book *No Money Down: How to Buy a Sports Franchise — A Journey Through an American Dream*. The Avalanche lasted two seasons (1980-82) and never played .500 ball.

One of the more pleasant experiences during that time was working with Esse Baharmast in his first on-field assignment, albeit a pre-season game in Wichita against Kansas City. Esse was so nervous the day of the game that we had to go for a walk along Wichita River Park to calm his nerves. However, once on the field, he easily asserted himself and took over the game. I took a "back seat" and watched him work.

Esse then went on to become a member of the MISL full-time officiating staff, while also accepting outdoor assignments in the off season. He caught the eye of FIFA Referee Committee member, Fernando Alvarez, who was living in the States and then Esse proceeded to have a meteoric rise in the international game leading to his appearance in the 1998 World Cup in France, during which his penalty-kick decision against Brazil was highly criticized for several days. Until, of course, the call was substantiated by a photograph from behind the goal which showed a clear and obvious, blatant pull of Norway striker Tore André Flo's shirt. The penalty kick decision is ranked in the "Top 20 Calls of All Time" by the National Association of Sports Officials (NASO) for all sports!

Prior to officiating at the World Cup, Esse had already established himself as the best referee in the country and he was assigned the first game in Major League Soccer (MLS) and the maiden MLS Cup Final match after officiating both semi-finals.

When he returned from France, he officiated the MLS All-Star Game as his final on-field assignment. He then became renowned as a CONCACAF and FIFA Instructor, working multiple international tournaments and also leading US Soccer's Referee Department until his retirement in 2022.

Esse and I stayed in touch over the years, and he asked me to deliver his introduction speech at US Soccer's Annual General Meeting (AGM) when he was honored with the Werner Fricker Builder Award in 2020, the organization's highest honor.

I had the privilege of performing the same duty when Baharmast was inducted into the National Soccer Hall of Fame in 2022 and honored with a Lifetime Achievement Award by the Walt Chyzowych Fund the same year!

On the operations front, the indoor league suffered from various issues with its carpet and whether it was laid on top of the ice directly, or when time permitted, on boards laid over the ice. There was always the difficulty of uneven seams and bubbles, to the point in one game where a player slid, and his body wound up halfway under the carpet.

The New York Arrows shared their facility with the NHL NY Islanders, who were on a run of four straight Stanley Cups, which meant that the ice was still down at the Nassau Coliseum when the Arrows were hosting playoff games of their own.

In the 1982 best-of-five Championship series between the Saint Louis Steamers and the NY Arrows, the carpet issue was the leading story. The opening game was played on Friday night, May 14th on Long Island. Because of the warm weather outside and whether the air conditioning was put on in time, or the doors were left open too long, a layer of fog and mist developed above the carpet and then froze, causing a slippery and dangerous surface. Players could not keep steady on their feet and more than once the game had to be stopped to deal with a non-contact floor-related injury. The Steamers won the first game, which was attended by 7,921, by a score of 3-2, with Tony Glavin scoring after five minutes and 55 seconds of overtime.

The second game was played on Sunday, May 16th before 7,431 spectators, and the temperature outside reached 79 degrees with 70% humidity, exacerbating the issues with the ice forming on the carpet. The Arrows won this game 5-3 and the next in Saint Louis, in front of 18,160, with Steve Zungul scoring at 4:13 of overtime. There were no ice/fog/carpet issues in the Checkerdome.

The Steamers won game four at home by a score of 6-4 before another sell-out of 18,118, meaning the MISL Championship would be decided with a fifth match played in New York.

Earl Foreman sent me to Long Island to meet with the head of maintenance and the folks in charge of the ice and carpet situation. They assured me they had solved the problem and that since the game would be played at night when temperatures outside cooled, and that the air conditioning system would be on at full blast from noon that day, there would be no issues. I reported the good news to Foreman.

The temperature in New York that day hit a high of 79 degrees with humidity at 74%. A crowd of 11,023 attended the match. And the problem with ice forming on the carpet was not solved. Either I had been misinformed or the folks in charge did not know how to fix the problem, and as the Islanders were their top priority, they really did not care that much for indoor soccer or to fix the problem.

The Islanders won the Stanley Cup in 1980, 1981, 1982 and 1983. The Arrows won the MISL Championship in 1979, 1980, 1981 and 1982. The Islanders sold out all their playoff games while the Arrows attracted only 11,000-plus (in a 13,900-capacity arena) for their game-five Championship match in 1982. It was unbeknownst how fragile the flagship franchise of the MISL was at the time. The owners did not see a financial windfall or even an escape at the end of the tunnel.

One of the more interesting assignments issued to me by Earl Foreman was to meet with the newly appointed Commissioner of the NASL, Howard J. Samuels. Phil Woosnam had been relieved of his commissioner duties over issues of over-expansion to 24 teams and financial losses. Howard J. Samuels was a wealthy New York City businessman who made his fortune in the petrol-chemical industry as vice president of Mobil Oil. He also played a significant role in the establishment of the first Off-Track Betting (OTB) programs in America in New York City. When Samuels asked me what I did for Earl Foreman, I replied that "I was his soccer guy". He promised to get back in touch with me.

Samuels died suddenly at home in his New York apartment and Clive Toye, the original founder of the New York Cosmos and the man who brought Pele to the NASL, was named Acting Commissioner. The NASL folded in 1985.

The fourth MISL All-Star Game was played on February 22, 1983, in Kansas City. Knowing I had to be in Kansas City for the concurrent Board of Governors and other meetings, I scheduled myself to officiate, along with Anatol Popovich, the regularly scheduled league game a few nights earlier between Memphis and the KC Comets. I had no idea at the time that it would be my last MISL game.

I did realize, however, that the time might be appropriate to discuss a contract extension, and I was looking forward to the continued work for a league which was now averaging more than 7,000 spectators a game (the first season's average was just a little above 4,000).

The big news around the All-Star Game was not the match itself but the news that the New York Arrows were breaking up.

The former owners abandoned the four-time champions, and the League took over the team prior to the season. Commissioner Foreman appointed Terry Leiweke to serve as President and 22-year-old Todd Leiweke as Vice President and Director of Sales. Kansas City owner Dr. David Schoenstadt took over the club on the premise that what is good for the New York team is good for the League.

In an article in the Sunday, December 5, 1982 edition of the *New York Daily News* written by Jerry Cassidy, the Leiweke brothers outlined their plan to make the Arrows profitable. The headline read, *Arrows are hoping to score with L.I. Fans*. The Leiweke brothers hoped to mobilize the Long Island Junior Soccer League by writing public appearances into the player contracts and to work with goalkeeper Shep Messing, a Long Island resident, in the promotion of an indoor facility in Syosset that would become the team's practice facility and hopefully youth soccer hub.

"We just took over the team one week before the season began," Todd Leiweke is quoted as saying. "So, we haven't had much time to promote the sport. But this summer we are going all out to introduce our players to our fans. We intend to work with the Long Island Junior Soccer Association, and we will be holding clinics all over the island."

In a *NY Times* article which appeared on January 13, 1982, written by William C. Rhoden, the headline read, *Arrows Are Seeking to Americanize Soccer*. There was a picture of the brothers heading the ball with coach Don Popovic. The article reported that the previous owners had lost ten million dollars over the past four years. It also stated that Steve Zungul was put on waivers and that the team was signing Joe Ulrich, Duke University's All-American player from Poughkeepsie, NY, and the winner of the 1982 Hermann Award given to college soccer's best player. "Joe Ulrich is the kind of player we have in mind," said Todd Leiweke. "Born and raised in America."

Already missing from the 1982-83 version of the Arrows were Branko Segota, Juli Veee, Luis Alberto, Omar Gomez and Renato Cila. At the time of this article the Arrows' record was 10-7 and they had just lost at home 5-0 to Memphis. "Motivation is the problem for us right now," Popovic said. Shep Messing ends the article with: "If we get young American players, it might mean we'll have to fight harder to win the title, so we'll fight. The important thing at this point is that we put fans in the seats."

At the time of the All-Star Game, coach Don Popovic's record was 17-13. When he left for San Jose, Dave D'Errico and Shep Messing each coached a game but the Arrows recorded two further defeats.

Tracy Leiweke was representing the Kansas City team in the MISL Board meetings and obviously was privy to all the inside information. After one such meeting, he cornered me at a function and reported on a conversation where one of the owners accused me of flirting with a "blond woman" at the bar. Leiweke reported that he set the owner straight and told the Board that the blond was indeed my wife, Barbara, thus embarrassing the accuser.

I guess I should have seen the "handwriting on the wall". I thought by now that I was savvy and street smart thanks to the education I received nightly in the apartment I shared with the Commissioner. Evidently not!

I was called to a meeting attended by Commissioner Foreman and the representatives of Wichita and Cleveland. The three sat in a line facing the one chair that I was asked to sit in! "We want to discuss your contract," is how the meeting started.

It was explained to me that while they wished that I continue to work in the same capacity for the League, they were not prepared to extend my contract. This news came as quite a shock. I was not prepared for this. Did they want me to finish the season and then let me go?

I had given up a great job as Athletic Director at the University of New Haven and, worse, a tenured position on the faculty.

I was of the firm belief that the position I held and the duties and responsibilities that came with it required the security of a contract. After all, as part of the Discipline Committee and dealing with protests and the like, a contract is something the League should have demanded to provide security and to make sure there was no undue influence expressed by any owner whose interest I might favor in support of retention of my employment. I could see that Foreman was beside himself. This was not his idea. But he was not able to challenge the owners in my support.

The following evening, Tracey Leiweke came to me with a proposition that I take over as coach of the New York Arrows. This also came as a shock. But it also came with a contract. Three years as Head Coach and Vice President of Player Personnel. Without negotiation, the offer was $20,000 more than I had received from the League. I didn't think of it at the time but having been born and raised in New York and having been named an All-American at Long Island University with a successful college coaching career, I was a perfect fit for the new NY Arrows "Team Long Island". But it was never about money. There was principle involved. I would have gladly stayed at the League office with the security of a contract.

I accepted the coaching offer and traveled to Philadelphia to clear out my office and say goodbyes. There were tears in my eyes when I shook hands with the Commissioner for the final time in my capacity as a League Office employee. I could see that he was touched as well.

I asked Commissioner Foreman who would replace me. I had deep concerns for the referees and the program. Foreman stated that he could not tell me at that time but indicated I would be most pleased with the appointment. He also asked that I call each full-time referee and announce my departure personally, which I had planned to do anyway, of course.

Two days later, Walter Chyzowych was announced as MISL's Director of Soccer Administration.

When I was introduced to the Arrows team, I sensed a sigh of relief on their part that at least the state of transition was coming to an end. There was also skepticism as to how the former Referee-in-Chief would coach. And throughout the League, coaches were reportedly nervous that the officials I had guided since the inception of the competition would give us, the Arrows, all the calls. No one could remember whether there was any such transition in a professional sport league where the head referee, or any referee for that matter, would go on to coach in the league. In my calls to the officials, they expressed surprise and disappointment. And speculation of their own as to how Chyzowych, a former coach with no officiating experience and a reputation for being tough on officials, would lead them. They wound up pleasantly surprised.

The Arrows had been on a three-game losing streak and the first match under my leadership was against the San Diego Sockers, who were tied for first place. The players responded greatly, and we managed to win and perhaps celebrated too hard. We lost the next game to lowly Los Angeles Lazers, which had the worst record in professional sports at 5-29. I thought the "Cinderella Effect" of a new coach would last more than one game.

The rest of the season was up and down as well, finishing with seven wins and nine losses to bring the overall record to an even, 24-24. Finishing fourth in the division, the Arrows were eliminated by Baltimore in the first round of the playoffs in a best-of-three series with each team winning its home games. Baltimore went on to defeat Cleveland before narrowly losing to San Diego in the Championship round of five games.

The "losing season" took its toll on attendance as the average Arrows home crowd of 5,623 was some 800 spectators fewer than the year before.

Developments during the off season had an impact, as well. Several agents were successful in relocating their players away from the Arrows, which was beginning to look like a failing franchise both on and off the field. Certainly, the disappointment of not going further in the playoffs and not winning a fifth consecutive Championship was out there. Among the players who were able to leave were Paul Kitson, Gordon Hill, Fernando Clavijo (a true gentleman and a pleasure to coach), Franz St. Lot and Juan Carlos Michia.

Michael Collins, the son of LI Junior Soccer's leader Peter Collins, was earmarked to play a bigger role on the team both on and off the field, as was newcomer Tom Mulroy, a master of soccer-related entertainment who would oversee the clinics and other promotional activities, such as attending club functions and even birthday parties.

The team still had a strong nucleus with forwards Fred Grgurev, Mark Liveric, newcomers Njego Pesa and Mike Laschev, with support from midfielders Gary Etherington, Claudio Rocha, and a strong defense led by Val Tuksa, Nick Megaloudis, Doc Lawson, the return of Renato Cila and youngsters Joey Ulrich, Long Islander, Ray Vigliotti and draft pick David Lischner from the Walter Chyzowych coached youth national team.

And of course, two top goalkeepers in Zoltan Toth and Shep Messing.

During the summer, the Arrows were asked by the Cleveland Force if they wanted to play an outdoor game in Ohio. All expenses would be paid and there was a $2,000 guarantee. There was no obligation for any player to play in the match as their Union agreement did not require them to be at practice before a certain date in the fall. A nice complement of players showed up for the game, which we won, taking Cleveland's money as well! Also in the pre-season, our trainer, Mark Steffans, had access to an aerobics facility at which his wife, Diane, was the lead instructor. So, for a month or so, many of the players volunteered to attend aerobics sessions, although they were not obligated to do so by virtue of their Players Union Agreement.

To ease my commute from Connecticut and to provide greater presence in the Long Island market, the Arrows rented a house on Long Beach (Lido Beach) for the winter, where I would stay most of the season. Long Beach was noted for its winter rentals to sports personalities. The island hosted the New York Rangers players when they practiced at the Long Beach ice rink facility and many members of the New York Jets when they trained at Hofstra. In fact, there was a bar/restaurant at the entrance to neighboring Point Lookout where I often saw members of the "NY Sack Exchange".

The Arrows hosted a party at my new Leamington Street address a few nights before the season opener. The thought process being that it was a good way to reward the players for their strong pre-season and for their work promoting the team and the sport in the greater Long Island community.

Also, during this period, I was approached by an agent familiar with working with European players. He was representing a Yugoslavian midfielder he was shopping around the League. The player in question was excellent and reminded me of the Baltimore Blast defender Mike Stankovic, a perennial All Star. Obviously, all the Arrows' players saw the benefit of his being a teammate.

When I discussed the purchase and impending contract with owner Schoenstadt, he was not amenable to the arrangement. I was disappointed with the result of the conversation, and I knew it would send the wrong message to the team. Both the player and the agent were equally disappointed. It was then that I was offered $5,000 from the player's salary if I could get him signed. I had heard rumors about these kinds of transactions (I heard that one coach already had amassed five sets of golf clubs) but in no way did I want to be a part of it, and I immediately reported the situation to Schoenstadt, who did not seem surprised.

Despite all the other good vibes, we opened the season with a home loss to Memphis. We continued to play barely .500 ball and were in danger of not making the playoffs. I even got fined by Chyzowych the same amount that I fined him, this time for coming onto the field when a referee took back an opponent's yellow card realizing it was the player's second of the match meaning that player would have to be ejected, and his team would play down a man for the next five minutes.

I recognized that if we had a chance at making the playoffs, we would have to get more out of the players who could take over and win the game on the field, namely, Grgurev, Liveric and Tuksa.

Fred Grgurev and I discussed how to get some more positive results over lunch. He was disappointed in his playing time and suggested that I incentivize him with a goal scoring bonus. I was happy to oblige, it could only help. As Vice President of Player Personnel, and having input on other acquisitions and salary determination, I did not see an issue with this. The bonus structure was added to Grgurev's contract and filed with the League as required.

The general system of play used by most teams can best be described as a "box and one". Four players in a box defended and tried to spring the one forward either on a break or to hold the ball while others joined in attack. The system made Steve Zungul the "Lord of All Indoors". Grgurev would play "the one". Of course, his increased playing time and the change in system would minimize the time on the carpet for some of the players who had been doing all the clinics, parties and promotions.

We would start to win games, but there was no increase in attendance.

We were fighting with Buffalo for the last playoff spot, playing a game in the Aud. During warmups, I grabbed Tuksa by the arm. Val was a physical specimen, who could overpower opponents and could not be knocked off the ball. I often felt that he played at 60% just so he wouldn't hurt anyone. I asked him for a favor, "Give me your "A" game tonight...you can be the difference." Tuksa turned it on, and we won an important away game putting us clear ahead of Buffalo for that last playoff spot.

When we returned home, I was criticized by management for not using the full complement of players and for over-relying on Grgurev, Liveric and Tuksa. I retorted that without them we "could not make the playoffs", upon which Schoenstadt replied that he was not interested in making the playoffs.

I got on the phone immediately after that conversation to report to Commissioner Foreman that the Arrows were in a situation where the owner was hoping to lose. Not making the playoffs would mean less money spent, fewer bonuses to pay. Who knows how far we would go in the playoffs; each series was scheduled now to be best of five.

Compounding the precarious situation was that the next game was scheduled in Kansas City, against Schoenstadt's Comets. In addition to the game, a party was scheduled for both teams in the good doctor's house. The Arrows were fully expected to lose. Kansas City was particularly strong at home, finishing the season with an enviable 15-9 home record.

Prior to the game we had a walk-through practice session on Kemper Arena's floor for one hour. We did not know that Schoenstadt was high up in the stands observing. The Comets followed us on the field. Our practices were always business-like, goal-oriented and no nonsense.

We won the game on the strength of a Zoltan Toth performance and a penalty kick awarded by the referee team of Bill Maxwell and Esse Baharmast. After the game, I suggested not going to the party in defiance of what was happening with the team and Schoenstadt's stance on not making the playoffs, which, of course, I used to motivate the players even further. Gary Etherington was adamant that we attend but not for the reason of gloating but because, as he explained: "It was the right thing to do."

At the party, Schoenstadt asked that I come up to his upstairs office. He told me he had never seen me so relaxed and that our practice was very much different than that of the Comets, which he described as a "hug fest". He again reverberated that he did not want to make the playoffs. He informed me of his intention to trade Njego Pesa to Saint Louis, the team he had played for previously. I disagreed with that intention.

Upon our return to New York, I went to my Arrows office after practice, as was my routine. I must have gotten there a little early because as I arrived, I saw local club coach Jim McGeough leaving the office. McGeough had been hanging around practice, which was often open to the public; it was a good gesture, and coaches would often come to see what was going on or to just marvel at the players. Ray Klivecka would come by and sometimes we would have lunch thereafter.

When McGeough left, Todd Leiweke called me into his office to inform me that I was relieved of my coaching duties. However, I was asked to stay on and help with the community and I traveled with the team to do radio and TV commentary. My record at the time was 13 wins 14 losses.

McGeough coached the team to a 2-8 record, was let go and Shep Messing took over and won five games while losing six. The team finished 20-28 and ironically made the playoffs.

The Arrows once again met Baltimore in the playoffs, losing the five-game series three games to one. The attendance for their first home playoff game was 2,353 and 1,779 for the second.

The following year the MISL Media Guide made no reference to the fact I was ever employed by the League. I was persona non grata.

The MISL lasted until 1992. Earl Foreman was replaced as Commissioner in 1985 by Francis Dale, who in turn was replaced by former Wichita Wing operative Bill Kentling from 1986-1989. Foreman was brought back in 1989 and remained as Commissioner until the League folded. Significantly, with the demise of the NASL and professional outdoor soccer, Foreman changed the MISL's name to the Major Soccer League in 1990, with the presumed intention of playing both indoors and out.

With the reorganization of the USSF into three components, Senior/Adult, Youth and Professional; Foreman controlled one-third of all the votes. As such, he would play a huge role in the outcome of the USSF elections of August 1990, and the control over the 1994 World Cup which was to be played in the United States.

Escape From The Bench

Listen Lester Patrick, Sir— Joe Machnik Tops Your Story

Remember one of the great, true stories that is part of National Hockey League tradition—the time New York Ranger coach Lester Patrick had to leave his job behind the bench, dash to the dressing room to put on the goalkeeper's gear and then finish the game in the nets because his only goalie was injured during a critical Stanley Cup playoff game. The Rangers won.

Joe Machnik, a former hockey player and coach, may be one of the only guys in professional sports who can top that story.

As Machnik recalls it, "It just happened a few months ago, in the summer of 1978. I was serving as assistant coach of the U.S. Olympic soccer team that was playing a three-game series against the Puerto Rican national team.

"In the first two games, the officiating was horrible and our head coach, Walt Chyzowych, was really upset. He called for a meeting with the Puerto Rican Soccer Federation to plead for a U.S. official. Fortunately the Puerto Rican Federation agreed the officiating was not good, but it was a question of who could they get from the U.S. on short notice."

Chyzowych had the answer. He remembered that his assistant coach, the same Mr. Joe Machnik, was one of the top referees in U.S. College scoccer and, alas, he was on the scene. Yup, right there behind the U.S. bench.

Chyzowych recommended Joe Machnik.

And because there was a solid trust among the soccer people, the Puerto Ricans respected the idea that Machnik would not only be good, but fair.

So, depart Machnik, the assistant coach; enter Machnik, the head referee.

"I handled the third and final game of the series," recalls Machnik.

Who won the game, Joe?

"The U.S. team won, 4-0, but everyone was satisfied, and, personally, I felt good about the game," Machnik said. "I've been working some of the top U.S. college games and a referee knows when he has called a good game. It's a code, the honor of the sport. The teams really make no difference to a man who is doing his job. You don't see the numbers or the players or personalities. You just watch for infractions and to see that the job gets properly handled."

It was an interesting experience for Machnik, but it had an even greater significance. It is probably the main reason why he is referee-in-chief of the new major Indoor Soccer League.

Says Machnik, "When the MISL first organized, it hired Chyzowych as a consultant on many matters pertaining to the sport. One of Walt's duties was to recommend a referee-in-chief. He watched me work the U.S.-Puerto Rican game and he thought I could handle the MISL job. I guess there was another ingredient. Walt knew I had played and coached hockey and he was aware of certain similarities between the rules of hockey and indoor soccer, such as penalties, serving time in the penalty

box, substituting players during game action. He thought the blend of the two qualified me to hire and instruct an MISL staff of referees."

Once he accepted the assignment as MISL's referee-in-chief, the 36-year-old Machnik, who is athletic director and soccer coach at the University of New Haven, selected 12 top officials to attend a pre-season training camp.

"The astro-turf for indoor soccer was already down in the Riverfront Coliseum in Cincinnati, so we held a three-day clinic there," he remembers. "We had to run through the rules, point out the differences, give demonstrations on the techniques, etc."

With a chuckle he recalls one of the problems, "We went through a series of scrimmages and the referees had to learn to get out of the way of the players and the ball. That was not a major problem for them in outdoor soccer, but in indoor soccer the pace is much faster, quicker and with the ball caroming off the sideboards it really brings in an entirely new aspect for the officials. They had to learn to grab the plexi-glass, pull up and lift their bodies out of the way so as to not obstruct the flow of the game. This action is natural to hockey officials, but strange to the outdoor soccer officials. But they learned quickly. From the 12 top guys we selected nine who will handle the MISL games. We've got top men."

Machnik himself will referee "about nine or 10 games." But, for the most part, his role will be administrative. "I will spend a lot of time on the road, evaluating performances to make certain we are getting our best, most competent people assigned to the games. I'll handle the assignments, reviews and evaluating the performance cards that each coach will submit after each game."

Does Joe Machnik think MISL will go?

He states, "If I didn't, I wouldn't have taken the assignment."

N-8

Article from MISSILE Magazine the MISL gameday program which explains the circumstances surrounding how I became Referee-in-Chief.

MISL Referee signals and a listing of the members of its officiating staff.

The Referee-in-Chief in action.

MISL Publicity photo card for the Referee-in-Chief.

Earl Foreman, MISL Commissioner

The Blue Card. I instituted the use of a Blue Card to signal when a two minute time penalty was issued. This eliminated confusion and the need for officials to point two fingers at players which at times seemed offensive.

MACHNIK IN AS NY ARROWS HEAD COACH

Dr. Joe Machnik, Director of Operations and Referee-in-chief for the Major Indoor Soccer League, has been signed by the New York Arrows as their Head Coach and Vice-President of Player Personnel, it was announced by Arrows President Terry Leiweke. Machnik was signed to a three-year contract with a one-year option. The salary was not disclosed.

Machnik replaces Don Popovic, who was relieved of his duties as coach last week. Machnik becomes only the second coach in Arrows history. Popovic coached the Arrows to four straight MISL championships, compiling a regular season record of 131-39 and a playoff mark of 17-4.

The 40-year old Machnik was born in New York City but raised in Brooklyn. He attended Brooklyn Tech and graduated from Long Island University in 1964. He was All-American goalkeeper at LIU. Teammate Ray Klivecka, former Cosmos and Buffalo Stallions Coach, was also an All-American as a striker.

Upon graduating, Machnik became assistant soccer coach at LIU for two years and then served as varsity coach for the next three years. He guided the Blackbirds to the NCAA championship his first

Dr. Joe Machnik cheers his new team on at Nassau Collisium.

On the bench coaching the NY Arrows in the Nassau Coliseum.

From the Sandlots to the World Cup: INSIDE Seven Decades of American Soccer

Big news when the League's head of Referees becomes a coach during the same season. Soccer America's headline.

Journal-Courier SPORTS
TUESDAY, MARCH 1, 1983

Former UNH coach
Arrows name Machnik coach

UNIONDALE, N.Y. — Dr. Joe Machnik, former athletic director and soccer coach at the University of New Haven, has been chosen new head coach of the New York Arrows of the Major Indoor Soccer League.

Machnik signed a three-year contract with a one-year option and will also serve as the Arrows' vice president of player personnel.

The Guilford, Conn., resident, who left UNH in 1978 to become referee-in-chief for the MISL in its inaugural season, was named to the dual role of director of operations and referee-in-chief in 1980. Machnik, 40, replaces replaces Don Popovic, who had guided the Arrows to four straight league titles but was fired last week. Popovic was hired as head coach Sunday by the Golden Bay Earthquakes, where he'll be united with former Arrows stand- out Steve Zungul.

In accepting the Arrows position, Machnik will be heading back to some familiar territory. Machnik was born in New York City and raised in Brooklyn, where he attended Brooklyn Tech before going on to Long Island University. While playing goalkeeper for the Blackbirds, Machnik attained All-America honors in 1964. After graduation, he became the assistant coach of the Blackbirds, and two years later took over the head coaching chores. In the following two years, Machnik guided LIU to two straight NCAA championship games.

In 1969, Machnik took over the head coaching job at UNH and guided the Chargers to a 110-54-21 mark in nine years. He also became the director of athletics for five years.

"It's terrific coming back home and great to be coaching again," Machnik said. "Now I face a big challenge. The Arrows have been champions and I want them to continue. I want to harness the energy they have for the game."

The Arrows, who play in the Nassau Coliseum, said, through their president Terry Leiweke, "This has worked out the best for all concerned. Joe is the kind of person with an administrative background and coaching experience who can ensure our future success."

Though the Arrows have enjoyed success in the past, the 1983 season has been somewhat of a disappointment. They're currently in fourth place in the Eastern Division, six games behind front-runner Baltimore. Machnik will hope to break a three-game losing streak Friday when they host San Diego.

MACHNIK

It was big news in New Haven and all over the League.

Family photo taken in Kansas City the night before I was told that MISL would not be offering a new contract. Left to right: daughter Janine, yours truly, Barbara and daughter Colette.

From the Sandlots to the World Cup: INSIDE Seven Decades of American Soccer 165

Chapter 8

The American Indoor Soccer Association (AISA)

"The Handwriting Was On The Wall"

Shortly after my dismissal from the NY Arrows, I received a phone call from Peter Mahlock, President and General Manager of the Louisville Thunder, a team which was scheduled to start play in the inaugural season of the American Indoor Soccer Association (AISA) later that year. Mahlock wanted to know if I had any interest in being involved in the formation of an alternate league to the AISA that was to be called the Central Indoor Soccer League (CISL).

I did not know much about the AISA. But after a little bit of research, I decided to investigate further and take a trip out to Louisville. I still believed in the sport of indoor soccer. Maybe by focusing on smaller cities without NHL, NBA, NFL or MLB franchises and playing in smaller arenas, a new league might have a chance at success?

I was smarting from the pain of being let go by the Arrows after such a short period of time following five years in the MISL League Office and being involved in every soccer-related decision at the highest level sitting at the right hand of the Commissioner.

I was 41 years old, had a very successful soccer camp business (our next chapter), but felt a real need to "stay in the game".

After a few more days thinking it over, I asked to speak with the two owners of the Thunder, Attorney Joseph Bishop of Barnett & Alagia in Louisville and Allen Northcutt, a Senior VP at Hilliard Lyons investment firm. During that conversation I agreed to accept an offer with travel and housing expenses to be reimbursed.

On my first full day in Louisville, I toured Broadbent Arena, the 6,600-seat home of the Thunder. It was in the shadow of Freedom Hall, the home of the University of Louisville basketball team which sold out every game at over 18,000 per.

There were six teams in the AISA that first season. In addition to the Thunder were the Canton Invaders, Columbus Capitals, Kalamazoo Kangaroos, Chicago Vultures and Milwaukee Wave. I learned that the Commissioner was former ice hockey coach Bob Lemieux, who started the AISA in Kalamazoo. I vaguely remembered hearing his name mentioned several times by Earl Foreman in the MISL office.

I researched Commissioner Lemieux's background and learned that he was a solid hockey defenseman with a long, mostly minor-league career, but that he did play 19 games for the NHL Oakland Seals and recorded one assist. And for a period, he was the General Manager of the NASL's Ft. Lauderdale Strikers owned by Joe Robbie.

Starting sometime in 1982, Lemieux introduced "Soccer Leagues Unlimited", which later became the AISA, and approached arena owners and potential investors throughout the mid-west regarding his start-up. He set up an office at 3721 South Westnedge Avenue in Kalamazoo and prepared a presentation for the MISL Competition Committee to have the AISA serve as a developmental league. A year later, with six teams in place, just like MISL's start with six teams, the first ball was kicked. The date was November 25, 1984, and Louisville lost 8-6 away at Kalamazoo.

It was never made totally clear to me what the level of dissatisfaction was with participation in the AISA for some of the owners. But some seemed to think they had a better idea and stated that the owners of the Canton Invaders were on board and there was strong interest coming in from Memphis, Ft. Wayne, and Rockford, IL to start an alternate league.

On March 22, 1984, I received a contract offer of employment lasting until July 1 to serve as the Commissioner of the yet-to-be-formed CISL with an understanding that a further written contract would be executed upon confirmation that the CISL would start its season the following fall in 1985. The March 22 letter was signed by Doug Logan, Managing General Partner of the Rockford Metro Center, who signed it as "Initial Director and Chairman" of the CISL.

Logan and I seemed to hit it off right from the beginning. I had confidence in his leadership, goodwill and savvy understanding of the various small markets in the mid-west with arenas in need of a full-time winter tenant.

I was confident of the potential of the CISL and scheduled a May meeting in Columbus at which I hoped to have representatives from Peoria and

Springfield, IL, Ft. Wayne, Grand Rapids as well as Cincinnati, Dayton and Memphis. I wrote a letter outlining my contract needs which included the statement that Barbara and I would move to Louisville and establish residency by September 1st.

Office space in Louisville for the upcoming CISL season was secured at 3000 Mellwood Avenue in Louisville and Barbara and I secured a lease agreement in the fully furnished model apartment on the top floor of a new high-rise building across from Cherokee Park.

Our daughter, Colette, was scheduled to start college in Providence RI in the fall, and we had secured a place in the incoming class at Louisville Country Day School for younger daughter, Janine.

On May 21, 1984, I received a letter from AISA Commissioner Bob Lemieux answering a letter I had written to him seven days earlier suggesting an interest in a merger of sorts between AISA and the CISL. "Our purpose is to form a unified league in the Midwest and not split the enthusiasm and spirit of indoor soccer participants by creating a competitive situation between two groups," Lemieux wrote. "We are interested in total resolution," he furthered.

I was so confident in the future of the CISL that on July 3, 1984, I wrote a letter on CISL stationary with the Mellwood Avenue address to MISL Commissioner Earl Foreman offering a conceptual outline for MISL player and referee development in the CISL. The letter addressed roster size, salary cap, citizenship and other restrictions, a CISL draft, call up rules of players to the MISL, etc. It even outlined a referee development program like that which the NBA had with the Continental Basketball Association (CBA), citing that in the last three years the NBA has chosen all their rookie referees from the CBA.

However, despite the best efforts of all involved, the verbal commitments of several teams did not materialize in Letters of Credit and in the middle of August 1984, it was clear that a CISL ball was not going to be kicked the following fall.

Barbara and I were very fortunate to get out of the lease we signed for the apartment in Louisville. Then, during late fall, the Thunder management realized they needed help to run their front office and offered a contract to once again come out to Louisville for at least the balance of their first season.

The AISA's first season was well in progress. I visited the Thunder's practice session at Broadbent Arena and met with Head Coach Keith Tozer, the same Tozer who played for the Cincinnati Kids in that first MISL game. Also on the team were my former University of New Haven and No.1 Goalkeeper's Camp staff member Rick Schweizer, Connecticut College standout Jim Gabarra, who would go on to play for several US Five-A-Side National Teams, and Mike Noonan, the future coach at the University of New Hampshire, Brown University and finally Clemson University, where he would become a NCAA National Champion!

The Thunder finished the season in third place and averaged 1,915 spectators per game. They swept the Columbus Capitals in the first round of the playoffs but lost to the Canton Invaders in the best-of-five Championship series. Rick Schweizer was voted AISA Goalkeeper of the Year!

There was still a concerted effort to form the CISL and the Memphis market was considered key, as both the NASL Memphis Rogues and the MISL Memphis Americans had considerable success playing indoors at the Mid-South Coliseum, an early venue in Elvis Presley's career.

Kyle Rote Jr. had brought the former Hartford Hellions to Memphis, playing as the Americans, and with players like Toni Carbognani and German legend Bernd Holzenbein averaged a healthy 5,763 fans per game. However, these crowds were not sufficient to pay the MISL bills and the team relocated to Las Vegas, where they lasted only one year.

Before leaving Memphis and returning to Germany, Holzenbein sold his Mercedes-Benz to J. Wise and Joyce Smith, fans of the Americans who befriended him during his short stay in Tennessee.

During the AISA off-season and before the start of the 1985-86 campaign, Commissioner Lemieux was voted out of his position and Canton majority owner Steve Paxos assumed the position of AISA Chairman of the Board. According to all involved, it was no longer necessary to pursue an alternative league, the focus was now to make the AISA bigger, stronger and better!

Based on the work I had done in Louisville and the strong recommendation of the Thunder owners; I was offered the position of AISA Director of Operations. The AISA would now run out of the No.1 Camp office at 1200 Boston Post Road in Guilford, CT.

I immediately started to construct a schedule and to organize a referee program. Under Lemieux's tenure, the referees were organized and assigned by Rod Smithson, who resided in Michigan, with many of the games officiated by Ann Arbor-based Steve Olson.

We had a change of ownership in Chicago, where the Vultures became the Shockers with owner Leon Leibovich. They would have difficulty finding a permanent home and were forced to play some of their games at Doug Logan's Rockford Metro Center when the Odeum was not available. Regardless, I was able to construct a schedule where 76% of the games were to be played on prime weekend or holiday dates as reported in *A Message to AISA Soccer Fans*, my column which appeared in each team's game program. The match day programs, press releases, press conferences, etc. were organized by Canton-based AISA Director of Media and Public Relations, Paul Dangelo, who did a fabulous job with little resources.

We also organized the very first AISA College Draft. I had built a portable draft board with hinges that made it fold up and be transportable. There were Velcro strips for the placement of the names as each player was drafted. I asked one of the employees of the local team to assist in the placement of names and she replied in the negative, stating: "I am no Vanna White" in reference to the American *Wheel of Fortune* TV game show star who performed a similar task when she started her career in 1982.

My message in the AISA game program was signed as Director of Operations, Referee-in-Chief, although I had no intention of officiating in the League at that time.

Fortunately, I had remained in good contact with Herb Silva, who had taken over the MISL referee program from Walt Chyzowych, who was now working hand in hand with Werner Fricker to put a viable team on the field for the 1990 World Cup.

Herb and I worked closely to enable referees currently working in the MISL to also work in the AISA.

One of the great stories of that 1985-86 season is often told by Esse Baharmast, who was assigned to work a game in Kalamazoo, where the referees stayed in the Knights Inn which they referred to as the "Purple Palace" due to the overuse of that color in the hotel's decor. Two Kalamazoo players had been fined $15 each for multiple game yellow card accumulation and had not paid their fine prior to the day of game. I had been in touch with Mike Garrett, the now player-coach of the "Roos", informing him that the players were not to play unless the fines were paid and that in fact, if he insisted on dressing and playing the two, Baharmast would refuse to start the match.

Baharmast was instructed to attempt to collect the $30 in cash. When he knocked on the locker room door, he was requested to identify himself. Upon doing so, six $5 bills were passed through a small crack of an opening in the door. Baharmast then called me to report that the fines were paid, and he asked what he should do with the cash. I told him to keep the money and that I would deduct it out of his game fee, which meant that he would receive a check worth $55 for refereeing the match.

The 1985-86 AISA season ended with remarkably similar results to the initial year. Canton finished at the top of the standings, winning 33 out of 40 games, defeating the Chicago Shockers and Louisville Thunder in straight best-of-five games series to win their second consecutive AISA Championship.

The fact that the AISA survived its first two seasons was making news around the country. Although Kalamazoo folded, the Toledo Pride had already been announced with former Kalamazoo head coach Mike Garrett at the helm!

During the summer, overtures were received from around the country. Most significantly, the owners of the Tampa Bay Rowdies, once a leading NASL team, desired to continue operating their franchise playing indoor soccer, where they had success in the Bayfront Arena. A meeting was held with owner Cornelia Corbett and former Rowdie standout Rodney Marsh, after which a successful bid for a franchise for the upcoming season in South Florida was announced.

Then, an invitation to dinner in Memphis at the home of former NASL/MISL/AISA referee Don DeWeese led to an introduction to Joyce and J. Wise Smith. DeWeese's wife, Rita, made delicious seafood gumbo and served several glasses of wine; later an agreement was reached for DeWeese and the Smiths to own and operate a franchise in Memphis. The Smiths still owned the Mercedes that Bernd Holzenbein had left with them. I marveled at the uniqueness of the vehicle. It had a German license plate in front, wipers on the head lights, no seat belts and shades on the rear side windows. There was no other car like it in America. I offered to purchase the vehicle, and we settled on a price of $18,000. I then drove the vehicle from Memphis to Guilford, CT and surprised Barbara with a gift. I wish I still had that car today!

Thunder President Peter Mahlock successfully put together a group in Fort Wayne and the Flames overnight became the AISA's eighth team.

The AISA now had a Northern division of Canton, Chicago, Toledo and Milwaukee while the Southern Division consisted of Louisville, Memphis, Tampa Bay and Fort Wayne Flames.

In September 1986, I wrote to Jim Budish, now Director of Operations of the Major Indoor Soccer League, to use MISL referees in the pre-season exhibition games which were now being scheduled between the AISA and MISL teams. It marked the beginning of an arrangement whereby officials working a MISL game in Cleveland, for example, would be assigned to work in an AISA game in Canton or Toledo the night before or day after. The same was true for Milwaukee/Chicago, Memphis/St. Louis etc.

Partly due to the expansion success and the organization and administration of the league as Director of Operations, I was offered the position of Commissioner, signing a contract dated June 1, 1986, continuing through to June 30, 1989. The contract recognized that while I needed to "devote" my entire time, effort, skills and attention" to the AISA that I "may continue to operate the No.1 Goalkeeper's Camp under its present structure and format for eight weeks each summer.

The AISA office would continue to operate out of the Guilford, Connecticut office of the No.1 Goalkeeper's Camp.

Congruent with the 1986-87 AISA season, FIFA, the governing body of world soccer began to recognize the value of the game being played indoors. While FIFA would not recognize the American version of the indoor game played with hockey dasher boards, it was seeing the value of Five-a-Side soccer played on a basketball or similarly sized team handball court. The MISL did not recognize this version of the game, but the AISA released its players to participate in a Five-a-Side tournament in Spain representing the USA.

US Men's Five-a-Side team coach John Kowalski selected Louisville Thunder players Jim Gabarra and Zoran Savic, midfielder Chris Hellenkamp and goalkeeper AJ Lachowecki, who was also a No.1 Goalkeeper staff member. Also selected were Chicago Shockers player Rudy Glenn and Milwaukee Wave goalkeeper Tony Pierce. The team also featured Paul Caligiuri who was playing in Germany, and college players Eric Eichmann, Brent Goulet, Tom Silvas and Mike Windischmann. Kowalski's team beat Italy 5-3 and tied Belgium 1-1 before losing to Spain and Portugal by 3-2 and 4-3 scores respectively.

During the 1986-87 season, the Milwaukee Wave had their first sellout as 3,482 fans jammed the Mecca Auditorium for a game against Canton and the second All-Star Game was played, this time in Louisville.

Jim Gabarra was named interim coach of Louisville as Keith Tozer left the team mid-season to coach the Los Angeles Lazers of the MISL, another "feather in the cap" for the AISA. Louisville was also under new ownership as Attorney Richard Heideman and wife Phylliss were now principal owners, taking over from Allen Northcutt and Joe Bishop.

But there were problems with the Toledo Pride franchise from the get-go. And mid-season, I had the unique but unwelcome experience of traveling to that city to "pull" the owner's Letter of Credit from the bank to pay the players to finish the campaign.

Later that season, the Pride's general manager developed a half-time sponsorship arrangement with a local car dealership which caused major problems. Under the arrangement, fans at the game would be able to tear out a page of the game program, put their name on it and create a paper "airplane" for the purpose of attempting to sail the plane from the stands into a barely open car window. The task was deemed to be impossible. So much so that the car was offered as the prize should someone accomplish that feat.

As luck would have it, someone won the prize. However, the Pride had not yet purchased the car or an insurance policy against someone winning it. The car dealership sued the team and the general manager. The team folded and the GM was held legally responsible.

The 1986-87 regular season finished with Canton on top of the Northern Division with a record of 31-11 and the Louisville Thunder atop of the Southern Division with a record of 27-15. The Memphis Storm upset Tampa Bay in the playoffs before losing to Canton, the Louisville Thunder advanced past Chicago, creating another match-up between the Invaders and Thunder for the title. The series went the full five games with Louisville prevailing in the fifth game on the road 6-4. The entire match, as well as the post-game award ceremony, can be found on YouTube! It was the last game ever played by the Thunder as Heideman folded the franchise. Stalwart player Chris Hellenkamp had played in 140 of their 143 games. Three other teams also folded. Only four teams remained to start the 1987-88 season.

At the end of season League meetings, I introduced Ron Hagen of Hagen Marketing & Communications, a division of Pacific Rim out of San

Francisco, CA, to the ownership group. Hagen gave a presentation on the future of indoor soccer and how he and his companies and their contacts would help the AISA "turn the corner" to success. It was a brilliant and inspiring presentation. So much so that Steve Paxos turned to me in the middle of the meeting and said, "Where did you find this guy?"

Among the projects that Hagen would take over was the production of a game program which he entitled *American Soccer Magazine*. Five thousand copies of Vol.1 No.1 were produced and were ready for the start of the season. In my *Message to AISA Soccer Fans* which appeared inside the cover page, I announced a 48-game schedule for our four teams and a new concept called the "American Indoor Soccer Challenge Cup" which would pit AISA teams against 1988-89 expansion hopefuls and independents. I continued that the previous season saw nearly half a million in attendance at games which averaged nine goals per contest. And I touted the success of the USA Five-a-Side team, loaded with AISA players, which now had victories over Holland, Portugal, Peru and Italy.

But the biggest news of all was the announcement of a televised AISA "Game of the Week" on Tempo Television over 20 weeks of the season!

American Soccer Magazine was loaded with up-to-date AISA information including biographies of the team owners and management. As a filler, I wrote a two-page article on indoor soccer goalkeeping. Hagen was able to sell a fair number of ads to the soccer community but also to the companies he represented nationally like Cathay Pacific and Russel Athletic. Of course, No.1 Goalkeeper's Camp had a full-page ad with a map of the US detailing our 12 locations.

The page outlining the AISA Playing Rules was entitled *Soccer the American Way*.

That year, Hagen also introduced the official AISA ball manufactured by Wilson. The ball was mostly blue and red with white stars on the blue panels. The red panels had the AISA logo or the stamping as "Official Game Ball" with a number H-6008. One red panel had my signature as Commissioner with my full name underneath Joseph A. Machnik spelled out. The first edition of the ball had only my signature, which is a difficult read! The mostly dark blue and red paneled ball was difficult to pick up on TV against the green artificial turf and was abandoned after one year. It was replaced with a mostly yellow and red ball.

The 1987-88 season was completed somewhat successfully. The

regular season ended with each of the four teams playing 24 games. The Challenge Cup Series started on February 14th with potential expansion teams Jacksonville Generals and Dayton Dynamo each playing 12 games. A single Challenge Cup final was played between the top two teams on April 1st and Canton defeated Fort Wayne in front of 8,028 in the War Memorial Coliseum, the former home of the NBA's Fort Wayne Pistons.

The AISA conducted two days of meetings at which both Jacksonville and Dayton were admitted for the following season. The minutes reflect that Steve Paxos was authorized to attend the meetings of the Canadian Soccer League in Toronto in mid-April to investigate the possibility of inter-league play.

On the second day of the meetings, I introduced representatives from the Toronto International Soccer Club indicating their desire to apply for membership. Discussions followed concerning all the difficulties regarding border crossings, immigration, US Soccer's potential objection (the AISA was still considered a regional league) etc. The Toronto group was advised to investigate nearby US cities for a possible franchise. I then introduced a representative from the Hershey-Harrisburg PA area who advised that he was seeking to put together a group to invest in a franchise for the Keystone State. That group was successful in starting the Hershey Impact, which played three AISA seasons in the Hershey Park Arena from 1988 until 1991.

Unfortunately, the Canadian group which had all the credentials necessary to be a successful franchise and in fact submitted a deposit and Letter of Credit, insisted on only playing in Toronto and wanted "exclusive rights with respect to franchising any more teams to Canada", citing Montreal and Vancouver as further expansion cities. Their insistence on these details and US Soccer's hesitancy resulted in a denial of the Canadian's application for membership.

Shortly thereafter, Steve Paxos and I traveled to Las Vegas where former FIFA and MISL full time Referee Toros Kibritjian put together a group for possible expansion in the Nevada city where the Americans of Memphis lasted only one year. The meeting did not result in a successful application for membership.

On April 28, 1988, I received a letter from the AISA Board indicating a desire to renegotiate my contract. The letter detailed specific duties and responsibilities of the Office of Commissioner as follows:

1. The need for the Commissioner's position to be full-time and year-round.
2. For the Commissioner to be fully responsible for any and all expansion-related activities, including the identification of expansion sites, solicitation and credential verification of the ownership of these sites, and the submission of proposals pro or con regarding a given site.
3. For the Commissioner to be readily available to the front office staff of a given member in order to provide them with expert consultation and advice regarding the business management of a professional indoor soccer team.
4. For the Commissioner to design, develop and implement a league-wide program for team novelties, souvenirs and other sales promotional devices.
5. For the Commissioner to have complete responsibility for all league-wide marketing activities including the direct management of any outside consulting/marketing organizations.
6. For the Commissioner to design and develop proposals for a league-wide travel program which will assist the member in a major reduction of expenditures and/or an enhancement of revenue generation.
7. For the Commissioner to have complete responsibility for all national press relations and activities and to develop a regionally national television package acceptable to the management of the association.
8. For the Commissioner to have a base salary structure driven by the number of teams in the league as follows: six teams = $35,000; eight teams = $50,000; 10 teams = $60,000; 12 teams = $70,000.
9. For the Commissioner to not receive commissions for securing new expansion franchises, since this is perceived as part and parcel of the base line duties of the position.
10. For the Commissioner to assume the administrative duties of creating a league schedule, providing referees for the games, maintenance and management of the league headquarters, administration and collection of appropriate fines, monitoring the salary cap for teams and settling disputes.

Once again, the "handwriting was on the wall". For starters, item number one was not negotiable. The No.1 Goalkeeper's Camp was at the very height of its success. I was not going to give it up to fully concentrate on the AISA. And several of the other demands were far outside my area of expertise. After all, I was just a "soccer guy!" Neither did the contract mention that I could continue my college officiating career, which was clear in the original draft. In fact, none of these new demands appeared in the original agreement.

By this time, FIFA had already announced that the first Five-a-Side World Championship (not yet called a World Cup) would be held in the Netherlands from Jan 5-15, 1989. John Kowalski had asked if I would serve as his Assistant Coach. There would be preparation games both indoor and out leading up to the tournament being played, which would take most of the fall and early winter of 1988.

So, in early April and in anticipation of the inevitable, I met with James A. Nugent, my attorney, to discuss the possibility of his writing a Release and Termination Agreement from the American Indoor Soccer Association.

The legal document had two clauses. The first was to terminate the existing contract and the second, read as follows: "Effective immediately upon the execution of this Release and Termination Agreement, each party hereby waives, releases and discharges any and all claims or demands whatsoever against the other on account of any rights or obligations created by or arising out of said Employment Agreement."

A special meeting of the AISA was held on May 16, 1988, to discuss, among other things, my future with the League. When the topic of my contract came up, I surprised the board with the Release and Termination Agreement. While there was momentary shock among certain members, the others realized that I was making them an offer that, in essence, with the new demands placed on the Commissioner's Office, they were asking for in the first place.

After a brief consultation among the owners during which I was sequestered, I was presented the Release and Termination document signed by Steve Paxos as Chairman of the Board and the other three directors representing Milwaukee, Memphis and Dayton.

We all shook hands, and I left the meeting saying something to the effect that I was leaving to go to drive in my first stock car race, which is another whole story.

The 1988-89 AISA season included the newly named Chicago Power and the Hershey Impact. A total of seven teams each played a 40-game schedule. During the season, the league had to take control of the Memphis Storm and eventually their Letter of Credit was pulled. The quality of play continued to improve with players like Karl-Heinz Granitza and Batata in Chicago. John Dolinsky, now plying his trade in Milwaukee, was named Coach of the Year.

The league made headlines when it announced a new scoring system, with goals being worth as many as three points, depending on the distance of the shot or game situation.

In the Championship Playoff round, the Canton Invaders defeated the Chicago Power by the scores of 16-8, 16-7 and 15-9, with the Power winning two games by the scores of 8-6 and 22-6.

The American Indoor Soccer Association, with Steve Paxos at the helm as Commissioner (1988-2000), eventually changed its name to the National Professional Soccer League. Over the years there were 30 franchises in 32 cities.

Local press coverage of my work as AISA Commissioner.

The official Wilson AISA game ball.

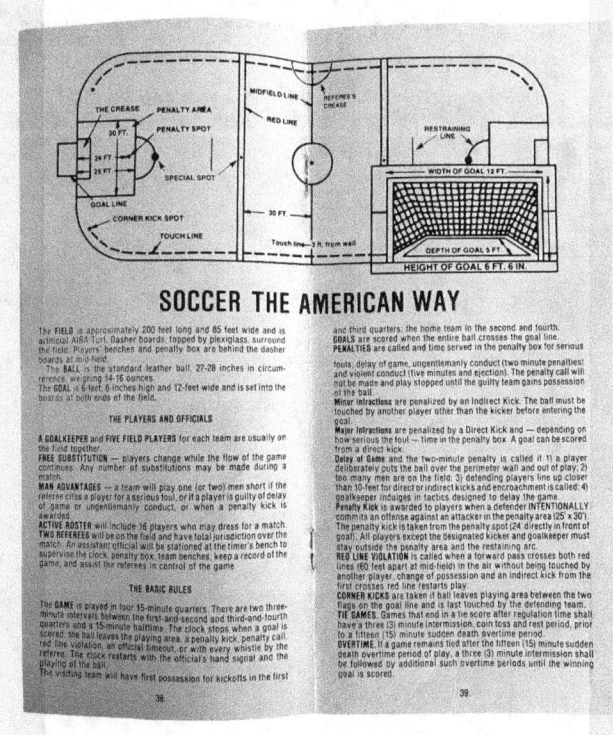

AMERICAN SOCCER magazine

Vol. 1, No. 1

A Message to AISA Soccer Fans

Dear Fans:

The American Indoor Soccer Association, Inc. (AISA) is proud to be commencing its fourth season with an exciting forty eight (48) game regular season schedule featuring the Canton Invaders, Fort Wayne Flames, Memphis Storm and Milwaukee Wave and an expanded new concept in playoffs; the American Indoor Soccer Challenge Cup which will pit AISA teams against 1988-89 expansion hopefuls and independents.

Last season nearly one-half million fans attended AISA regular season and playoff soccer witnessing a highly contested regular season and playoff race that featured high scoring games of outstanding quality. Better than nine goals per game were scored in the AISA during 1986-87, leading the United States Soccer Federation (USSF) to select AISA players as the foundation for its National Indoor Soccer Team, representing the United States in three International Tournaments in Hungary, Spain and Brazil. AISA players represented their League well in victories for the United States over Italy, Portugal, Holland, Peru and several other world soccer powers.

For the first time AISA fans will be able to view a nationally televised AISA Game of the Week over Tempo Television Network and affiliates bringing AISA soccer into thirty-two million homes weekly. Major sponsorships have been arranged with national companies such as Wilson, provider of the new official game ball of the AISA and Eiger uniforms.

Nine-one percent of AISA games are scheduled on prime weekend dates as the AISA continues to endeavor to reach you, the soccer fan. The AISA is structured with you the fan in mind with goals and goal scoring chances galore. So sit back if you can and enjoy the game.

The AISA is ready for 1987-88.

Joseph A. Machnik, Ph.D.
Commissioner

american indoor soccer association
1200 Boston Post Road
Guilford, Connecticut 06437
203-453-9089

AMERICAN SOCCER MAGAZINE is published by Hagen Marketing & Communications, a Division of Pacific Rim, Inc. © 1987, 450 Sansome, Suite 210, San Francisco, CA 94111; Ronald Hagen, Publisher. Designed by Carolyn Hughes.

Tempo Television to Kick Off Exclusive Schedule of Indoor Soccer Games

TULSA, OK—On November 7, TEMPO Television kicks off a 20-week schedule of indoor soccer games. It's **American Soccer,** a weekly series of soccer matches from the American Indoor Soccer Association (AISA), airing exclusively on the TEMPO TV network.

The AISA is one of only two indoor soccer leagues operating in the United States. AISA Commissioner Dr. Joseph A. Machnik recently released details of a new five-year plan intended to give the league more prominence and substantially increase its size to include a total of at least 20 teams. The league is currently comprised of four teams: the Milwaukee Wave, Ft. Wayne Flames, Memphis Storm and Canton Invaders.

Each team wil play a 24-game schedule during the 1987-88 season. A total of 20 matches will be televised on TEMPO. The schedule of telecasts through the end of the regular season is noted here. The remaining six telecasts will be taken from the league's 1988 Challenge Cup series.

TEMPO Television is a 24-hour cable television network delivered to more than 12.5 million homes nationwide. The network caters to viewers in the "45 plus" age demographic with four major blocks of programming: Entertainment, International/Travel, Sports/Outdoor and Information/How-To.

TEMPO TV is a subsidiary of TEMPO Enterprises, Inc. (AMEX:TPO), headquartered in Tulsa, OK.

American Soccer Magazine was our game day program. Here is my message to our fans!

Soccer America, March 17, 198_

AISA

AISA survives growing pains under Machnik

By David Tanner

AISA commissioner Joseph Machnik doesn't view nor does he want anyone else to perceive the four-year-old league at his exclusive enterprise.

"It's not at all a personal thing. I don't want to leave that impression. That's just the way I do business," said Machnik from the league's Guilford, Conn. offices where he was found between the end of the four-team 48-game regular season and the start of the six-team, 36-game Challenge Cup tournament.

Perpetually tan and svelte, the 45-year-old Machnik fits the cut of a commissioner as well as he does his European suits.

"He's both intelligent and a hard worker," said a longtime associate, "attributes that are often in inverse ratios in many people in soccer. I find him admirable and he's willing to give that extra something when others might be satisfied."

A hands-on administrator with a glittering array of credentials in several aspects of the game, Machnik is known through his dealings as thoughtful and fair, but firm.

He was an all-American at LIU where he would later coach the Blackbirds in the 1966 NCAA final at the age of 23. Over the next 12 years, Machnik found similar success at the University of New Haven as head coach and ice hockey coach and athletic director before moving on to the professional ranks with the MISL's New York Arrows. Later he served as the MISL's director of operations and referee in chief.

Since 1977 Machnik has operated the "No. 1 Goalkeeper's Camps" at sites throughout the country and has co-authored two books on goalkeeping as well as having produced instructional videotapes.

His firsthand experiences with the genesis of MISL have served him well in the birthing of the AISA. Having "been there before" has proved a valuable commodity in solving crises that have beset the league.

But his critics would argue that in trying to please the troika of owner/player/referee, Machnik's close associations with officials cause him to sway in favor of referees first, then owners, leaving the players last. Others — more harshly — claim no matter where Machnik's priorities lie, his job is akin to rearranging the deck chairs on the Titanic.

Machnik insists the success of the AISA so far — its survival — is because of the prudent following of the league's overall philosophy and

Taylor satisfied with Canada's Bermuda tour

The opposition was not exactly immense, but Canadian national coach Tony Taylor was more than satisfied with his first kick at the cat.

Taylor, appointed to succeed Bob Bearpark in December, took Canada's squad to Bermuda for three games, to get his feet wet in the new job and start preparation for World Cup qualifying play.

Result: Two wins and a tie; five goals for, none against.

"We accomplished what we set out to do," said Taylor. "This was our first tour of the season and I had the opportunity of evaluating players in game situations. And I was more than pleased with our performances."

Taylor singled out for special mention, defender Steve Jansen, midfielder Jim Easton and forwards Lucio

AISA Challenge Cup

Team	W	L	Pct.	F	A
Milwaukee	4	2	.667	24	21
Fort Wayne	4	2	.667	33	24
Canton	4	2	.667	27	25
Jacksonville	2	2	.500	14	15
Dayton	2	5	.286	20	26
Memphis	2	5	.286	20	27

Results
(Home team listed first)

Feb. 26
Milwaukee 7, Memphis 3
Fort Wayne 9, Canton 4
Feb. 27
Fort Wayne 5, Memphis 2
Jacksonville 6, Dayton 4
Feb. 28
Milwaukee 4, Fort Wayne 7
Canton 6, Dayton 2
March 2
Dayton 4, Fort Wayne 3
March 4
Memphis 3, Dayton 2
March 5
Jacksonville 2, Milwaukee 4
March 6
Dayton 5, Milwaukee 1
Canton 5, Jacksonville 3
Memphis 3, Fort Wayne 4

aside notions that it is a developme_tal league for anyone. But there's escaping the obvious financial d_ferences that separate the two ind_leagues and spell the difference m_jor vs. minor. The AISA reporte_ has a salary cap of $130,000 per te_ while MISL franchises must adh_ to a $1.275 million ceiling, althou_ that figure may be soon drastic_ reduced.

No formal agreements exist l_ween MISL and AISA clubs in_ classic "farm system" sense, but_ a fact that MISL managemen_ found AISA talent recruit_ Former AISA players like T_ Hayes, A.J. Lachowecki, M_ Evans, Jim Gabarra and_ (Zolgharnian) now contribu_

CANTON
INVADERS
129 14th Street, NE
Canton, Ohio 44714
216-455-6060
Steve Paxos – President/GM
Trevor Dawkins – Coach
Mike Siberini – Public Relations
Mohammed Attiah – Sales/Asst. GM
Canton Memorial Civic Center
Seating – 4,070

american indoor soccer association
LEAGUE OFFICE
1200 Boston Post Road
Guilford, CT 06437
203-453-9089
Steve Paxos, Chairman of the Board
Dr. Joseph A. Machnik, Director of Operations/Referee-in-Chief
Paul Dangelo, Director of Media and Public Relations

741 No. Milwaukee Avenue
Suite 329
Milwaukee, Wisconsin 53202
414-347-0684
Dr. Pernell Donahue – President
Mike Custer – Coach/GM
Dave Boucher – Public Relations/
Karen Heinig – Sales   Asst. GM
Mecca Auditorium
Seating – 3,482

CHICAGO SHOCCERS
316 No. Michigan Avenue
Chicago, Illinois 60601
312-346-8948
Leon Leibovich – President/GM
Aleks Mihailovic – Coach
Donn Green – Public Relations
Jack Taylor – Sales
The Odeum
Seating – 4,000

COLUMBUS CAPITALS
6800 Oak Creek Drive
Columbus, Ohio 43229
614-890-0055
Bob Jerles – President/GM
Ron Wigg – Coach
Mark Bishop – Public Relations
Roy Thibideau – Sales
Fairgrounds Coliseum
Seating – 5,124

Kalamazoo Kangaroos
P.O. Box 1538
309 Water Street
Kalamazoo, Michigan 49007
616-344-7030
Ron Creager – President
Chris Bartels – Coach/GM
Dave Wing – Public Relations
Gail DeWitt – Sales
Wings Stadium
Seating – 5,123

LOUISVILLE THUNDER
Legal Arts Building – Suite 600
200 South 7th Street
Louisville, Kentucky 40202
502-584-6762
Richard Heideman – President
Keith Tozer – Coach/Asst. GM
Craig Barnes – Public Relations
Tim Paulus – Sales
Broadbent Arena
Seating – 6,800

Chapter 9

No.1 Goalkeeper's Camp
No.1 Soccer Camps
"No.1 For A Reason"

Even through my tenure at the University of New Haven, and the years at the Major Indoor Soccer League (MISL) and at the American Indoor Soccer Association (AISA); there was always the presence of our soccer camps, referred to here going forward as "No.1".

While I have not been able to chronicle the very first soccer specific camp in America, soccer as a sport was being played in various residential and day camps across the country as far back as their history would detail. I have already related my "soccer counselor" experiences at Pine Forest and Silver Birch Camps in the 1960s.

And my father even told me about being taught soccer at a YMCA camp at Lake Winnipesaukee, New Hampshire, where he must have spent a week or so during his childhood in the early 1920s.

When Walt and Gene Chyzowych, Lenny Lucenko and E. Wayne Sunderland started the All-American Soccer Camp and School at the Ukrainian Workers Association (UWA) resort in Glen Spey, NY, it certainly wasn't the first-ever soccer specific camp. The previous year, Hubert Vogelsinger started his soccer schools, which were preceded by Brown University head coach Cliff Stevenson's camps.

I was assistant coach at Long Island University when Lucenko first invited me to work at the first All-American Soccer Camp and School. Walter and Gene were there as was Sunderland, who left his partnership in the camp a few years later to concentrate on his Athletic Directorship at Pratt Institute and his political career which led to his election as mayor of Massapequa on Long Island.

Lucenko oversaw the coaching school segment of the camp, and I remember teaching a classroom section for the coaches reviewing the recently completed 1974 World Cup. I loved saying the name of Jurgen Sparwasser, the player who scored East Germany's goal in their 1-0 victory over their West German neighbors.

There was one soccer field at the UWA resort and several bunks to house the participants. The senior staff stayed in one of several houses adjoining the facility. Of course, there was a dining room and auditorium where evening lectures and films were shown. Somewhat unique to the site was a saw dust pit used for track and field activities which I immediately adopted as the center for my goalkeeping instruction. In subsequent All-American Camp brochures there is a picture of me in a LIU warm-up suit holding a ball with a young camper about to turn, dive and grab the ball before landing in the saw dust.

Walter used to say that I would come to lunch covered in dirt and dust only to prove that I had been working!

Walter's contacts in the NPSL and NASL enabled him to bring current top players to the camp as guest coaches. I remember Colombian international goalkeeper Ernesto Lopera being there and early Cosmos standout Randy Horton. The All-American Camp and School began to attract a following of coaches who wanted to work there and learn at the same time, and after a single week that first season, additional camp weeks were added the following summer.

When the enrollment got too great for the UWA resort to handle, All-American moved to the New York Military Academy in Cornwall on Hudson, NY.

By this time, many other soccer specific camps were being organized. Some were conducted by college coaches on their campus, others by pro teams such as Tampa Bay Rowdies' "Camp Kick in the Grass". I worked at many of these camps, trying to learn as much as I could about camp organization and administration. I learned enough, I guess, to teach the course "Modern Camp Administration", my last classroom assignment taught at LIU in 1969.

Of course, I worked at Hubert Vogelsinger's camp several times and the Pocono Soccer Camp, which was run by Al Miller and John McKeon.

I remember working at All-American Camp with the famous former Olympic (1956) and Haverford College coach Jimmy Mills, who also coached and won championships with the Philadelphia Nationals of the American Soccer League (ASL).

There was a bar at the UWA resort where the staff would gather every night after the campers were put to bed and "lights out" decreed. It was fantastic to listen to Mills and some of the "old timers" talk about Walter Bahr, Benny Mclaughlin, Lloyd Monson and games involving the Philadelphia Nationals and Uhrik Truckers. One of the regulars back then was William "Billy" Charlton, who was a first-team All-American forward for Temple University one year after Walter Chyzowych received the same honor.

Charlton was associated with the US Army, and we called him "Colonel". His relationship with Chyzowych led to the promotional agreement between the US Army and the NSCAA to arrange a series of weekend soccer clinics across the nation and also to sponsor the first-ever High School All-Star Game, played at West Point, which I officiated in 1982.

Among the others around the bar those evenings were All-American Camp staff members Bob McNulty, Arvi Saar, Ron Gilbert and Jerry Sheska.

One day when I arrived at All American Camp in Glen Spey, I was told I was not needed, that they had a new goalkeeping coach who went by the nickname "the Cat". Of course, they were "putting me on" but I fell for it for a while. The "Cat" turned out to be Bob Barry, coach of the Iolani School in Hawaii, and after that we became lifelong friends.

Another of Walter's teammates at Temple was "Dick" Kessel, father of Rick Kessel, a camper at All-American who I worked with and eventually recruited to the University of New Haven, where he shined. Mr. Kessel told me he had been in touch with the camp administration asking when, specifically, I would be on campus working with the goalkeepers as that was the only time he would consider sending his son.

I began to realize there was a need for real goalkeeping instruction and what I was doing working one or two days at various camps was only scratching the surface. I approached the Chyzowych brothers and Lenny Lucenko about the possibility of becoming their partner in All-American, where I would be then featured as a permanent full-time goalkeeping coach. Once the word got out, I believed the camp would be flooded with goalkeeper applications.

The general consensus of the day was that goalkeepers could not be fully occupied at a camp, three sessions per day for an entire week. Most saw goalkeeping as only requiring the technical training of shot-stopping with little appreciation of the physical, tactical and psychological demands that needed to be addressed.

As we were not able to come to an agreement, I began to consider starting out on my own with a camp designed specifically and only for goalkeepers

I discussed the idea with Hubert Vogelsinger, who was also skeptical of the idea; but at least he allowed me to run our first No.1 Goalkeeper's Camp session at the Taft School in Watertown, CT, where he had multiple weeks of his own camp scheduled.

John Kowalski and I ran an indoor tournament in the University of New Haven gym to raise funds to pay for incorporation in the State of Connecticut and to get a license to run a residential camp from the State Department of Health/Child Services.

We put together a program which included all the catching skills, diving for low and high balls, dealing with crosses and breakaways, reading the game and a series of footwork exercises over cones and between corner flags and other obstacles. And of course, each session began with warm-up exercises to increase flexibility and agility and finished with a match-related game or competition which always involved goalkeepers playing in front of a full-sized goal. We also developed a field session which we named "pressure training", in which the keepers would work at maximum activity for 40 seconds and then rest for the next 40 seconds. It was a test of mental toughness and fortitude which challenged the campers to see how many stints they could accomplish. Sixteen stints were the objective.

And for the evening classroom sessions, I had collected a series of eight and 16mm films which included the entire set of the instructional series from England's Director of Coaching, Charlie Hughes, using highlights of the 1966 World Cup. One of my favorites was always *Why Are Goals Scored?* In addition, I also had goalkeeping instructional films featuring England legend Peter Shilton and German great Sepp Maier, and goalkeeping films distributed by Budweiser and the US Army. A film distributed by King Soccer was entitled *They Call Him Number One*. It may have been what led to us naming the camp from the start the "No.1 Goalkeeper's Camp".

Goalkeepers always wore number 1 back then as typically the players were numbered by position on the field. Looking from the goal out and going from right to left: the right back was number 2, the left back number

3. Half backs were numbers 4 and 6, which surrounded the center back, who wore number 5. Up front the forwards wore 7 at outside right; inside right was number 8 and the center forward was number 9. That left the number 10 for the inside left and 11 for the outside left or left wing. The back-up goalkeeper, if there was one, wore number 12 or 13.

I had to explain to the campers that Argentina made a mistake when submitting their roster for the 1978 World Cup. In error, they listed the players alphabetically, which meant that midfielder Osvaldo Ardiles had to wear number one as a field player while goalkeeper Ubaldo Fillol wore number five.

I knew that the opening night lecture and film had to be very important, not only to discuss the rules of behavior on and off the field but to "set the tone" as to how the camp was going to be run. There was to be no fooling around, no horseplay.

I developed a four-part presentation taking Dettmar Cramer's four elements that apply to every soccer player and tailored each to the goalkeeper position. In the technical realm were all the skills of goalkeeping; the "how" to perform. In the tactical realm were the "when, where and why" of goalkeeping which included starting position, angle play, the decision to catch or box (punch) the ball one-handed or two, penalty-kick theory, distribution etc. The physical realm included flexibility, agility, strength and power and we stressed vertical jump. Lastly, the psychological realm would include courage, concentration, mental toughness, leadership and more.

There was so much to teach and so much to learn. It defied the imagination of non-goalkeepers who wondered, "What are you going to teach goalkeepers for a full week, there's hardly more than a day's worth of material?"

After our indoor tournament, Kowalski and I secured several mailing lists from the neighboring state soccer associations, and Barbara neatly developed pages of labels which we had to then affix to the two-sided, single-page brochure which announced one week of a camp specifically for "Soccer's Forgotten Player", the goalkeeper.

We did not know anything about bulk mailing permits, so in addition to affixing the labels, we also had to attach stamps. I was sure this time not a single piece would go out through the University of New Haven mailing room. Lesson learned!

We also took out a couple of ads in what few soccer-related publications existed at the time. *Soccer America*, which started in 1971 as *Soccer West*, was slowly becoming the go-to publication for soccer when it started covering the NASL and US soccer fortunes nationally.

One day Barbara answered the doorbell at our Guilford home and there was a young high school player from Old Lyme, CT, who found a discarded copy of *Soccer America* in the locker room trash, saw the ad and convinced his mother that he had to hand deliver his application and payment for enrollment, personally, to be sure he would be admitted. Scott Saunders later became a No.1 Staff Coach and an important family friend to this day.

Slowly the applications for that first camp came in. The start date for the camp was Sunday, August 21, 1977. The week before I took a job working at George Herrick's camp conducted at Colgate University. I had decided to leave the camp after the morning session on Wednesday to get everything ready for the first No.1 Camp. Driving home, every radio station was playing Elvis! It was the day he died.

For many years later, we played only Elvis' music in the No.1 Camp store.

Thirty-nine goalkeeping campers, all boys, enrolled that first year. In addition to John Kowalski, we hired four goalkeepers to serve as group coaches. It was an important component of the camp that after the campers viewed the "Master Lesson", mostly from behind the goal, they would break up into small groups to practice what they had seen demonstrated. The groups were divided by age but also by size and numbered approximately ten per group. It was important to keep the groups small as individual attention was necessary. Each staff coach was also charged with writing a detailed evaluation of each camper in their group.

Kowalski's role was uniquely important as described in the second year's brochure: "Kowalski will again co-direct the camp's operations and provide his unique insight into the total role that the goalkeeper must play in team tactics and full team preparation." We were years ahead of the times!

The other staff coaches were Mickey Cohen, who was my goalkeeper at LIU for those NCAA title runs; Danny Gaspar, who later played in the 1978 Senior Bowl and became a goalkeeper coach extraordinaire, serving in that role for several countries in World Cups; Peter Johnson, the goalkeeper for Quinnipiac College, and Roy Messing, who was goalkeeper at Yale and later for several NASL and MISL teams.

As a special guest coach, we brought in Shep Messing, Roy's brother, who was goalkeeper for the NY Cosmos. After putting Shep through a difficult workout which he admitted was tougher than a Cosmos' training session, I heard Shep vow to his brother that he would never come back to do another such guest appearance. I guess Cosmos players were used to just signing autographs. Years later when we crossed paths in the MISL and even later with the NY Arrows, we always joked about it!

It was no surprise when we started to plan for our second season, we were told the Taft School was not available to us. After all, we were now in competition. Plus, we were going to need more rooms, more beds and a bigger field with more goals as the feedback we were given by the departing campers was that they would all be back next year and would bring a friend or teammate, perhaps a brother, and that they could not wait to show their coach all the stuff they learned.

A huge part of the camp's success must be attributed to Barbara, who took care of all the registrations, paperwork, medical forms, parental permissions, insurance, phone calls (no cell phones back then, not even beepers) and made sure the staff was comfortable, and well fed with a late-night snack at the day's debriefing and next day's planning session which began at 11pm. The staff, after all, was asked to work 16-hour days.

Searching for a new site for the following summer began right after the end of camp at Taft. And of course we needed to enhance our brochure offering. We had photos from the first year, including an impressive image of the first-year campers and staff, testimonials and new regulations to deal with.

The soccer camp "industry" was taking off like wildfire. Soccer camps were the place to go to get the next level of coaching. Neighborhood and town club soccer programs were years away from becoming a factor. Even my former teammates at the NY Ukrainians, Gordon Bradley, Ted Purdon and John Young advertised a camp "The American Professional Soccer Camp" at Gardner Lake in Connecticut. Bradley had played for the NY Generals and was now the playing coach of NY Hota. Ironically, their green and white camp flyer did not specify the exact dates or price. But it is quite a collector's item.

With good fortune, a soccer jamboree of local college teams was being held in the fall at the Loomis Chaffee School in Windsor, CT, just north of Hartford. The facility was fabulous. Multiple green soccer fields with goals and turf nourished by the adjoining Farmington River, a tributary of the mighty Connecticut River. And there were more than 100 dorm rooms which slept two or three, several meeting rooms, two gymnasiums and a very important swimming pool. I always believed the pool was important for the campers to soak their bodies at the conclusion of the afternoon session, before dinner and the evening sessions.

The following Monday I made an appointment to visit the school's headmaster, Aubrey Loomis, and went out on a limb by guaranteeing a minimum 100 occupants for one week in August. That was Loomis' minimum to open the kitchen, groom the fields and maintain the dorms.

Also of simultaneous good fortune was the success being achieved with the soccer team at the University of New Haven; NCAA Div II runner-up in 1976 and third in 1977. This led to additional speaking engagements and welcoming clinics at which to promote the camp.

When I look at our brochure for 1978, our second year, there is still no bulk-mailing permit. The camp was advertised as taking place from Sunday, August 20, through to the following Saturday, and full tuition was priced at $185. It advertised that Don Wynschenk would join the staff, highlighting his USSF "A" license and experience as being twice selected as Coach of the US Maccabiah Team. In fact, the Maccabiah team practiced at the University of New Haven prior to leaving for Israel. It was at one of those practices that I first met a young player from Dallas by the name of Dave Rubinson, who would play a huge role in our camp's future in Texas. I still find it a bit of a coincidence that both at LIU and New Haven, the US Maccabiah coach was selected from our staff during my tenure as head coach. Gary Rosenthal also served in that capacity.

We increased the range of our mailings throughout New England and the Mid-Atlantic region and took ads in every soccer publication and/or state association newsletter we could find. In the end, we must have done a very good job in year one. Our 39 graduates and their parents were our best advertisement both through their play on the field and through word of mouth. We were swamped with applicants for year two and when we stopped counting, 221 goalkeepers enrolled, representing 39 states. "The largest assembly of goalkeepers in the United States and perhaps the world," I boasted. And that meant the need for 25-plus staff, some of which we had to house in the gym so that each camper would be able to bed in a dorm room. Mr. Loomis was blown away. We were even picking up campers at nearby Bradley (Hartford-Springfield) airport.

I thought at first that Don Wynschenk with his CPR/First Aid and other certifications would be able to handle the role of trainer by himself. That proved a miscalculation. We were so fortunate to be able to hire the trainer from the Loomis-Chaffee School, Ted Plamondon. Ted had all the credentials, could also serve as a lifeguard, and had "all the keys". By that I mean that he knew everyone and could get us access to anywhere on campus. He also worked part-time with the State of Connecticut Health Department camp inspection team. We had no problem passing inspections at Loomis for years to come!

In 1971, *Soccer America* printed its first *Camp Issue*. Ten years later its Summer Camp Directory listed every camp by region (eight such regions) in the US and most camps took out an ad. Vogelsinger had the entire back page. No.1 had a quarter page ad on page 27, right under Joe Morrone's Connecticut Soccer School ad, which featured four six-day training sessions and the first session for girls only. The times were changing!

By year three, expansion for No.1 was on our mind and John Kowalski traveled out to Aurora, Illinois, in the middle of winter to visit the Marmion Military Academy on Butterfield Road. The field was covered in two feet of snow, the single dorm building was barracks-style housing and there were tunnels underground in case of tornados. The showers were in one large room with a chain to pull the water on from a spigot above. If you let go of the chain, the water stopped. And it was well water at that, difficult to get up some lather! There was a gymnasium for indoor play if needed and a swimming pool. There were cannons and crucifixes. It was a Catholic Military Academy. If Loomis was Athens, Marmion was Sparta!

Marmion's Headmaster, Father Barnabas Lundergan, a Benedictine monk, was surprised to learn that several females would accompany us to Marmion, including Barbara, our two daughters and several female companions of our staff coaches. It was also anticipated that we would be enrolling several female campers. It would be the first time that any girls or women occupied their dormitory. And of course, we had to establish special hours when the shower facility was for "Girls and Women Only", with Barbara standing security during that time.

Bob Barry (the Cat) was a regular staff member by this time as was Rick

Kessel, who challenged Chicago Sting goalkeeper Paul Coffee in a staff demonstration game of "Goalie Wars".

It was common practice that goalkeepers would bring two full size portable goals together approximately twenty yards apart and attempt to score on each other by throwing the ball or taking shots. We didn't invent the game or give it the name "Goalie Wars", but we certainly perfected it with what I termed as "international rules". These rules included how many steps a goalkeeper could take with the ball after making a save and how the ball went back to the original shooter if the ball rebounded off the post or crossbar and crossed the mid-field line. The game became our Tuesday night staple activity going to a Camper Championship at each camper age/group level.

But before the campers got to play there was always a staff demonstration which I motivated with a $100 bonus for the winner.

The best Goalie Wars staff demonstration game in the history of the camp was between Zoltan Toth v Richard But, both full time current professionals in the MISL. Coming in a close second was former Dutch pro Frans Hoek v Dave Vanole, a US Men's National Team goalkeeper and/or AJ Lachoweki, goalkeeper for the US Five-a-Side Team. Their athleticism, distribution skills and refusal to lose attitude inspired the campers to higher levels. "A picture is worth a thousand words."

In the 1981 *Soccer America Soccer Camp* issue which came out in February, 121 soccer camps were listed. Our advertisement lists three locations starting July 5th at Chapman College in Orange, CA; Marmion Military Academy and two sessions at Loomis Chaffee, the first being for campers aged 15 and under. It also illustrated a slogan "So You Want to be a Goalkeeper" and had a stick figure goalkeeper logo in a goal with the words "Machnik Saves" to either side. Several years later, at the request of a few parents, we removed the "Machnik Saves" part as it was deemed to be offensive to certain religious ideologies.

"So You Want to be a Goalkeeper" was something I often said when a young goalkeeper was having difficulty with a drill or exercise and needed a little motivation to get past the challenge. So, it became an easy selection for the title of our first book.

Paul Harris was a Manhattan Beach, CA former high school and college goalkeeper and current referee who had already written ten books on various aspects of soccer under his "Soccer for Americans" brand. Harris introduced himself to us at our Chapman College camp location with a proposal to bring a photographer to take a series of photos of the various drills and exercises, and co-author what would turn out to be his 11th book. Among his other titles were *America's Soccer Heritage* and *Fair or Foul*.

I dedicated my first book to my parents, to Barbara, daughters Colette and Janine, and two of my early mentors, Gary Rosenthal, my LIU coach, and Walter Chyzowych. It contains not only pictures from camp but also NASL and MISL action and shows that by this time, yes, there were female campers at No.1 and called it *"So You Want To Be A Goalkeeper"*.

Several of the photos in the book are of yours truly training a young Greg Andrulis and California native Tim Harris, among the first of our traveling staff coaches. It was important to establish a trustworthy cadre of young coaches who believed in the "Machnik Method" to travel from site to site to bring consistency to the instruction on a national level, especially in the small group breakouts. I was still doing all the so-called "Master Lessons" with John Kowalski adding "Reading the Game" and other tactical sessions. And on page three, there is a photo of young camper Dave Vanole diving over two goalkeepers on all fours to make a save. Vanole would later play a huge role in the success of No.1 (he was a five-year camper) but also as goalkeeper on the US Olympic and national teams.

Among the others who traveled with us from site to site were Rick Schweizer, Jon Halliwell, Tony Pierce, AJ Lachowecki, Silas Boyle and Michael Sheparovich. Alex Prus, an active MLS referee at the time, traveling with his wife Ewa and camper son Filip, brought a unique family perspective to the camp.

During one training session when I was coaching the New York Arrows, Shep Messing suggested that I meet with the proprietors of Action & Leisure, Inc., representatives of Uhlsport in New York. Uhlsport was a German firm founded by Karl Uhl in 1948 and was the leading provider of goalkeeping gloves, jerseys, padded shorts, knickers, training pants, etc.

Barbara and I met with Uhlsport representatives Eric Bodinet and Craig Zelinske and immediately hit it off. The two gentlemen saw an opportunity to have their products spread nationally to what was a "captive audience" at No 1. Before the internet there were barely any sporting goods stores in

America that carried specific goalkeeping gear of various sizes, colors and price points. We quickly came to an arrangement to make Uhlsport the official supplier of No.1 Goalkeeper's Camp. The first year was so successful at the camp store that Uhlsport agreed to a second publishing of *So You Want to be a Goalkeeper*, of course with their logo front and center. The book was republished several times and was first offered for free to every enrolled goalkeeper starting in 1982. A fourth edition was later published with a grant from Peter Carli who represented the German goalkeeping equipment brand Reusch.

My parents and Barbara's mother loved working in the camp store. They constantly folded all the jerseys and kept others on hangers. My dad worked the check-out desk, which was cash only until we were forced to accept credit cards. He struggled how purchases could be made and signed for by someone whose name was not even on the credit card.

By 1982 we were up to five sessions per summer with the addition of the George School serving the Philadelphia and Trenton areas and Miami-Dade Community College in South Florida. The camp brochure was now printed on glossy paper and advertised the Machnik/Harris book at $6.95, as well as an assortment of Uhlsport goalkeeper jerseys and gear which could be ordered from No.1 Goalkeeper's Supplies. The supplies company was managed by my sisters, Madelyn and Debra, out of Debra's basement. Much of the equipment which was not sold at the various on-site No.1 camp stores was shipped to Debra's house in Middle Village, New York, where once a week she and Madelyn worked on the orders and sent the gear out by UPS.

An addition at each camp was the use of a JUGS Shooting Machine which could accurately serve crosses, inswingers and outswingers as well as simulate long-range shooting. The campers loved their individual time with the machine. Staff coach David Smart and I built four wooden shipping boxes for the machine which we shipped via Yellow Freight all over the country.

The year 1984 was a pivotal one for the camp! I had received a letter from Hans Ooft about a goalkeeper in Holland, Frans Hoek, who was finishing his playing career with Volendam but also had a teaching certificate. Ooft was invited as a guest coach at a USSF winter coaching school by Walter Chyzowych and we became friendly over the week and must have talked about No.1 Goalkeeper's Camp. Hoek then wrote to me and indicated that he wanted to come to camp at the Marmion School in the Chicago area, to which he could get a direct flight from Amsterdam.

We picked Hoek up at O'Hare airport and he settled in at camp. He brought bags of equipment, notebooks and paraphernalia. He attended every session, even the film sessions with Bob Barry at the projector. Hoek returned for several weeks during each of the next five or so summers. He brought goalkeeping tactics into the program and added so much more. He took what he learned about camp organization, administration and management with him and started his own camp programs throughout Europe. He became famous as a goalkeeping coach and served under legendary manager Louis van Gaal at Barcelona, Manchester United and Bayern Munich. Hoek was also on the sidelines with Van Gaal during his international appointments with Holland and could be seen giving instructions to entering substitutes in the 2022 World Cup game during which the Netherlands eliminated the USA.

Hoek brought with him a book he wrote in Holland which contained many photos of his playing days in Volendam. I thought the book to be very special and offered Frans the opportunity to have it published in English in the United States. I asked my friend Don Wynschenk to translate the work and then I sat down to "Americanize" it. For example: a chapter in Dutch translated as "What's in a Bag", which was really meant to illustrate the equipment a goalkeeper must have and be ready to use depending upon the circumstances of weather, field conditions and more. I added pictures taken at camp to the pictures of Frans both in training and game action, and a few professionally done by Reusch USA, and completed the book which would now be called *So Now You Are a Goalkeeper* by Joe Machnik and Frans Hoek.

No.1 Goalkeeper's Camp financed the initial print run of 5,000 copies at Phoenix Press. The book was an immediate success and is still valuable today in many of its insights. I believe that if I added a few chapters on the new role of the goalkeeper in attacking play, changes in the Laws of the Game, modern training techniques, the use of analytics in penalty kick theory etc. volumes would fly off the shelves. Twenty thousand copies over four printings were sold. It is still possible to find some used copies on eBay!

In 1984, 12 year old Skye Eddy was dropped off at Loomis Chaffee School by her parents after not making the final cut in the Olympic Development

Player (ODP) pool that summer. Skye was one of four attending girls and was highly motivated. She made it to the final of the NASL Shootout/Breakaway contest held each Wednesday night at camp. Skye attended several more years, became a staff coach, an outstanding goalkeeper who played at the University of Massachusetts. She was named an All-American and appeared in the NCAA final. Skye is now known as Skye Eddy Bruce and her organization Soccer Parenting helps parents navigate the intricacies of youth soccer through the college recruitment process.

I thought it necessary to start video recording the sessions at No.1 Goalkeeper's Camp. I made an arrangement with Southern Connecticut University's Film Department and their crew was sent to Loomis Chaffee School to film an entire week's work. I then spent weeks editing the hours of the film, adding commentary and music. The result became two VHS cassette tapes of two hours each, entitled *The Skills of Goalkeeping* and *Goalkeeping Fitness and Tactics*. They sold like crazy! They are a record of the glory days of No.1 Goalkeeper's Camp when it was customary to have over 100 goalkeepers on the field at the same time, locked in attention to the lesson and practicing what they had learned.

Several years later, we produced a one-hour VHS tape entitled *Goalkeeping: The Next Dimension*, which addressed the tactical concerns which face goalkeepers. These developments over the next 30 years, have led to a new type of goalkeeper which our friend Frans Hoek named a "Goal Player".

The first No.1 Goalkeeper's Camp brochure to possess the appearance of a Bulk Rate stamp was for the 1988 season: Bulk Rate Permit # 179 out of Guilford, CT. It also lists that the office was now at Unit 2C Cedar Crest at 2414 Boston Post Road in Guilford. The same office that would be home to the American Indoor Soccer Association (AISA). To help with the sorting and assembling of the 70,000 brochures that we printed, my sisters came to Guilford for the weekend. With the help of Colette and Janine, we placed 50-plus shopping bags on the living room floor and began the process of labeling each brochure and placing it in the appropriate shopping bag, each naming a different state. Then later we had to sort by zip code for further bundling. That is the only way the post office would accept them. The process took the entire weekend.

When we learned that we could start before Memorial Day weekend in Texas at TCU because potential campers had already been out of school for the summer, we opened prior to the holiday and scheduled 12 straight weeks on the road with multiple camp locations. During that time, I would attempt to visit each campsite for a few days, but obviously, I was not present at any camp for the entire week. This meant we had to train certain staff coaches to teach in the Machnik Method, and they became proficient at it. It also meant we would have to trust the off field management of such campsites to our now teenage daughters Colette and Janine and others as Barbara would have to focus on a single location.

It became a tradition that we would invite all our potential leaders in camp for orientation days prior to the first week of camp in Texas. Several days of meetings but also lessons on the field were practiced and rehearsed. It would also mean several days additional housing for the staff and restaurant meals etc. It was a major expense for the camp but worth the investment. So many of these coaches (like Scott Calabrese, Mike Idland, Nick DeMarsh, Bobby Kramig, Todd Bramble and Darren Ambrose) went on to careers in the game, either through the development of their own camps or in the professional ranks, but especially as men's and women's coaches in the college game. A referral or recommendation from No.1 carried a lot of weight in the soccer community.

It was at these pre-camp orientations that we introduced the first handbook for our coaches with the daily program and all the approved exercises and drills. The handbook also contained my articles entitled "The Goalkeeper's Diving Save" and "The Soccer Specialty Camp" as well as one co-authored with Lenny Lucenko, "Some Thoughts About Soccer's Goalkeeper", which first appeared in the periodical *The Coaching Clinic* by Prentice Hall.

When Reusch replaced Uhlsport as our official supplier of goalkeeper gear it helped underwrite the formation of the Reusch No.1 Goalkeeper's Club. Membership included the receipt of a bi-monthly newsletter with specific articles and news about goalkeepers worldwide as well as an official pin and discounts on Reusch gear. It was in the first of these newsletters that I wrote a goalkeeping crossword puzzle.

In 1988 we introduced the Star Striker's School under John Kowalski. In many ways the striker's curriculum was designed to increase attacking prowess in front of the goal with the added benefit of being able to create tactical situations for the goalkeepers at the end of every lesson. The campers were amazed that we even taught the toe-poke shot and how beneficial that tool was when attacking the goal at speed. Most had been taught never to kick the ball with their toe.

The Striker program, of course, was designed by Kowalski, who a year and a half earlier had taken the US Five-a-Side team to Hungary for the first-ever FIFA indoor soccer tournament. John was now the US Soccer Federation Developmental and Five-a-Side Team Coach as listed in the 1990 National Teams Media Guide. The striker program was organized under the same guiding foundations as the goalkeeper program. The physical, technical, tactical and psychological dimensions of going to goal. Yes, we were beginning to talk about a striker's need for "killer instinct".

Among the lessons were: power shooting from distance, movement with the ball, dribbling, shielding and taking players on, breakaways, the killer pass, numbers up (2v1, 3v2) and numbers down (1v2, 2v3) attacking. Every lesson ended with going to goal against real goalkeepers to full size goals.

We needed lots of goals and nets to facilitate this new program. Shooting at a goal made up of coaching sticks was not going to cut it. Fortunately, Andy Caruso's Kwik Goal company had the answer: a two-sided portable goal with its own shipping bag with spikes to secure the goal to the ground outdoors and/or a platform piece which permitted their indoor use. Over the years we purchased more than 20 of these units for use around the country. They were made of lightweight aluminum pipes with snap-on components which enabled the goals to be broken down and put together easily as well as moved on the field wherever we needed them.

When we arrived at an airport for trips between camps with half a dozen goals in canvas/nylon shipping bags plus up to 20 boxes of cones, bibs, balls and equipment for the store, Barbara would get out of the van with a $50 bill and approach the baggage service outside with a proposition of shipping everything on the same flight. There was never a problem! This was also a time when they did not check IDs at the airport, there were no security lines and she was able to hand staff members a ticket that may not have been issued in their name.

We often picked up unaccompanied minors at the airport when they were able to be met at their gate when they deboarded. We asked each arriving camper to keep their soccer ball out for easy identification. Over the years, we only made one mistake as we picked up a camper going to computer camp who was also carrying a soccer ball. He never said a word until after the first field session when he asked for the computer lab. Today, airlines are refusing unaccompanied minor travel, and you can't get near a gate without a ticket.

John Kowalski brought some great striker coaches into the camp including Dave Kasper, Jim Gaberra, Chris Hellenkamp, Marcio Leite, Eric Eichmann, Caleb Suri and Hylton Dayes. Under a previously negotiated arrangement, Star Strikers would separate from No.1 when it achieved 700 campers.

In 1992 the concept of No.1 Goalkeeper and No.1 Striker Camp was introduced. Later, as field players outnumbered goalkeepers and the number of local and national goalkeeping camps appeared, our business was renamed as No.1 Soccer Camps. Also, that summer, we introduced the two-week Academy program at the sites that were available for longer periods. The second week's program was completely different and more advanced than the first. And where possible we would bus the campers to an indoor center for MISL-styled instruction with an accomplished indoor specialist like Krys Sobieski or AISA veteran Rick Schweizer. When I was associated with MISL we had their goalkeepers working at camp along with NASL stars; my association with the AISA brought new talent into the camp program, such as Manny Sanchez, Eddy Carvacho, Yaro Dachniewski, Joe Papelo and Scoop Stanisic, and we still had guest appearances from the likes of Brad Friedel and Tony Meola.

It took a while for the No.1 Striker's Camp to take off. Clark Brisson was one of our first coaches for the striker camp. He was the second-leading scorer in NCAA DI soccer playing for the University of South Carolina as a junior. He remembers working the camp with only four strikers at Coco Expo, a campsite outside of Cape Canaveral in FL. This site would also be the home of the US National Team for a week before their most important game against Trinidad and Tobago in 1989.

By the year 2000, the *Camp Issue* of *Soccer America* listed 549 camp organizations, most of which had multiple sessions at several locations. Some were simple day camps while others competed on the national level. Many were run at colleges and universities by their coaches. It was a good recruiting tool. Most advertised specialized goalkeeping instruction, yet others were specific goalkeeping camps or provided coaching for both goalkeepers and strikers.

There is no doubt that the most formidable and worthy of these camps was created by Dan Gaspar and his partner Tony DiCicco in the form of Soccer Plus Camps. Both excellent instructors! Later Gaspar organized Star Goalkeeping Academy. When DiCicco was named coach of the US Women's National team which achieved huge success, Soccer Plus became the camp of choice for aspiring young female players and coaches. I always thought of how coincidental it was that three of the earliest goalkeeping coaches in America lived and worked in Connecticut.

Starting in 1997, we produced a CD-ROM advertisement for the camps and would send these out to any requests for more information. It was a game changer, as was our toll-free telephone number; the very pompous 1-800-MACHNIK.

In 1998 we held our first sessions at a facility in Port Jervis, NY, called "Team USA". Based on 500 acres, it provided bunk housing around several playing fields but also the adventure activities of zip lines, a climbing wall called the "Schmatter-horn", and a "Black-Forest Ropes" course. One of the zip lines allowed the rider to let loose and land in the swimming lake. And there was the giant inflatable called the "Blob" which could propel an individual several stories high before a lake landing. During the first summer at Team USA we offered five consecutive weeks of coaching, and six weeks the summers after. Each week there was a sellout of 125 campers, many from nearby New York City who would not have enrolled in a strict, soccer-only camp. We called the combined soccer and adventure activity program "Soccer in the Wild" .... where "Wild Things are Happening".

The years that "Soccer in the Wild" was part of the No.1 program, we enrolled in excess of 3,200 campers over those summers.

Arguably, one of the things which separated No.1 Soccer Camps from the rest was its attention to detail, especially in the Evaluation and Personal Development Plans which were given to every camper upon completion of their camp week. Printed on hard, cardboard-like paper for permanency, each evaluation was signed by the camper's immediate coach but also by the director of that camp's program. If I was present at a camp's closing, I wanted to sign off on these as well.

Not only did the campers show their "evals" to their parents but also to their school and club team coaches. It provided coaches with information on the pros and cons of each player and often specific drills to improve each aspect. The evals have had such lasting value that we often receive copies written forty or more years ago, submitted by former campers who have sent their children to No.1 and in some cases, their grandchildren. If a camper went into coaching, even as a parent-coach, they would often send one of their players to camp. Many sent a full roster of players when we began full team training programs at No.1.

No one could state that the camp didn't have some unique locations over the years with the various challenges each presented. At the Valley Verde School in Arizona, we had a tarantula scare. At the University of Northern Colorado, we had to deal with the horrific odors coming from a nearby slaughterhouse and meat packing facility. Each day we prayed for the wind to blow in the opposite direction. At the Blue Ridge School we walked past a field of cattle to get to the soccer field. At Oglethorpe University, we ate our meals in the same dining facility as the medical students and the doctors in their gowns who taught them. At the Sauk Valley Sports Center, the campers claimed they saw a snake in the lake we used for swimming. At the University of Missouri-Columbia, the campers had to walk through a tunnel under a main road and then up a long hill to get to the field. At the Marmion Military Academy, one year we were told there would be a temporary water shut-off for a couple of hours as they transferred from well water to municipal supply. Turns out we had no water for showers or toilets for three days. At the Darrow School near Albany, NY, we were told by the NY State Health Department inspector that each dorm had to have a bat-catching net and equipment. Trying to find them drove us bat crazy! And then there was Historic Dodgertown, the former spring training site of the Brooklyn Dodgers. Exclusive two-bed private rooms with a TV and more but no soccer fields. We created them in the outfield that used to be the home of Sandy Amoros, Duke Snider and Carl Furillo.

At Marmion one year it was so hot that our trainer, Ted Plamondon (now traveling with us), asked if he could use the thirteen passenger camp van as his base on the field. Of course, he would keep the engine running so the air conditioning would keep him and his supplies cool. Over that week the van used up three tank-loads of gas and was driven only seven miles.

We always felt best about coming back to Loomis Chaffee. It had everything, including a perfect location, lush fields, good housing, great food, a beautiful swimming pool, a track, you name it! Loomis Chaffee was more than happy with us, as well. We were bringing in large numbers of campers and staff. And we cared for and respected their facilities. In 1985 Loomis Chaffee issued a bulletin entitled "Summer Activities at Loomis Chaffee". It highlighted our eight consecutive years at the Windsor facility and stated that, "Director of the camp, Dr. Joe Machnik, is also a member of the year-round Loomis Chaffee community as parent of junior Janine Machnik." We loved the place so much that our youngest daughter, Janine, enrolled for her junior and senior high school years.

In 1989 we moved from our Guilford home and office on the Post Road to nearby Branford. At first, we tried to run the camp out of our basement, which also had room to store all the gear. But after a trial period of a year or two we moved to office space on top of the Branford Movie Theater at 19 South Main Street.

The field-player/striker program really took off and there were now more field players in camp than goalkeepers. Of course, that made sense as field players generally outnumber goalkeepers by ten to one in any team environment. And, because of the success of the women's national team, in part at least, female campers were signing up on a regular basis. As a result, it became necessary to hire female staff, for dorm supervision and for on-field training.

Women's national team goalkeeper Briana Scurry paid us a visit to our Wisconsin-Parkside location. I put her through a vigorous workout, and I believe to this day that her athletic ability surpassed any of the male counterparts who had previously visited with us, including NASL, MISL and national team goalkeepers.

In the March/April 1998 edition of *Women's Soccer World*, a special camp issue, No.1 was cited as one of six camps recommended for attendance. And *Sports Illustrated for Women* named No.1 a "Top Camp" in their May 1996 issue. And we were listed among "The Best Camps" in the 1993-1996 publications by the Student Athlete Scholarship Foundation, regular publishers of *Instep* magazine.

Clark Brisson was beginning to show real leadership in the Striker's Camp, and I began to rely on him for programming details and staff hirings. He brought his friend and former University of South Carolina teammate Mike "Goose" Gosselin into the fold which now included regulars such as Brown University's Elizabeth Lyons, Danny Bacon, Hylton Dayes, John

Dolinsky, Colleen Farrell (one of our first female striker campers), Dave Anderson, Tom Poitras, veteran pro player Brian Kohen, Richard Poole, MLS referee Alex Prus and Andrea Lockhardt. And when I was asked to start the women's soccer program at the University of New Haven, several of our players became regular staff members including Mireille DeRose, Sheila Ringbloom, Jenn Kulmann and Christine Huber.

In 1994, our daughter Janine and Clark Brisson started a relationship which led to their engagement and marriage. Clark was raised in the South, played at the University of South Carolina and was an original member of the Charleston Battery, where his scoring prowess earned him the nickname "Clark the Shark". After living through a harsh Connecticut winter without golf, Clark, Janine and their infant daughter Olivia moved to the Charleston area of South Carolina.

Naturally, as grandparents, we were soon to follow. We purchased a home on the Isle of Palms and soon set up a camp office in a two-story wooden structure that we learned had served as the island's first hotel.

As a high school student, granddaughter Olivia also worked at camps run by her dad. While working a camp in Colorado during the time I was employed by Major League Soccer, I arranged for her to have VIP access to their All-Star game, where she met David Beckham! She likes to emphasize her visit with, "I touched him."

The internet came on the scene and changed the way we live and had to work. We soon had to hire a web page company to put together our first No.1 website. And we had to learn how to get into the back of the site to adjust and make changes. Registrations were now done online, credit card companies would have to be contacted, and business arrangements made. Startup companies such as EuroSport began to offer every possible piece of goalkeeping equipment which could be purchased online and delivered in a matter of days. They were like soccer's Amazon! As such, the No.1 Soccer Camp store was virtually put out of business overnight. Suddenly, the soccer camp business was becoming more like work.

Barbara had a great idea to relieve some of the pressure and responsibility. At first we thought of franchising but after investigating the federal rules and regulations, thought it not feasible. Instead, we would offer key staff members the opportunity to become Regional Directors (RDs); a position whereby they would share in the profits after securing their own facilities, insurance, shipping, local advertising, facility payment and staff. Each would have to form their own corporation. And of course, they would also have to prescribe to the Machnik Method of teaching and coaching and the No.1 curriculum.

The idea was brilliant and was quickly accepted by staff coaches Greg Andrulis, Clark Brisson, Mike Potier, Christine Huber, Chad Liddle, Graham Orr, Billy Gordon, Tony Pierce and others. The system worked well for all involved for many years.

In 2013, we had an offer from a national company to outright purchase No.1. Barbara and I brought most of the RDs to our Isle of Palms home for a meeting. Others participated via conference call. We discussed the potential imminent sale. They were flabbergasted, floored to say the least. They stated they would not work for the new owners as a matter of loyalty. No.1 would not be the same.

As a result, the sale did not take place. Instead, Greg and Lorrie Andrulis, assisted by Greg's brother Rob, a successful high school coach in Connecticut, would take over the organization, administration and management of the camp through their newly formed No.1 Soccer Camps Management Company, which they would run from Manassas, Virginia.

Many of the RDs continued to work for Greg and Lorrie under the same format. And new RDs were recruited around the country. The Machnik's still own the camps and would receive a royalty for every camper registered. The system is still in place today.

The sport of soccer in America has changed dramatically since the inception of the No.1 Goalkeeper's Camp almost half a century ago. Good coaching can be achieved at the club level in almost every community. The internet provides instruction, regardless of the position played, using up-to-date game footage. There is a soccer game on TV in America almost 24 hours a day. Clubs play in an alphabet soup of leagues. There are more women's college soccer teams than men's. The USA will host its second FIFA World Cup (along with Canada and Mexico), the biggest ever, in 2026. TV ratings for international soccer competitions break records every year.

But there still is something special about the No.1 Soccer Camps environment!

No.1 Soccer Camps is still alive and kicking!

It's No.1 for a reason!

Our first camp at the Marmion Military Academy in Aurora IL, outside of Chicago. Our staff included guest coach Paul Coffee of the NASL Chicago Sting.

Typical goalkeeper clinic held all over the country to promote the No.1 Goalkeeper's Camp. Note all the participants holding up the number 1!

Conducting sessions at the No.1 Goalkeeper's Camp held at the Loomis Chaffee School in Windsor CT. Note: the controversial "Machnik Saves" on the back of my shirt.

Our first goalkeeping manual; lots of pictures taken at Chapman College in Orange CA. Thank you Paul Harris for your work putting it all together.

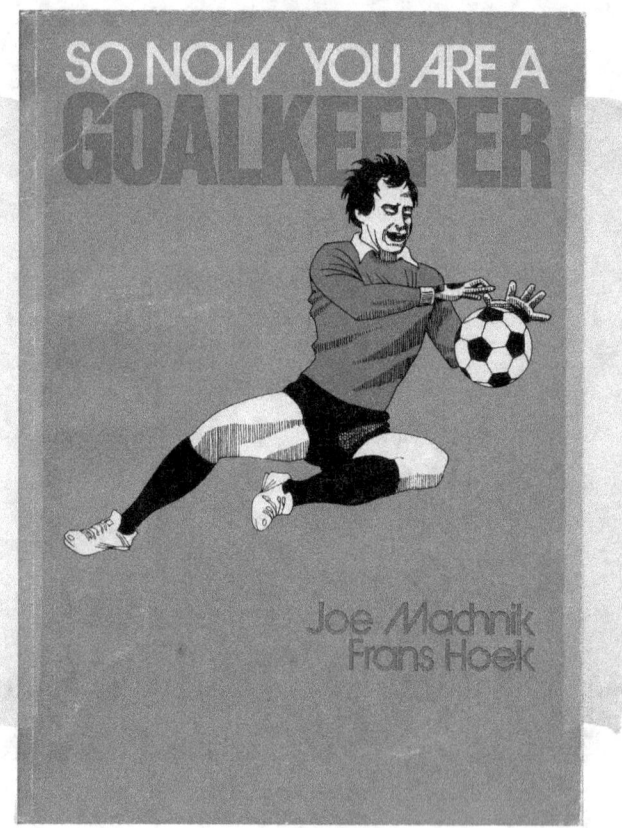

"So Now You Are a Goalkeeper" with legendary Dutch coach Frans Hoek. In many ways, it is still relevant today.

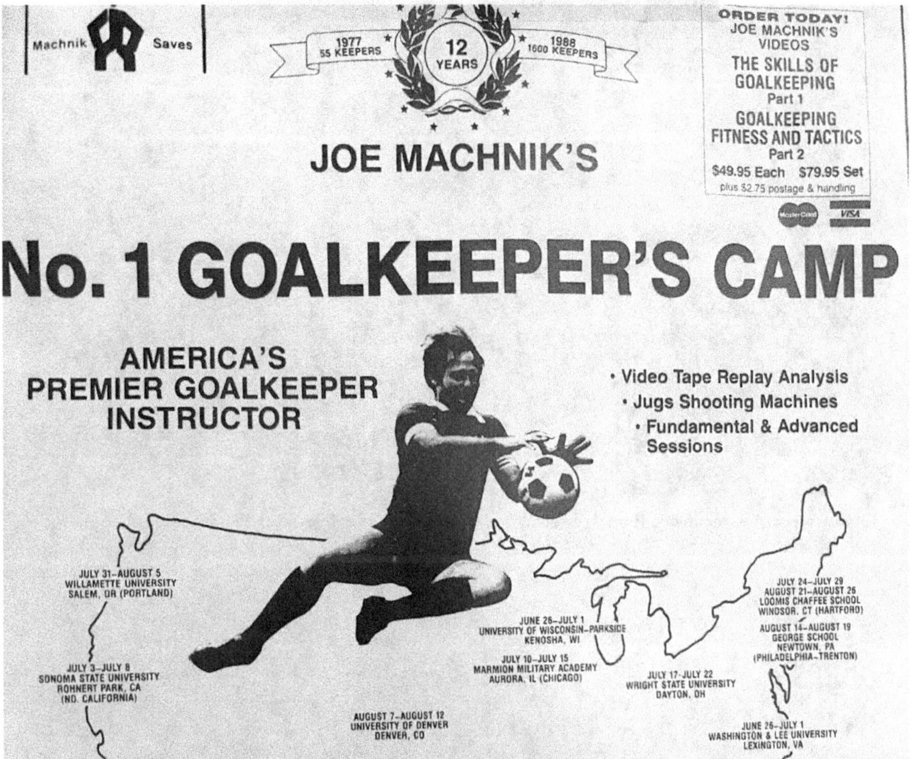

A typical 1988 full page add illustrating twelve camp sites across the nation.

Our three-tape video instructional series filmed at camp with over five hours of material.

When we added the striker component to camp, the numbers just exploded as evident by this photo of campers and staff at the Loomis Chaffee School.

Barbara and I had a lot of fun posing for this photo wearing our sponsors Uhlsport gear!

At camp with guest coach Brad Friedel who went on to win over 80 caps for the full US National team and a career in the Premiership.

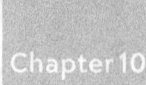

Chapter 10

NCAA Officiating and a NASCAR Career

"Let's See If Joe's Alright"

After taking the NCAA Soccer Rules exam which enabled me to referee in the first-ever National Soccer Coaches Association of America/US Army High School All-Star Game at West Point; I was encouraged to register at a local chapter of the National Intercollegiate Soccer Officials Association (NISOA) in Connecticut. At the time, I did not realize the ramification of that move.

I continued to serve as a referee in the Connecticut State League every Sunday and was getting some choice assignments, often working at Dillon Stadium. The Connecticut State Referees Association had some excellent officials and that included David Socha, who was working in the NASL and would go on to officiate at the 1982 FIFA World Cup in Spain. I often served as a linesman for Socha in the American Soccer League.

As a coach at the University of New Haven, I was one of the first to support the three-person diagonal system of control for our home games. Being Athletic Director as well ensured that we had the added budget for a third official. Sometimes, however, we would get an official who was unfamiliar with the system and who, you could tell, had never seen a game officiated with three officials, two with flags and one with a whistle. I will never forget when an official, serving as a linesman, tried to influence the referee to award a penalty kick by running onto the field with his flag and almost planted it on the penalty spot.

When the NCAA mandated that its post-season tournament games be officiated with the three-man system, and the major colleges suddenly wanted to follow suit, there was a sudden surge of officials trying to learn the mechanics.

Since I was already thoroughly familiar and competent in the system,

I was urged to attend a pre-season NISOA referee clinic conducted at the University of Hartford. The session was conducted by Gus Constantine, who worked for me in the indoor MISL. I passed my practical field exam with flying colors according to Gus.

College and university officiating assignments in the Northeast and Mid-Atlantic states were coordinated through the Eastern College Athletic Conference (ECAC) and their assignor "Scully" Scandrett. Most of the assignments for the fall season had already been made as each official at the clinic had received a fax with their schedule. Having just completed my course, I started the season without any assignments.

One afternoon in the middle of September, I received an emergency phone call from Scandrett. Could I get to the University of Rhode Island for their match against rival Brown University in time for their 7pm start? "Of course," I said and immediately got in the car for the hour and a half drive to Kingston. Evidently the game went well, sufficiently so that Brown coach Cliff Stevenson called Scandrett the next day and stated: "Get this guy some more games, he knows what he is doing out there."

I wound up officiating ten games that fall. At the end of the season, I received a fax stating that I received a rating of 8.80 from the coaches, which placed me at the top of the 53 officials rated. In fact, the losing coach rated my performance as 9.25 while the winning coach rated 8.50. The document came from Bill Fortin, NISOA Evaluation Chairman, with a handwritten note at the top: "Great job Joe." Evidently, the losing teams believed they got a "fair shake".

During the following college soccer season, I received 50 games. I never worked more than one game per day. Except, after finishing an afternoon game at UCONN and having already showered, I was notified that there was a phone call from Scully Scandrett. I thought I was in trouble!

Instead, Scully asked if I could rush over to Worcester Polytechnic Institute (WPI) for a 7pm start of a game that he forgot to assign. It was a one-hour drive, and it was already 5:45pm. When I got there with barely enough time to dress in the car and walk out onto the field, I learned that I was the only official and would referee solo. Fortunately, WPI was coached by the great Alan King, a former GASL and Eintracht FC player who had seen many games officiated by a single referee in his day.

I selected two students (one from each school) to serve in the position known back then as "Club Linesman". They would be responsible for flagging when the ball crossed the touch or goal line, and I would make the decision on the direction of a throw-in, goal kick or corner. I would also adjudicate offside.

The game went great! Suddenly, I was in line to get post-season NCAA tournament games in DI and DIII, and good ones at that. North Adams State at Williams, Columbia at Dartmouth, New Hampshire at Brown, Boston University at Harvard. I didn't get any DII playoff games because of my affiliation with the University of New Haven which played in that division.

At one match at Dartmouth, one of their fans yelled out: "Hey Machnik, my brother spent a lot of money at your goalkeeper camp; you better give us a call today!"

In 1986, Walter Chyzowych became head coach at Wake Forest University in Winston Salem, NC. The Demon Deacons played in the Atlantic Coast Conference (ACC) with soccer powerhouses Duke (John Rennie), Virginia (Bruce Arena), North Carolina State (George Tarantini), North Carolina (Anson Dorrance-coached both men's and women's soccer), Clemson (Ibrahim M. Ibrahim). It was the top college soccer conference in the country and an argument could be made that it was the best overall soccer in the country. Chyzowych and the other coaches believed it was necessary to upgrade the officiating in the conference and convinced Dr. Ray Bernabei, President of NISOA, to begin assigning officials from out of the region. I believe I was the first such official selected to make the journey.

I loved working at the ACC regular season games and was also selected to officiate in several of the conference's post-season tournaments, the winner of which had an automatic qualification into the NCAA tournament competition. I worked two games at Wake Forest, the second of which was against Arena's University of Virginia. I disallowed a Wake goal on the advice of a local linesman and Chyzowych was furious. He came out at me at half-time and I had to show him the yellow card. I believe the game ended in a tie. Regardless, Chyzowych invited me to his townhouse across from the field after the game. I was reluctant to go at first, not knowing what to expect. Over several glasses of white wine, he told me that he would prefer me not to accept any more games involving Wake Forrest. Jokingly, he said: "Because you are too honest."

In 1988, I was assigned as one of the referees for the NCAA final tournament which was being held at Indiana University. I ran the line on one of the semi-finals and was assigned to the final. Years later, I learned that Clark Brisson also played in that tournament, South Carolina being eliminated by Howard 2-0 in a semi-final.

It was a cold day on December 4th in Bloomington, Indiana. The Howard players did not come out for warm-ups, choosing to get ready in their locker room. I learned much later that their bus had issues, and they were late getting to the game.

In the 31st minute, I awarded a penalty kick against Howard, which was scored despite the efforts of their great goalkeeper, future Trinidad and Tobago international Shaka Hislop. The decision was controversial back then as the fouled player had his back to the goal, was near the edge of the penalty area and was dribbling away from the goal. I had looked away from a previous foul in the penalty area minutes before and felt compelled to award a spot-kick this time.

At half-time, in the referee locker room, I asked the nearest linesman what he saw on the play. "I didn't see anything," he said. Then I asked the fourth official who was next closest. He said: "Great call, they are making penalty kick calls on plays like that in Italy all the time." The problem was, we were not in Italy!

The game was taped for delayed broadcast during Christmas week, which meant waiting more than 20 days to see what was said about the call on ESPN. The color commentator Seamus Malin said: "Wow, that's a tough call." Until he saw the replay and added: "Well, he definitely got him."

When I finished the game, someone mentioned to me that I may have been the only person to play in the NCAA soccer tournament (LIU '63); coach in two NCAA finals (LIU '66, New Haven '76) and referee a NCAA final.

I thought I might have had the distinction of being the only person to coach, referee and play in a pro-league (MISL) had I taken the kick-off one game when our Arrows roster was reduced by injury. I didn't do it, because I had too much respect for the game.

During my last college refereeing experience, I had back-to-back Saturday/Sunday matches at UCONN. The first was a women's fixture and the second was a men's game against Penn State. Lou Labbadia was the referee, and I carried his bags. Both were NCAA tournament games.

Those were my last officiated games.

Changing Gears

From the day I saw my first stock car race in Connecticut at the New London Waterford Speedbowl (the "Bowl") in 1953 as a ten-year-old, I just loved every minute of the sport. I insisted that my father take me to the tracks all around the New York area. I have been to 65 tracks in America, many which are now extinct. The sport is in my blood.

Upon the 50th anniversary of the Speedbowl in 2000, a pictorial history of the Bowl was published by Dave Dykes. On page seven is a picture of the #5 "Machnik Express" driven by Dick Beauegard and sponsored by Machnik Bros. Construction Company of Old Lyme, CT. That picture is from the early 1950s. There must be a blood line.

One Saturday afternoon as a spectator at the "Bowl", they announced the formation of a new entry-level economical division of racing that was to start the next season. It was to be called "Strictly Stock". This was my chance to fulfill a lifelong dream to drive in a stock car race. I began to investigate further. I saw a beat-up old race car behind a fence at Grand Prix Auto on Route 1 (Connecticut Post Road) in Branford and inquired about it. The owner of the garage, Ignazio Puleo, explained that it was an "Enduro" car that belonged to a friend. I further inquired as to whether he would be interested in supporting me as my mechanic when I started a racing career. The Puleo's had a 12-year-old son, Eddie, who with a friend, Steve Godfrey, hung out at the garage and Ignazio liked my request as a possible hobby for the two boys, perhaps "keeping them off the streets".

I found a car for sale in Stamford, CT, and convinced Mr. Puleo to drive with me in my two-seated Mercedes, with young Eddie barely being able to fit in the back.

I paid $1,700 for the car and trailer and returned the next day to tow it back to "Nazio's" garage. The next step was to attend a pre-season meeting at the Cohanzie Firehouse near Waterford, to learn more about the rules, register the car and secure a racing number. All my favorite numbers were taken; I couldn't have No.1 or 11 or 13 or 21 so I had to settle for 46, which was my age at the time (1989). I got my first Speedbowl competitors license numbered 9048. And when the track became sanctioned by NASCAR, I had to get a NASCAR license. Imagine!

The first time I was in the car was for eight laps of practice on the one-third mile asphalt Bowl. And soon after, I was attempting to qualify for the feature race in an eight-lap heat race. I started in tenth position out of nearly 20 cars. The green flag dropped, and I hit the gas. Unfortunately, I went into the first turn too hot and I hit the brake, briefly losing control and doing a 360-degree spin on the 12-foot banked turn. Fortunately, I finished the spin headed in the right direction and kept going. No one crashed into me and the yellow caution flag did not fly. And I later passed two cars before the checkered flag dropped. That was exhilarating! The finish was not good enough to qualify for the feature and I did no better in the last-chance consolation race.

I began to realize there was a big learning curve to be had. Not only for the driver, but for the crew. Setting up the car to make left turns at speed was a science. A combination of wheel balance, stagger, caster and camber. Over that first year, I think I qualified for the lesser second level "B" feature twice. No money was won. And quite a lot of money was spent. I was the driver and Chief Financial Officer. By the end of the season, there were 90-plus Strictly Stocks in the pits every Saturday night. Ninety nine percent of the drivers were younger than me and had been driving go karts since they were four years old. I also learned what the blue flag with a yellow stripe meant: get low so the faster cars can pass. And the black flag: get off the track because you are leaking oil or dragging a part that could become dangerous to the other cars or even fly into the stands, endangering spectators.

But I loved every minute of it. The adrenal rush was more than I ever experienced. I would lose on average ten pounds on a given Saturday night, mostly sweat and the burning of nervous energy. My daughters Colette and Janine were my biggest fans, Barbara wasn't that excited! But in many ways, it was a family affair!

The next year we built a new car from scratch out of a Monte Carlo and souped it up to gain a little more speed and much better handling. Handling was the key. I started the season off well, finishing fifth in the Blast Off consolation race and 21st out of 30 cars in the feature. I was moved up to 19th when two cars ahead of me were disqualified for failing the post-race inspection for illegal cylinder heads. However, at the end of the season, I finished near the bottom of the table in points.

Points were allotted for each position finished, and at the end of the year there would be a points-based champion named with additional prize money awarded. There was also a handicapping system which positioned cars at the start of a race based on points won over the previous three weeks. The cars with the most points started at the back. However, if a driver missed a Saturday night race it was counted as a win with no money or points awarded but the next week the driver would start at the back of the field as if he had won the race. It was an incentive system to race every Saturday night. Since I was away with the national team a lot, I often started at the back!

I was able to schedule a visit to the track by the US Men's National Team the night before our game played against Partizan Belgrade at the Yale Bowl in New Haven. It was our last practice game before heading to Italia '90. The team was able to go out onto the track during intermission and was introduced to an appreciative crowd, the majority of which did not know there was a game the next day.

By my third year of racing (1991), we had learned most of the tricks and I was learning how to drive at speed and keep the car away from the wall. On the opening weekend, I finished third in the first qualifying heat (which took 12:29 to finish eight laps) and 11th in the 30-car feature of 25 laps. Since two cars ahead of me failed post-race inspection, I started the season off ninth in points. Since there was limited national team duty, I was able to make the races most Saturday nights. On September 28th that year, I won the qualification heat and finished fourth in the feature.

At the end of the season Awards Banquet, I was honored with a plaque citing my record as "Sportsman of the Year" in the Strictly Stock division. I have joked in many of my speeches and presentations that "Sportsman of the Year" is given to the driver who spends the most money and accomplishes the least. But we accomplished a lot that year. And I was proud that my driving skills and the way I treated my fellow competitors on the track was appreciated. There were 126 cars registered in the Strictly Stock division. I was not your typical driver. I knew nothing about cars, did not work in a garage and had an advanced college degree.

I was so different from the other drivers that *Trackside Magazine* in October 1992 published a three-page article, written by former *New Haven Register/Journal Courier* sportswriter Pete Zanardi, with photos by Steve Kennedy entitled, "The Doctor is In." It chronicled my racing story. It starts with: "Joe Machnik might be the last person you'd expect to find banging around the Waterford Speedbowl in a Strictly Stock feature. His Ph.D. and his background in soccer are hardly standard training for a stock car shoe. But at age 49, Doctor Joe is having the time of his life."

In 1992, the Bowl changed the name of our division to "Limited Sportsman" and allowed for a fair number of upgrades, all of which cost money. We built another new car, our fourth. I regularly finished in the top ten in all the features and in the top five in a few. The highlight of the season happened on the sixth night when the Bowl hosted time trials for the top ten Limited Sportsman cars and I was third in points at the time. I had never participated in time trials before. It started by coming out of the pits and taking a green flag. On the first lap, I hit the gas too hard coming out of the fourth turn and spun the wheels, almost scraping the wall in front of the main grandstand. But I nailed the second lap and finished with a time of 18:32 seconds, which was a new track record for the division. John Faulkner finished second at 18:37 and Bob Bruce third at 18:38. I won $150 for the effort and got a chance to be interviewed on the track, during which I thanked my crew at Grand Prix Auto. For the record, 18:32 translates to an average speed of 65.57 miles per hour on the one-third mile track, which at the Bowl translates to approximately 80 mph on the straightaways and 45 mph in the turns. If it doesn't sound fast to the reader, I can understand. The faster "Late Model" division averaged two seconds fewer and the open wheel modified division two seconds less than that.

We felt so good about our performance that, the next day, we decided to bring the car to Thompson International Speedway, where there was a big program of racing including a NASCAR Modified Tour event. To pass a pre-race inspection, we had to add 200 pounds of weight to the car. And of course, change the transmission. Thompson is a $5/8^{th}$ mile track, highly banked with much longer straightaways. It is shaped like a paper clip, something like Martinsville on NASCAR's big circuit.

I qualified for the 20-lap feature and was doing well starting from the back. I was picking off cars one at a time and passed a slower car coming out of turn four. Unfortunately, I couldn't get the car down low enough and a vehicle that I passed just clipped the #46 in the right rear quarter panel forcing a hard-right turn into the wall, putting the car on the driver's side down on the track. Then another car which could not stop in time pushed my machine on its side for about 60 yards before letting up, which caused the car to rotate on its side and flip five and a half times. It was a horrific accident for that level of racing. So much so that my daughter Janine was allowed on the track as the ambulance came out and the PA announcer said: "Let's see if Joe's alright." The car stopped rolling right in front of the stands where crew members were able to monitor the race and right in front of Barbara, who was wondering at first if my arm got caught outside of the car when it was on its side, and then whether I was alive when the car finished its fifth rollover upside down.

I crawled out of the car through the open window space on the passenger side facing the grandstand. The announcer then said: "Let's give Joe a big hand as Joe is alright." Joe was alright except for a concussion and the bruising caused by the pressure of the shoulder straps and harness. The car was totaled.

Barbara was so angry that she left the track, and I caught up to her on the road outside as she was attempting to walk home, which was 50 miles away. I cannot repeat what she said to me in a book that will hopefully be read by a family audience.

The nasty accident was caught on video, and I made a practice of showing it to anyone who wanted to watch when they came to our house for the first time. Barbara refused to watch it!

I was not sure if I was going to race again. But "Nazio" and the boys started to rebuild the car, which took about a month. The vehicle was ready, but the driver was not yet! Other drivers came by the garage and volunteered to drive the car. They knew it was a great car!

Finally, about two months later, I was ready. I got back in the car and finished the season at the Bowl. The only way Barbara would allow me back in the car was if we purchased mortgage insurance. I finished the season but lost the support of my family, which for the most part no longer came to the track to support my folly.

I started the next season, but without family much of the fun was gone. Racing every Saturday night takes up a lot of time as there is work to do at the garage in the days before and after. It's a time-consuming, expensive hobby at most grassroot levels. Even then, I won a couple of qualifying heats. But I never won a feature event. But I had the time of my life and loved every minute of it.

Puleo's son, Eddie, became a driver in his own right, winning the Limited Sportsman division at the Bowl and then moving up to the modifieds where he won at that higher level as well. Eddie's son, Jonathan (JP), is now a regular in the modified division at all three Connecticut tracks and has won features at all. I try to make it up to see him race at least once a year. I feel good about the legacy I left in racing because if I hadn't stopped at Grand Prix Auto way back in 1988, JP most likely would not be racing today.

Twenty years later, during Speedweeks at Daytona, a track in New Smyrna sponsors a week-long event for cars that come from all over the North. Upon entering the track at New Smyrna, several vendors sell programs, souvenirs, etc. One sells pictures of race cars. Almost in jest, I asked him if he had any pictures of the #46 that raced in the Strictly Stock/Limited Sportsman divisions in Connecticut in the late '80s, early '90s. "Of course," he said and then proceeded: "Hey, I know you, I was at your big crash at Thompson." Barbara could not believe it. But at least she was there and could verify the story!

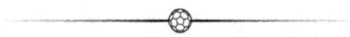

In 2017, I was contacted by John Kowalski, who was now coaching the women's soccer team at Robert Morris University. Kowalski had a long relationship with Robert Morris, having previously been the men's coach. He asked if I was interested in becoming the assignor of game officials for women's soccer for the Northeast Conference (NEC), of which Robert Morris was a member. I was interviewed for the position at the NEC by the Conference Commissioner, Noreen Morris, a former soccer player at Cornell, and later visited their offices in Summerset, New Jersey.

Over the years, I have put together a competent cadre of officials for the conference. One of the referees, Randy Vogt, wrote regularly for *Soccer America* about the trials and tribulations but also the joys of officiating, of which there are many. Several of Vogt's articles addressed the concern that referees were working multiple games at tournaments etc. without protection from the sun. US Soccer had a firm policy that hats or caps were not part of the official's uniform and, in fact, were prohibited. I informed Vogt of my battle with melanoma and showed him a picture of the 50-plus stitches on my scalp resulting from surgery. Vogt asked that I join in his crusade, and he included a reference to my surgery in one of his articles. I then sent the same picture to Sunil Gulati, president of US Soccer, who immediately recognized the danger of US Soccer's stance on hats, legal and otherwise, and in one day the prohibition was lifted.

The Doctor Is In!

He has just passed his 49th birthday and, on the subject of auto racing, anyway, he sounds like a teenager. Dr. Joe Machnik just bubbles over talking about driving Street Stocks at the Waterford Speedbowl.

"It is the biggest adrenalin kick I've experienced in all my life," says the owner of a Ph.D. from the University of Utah. "That is true every time I get behind the wheel."

Machnik, in his fourth season in Strictly Stocks, is no stranger to those in the soccer world. He is the owner of the "No. 1 Goal Keepers Camp," generally regarded as the best there is.

"I've done a lot of things," says Machnik, of Branford, CT. "I was the referee at a Major Indoor Soccer League All-Star Game at Madison Square Garden; I was the referee in the NCAA Division I College Soccer Championship game between Indiana and Howard Universities, and I was an assistant coach with the United States World Cup team."

Machnik's 1989-90 racing seasons, in fact, suffered a bit. He spent much of the summer of '90 with the US team at the World Cup in Italy.

Machnik played a major role in the MISL, serving as director of officials for a time. He was an All-American goalkeeper, as well as a very successful coach at the University of New Haven (where he was also Athletic Director) and with the New York Arrows of the MISL.

He has found new things to get excited about. He was named 1991 Waterford Speedbowl Strictly Stock "Sportsman of the Year." That qualifies as exciting.

"Yes it does," he says. "We won a heat. We got a fourth and finished 18th in points. We even collected some point money. I felt pretty good about it all."

Machnik "got a tremendous kick out of reading his name in the racing papers for the first time. I was included in 'rounding out the top 10' and I was excited."

Joe Machnik might be the last person you'd expect to find banging around the Waterford Speedbowl in the Strictly Stock feature. His Ph.D and his background in soccer are hardly standard training for a stock car shoe. But, at age 49, Doctor Joe is having the time of his life.

By PETE ZANARDI
Photos by STEVE KENNEDY

Trackside...37

Trackside Magazine article by Pete Zanardi who also covered soccer in Connecticut. What was I doing driving stock cars at a local bull ring?

Sportsman of the Year Award in 1991 at the Waterford Speedbowl! Meant a lot to me. It was more than Mr. Congeniality!

Time Trial Winner: I won a Time Trial Award the night before I crashed at Thompson International Speedway.

The "Big One" at Thompson International Speedway. Five and a half roll-overs and finishing upside down. "Let's see if Joe's alright"?

Actually won five heat races in three different cars over my six year racing career.

Another heat race win at the Waterford Speedbowl.

NCAA Certificate in recognition of being the Referee in the 1988 Division I Soccer Final.

Chapter 11

US Men's Five-a-Side '89 Bronze Medal and World Cup Italia '90

"The Long Wait Is Over"

After the failure to reach the 1986 FIFA World Cup with the ill-conceived NASL Team America debacle, attention quickly turned to qualifying for the 1988 Olympics in South Korea.

Also, US Soccer, with John Kowalski leading the Five-a-Side national team, began to enter international indoor tournaments in preparation for the first FIFA Five-a-Side World Championship. That tournament was scheduled for early 1989 in the Netherlands. Even though I was still employed by AISA, Kowalski asked that I serve as assistant coach.

With that in mind, Kowalski and I decided to attend the first qualification game for the Olympics which was played on May 23, 1987, in Saint John, New Brunswick, Canada. Walter Chyzowych and Werner Fricker would also attend the match. Chyzowych had recommended the appointment of northern California-based coach Lothar Osiander, who had led the San Francisco Greek Americans to US Open Cup success in 1985 as Olympic coach.

The US was badly outplayed in the match, losing by a score of 0-2. After the game, John and I joined Fricker and Chyzowych for a late snack, and since we had not booked a hotel room, the four of us shared a room, with John and I sleeping on the floor. Fricker was not happy with the team's overall performance but, fortunately, they turned Canada around one week later in Saint Louis 3-0.

In August 1987, I attended the Pan-American Games in Indianapolis, where we defeated Trinidad and Tobago 3-1, tied El Salvador 0-0 and then lost to Argentina 0-2. After the El-Salvador match, Lothar Osiander, Chyzowych and I had dinner with Art Walls who was appointed by Fricker to oversee the coaches' performances at various tournaments.

His title was Director, National Teams Management Group. It was at that dinner that I first heard Chyzowych use the term "Cornucopia Kids" in describing our players, meaning that they had all the benefits of a soccer and cultural upbringing but weren't hungry enough. I strongly urged the discontinuation of that description. Later, my future role as goalkeeper coach with the national teams was discussed but as there was no budget for such a position, going to South Korea with the Olympic team was not in the cards. This was the case even though Dave Vanole was the starting goalkeeper, a player who had attended the No.1 Goalkeeper's Camp for five summers.

The 1988 Olympic team roster was a forerunner of the 1990 FIFA World Cup qualification process lineup. All familiar names now: Vanole, Trittschuh, Doyle, Crow, Windischmann, Klopas, Gabarra, Davis, Goulet, Vermes, Eichmann, Krumpe, Harkes, Stollmeyer, Ramos, Murray, Armstrong, Duback, Bliss and Caligiuri. The results in South Korea were favorable: 1-1 vs. Argentina, their goal being scored via a penalty kick in the 83rd minute; 0-0 against the hosts South Korea and 2-4 vs. the Soviet Union, a game that could have been won except for a harsh penalty kick decision just before half-time which turned the result. Watching Vanole's attempt at saving those penalties, during which he seemed to forget the strategies taught at camp (much more on this later), convinced me that I could help improve the performance of goalkeepers at the national team level and thus influence results, even more.

The US men's national team, coached by Lothar Osiander with Len Roitman as his assistant, opened the Italia '90 qualification process with a home and away series against Jamaica, the winner of which would move onto group stage of qualifying. The first game finished 0-0 in Kingston, Jamaica on July 24, 1988, with a rematch set for the Saint Louis Soccer Park on August 13th in the heat of the afternoon to satisfy television commitments. This game would be my first as an assistant to the full national team, as Osiander requested Chyzowych assign me to help the 'keepers.

There were two days of practice with goalkeepers Vanole, Duback and St. Louis native Steve Fuchs before the game, which remained delicately poised at 1-1 until Hugo Perez's penalty put the home side ahead in the 68th minute, before three further goals gave the USA a handsome 5-1 victory.

Several days later while at our No.1 Soccer Camps site at the George

School in Newtown, PA, Kowalski suggested that we have dinner with Werner Fricker at his restaurant in Horsham. During that dinner, I made a comment about how foolish and risky it was to play the game against Jamaica in the heat of the day. Fricker took exception to my comments and slammed his fist on the table, citing my ingratitude and lack of knowledge of what went on behind the scenes, especially with the financial pressures he was under in attempting to qualify. Evidently, the TV revenue was essential for the continuation of the process. And there was the added pressure of the USA being awarded the World Cup in 1994, to a country that hadn't qualified for the sport's biggest tournament since 1950. If the USA didn't qualify for Italia '90, there was a threat that FIFA would move the 1994 World Cup and award it to another country.

Defeating Jamaica meant that the next round of qualification would take place in April 1989, which bought some time to enhance the program, solicit new sponsorship revenue and consider changes to the team. The qualification process would include eight games, two each home and away against Costa Rica, Trinidad and Tobago, El Salvador, and Guatemala. And there was a question as to whether Lothar Osiander could continue in the role as head coach due to his full-time job commitments as a head waiter and maître d' at leading lunchtime restaurant, Graziano's which was in the San Francisco business district. Coaching the USMNT was still a very part-time job. Different times indeed!

Werner Fricker and Walter Chyzowych thought it wise to consider the full national team for the indoor world championship, keeping the team fit and focused. A fund-raising outdoor exhibition game was scheduled for the Santa Ana Bowl against Mexican team Chivas of Guadalajara. Kowalski added Ricky Davis to the squad and despite playing a man down for the better part of the second half, a 2-2 tie was managed. There was a penalty kick shootout after the match, which we lost. The Santa Ana Bowl reminded me of my playing days at the various "ovals" in New York City, especially Eintracht Oval. A sandlot even then!

The previous month, in October, a three-day training session for the Five-a-Side tournament included another fund-raiser, an outdoor game vs. the Washington Diplomats at RFK stadium. Then an indoor session at American University gymnasium included a game that I chose to referee. The memorandum announcing this training period was written by the Chairman of the International Games Committee, Sunil Gulati.

It announced that in addition to transportation, room and board, the players would receive a per diem of $10 per day. Included in the squad for both trips was Ricky Davis, who Kowalski had thoughts of playing as an attacking goalkeeper. However, an injury to Davis kept him out of the final selection of players for the tournament.

We received all the planning documents from FIFA and the Dutch soccer federation (KNVB) and learned that we would be housed at the Papendal Sports Complex, outside of Arnhem, near the German border.

Sixteen teams were invited to the tournament and were divided into four groups with the first and second-place teams in each group advancing to the next round. The US was placed in Group D along with Australia, Italy and Zimbabwe. Group A had Algeria, Denmark, Netherlands and Paraguay. Group B had Brazil, Hungary, Saudi Arabia and Spain while Group C had Argentina, Belgium, Canada and Japan.

In addition to national team players Vanole, Vermes, Ramos, Windischmann, Gabarra, Eichmann, Goulet, Trittschuh, and Murray, John Kowalski added Peter Smith of Pittsburgh, MISL players Doc Lawson and Juli Veee, and AISA goalkeeper, AJ Lachowecki. AJ had good field playing skills and Kowalski saw him as a fifth attacker in the tactical plan.

Former Pittsburgh Spirit athletic trainer Jim Kittlelberger was our "physio". Our head of delegation was Chuck Blazer, and our doctor, Mel Hayashi. Since we would be playing in Holland, we recruited the services of Frans Hoek as scout and unofficial assistant coach. Our Press Officer was the Federation's John Polis.

The Opening Ceremony and first games were to be played on January 5th. The USA would not play until the next day. As part of our preparation, the Federation arranged for us to fly into Paris for two exhibition matches in Brest, France. We won the first game easily, but the second game was a nightmare as the referee seemingly did not know the indoor rules and allowed slide tackling and reckless challenges all over the field. We picked up several injuries, including a knee injury to Peter Vermes, and Dr. Hayashi questioned whether he would be able to continue. After spending New Year's Eve in Paris, we bussed up to Arnhem for several days' training.

When we submitted our roster and participated in the obligatory passport check, FIFA was not going to permit Juli Veee to play as his passport used his real name, Gyula Visnyei. It took Chuck Blazer several days to clear the issue.

Prior to the first game, all team representatives were required to attend an organizational meeting conducted by FIFA General Secretary Sepp Blatter and Walter Gagg, who would oversee game administration and write the technical report. I informed Blazer that there were still some issues with the playing rules and that I had questions. When Blatter asked if there were any questions near the close of the meeting, Blazer raised his hand. No other team representative did so. "The USA has questions?" Blatter asked in a derogatory tone. "Only the USA?"

He then stated that we could come up to the podium at the end of the meeting and ask the questions privately. I took it as he was unprepared to answer the questions publicly. When at the end of the meeting, Blazer, Kowalski and I went up to the front of the room, eight other team reps followed us. I guess they were afraid to ask their questions publicly as well.

Similarly, I felt we were disrespected as a soccer nation and as coaches when in our mandatory technical meeting with Walter Gagg, he refused my answer as to where we expected to finish in the competition. "What are your objectives in coming to the tournament?" he asked. "We came here to win it," I replied. He then rudely dismissed us.

Our first game was in the Sporthallen Zuid in Amsterdam, and we were up 1-0 on Australia with less than a minute to play. Under pressure, Doc Lawson inadvertently handled the ball in the penalty area and the penalty kick was easily converted against AJ Lachowecki. The game finished 1-1.

An important lesson was learned from this game. If another penalty was called against us, we would immediately change goalkeepers, bringing in Dave Vanole, who had a much larger physical presence in front of the smaller indoor goal.

With a tie and only one point in our first game, Chuck Blazer began to think about our trip home, thinking that we weren't going to get out of the group. He was investigating flights. I relayed this to the players in much the same way that I had used the phony airplane ticket jackets to motivate the teams at LIU and New Haven.

The next night we played Zimbabwe in Arnhem and were leading when a penalty was awarded. When we substituted Vanole, the crowd, the opponents and even the referee were stunned. When the spot-kick was saved, everyone then understood the move. Walter Chyzowych got a big kick out of it. Many years later, Frans Hoek, assistant coach of Holland at the 2014 World Cup, used the same tactic successfully against Costa

Rica, subbing in Tim Krul to win the PK tiebreaker.

With a 5-1 win over Zimbabwe, we now had three points (two points for a win back then) while Italy, which defeated the African nation by the same score but also had a big 6-1 win over Australia, had four. It meant that both teams were going to get out of the group before playing each other in the third group game.

When we saw the Italian players in the locker room area before the match between us, they kept repeating "Tranquillo, Tranquillo" — which we interpreted as "take it easy on us" — as both teams would move on to the next round regardless of the result between us. We won the game 4-1 and the highlight was AJ Lachowecki scoring what was thought to be the first-ever goal scored by a goalkeeper during live play in a FIFA tournament!

Winning the group put us in the second-round group with Brazil, Paraguay and Argentina while the other group consisted of Netherlands, Belgium, Italy and Hungary. We had played three games in three nights with travel, and it was good to have one night's rest as we were scheduled to take on Argentina on January 10th.

Simultaneous to this tournament was the annual NSCAA Convention back home. Werner Fricker and Walter Chyzowych had gone back to the States to attend the event and take care of other Federation business. When we opened the second round with a 3-1 win vs. Argentina, we became the talk of the Convention. The pair felt obligated to come back. On January 11th we defeated Paraguay 2-0 with a spectacular goal from Peter Vermes, who had his first shot blocked by a defender, completely knocking him over, before blasting in the rebound.

AJ Lachowecki received a yellow card for a slide tackle in this match, so we decided to play Dave Vanole against Brazil to protect AJ from the possibility of being suspended in a semi-final. The USA won that match 5-3. We had defeated Argentina, Paraguay and Brazil in soccer. USA! USA!

Since we won the group with three wins, we had to play the second-place team from the opposite group, the Netherlands. On January 14, 1989 the home team, playing before the biggest crowd in the tournament, took the lead thanks to two goals by Vic Hermans in the 23rd and 26th minute before Jim Gabarra pulled one back in the 33rd minute. After that goal, we started to take over the match and were pressuring right up to the end. Mike Windischmann hit the crossbar with the goalkeeper beaten.

Then two players fell in a heap and the Spanish referee, Emilio Soriano Aladren stopped the game to wipe up the sweat. The clock kept running as he continued his janitorial service. When I asked Walter Gagg at the official's table if time would be added as is customary in the outdoor game, he replied: "For sure, no problem." The clean-up took a full half-minute. The game was restarted, and we were all over Holland when the whistle sounded for full time. No time was added! We lost the game 2-1. The players were devastated.

The next night we had to play the third/fourth-place playoff. It was a credit to the players how they responded. Our opponent, Belgium, lost their semi-final to Brazil (whom we had beaten). We wondered whether Brazil let up purposely against us to avoid meeting Holland in the semi-final? We won the playoff game 2-1 in extra time. On the same night, January 15th, Brazil beat the Netherlands 2-1 in the final.

After the match, an award ceremony was conducted and FIFA President Joao Havelange presented us with our bronze medals, the first medals won by a USA men's team in a FIFA competition (while the USA finished third in the 1930 World Cup, no medals were awarded).

The USA was also awarded the "Fair Play" trophy, which was cool to think you could medal and be honored for sportsmanship at the same time. We were disappointed, however, that AJ Lachowecki was not honored with the tournament's "Best Goalkeeper Award". He deserved it over the keeper from Belgium. And Peter Vermes, who had scored six goals, missed winning the Golden Boot by one goal. Back in the locker room after winning the third-place game, I remember the always emotional and patriotic Vanole in tears, reminiscing about all the previously unrecognized hard work without reward and cherishing his third-place medal despite starting only one game and subbing to save a penalty kick in another. He was the ultimate team player and was loved by his teammates.

Bob Gansler had been assistant coach for Walter Chyzowych going back to the qualification processes for international tournaments including the Pan American Games, 1980 Olympics and 1982 World Cup. Bob was also a former national team player who had achieved his US Soccer "A" coaching license that same year as me at Hartwick College in 1974. And, he was a regular participant, thereafter, as a staff coach at the Federation's hugely successful coaching schools.

One day after the conclusion of the Five-a-Side tournament, Werner Fricker and Walter Chyzowych named Bob Gansler as Head Coach of the US national team, taking over for Lothar Osiander, who had brought the team to the final qualifying round for the 1990 World Cup.

But before starting to work on the senior side's attempt to qualify for Italia '90, Gansler, with assistant coach Ralph Perez, had to finish their work with the national youth team which had qualified for the 1989 FIFA World Youth Championship being played in Saudi Arabia in late February, early March. The USA's fourth-place finish was the highest ever in a FIFA (non-indoor) soccer tournament. Goalkeeper Kasey Keller won the Silver Ball as the second best player in the Tournament and the USA again won the Fair Play Award!

Gansler was coaching two teams at the beginning of 1989. The national team got together for a training session in Los Angeles and played a friendly against UCLA and the California South Select team in late January. He then left the team to join the U20s for their tournament in Saudi. During that time, he asked that I come out and work with the goalkeepers, a role I assumed again during training sessions in South Florida in mid-February when Jim Lennox, a successful coach at Hartwick College, was temporarily put in charge. During that time, we played two successful games against the University of South Florida and the University of Tampa.

I still had no idea as to what my role would be, if any, until just before a trip to Paraguay, when Bob Gansler asked that I serve as his assistant during the qualification process. I was shocked to say the least. Neither Walter Chyzowych nor Art Walls had given any indication that I was being considered for this role. Selfishly, I said to Bob that I would be most pleased to serve in this capacity with the caveat that when we qualified (not if) I would also be on his staff for Italia '90. We shook hands on it. Later, I was told that my salary would be the same as that which I had earned with the Five-a-Side team; $100 per day.

We had one more training session with friendly games before qualification started, going up first against the pro team Miami Sharks before facing two Columbian first division sides, America Cali and Santa Fe, in Miami in what was known as the Marlboro Cup.

Our first Italia '90 qualification game was played on Sunday, April 16, 1989 in the Estadio Nacional de Sabana in San Jose, Costa Rica. When I woke up in the morning on the day of the game, I turned on the TV just to see what was happening. On almost every channel, there was a full soccer stadium of fans celebrating the start of a game. This was at 8am in the morning. Our game wasn't until later that afternoon, so it couldn't be our stadium, or our game. I was wrong!

Our lineup that day: Duback in goal, Balboa, Trittschuh, Windischmann, Bliss, Stollmeyer, Harkes, Ramos (Klopas,88) Murray, Goulet (Gabarra 54) and Vermes.

Costa Rica's Gilberto Rhoden scored in the 14th minute, and we never seriously threatened. If anything, we seemed uninspired, and the match ended in a 1-0 defeat. A crowd of 26,172 was announced.

Just before leaving the stadium, the President of Costa Rica asked to address the team on our bus. Oscar Arias had just won the Nobel Peace Prize in 1987 for his Central American Peace Plan. In excellent English he explained how Costa Rica was "America's best friend in all of Central America" and that he wanted us to deliver that message back home. I guess he thought that someday we might visit the White House.

Two Sundays later the return match was scheduled, this time at the Saint Louis Soccer Park, sponsored of course by Budweiser. A sellout crowd of 8,500, many of which were standing, attended the game. Our lineup was the same, except it was decided that Dave Vanole would start in goal. Vanole, a favorite of the players, with his charismatic personality winning them over. He would come onto the field with small American flags sticking out of his gloves and he would plant them in the goal during warm-ups.

Tab Ramos, with an assist from Bruce Murray, scored in the 72nd minute. Costa Rica appealed for several penalties from the referee, Rodolfo Mendez of Honduras, only to have him look away. Then in the closing minutes, Vanole mishandled a crossed ball which fell to a Costa Rican forward who shot at the goal which was now only protected by Steve Trittschuh. The defender had no choice but to knock the ball down with his hand and give away a penalty. (Under today's Laws of the Game, Trittschuh would be sent off for denial of an obvious goal by handling and be suspended for our next match during which he would score our team's only goal).

Our World Cup qualification hopes were on the line during the next several minutes. We could not afford to lose a point at home. We were all surprised when Mauricio Montero, wearing the number five, stepped up to take the penalty kick.

Vanole was prepared this time with the knowledge that when a defender steps up to take a penalty, there is a strong chance that he will hit the ball with power and that placement is less of an option. Vanole held his ground. He did not guess or dive to either side. He stood square in the middle of the goal. The ball was hit with such power that Vanole almost didn't have time to raise his hands, it hit him square. The rebound came out to his left side, and he challenged the ball again until it was played out for a corner. Shortly after, the final whistle blew. Vanole was now the starting goalkeeper. Two points were awarded for a win in 1990, and we had two in the bag!

An estimated 10,700 attended our next qualification game, played in Murdock Stadium on the campus of El Camino College in Torrance, California. If the stadium sounds familiar it is because it is the same ground where the US lost to Costa Rica in qualification for the 1986 World Cup.

The opponent this time was Trinidad & Tobago (T&T), with a star-studded line-up including Russell Lataby.

Steve Trittschuh beat an offside trap after a corner kick to score for the US in the 48th minute. The game was nearly won until, two minutes from the end of normal time, Hutson Charles scored for T&T after the Italian referee, Luigi Agnolin, missed what looked to me as an obvious handling offense by an attacking player. A home point lost, Gansler was furious, and we were in trouble.

Before we were to play our next qualification game there was another Marlboro Cup engagement, this time at New Jersey's Giants Stadium, in early June. Dave Vanole showed up with an injury and Jeff Duback was scheduled to start in goal. But we needed a back-up goalkeeper.

John Harkes and Tab Ramos suggested that we call Tony Meola, their friend from recreation league play in Kearny, New Jersey and later teammates at Kearny Thistle FC. Meola lived nearby and was home from the University of Virginia. Tony came in and we had a private workout the day before our first game against Benfica, the Portuguese side that would go on to reach the final of the 1990 European Cup. During the game, Duback was violently challenged and injured coming out for a crossed ball and Meola was called upon to enter the game. His strong play solidified a 2-1 victory. Meola would start the Championship Game two days later against Peru.

An interesting fact (at least to me) about this game is that it represents my debut and only game as Head Coach for the national team. Although the records do not show it. Bob Gansler had received permission from the Federation to return home after the Friday night game against Benfica to attend two graduations of his sons: one from high school and one from college. This must have come as somewhat of a surprise. Suddenly, Walter Chyzowych was concerned and asked if I needed help on the bench? I turned him down.

Arrangements were made to be able to reach Gansler by telephone at half-time for guidance. We opened the game with first-half goals by Bliss, Ramos and Murray and led 3-0. When Gansler was reached by phone, I jokingly asked "How am I doing?" We locked down Peru in the second half and won the game by that same 3-0 score.

Many years later, when I told the story to a reporter, he questioned its authenticity. Then, somehow, he was able to get a copy of the line-up card with my signature on it as Coach! US Soccer still hasn't corrected the record.

Thirteen days later, Vanole was healthy enough to start our next qualification game, which was played in New Britain, Connecticut, against Guatemala. Additional grandstands had to be brought into Veterans Memorial Stadium, and many possible attendees were turned away for security reasons and the fact that they did not have tickets. The crowd of 10,516 saw a great early goal by Murray in the third minute, only to see Raul Chacon tie the game 19 minutes later. The match was finally decided when Eric Eichmann got on the end of a scramble to score in the 67th minute. The game was officiated by former MISL referee Gordon Arrowsmith, of Canada, who had to issue three cautions and send off Guatemala's Juan Manuel Funes in the 87th minute. Two more points in the bag.

There was a slew of friendly games to be played, including a Marlboro Cup fixture in Chicago, a trip to Italy, two games in LA, and matches in Philadelphia and Miami, before our September 17th engagement with El Salvador in Tegucigalpa, Honduras. El Salvador was barred from playing at home due to fan disruptions in their previous match. A goal by Hugo Perez in the 62nd minute iced the 1-0 win with Meola in goal. It would be the first of his four consecutive shutouts in World Cup qualifying.

His second came in a 0-0 tie in Guatemala City against a team that was mathematically eliminated and which we outshot 16-7. Goal scoring continued to be a problem, and that was an understatement, exemplified in detail when we faced El Salvador again on November 5th at a sold-out Saint Louis Soccer Park. Another 0-0 tie, another point lost. Shots were 12-5 in the US's favor and corner kicks 13-3. But another shutout!

Whether the USA was going to qualify for Italia '90; whether the country would keep the right to host the World Cup in 1994, would all come down to the final game of World Cup qualification; not only in CONCACAF but worldwide. So much has been written about this game against Trinidad and Tobago, and documentaries produced.

The Federation decided to host a full week of training prior to leaving for Port of Spain. We practiced double sessions at Coco Expo and stayed at a nearby hotel. Preparations were enhanced by bringing in the Bermuda national team on Wednesday for a final tune-up. Werner Fricker and Walter Chyzowych were present as we barely scraped by 2-1 thanks to a goal by defender John Doyle and another by Erich Eichmann. A lot more was expected. Our two visitors left dejected. Pessimism reigned.

On Thursday, we learned that FIFA had changed the referees for the game, taking off the scheduled officiating team from Venezuela and replacing them with one from Argentina led by Juan Carlos Loustau.

There was a celebratory atmosphere when we landed in Trinidad for the big game. So confident were the Trinidadians that they declared the day after the game to be a national holiday. They only needed a tie to get to Italy. The USA, which had scored only one goal in its last 208 minutes of play, would need to score a goal and win.

Our bus had a difficult time getting to the stadium through streets crowded with red shirted T&T supporters who could not get into the game. When we finally got to the gates at the stadium entrance, I got up and was first off the bus! "Let's get this done," I said!

Paul Caligiuri scored the miracle goal in the 31st minute, taking a shot off a bounce that floated into the goal behind Michael Maurice.

Our bench was in the half of the field where the goal was scored. The moment the ball was hit, I jumped up and yelled: ***"Trouble!"*** I saw the trajectory of the shot, where the goalkeeper was standing, and had judged the combination of wind and sun to know that he was in trouble. Sure enough, the ball floated into the goal and bounced over the goal line before even hitting the net. The USA was in front!

There was a play still in the first half that referee Loustau had to look at for a penalty as John Doyle had made contact with a Trinidadian forward as he was running onto a through ball. Loustau looked away. He was later rewarded with three center assignments at the 1990 World Cup and his son, Patricio, became a top referee and appeared in Copa America Centenario.

Even though we had scored that early goal, there was no panic in the crowd nor amongst the Trinidad players. They had come from behind in several qualifiers leading up to this game and had scored an 88th minute goal against us in our previous meeting. However, our defense and Tony Meola held on, and when the final whistle blew there was shock amongst the crowd and jubilation amongst the handful of US supporters that had made the trip. Our players threw themselves on the ground and on top of each other.

When we finally made it back to the locker room and reality set in, we realized we didn't even have champagne to celebrate. Then the Trinidadian team brought us their bubbly as they had no use for it.

Several US Soccer dignitaries came into the locker room, including Sunil Gulati, Chairman of the International Games Committee. Sunil shook each player's hand and that of coach Gansler before coming to me with a simple, "Thank you." He recognized the difference goalkeeping had made in the qualification process as in eight games we had scored only six goals but had given up just three, conceding none in the last four games.

Our celebration back at the hotel was a quiet one, we were exhausted physically, but mostly mentally, from the pressure and the strain. And not knowing what was going to happen next. We were about to enter uncharted territory, preparing for the USA's first World Cup appearance in 40 years.

When we finally arrived at Miami airport after much delay, there was no crowd to greet us, no photographers, no newspaper columnists, no family, friends or fans. From there, each player would head to their home destination flights separately and be prepared to have Thanksgiving dinner three days later with family and friends, hoping to reflect on what just happened and giving thanks for Paul Caligiuri's "Shot Heard Around the World", as his all-important goal was dubbed in the American media.

The day before the game, George Vecsey's *New York Times* article was headlined with "US Pride Rests on One Game."

But after the game the headlines read as follows: *Soccer International:* "A Gift From The Gods." *Soccer Week:* "America's Dream Comes True." *New York Times:* "US Advances to World Cup and US Gets Cup Slot." *USA Today:* "USA ends 40-Year Cup Absence 1-0 and US Soccer Gets A Lift." *New York Post:* "Gutsy US Wins World Cup Bid." *New Haven Register:* "US Soccer Team Ends 40-Year World Cup Drought." *The Hartford Courant:* "US Reaches Finals."

Many of the newspapers used a picture of the team celebrating the final whistle, or of Dave Vanole, American flag in hand being hugged by Brian Bliss. One, the *New York Daily News* with the headline "Yankees Win!" badly misspelled David's last name as "Danola".

If 1989 was busy, 1990 would be so much more so! Suddenly there was local, national and international media coverage and expectations. Equipment companies were now looking at individual players for endorsements. There was controversy over the shoe contract signed by the Federation with adidas while Puma attempted to sign individual players. The goalkeepers were offered glove contracts. There was a player "strike" of sorts as the players were unhappy with the terms of a "full time" contract offered by the Federation. And there was dissention in the ranks as some players felt the need to sign a contract while others held out.

Dave Vanole seemed to be in the middle of it all to the point that he was initially excluded from the team's early training dates. His contract offer was eventually withdrawn by the Federation, and we started camp without him. This did not sit well with many of the other players and became even more public when David's mother wrote a letter which was printed in the February 8, 1990 issue of *Soccer America*. One of the goalkeepers brought in as a possible replacement was Jurgen Sommer, who appeared in the 1988 NCAA Championship Game for Indiana University. Over time, the situation was resolved and Vanole was brought back into the team, but as the third-choice goalkeeper with Tony Meola as the starter and Kasey Keller as his principal back-up.

Now that the Federation was guaranteed income from its anticipated appearance in Italy, there was enough money to add a second assistant coach. Bob Gansler chose Ralph Perez, who was his assistant during the successful U20 Saudi Arabia campaign when the USA finished fourth.

The Federation printed a beautiful 66-page full color guidebook for the 1990 World Cup with biographies of all the players and staff. Ralph Perez was now listed as Assistant Coach, and I was listed as Goalkeeper Coach.

The players listed were Desmond Armstrong, Marcelo Balboa, Jimmy Banks, Brian Bliss, Paul Caligiuri, Neil Covone from the U20 team along with Troy Dyak, Kasey Keller and Chris Henderson, goalkeeper Mark Dodd, John Doyle, Ted Eck, Eric Eichmann, John Harkes, Paul Krumpe, Tony Meola, Bruce Murray, Hugo Perez, Tab Ramos, John Stollmeyer, Chris Sullivan, Steve Trittschuh, David Vanole, Peter Vermes, Mike Windischmann and Eric Wynalda.

Our traveling support staff was made up of Equipment Manager, Gary McGuire; Director of Communication/Press Officer, John Polis; Athletic Trainer, Rich Riehl, and National Team Coordinator, Doug Newman. But everything was held together by the National Team's Program Administrator, Jan M. Wooles. It was Wooles who would issue the memos to the national team players for each training session leading up to the departure for the World Cup.

For instance, in Wooles' note written to the team ahead of a week of training and games against the Ft. Lauderdale Strikers, Miami Freedoms and the Colombia national team in April, the following was written regarding shoes: "Adidas studded, molded and flats for this and all future trips. Adidas is the official supplier of the National Teams, and all players are required to wear adidas. NO EXCEPTIONS."

The memo included a full roster of the players invited and a listing of the teams or organizations each represented. Billy Thompson of UCLA was added. It is interesting to acknowledge the affiliations of the players which included the Universities of Portland, Virginia, Wake Forest and San Diego State, the indoor teams of Baltimore Blast, Milwaukee Wave, Chicago Sting and Cleveland Force, and the outdoor teams San Francisco Bay Blackhawks, Tampa Bay Rowdies, Albany Capitals, Miami Sharks, Washington Stars and Colorado Foxes. Only two players had been playing abroad at the time: Paul Caligiuri, with S.V. Meppen in Germany, and Peter Vermes, who had a stint with Dutch side Volendam, arranged by Frans Hoek. The national team was primarily a side of college kids, indoor players and semi-pro amateurs.

The World Cup year kicked off with February exhibition games in Miami, Florida, against Costa Rica (0-2) and Colombia (1-2), with newcomer Eric Wynalda scoring. Whenever we played in the Orange Bowl, I always went to the field exit where Joe Namath showed his No.1 signal to the fans after the New York Jets' Super Bowl win over the Colts in Super Bowl III. I reminisced and still root for the JETS and did so even when they were Harry Wismer's Titans.

A week later we were in Bermuda to return the favor of their coming to Coco Expo to help us prepare for our big game in Trinidad. We beat Bermuda 1-0 after a goal by Chris Sullivan and then beat club team Hamilton 4-1 thanks to goals by Wynalda, Harkes, Sullivan again and U20 player Neil Covone.

Then off to Palo Alto, California, for a match against the Soviet Union which we lost 3-1. The game was officiated by Vinnie Mauro, who was to be the US representative referee in Italy. I remember the Russian players coming home from a shopping spree as we stayed in the same hotel. They had TVs, toasters, mixers and all kinds of appliances they couldn't get back home, and lots of pairs of Levis, Lees and Wranglers.

In March, we had a nice 2-1 win over Finland in Tampa with Caligiuri and Murray scoring. Then it was off to Hungary, where we were defeated 2-0 in Budapest, before going to Berlin, to play East Germany, who beat us 3-2. The experience of playing in that country right after the collapse of communism and the Berlin wall was a highlight for the team. We still had to pass through "Checkpoint Charlie" and have our passports examined. We stood on the wall, and with the use of a hammer provided by Paul Krumpe, we each took home several chunks.

Stepping into East Germany was like stepping back in time 25 or more years. There was no color. Everything was dark, grey or black. The cars were old and the trolleys older. The crowd at the game was a meager 4,000, many of them were US servicemen who had come across the border to see their team play.

A week later we were home in Saint Louis for a nice 4-1 win over Iceland with goals by Wynalda (2), Trittschuh and Murray. We lost an April game to Colombia 1-0. The South American nation was becoming one of the better teams in the world with flamboyant goalkeeper Rene Higuita (injured and unavailable for this match), Carlos Valderrama and Leonel Alvarez.

As a final tune-up for the World Cup, the Federation set up three games in ten days, scheduled to replicate what we would go through in Italy (actually, four games in 16 days). We passed up an opportunity to play in the Marlboro Cup in Chicago to play on the East Coast against Malta, Poland, Ajax and Partizan Belgrade before leaving for Italy.

On May 5, 1990, we defeated Malta 1-0 in Rutgers Stadium, where the NCAA Championship Game was played the season before, to start the journey. Then a 3-1 victory over Poland in Hershey, PA, with Kasey Keller in goal. A crowd of 12,000 witnessed goals from Bruce Murray, a penalty kick from Vermes and a brilliant goal by Sullivan set up by Tab Ramos. Then, on to Washington for a 1-1 tie with Ajax at RFK Stadium.

Before heading up to New Haven for the final match on May 20th against Partizan Belgrade in the Yale Bowl, the Federation arranged a send-off party in the "Little Italy" section of New York City. We were advised to wear our mostly red adidas warm-up suits specially designed for the World Cup, with USA on the back and World Cup Italy 1990 on the front. There was entertainment and the team members got up to present their rap song recorded in Hollywood with the help of the LA Raiders star, Marcus Allen. The Master of Ceremony was New York sport celebrity and storyteller Dick Schaap, who seemed a little bit out of his element dealing with soccer people but worked hard keeping the party moving along. (Schaap died from complications during hip replacement surgery in 2001, aged 67.)

After the party we bussed up to New Haven for our game at the Yale Bowl, where 30,000 fans turned out for our final encounter before leaving for Italy, and they witnessed a 1-0-win courtesy of a goal by Peter Vermes.

After the game there was supposed to be meal arrangements for the team, but when we got there most of the food had already been eaten by the press and so-called VIPs. I knew that Barbara and I were going to host a post-game party for our friends who attended the match and that she would have more food than necessary. Without giving her a heads up, I directed our bus driver to our Branford home in the Indian Neck section called Linden Shores. All our guests were surprised and shocked to see the team bus pull up for dinner. And true to form, Barbara had prepared enough food for the entire team and there was no shortage of drinks either.

One of the nicest things the Federation did that year was organize an itinerary called "Italia '90 Family Style", a program for the players' wives, family and friends to attend the games and follow the team through their Italian adventure. The literature thanked the families of the players and staff "for being the wind beneath their wings and allowing them to dream...now live their dream with them".

The families and friends would meet at New York's JFK airport for a TWA flight to Rome on Friday, June 8th, then transfer by bus to Florence the following day. Our first game was to be on Sunday, June 10th vs Czechoslovakia. The organized tour ended after our last group game vs Austria with a departure back to the USA on Wednesday, June 20th. Were there no plans for us to get out of the group?

I reminded Barbara of the World Cup that we went to in 1982 in Spain. We were in the street outside of the stadium when the Argentine bus arrived and thousands of fans with flags, banners, blue and white jerseys were there to greet their team and their hero, Maradona. Barbara would need to rally the group of American supporters to be at the stadium entrance in Florence when we arrived for our first game.

The Italian Federation offered the US the possibility of using their national Coverciano training center as our home base and training site during our stay in Italy. This was the best of all worlds as the Italian team would train there as well. Then, as fate would have it, we were drawn into the same World Cup group as the hosts, along with Austria and Czechoslovakia. Now the Italians could not have us training at Coverciano as we would be their opponents in the second group game. Talk about the potential of "spy gate". And, as the draw took place on December 9, 1989, there was precious little time for the US to find another training site. Instead, the Italian Federation offered us its former Olympic training center located in Tirrenia, a small beachside town close to Pisa and the US Army Camp Darby. It left a lot to be desired.

Our Italian journey would start with a detour to Switzerland for a game against the Swiss and Liechtenstein. We were housed in the beautiful spa town of Bad Ragaz in the Swiss mountainside St. Gallen region. Our Hotel Bristol was first class in every regard and worthy of those guests who came for the natural spring as a health resort destination. And of course, the training field was flush, and the meals and other accommodation were fitting for the location.

We were tied 1-1 at half-time during our May 30th game against Liechtenstein but pulled out three second-half goals. Chris Henderson and Neil Covone both saw action in the match. And we scored first in our game against Switzerland before surrendering two goals in a 2-1 loss. Keller and Meola split the first game in goal, while Meola remained between the sticks through the match against Switzerland, which was played in front of 4,500 in St. Gallen on June 2nd.

Our bus ride from Switzerland, through the Swiss and Italian mountains and the Lake Como region, was as spectacular as anyone could imagine. And occasionally we could hear and see a security helicopter overhead. We also had State Department security with us on the bus.

To state that the players were disappointed with the accommodation in Tirrenia is an understatement. Most said that it reminded them of the sparse conditions in Colorado Springs, where the first sports festivals were held. Going from Bad Ragaz to Tirrenia was like going from Athens to Sparta, one commented. The conditions were Spartan to say the least. But at least we were close to Pisa, which we visited on June 4th, the day after our arrival in Italy. That helped break the tension and put everyone in a more relaxed mood.

Czechoslovakia's preparation for the World Cup was not impressive. There was reported dissension in their camp between the players who were already playing elsewhere in Europe, at high salaries, and those who were required to remain in the once communist country that typically would not release players to play elsewhere under the age of 29. Our thought process regarding getting out of the group was that it was possible to get a win against the Czechs, and thought it was unlikely we would get anything from our game against Italy in Rome, we could then hope for the best by maybe getting a tie against Austria, which had beaten Spain, Hungary and Holland in their tune-up games.

I remember lining up in the tunnel before coming out for that first match at Stadio Artemio Franchi in Florence. There was an underground entrance to the field where the teams came out from under the playing surface behind one of the goals. Strange!

The Czech players looked bigger and stronger for the most part. But we stayed with them for the first 20 minutes or so. Tomas Skuhravy scored after 24 minutes, and we were still in the game until the 30th minute penalty kick decision made it 2-0 at half-time. Then Eric Wynalda was foolishly sent off in the 52nd minute when he retaliated with a push right in front of the fourth official after having his foot stepped on. When the referee first came over, he seemed to be wanting to show the red card to John Harkes, but the fourth official intervened and pointed to Eric. Even though we were down to ten players, Paul Caligiuri scored one of the better goals of the tournament to bring us to 3-1. Skuhravy scored his second in the 78th minute. The referee, Kurt Roethlisberger of Switzerland, showed us no mercy as he added five minutes of additional time during which the Czechs scored their fifth goal and even awarded a second penalty, which Tony Meola saved when he outsmarted Michal Bilek, who tried to chip the goalkeeper with a shot now known as a "Panenka". Of the five goals scored, two came from corners where we were beaten to the ball in the air and a third was from a penalty. The Czechs had shown none of their corner kick expertise when they were shut out two months earlier by Egypt in a friendly.

Soccer America's headline for the article describing our first World Cup game in forty years read: "Truly a Baptism of Fire."

After the game, FIFA General Secretary Sepp Blatter characterized the red card given to Wynalda as "too harsh" but there was no way his one game suspension could be appealed.

Prior to our trip down to Rome for our second match, the Federation arranged a family/team get-together with a meal in Pisa. This was very well received by the players and certainly sparked conversations as to what should be done in future tournaments to ensure the team was not sequestered in isolation as we were in Tirrenia. Once in Rome, the bus stopped at every intersection as our police escort in front stopped to allow the machine-gun armed guards out to make sure there was safe passage. The citizens of Rome must have known our route as the streets were lined with spectators who we at first thought were waving at us. Then we figured that they were showing us both hands with fingers spread, signaling that we were going to get beat by ten in our encounter with the mighty Italians.

Strategically, coach Gansler started the taller John Doyle in the back and replaced the suspended Wynalda with the speedy Jimmy Banks. We also had a CONCACAF referee on the match, Edgardo Codesal of Mexico (who would also officiate the final) who treated us more fairly, despite awarding a penalty which was shot wide. In fact, the US had a golden scoring opportunity to cancel out Giuseppe Giannini's early opener when goalkeeper Walter Zenga could not handle Bruce Murray's curling free-kick from the left side and the rebound fell to Peter Vermes, whose shot got under Zenga before it was cleared from behind him.

Having expected a flood of goals after watching their team take an 11th minute lead, the Italian fans started booing and whistling their Azzurri without mercy during the second half, and the game ended without the hosts adding to their tally.

The *Soccer America* headlines read "US Rises from the Ashes", "US Salvages Pride in Loss to Italy" and "Doyle Stifles Azzurri Strikers". The Italian line-up included world-class players Baresi, Bergomi, Maldini, Berti, Carnevale, Donadoni and Vialli. After the game the Italian players came into our locker room to swap jerseys. Former world middleweight champion boxer Marvin Hagler also came by to complement the team on how well they played.

Without any points from the first two matches, there was only a glimmer of hope of getting out of the group. It would take more than the points from a win against Austria but also a series of other favorable results. Although very pleased with themselves for their performance against Italy, and rightfully so, there was a state of depression when we returned to Tirrenia. Regardless, the team was up for the game against Austria, with Bruce Murray scoring a late goal on an assist from Tab Ramos. Austria scored a goal on a counterattack when, after a US corner, their player, Gerhard Rodax, raced past two defenders who had the opportunity to make a tactical foul and take a yellow card for what today would be called "stopping a promising attack". The game was poorly officiated by Jamal Al-Sharif of Syria, who issued three yellows and a red to Austria and three yellows to the US. Despite the two points for the win, Austria did not get out of the group as one of the best third-place teams as other results made three points necessary.

Of course, there was obvious disappointment all around as the team broke up. Some stayed in Italy for a while and toured with their families. I had purchased tickets for many of the knockout games, all the way to the final. Barbara and I traveled down to Milan to see Cameroon beat Colombia in a game that witnessed Rene Higuita being stripped of the ball outside of the penalty area for a goal which ended, at least for a time, the whole concept of attacking goalkeepers.

I left a handful of tickets with my former LIU captain, Carlo Tramontozzi, who had also served as our interpreter, after stopping at his hometown near Monte Cassino. Even he could not use all of them and I have many unused tickets for Italia '90 in a jar along with coins and paper currency from the many foreign countries I visited because of soccer related travel.

No.1 Goalkeeper's Camp was going strong, and our next campsite was in Atlanta at Emory University, which was also the home of Turner Network Television (TNT). Tony Meola was working that camp, and the TV station invited us for a post-World Cup interview. Little did I think at the time that I would one day be a member of broadcast teams commenting on World Cups.

Back in the United States, behind the scenes and off the field, there was trouble brewing within the Federation. Even though we had qualified for Italia '90, there was dissatisfaction with the performance. The expectations fueled by the media were far beyond the capabilities of this team of college players, semi-pro and indoor players. Much of the criticism was put on coach Gansler who had made the courageous decision to go with the players who had "brought us to the dance". Once we qualified there was pressure to add players from outside the US soccer community, some playing in Europe that began to surface as having dual citizenship. When evaluating these, Gansler said to me, "They are not any better than Bruce Murray." Loyalty to his players was a strong Gansler quality. And it was loyalty to Gansler on the part of Werner Fricker, who resisted any conversations about replacing his coach. But the tension inside the Federation went far beyond the coaching. There was dissatisfaction among many of the delegates who were going to attend the August Annual General Meeting (AGM) in Orlando, FL, with Fricker's leadership style and with the slow-moving plans for 1994. And FIFA came into the situation after Fricker allegedly sold the TV rights in America for the World Cup without the global governing body's permission.

The Federation was divided into three components, the youth, amateur and professional divisions. And because the MISL was the only remaining pro league at the time of the election for Federation President that would take place at the AGM, Earl Foreman, representing his eight owners, controlled one-third of the voting power. The rifts between Fricker and Foreman over the years were widely known. Foreman was inclined to cast his votes for Alan Rothenberg, who emerged as a FIFA-supported candidate at the AGM.

Fricker knew that Walter Chyzowych, John Kowalski and I had personal relationships with Foreman that might help convince him to support Fricker's candidacy. John and I were flown to Orlando to meet with Foreman the day before the election. Despite a warm welcome and a healthy conversation, we left doubting that our mission was successful. The next day, Fricker lost the election.

On Wednesday, August 29th, the Federation received a fax from UEFA's coaching arm with an invitation to send a representative to the "XI Simosio of the Unione Europea Allenatori Calcio" to be held at Coverciano in October. The USA was to be assigned the presentation topic: "What did you learn from this World Cup experience?" Each presentation would be translated over headsets into English, German, French, Spanish and Italian, and the invitation was going out to each Federation that participated in the World Cup the previous summer as well as all the head coaches in Serie A.

The symposium dates of October 8-9 conflicted with a scheduled men's national training camp in Europe with games in Poland and Croatia. As Bob Gansler could not be in two places at the same time, I was selected to go to Coverciano. At least, I would finally get to see the place. And, yes, it was everything a national training center should be. It would have made our Italia '90 experience so much more pleasant.

I would be accompanied to Coverciano by Ed Tremble, the State Coaching Director for Connecticut. Ed and I arrived on Sunday, October 7th, and participated in the opening ceremony and dinner. I recognized many of the top head coaches present. I was nervous, to be sure, to be included amongst them.

The following day, the Head of the FIFA Technical Department, Walter Gagg, welcomed the group and Sandro Mazzola gave the first presentation on the Italian team's preparation and a general overview of the World Cup. After a coffee break, the 15-minute presentations by each coach present began. Here was the first day's schedule: Josef Venglos (Czechoslovakia): "Philosophy applied to football and the relationship between afternoon and evening performances," Ivica Osim (Yugoslavia): "Why fantasy and talent are not enough in order to obtain success at a World Cup," Josef Hickersberger (Austria): "Differences in performance levels prior to and during the World Cup — Why?"

There was a brief discussion period after each presentation and then a lunch break. The conference resumed with presentations by Scotland's Andy Roxburgh ("Variations in Performance Levels — Why?"), Uruguay's Oscar Tabarez ("Characteristics of Uruguayan football") and me. I was listed in the program as "Bob Gansler's Assistant." The day concluded with a presentation by Piero Volpi, the Italian team's orthopedic specialist reporting on injuries during the World Cup.

Day two included presentations by (Italian Federation Technical Director Azeglio Vicini ("The different tactical systems during the World Cup"), Argentina's Carlos Bilardo ("The concept of short play"), Brazil's Sebastiao Lazaroni ("The new system of play"), Romania's Emerich Jenei ("Problems involved in inserting a champion (Hagi) into the team") and, finally, Colombia's Francisco Maturana ("The importance and meaning of the goalkeeper who plays like a 'libero' too").

Having an opportunity to talk with Czechoslovakia coach Venglos about our 5-1 defeat at his hands was most enlightening. He openly talked about the dissension within the team and how he finally was able to pull the team together for a unified cause despite the players' differences.

I thought Bilardo's presentation was interesting as he explained that if he could not see at least five Argentine players on a TV screen at one time then they were too far apart.

But the absolute best (or worse) was Maturana. He drew the penalty area with the 10-yard radius restraining arc (the "D") at the top and explained that since many goalkeepers have female characteristics (Higuita's long hair and avant-garde uniforms) and that the penalty area represents the female body (use your imagination regarding the "D") and that, as part of women's liberation, the goalkeeper must leave the penalty area to escape the confines and restrictions of their body. And that is why Higuita played the way he did. There were lots of chuckles.

My presentation was very well received, I even got compliments from the translators who stated that my deliberate delivery and choice of words made it easy for them. I discussed how FIFA's "Fair Play" mantra is abused and how very little fair play existed in the game at the highest level, with a general lack of sporting behavior exemplified by the diving, efforts to get opponents carded or sent off (as USA's Eric Wynalda was after retaliating against Czechoslovakia's Lubomir Moracik in our opening World Cup match) and the tactical fouling to stop promising attacks. It was one of the lowest scoring World Cups ever. And then I discussed our own naivete going into the tournament, using the example of Austria's second goal against us when at least two of our defenders could have stopped the play with a tactical foul, taking a caution for the team.

At the coffee break that followed, at least half a dozen coaches came over to congratulate me. In Ed Tremble's summary report letter to the Federation, he wrote: "I would be remiss if I did not mention Joe's presentation. It took place in the afternoon of the first day. His content and delivery were outstanding. Objectively speaking, he delivered one of the top three presentations. His address received rave reviews from all in attendance. I was proud to be a representative of the USSF, the entire symposium but especially after Joe's speech."

Somehow, my remarks made it back to the States and were published in several soccer journals. And as such, they were totally misunderstood. It led to one parent-coach writing a letter to the editor of *Scholastic Coach* magazine, to the effect that "Joe Machnik is one of the most dangerous coaches in America because he is teaching our kids how to foul."

I flew to Warsaw directly from Coverciano to join the team for our game against Poland (a 3-2 win) and then seven days later in Zagreb to play against Croatia. When we landed in the capital, we were met by State Department officials who were urging us not to play. It seems that Croatia was not yet an official country and that they were using the game for political purposes stating that the United States, by playing them, recognized their autonomy from the rest of Yugoslavia.

While in my hotel room in Zagreb, I received a phone call from the front desk informing me that someone wanted to see me in the lobby. I went down to meet a well-dressed elderly gentleman who introduced himself as the father-in-law of Val Tuksa, my former player with the New York Arrows. He invited me to dinner in their apartment later that evening where I met the rest of his family. The dimly lit apartment, with a single light bulb hanging from the ceiling, reminded me of the places in New York City's East Village where my Ukrainian friends and teammates from junior soccer lived. Tuksa's wife, Dunja, had been a former professional figure skater in Yugoslavia before coming to the States. Her father explained the significance of the game we were about to play and how their county was rallying around a statue of Ban Jelacic, which had been put back into the square only the week before. It had been removed in 1946 by the communist regime.

We played the game — which we lost 2-1, with Troy Dyack scoring our consolation goal before a huge patriotic crowd. But you could almost smell that revolution was in the air and, shortly after we left, fighting between the Serbs and Croats broke out.

It didn't take long after Werner Fricker lost the election to Alan Rothenberg for changes to be made. Rothenberg replaced Keith Walker as General Secretary with Hank Steinbrecher, who had the unpleasant task of informing Bob Gansler that he would no longer be the coach, and that Walter Chyzowych would be dismissed as Technical Director.

Still, there were games to be played. Somehow, John Kowalski and I survived the purge and were appointed interim coaches for the national team, John as head coach and I as his assistant. We took over the team which had gone scoreless in five previous games for a game in Tampa against Olimpia of Paraguay, the South American club champion. A crowd of 11,256 witnessed goals by Marcelo Balboa and Peter Vermes, with a fine performance by newcomer Dante Washington in a 2-0 win, which headlined in the *St. Petersburg Times* as: "US Pulls Off Surprise."

Then it was off to Los Angeles to participate in the North American Nations Cup, which started with a 2-2 tie against Mexico in the Los Angeles Coliseum, with goals by Washington and Bruce Murray, followed by a 2-0 win over Canada with the same two scorers. The line-up for both games included Alexi Lalas, Fernando Clavijo, Troy Dyack and Chris Henderson.

The entire time we knew that our appointment as interim coaches was going to be short lived. Rumors of the Federation already being in contact with Serbian coach Velibor "Bora" Milutinovic to take over the team were everywhere. Bora had successfully gotten Costa Rica out of their group in Italy. And Alan Rothenberg was quoted as calling Bora "a miracle worker". In fact, when we left for our next assignment, two exhibition games in South Korea, Bora came on the trip with us as an "observer". We left on Easter Sunday and had difficulty putting together a squad. Many of the regular players were with their club teams and did not see the benefit of making this trip. We were fortunate to recruit Mike Lapper, Jeff Agoos, John Maessner, Mark Santel, Dominic Kinnear and Mark Dodd to join us. We were so short on players that Mark Dodd, a goalkeeper, had to come off the bench as a field player in our second match.

When we landed in South Korea, we were met at a training session by Dettmar Cramer, the coach who started it all for the United States

20 years earlier. He was in Korea to train their Olympic team. It seemed he knew more about our current coaching situation than we did, as he told me in confidence that the word was out, and that Bora had already hired his long-time goalkeeper coach Milutin Soskic to be his assistant leading up to the World Cup in 1994.

I already had gotten the feeling when, in a private conversation on the plane to South Korea between Kowalski, Bora and me, Bora said something to the effect that people at the Federation told him to watch out for me as I was "very dangerous".

We lost both exhibition games in South Korea, but not without putting up a good showing and having at least two unique experiences. On the second day there, before we traveled to Pohang for our first game, I was called to a meeting in the hotel with members of the South Korean Federation. We were traveling without a head of delegation (no one wanted to go) and that since I was the senior person on the trip, I would represent the team accordingly at the meeting. It was then explained that we were to receive $40,000 as a guarantee and that, since the banks were not open, they had to give me cash? I did not understand it, either. I was handed 400 brand-new, crisp $100 bills and was expected to carry the money for the next ten days in Korea, before delivering it to Colorado Springs, the Federation's headquarters at the time. No one had told me about a guarantee and this additional responsibility was completely unexpected and unwanted.

I divided up the money and gave $10,000 each to John Kowalski, John Polis, our PR person, and Dr. Bert Mandelbaum, keeping $10,000 with me. We each carried the money in our underwear, slept with it at night and when we met for breakfast each day, asked each other if the money was safe.

I collected the money again on the trip home and completed the required paperwork on the plane to declare that I was bringing more than $10,000 back into the States. There was no issue at either airport. When we landed in San Francisco, I attempted to give the full amount to Polis to bring to Colorado Springs because, after all, he was the only full-time Federation employee with us. Polis did not want to take the risk handling that amount of cash, so I brought the full amount home with me. The next day at the Branford Savings Bank I brought the money to be wired and transferred to the Federation offices with suspicious eyes all around. I guess this was a very unusual occurrence. The wire transfer completed, I thought nothing of it until the next tax season when Barbara and I were subjected to a week-long IRS audit with an agent visiting our home. It wasn't funny!

What was amusing was the experience we had in Seoul being confronted by a tailor at the hotel who insisted on making suits for both Kowalski and me. He would not take "no" for an answer so we each gave him $200 and allowed our measurements to be taken for two suits each, knowing full well that we might never see him again. I gave the tailor my business card which had my name as President of the No. 1 Goalkeeper's Camp. When we returned to Seoul nine days later, there was a call to our room. The person on the other end asked for "Mister Camp". I told him there was no one with that name at our end of the line and hung up. He called again! He had our suits! And they were quite nice. And inside the jacket was a label sewn in that had my name, "Mr. Camp!"

Then one day when crossing the street ahead of Barbara on our way to a Broadway show, she noticed that one pant leg was significantly several inches shorter than the other. That was the last time the suits were worn!

Milutin Soskic served the US as goalkeeper coach for three World Cups and three different head coaches: Bora, Steve Sampson and Bruce Arena. He helped improve the play of Tony Meola, Kasey Keller and Brad Friedel. He had played in more than 600 top-level games with Partizan and FC Cologne in the Bundesliga and over 50 matches with Yugoslavia. I certainly held no resentment for my replacement, even bringing him to work at No.1 Goalkeeper's Camp when he had the time.

Upon the 32nd anniversary of our win over Trinidad and Tobago that led to Italia '90 and the start of a new generation of American soccer, Fox Sports showed a video clip of Paul Caligiuri's goal and the celebration at our bench. Commentator Rob Stone recognized me jumping up in joy shortly after I had yelled *"Trouble!"* the moment the goal was scored and gave me a "shout out" on the air!

USA Men's National Five-a-Side team at first FIFA World Championship in 1988 with our third-place medals presented by FIFA President Joao Havelange (top row in tan jacket).

The FIFA Bronze Medal

FIFA Five-a Side poster advertising the games of "Zaalvoetbal" in January 1989.

As assistant coach with the national team, along with Captain Mike Windischmann and Rick Davis with Marlboro Cup promoter Clive Toye and their representative prior to one of the many Marlboro Cups we played in.

With goalkeeper Kasey Keller during a muddy workout prior to a 1990 friendly game before going to Italy for the World Cup.

My first assignment, assisting Lothar Osiander and Lenny Roitman with the national team in an important WC Qualifying round game played in St. Louis Soccer Park against Jamaica.

In March of 1990 the National Team played in East Germany. Here we are at the Berlin Wall. We all took home a piece.

The official Poster of the USA 1990 World Cup Team

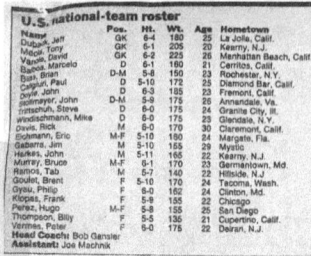

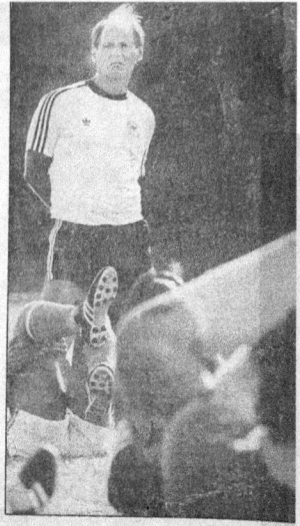

U.S. team facing test vs. Guatemala

Getting ready for the World Cup Qualifier played in New Britain CT.

The US Soccer Directory of Coaches-1988-89. I have not yet been named to assist the full national team.

Here is a poster commemorating our game in Croatia which was not yet recognized as an independent country.

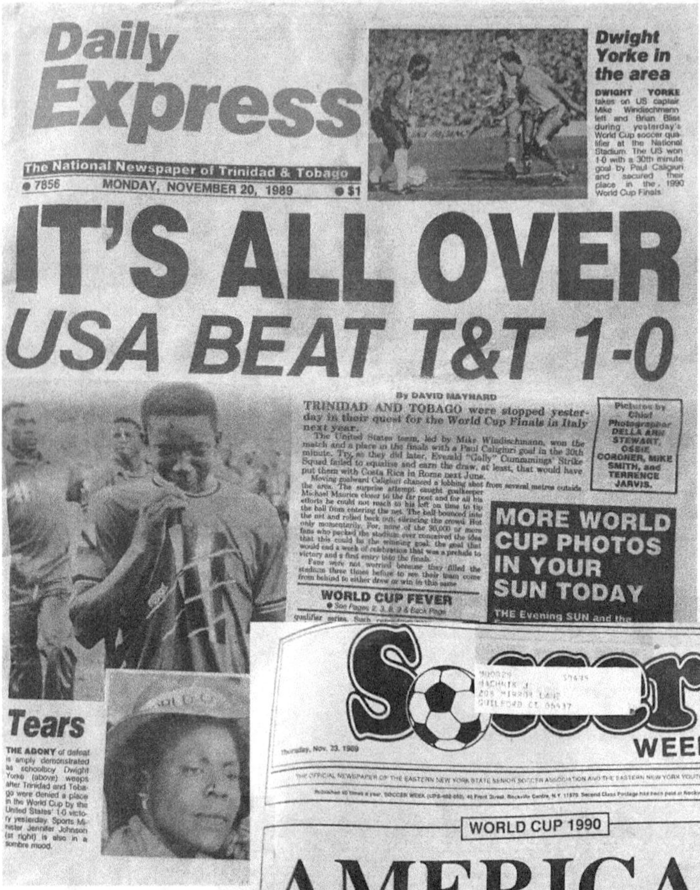

Daily Express

The National Newspaper of Trinidad & Tobago

● 7856 MONDAY, NOVEMBER 20, 1989 ● $1

Dwight Yorke in the area

DWIGHT YORKE takes on US captain Mike Windischmann left and Brian Bliss during yesterday's World Cup soccer qualifier at the National Stadium. The US won 1-0 with a 30th minute goal by Paul Caligiuri and secured their place in the 1990 World Cup Finals.

IT'S ALL OVER
USA BEAT T&T 1-0

By DAVID MAYNARD

TRINIDAD AND TOBAGO were stopped yesterday in their quest for the World Cup Finals in Italy next year.

The United States team, led by Mike Windischmann, won the match and a place in the finals with a Paul Caligiuri goal in the 30th minute. Try as they did later, Everald "Gally" Cummings' Strike Squad failed to equalise and earn the draw, at least, that would have put them with Costa Rica in Rome next June.

Moving goalward Caligiuri chanced a lobbing shot from several metres outside the area. The surprise attempt caught goalkeeper Michael Maurice closer to the far post and for all his efforts he could not reach to his left on time to tip the ball from entering the net. The ball bounced into the net and rolled back out, silencing the crowd. But only momentarily. For, none of the 30,000 or more fans who packed the stadium ever conceived the idea that this could be the winning goal, the goal that would end a week of celebration that was a prelude to victory and a first entry into the finals.

Fans were not worried because they filled the stadium three times before to see their team come from behind to either draw or win in this same qualifier series. Such …

Pictures by Chief Photographer DELLA ANN STEWART, OSSIE CORDNER, MIKE SMITH, and TERRENCE JARVIS.

WORLD CUP FEVER

● See Pages 2, 3, 8, 9 & Back Page

MORE WORLD CUP PHOTOS IN YOUR SUN TODAY

THE Evening SUN and the

Tears

THE AGONY of defeat is amply demonstrated as schoolboy Dwight Yorke (above) weeps after Trinidad and Tobago were denied a place in the World Cup by the United States' 1-0 victory yesterday. Sports Minister Jennifer Johnson (at right) is also in a sombre mood.

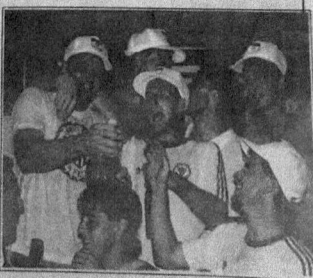

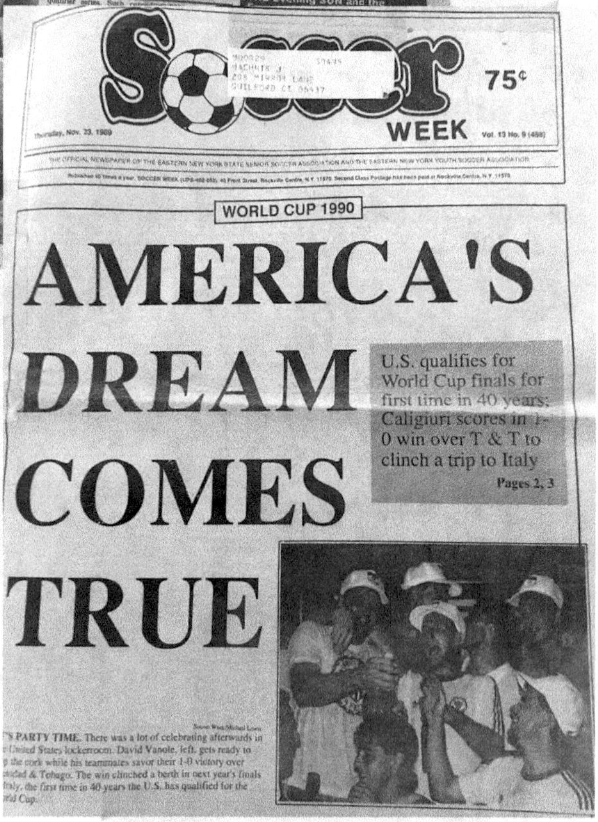

Soccer WEEK 75¢

Thursday, Nov. 23, 1989 Vol. 13 No. 9 (498)

THE OFFICIAL NEWSPAPER OF THE EASTERN NEW YORK STATE SENIOR SOCCER ASSOCIATION AND THE EASTERN NEW YORK YOUTH SOCCER ASSOCIATION

WORLD CUP 1990

AMERICA'S DREAM COMES TRUE

U.S. qualifies for World Cup finals for first time in 40 years; Caligiuri scores in 1-0 win over T & T to clinch a trip to Italy

Pages 2, 3

…'S PARTY TIME. There was a lot of celebrating afterwards in … United States lockerroom. David Vanole, left, gets ready to … the cork while his teammates savor their 1-0 victory over … Trinidad & Tobago. The win clinched a berth in next year's finals … Italy, the first time in 40 years the U.S. has qualified for the … World Cup.

T&T Newspaper the day after the US won the deciding game to qualify for its first World Cup in 40 years and play in Italia '90.

Machnik Analyzes Goalkeeper's Future in Soccer

At the request of Arthur Walls, chairman of the National Coaching Committee/Competitive, I was asked to contact various goalkeeping coaches across the country in an effort to submit articles on goalkeeping for *United States Coach*. Some 35 coaches have been contacted to date, and I am pleased to report that we have received articles from the likes of Dartmouth's and Scotland's Bobby Clark, Eckerd College's Jim DiNobile, Soccer Plus's Tony DiCicco, University of Virginia's Mark Newman, and Wright State University's Greg Andrulis. Additional articles are anticipated in the hope that an article on goalkeeping will appear in each of the next twelve issues (two years) of our USSF's coaching newsletter.

I would like to ask the readers' indulgence in starting off this series with my thoughts on goalkeeping's future in light of the current and projected changes in the laws of the game. Goalkeeping is changing and the new demands placed upon the goalkeeper require adjustments in training and conditioning.

The following article should be helpful to the reader in contemplating what will be necessary for the goalkeeper to successfully meet the challenges of a changed game.

On page 19 of the Dec. 24, 1973, issue of *Sports Illustrated* (some 18 years ago), then Senior Editor Robert W. Creamer reported on a fan's simple but radical idea for making soccer more popular in the United States: "Get rid of the goalie." Continuing, "...I can see the team on offense moving in to score with interesting passing plays and a defense organized to intercept. Some rule changes would be necessary, but it would be worth a trial....I'd like to see two teams play this way. It could reveal a very interesting new game."

Well, the rule changes have come fast and furious as FIFA scrambles to uncover through experimentation the secret to bringing excitement back into the game we all know and love. Excitement in the form of goals.

And, of course, once again it is the goalkeepers who must

Joe Machnik, former goalkeeping coach of the U.S. National Team, talks to goalkeeper David Vanole.

shoulder most of the 'blame,' the need for such rule changes either through their circumvention of existing rules to waste time or through the proper performance of athletic ability used to thwart goal-scoring chances.

Certainly goalkeeping changed since 1973. Goalies are generally more agile, fluid athletes taking up the position, some with relatively good soccer playing skill. One of the most controversial, Columbia's Rene Higuita, was selected by FIFA to the All-World Team to play against Germany Oct. 8.

It's interesting to note the direction FIFA seems to be taking in plotting a course for 1994 and beyond in regard to rule changes. Most change experiments leading to change are an attempt to minimize goalkeeper's prerogative to handle the ball.

The current issue of *F News* outlines the instructions to referees in interpreting some recent rule changes. "Possession of the ball" now includes intentional parrying of the ball and the goalkeeper being prohibited to handle the ball again after such action, in or

As Goalkeeper coach for our Italia '90 team, I was asked to write many articles. Here's one on the future of goalkeeping working with national team goalkeeper Dave Vanole.

NATIONS CUP NOTEBOOK
BY RIDGE MAHONEY

Goalkeeper coach Joe Machnik (left) now assists interim coach John Kowalski (right), who's undefeated in three games. (Photo by Milton Crossen)

Coaching announcement expected at March 27 press conference

■ The long-awaited appointment of **Bora Milutinovic** as head coach of the U.S. national team was seemingly assured when the USSF announced a press conference to be held in New York on March 27.

The USSF sent out notification of the press conference on March 22, six days after the U.S. beat Canada 2-0 in the North American Nations Cup played in Los Angeles.

■ The U.S. national team leaves April 1 for two matches in South Korea.

The U.S. will play the South Korean Olympic Team April 5 in Chunju and South Korea's national team in Kwangju April 7. Kwangju was one of the sites for the Olympic soccer competition, although the U.S. didn't play there. South Korea and U.S. played a scoreless tie in Pusan Oct. 20, 1988.

Nearly a year later, the U.S. played South Korea in the Marlboro Cup of Los Angeles. **John Harkes** scored the only U.S. goal in a 2-1 defeat.

After the World Cup, I assisted John Kowalski, interim coach for the National Team in a series of games.

Chapter 12

University of New Haven (Part 2)
"We Will Truly Miss You"

With the loss of the US Soccer Federation election at the AGM in August of 1990, Werner Fricker was no longer in charge of the 1994 World Cup, which he helped secure with his personal finances. Walter Chyzowych was also summarily dismissed.

As early as November of that same year, newly elected Federation President, Alan Rothenberg, with his appointment of Hank Steinbrecher as Executive Director of US Soccer, announced the formation of several new committees. Art Walls was appointed Co-Chair of the Coaching Committee alongside California-based Steve Sampson. The 12-person committee did not include the names of Bob Gansler, Walter Chyzowych or Joe Machnik. Ralph Perez's name could only be found as a member of the Minority Development Committee.

Obviously, I was disappointed not having a role in the planning of the upcoming World Cup, much less a role with any of the national teams moving forward.

I was interviewed for the position of General Manager of the United States Soccer Federation National Teams. I was told that my experience as an Athletic Director, manager of a referee program and former League Commissioner could provide an inside track to the position, which was designed, in essence, to manage their new national team coach Bora Milutinovic. The job went to Bill Nuttall, a former teammate of Steinbrecher's at Davis and Elkins. Regardless, I continued to pursue all options.

I received a phone call from Debbie Chin, now the Athletic Director at the University of New Haven. Chin had originally been passed over for the position, despite my strong recommendation when I left the university to work full-time for the MISL in the early '80s. She was now being charged to bring the university in full compliance with Title IX.

Chin asked if I would be willing to organize a women's soccer program at the university! I had certainly become more comfortable working with female players as the number of girls attending No.1 Soccer Camps was increasing by leaps and bounds, as was girls and womens soccer all over the country following USA's win over Norway in the 1991 Women's World Cup Final.

I accepted the challenge and began posting ads in the cafeteria and UNH student paper about the formation of a team in women's soccer to ascertain student body interest. I received a few replies and conducted some training sessions and practices, sometimes with as few as six participants.

On Tuesday, October 20, 1992 we had sufficient players to play a game, even if small-sided. I called my friend, Efrain "Chico" Chacurian, a former teammate at New Haven City and Hall of Famer who was coaching women at the University of Bridgeport. Would he agree to play us in a "friendly" match? The game was played at Seaside Park on a short field (50 yards) with six players per side, for two 30-minute halves. At half-time we were leading 5-0 after four first-half goals by Nikki Tierny, arguably our best player. The final score was 6-1. For the record, I want to note the players that played in that match: Melissa Flynn, Nikki Gugliotti, Jessica Hyde, Peggy Izaquirre, Susan Lane, Bernadette Phillip, Karyn Smith, Ann Straut and, of course, Nikki Tierney.

It was now time to go out and recruit the best high school players in the region because the following fall we would begin our first varsity full schedule.

It was extremely helpful that on January 31, 1993, the *New Haven Register* ran an article by Dan Nowak with a photo, headlined "UNH Women's Soccer a Machnik Challenge", and followed on September 3rd with Paul Marslano's article, "Machnik Excited about Prospects at UNH", which listed some of our recruited players: Isabel Demers, Jenn Kulmann and Melissa Jolly. The other team members of that very first varsity season were Marian Addotta, Kara Allen, Candice and Kim Carillo, Nikki Demorro, Mireille DeRose, Claudia Everone, Melissa Flynn, Ellen Hauan, Jennifer Leach, Tara Meagher, Angelique Murray, Jennifer Northway, Sheila Ringbloom and Nikki Tierney, who was now Nikki Devaney.

I was conducting a session of the Goalkeeper's Camp at the Loomis Chaffee School in late August before the start of that first season when we had a surprise visit from Professor Allen Sack of the University of New Haven. Allen and I had been friends back in the time of my first stint at UNH. He taught in the Department of Sociology and was somewhat responsible for my being asked to teach a course on the Sociology of Aging after achieving a Ph.D. with my dissertation focusing on recreation in planned retirement villages. Now, nearly 20 years later, Allen was being charged by the university to organize and develop a program major in the Management of Sports Industries within the School of Business. Being in the School of Business was a somewhat unique placement for the program as many, if not most, other sport management programs were administered by Physical Education, Health and/or Recreation Departments and some even by Athletic Departments. UNH always had a strong Business School and the emergence of so many sports-related businesses from gymnasiums to skating rinks, batting cages and bowling alleys, etc. made it a win/win situation for the university. Professor Sack asked if I would come on board in his new department as a practitioner in the field to balance his academic credentials and to get the department rolling. And of course, an association with the Athletic Department and its new women's soccer coach also made sense.

After meeting with M.L. McLaughlin, Dean of the School of Business, I was offered the position of Practitioner-in-Residence with a teaching load of six credits and the responsibility of organizing and administering the new department's internships program.

We opened the inaugural women's soccer season at UNH with a 1-2 home loss to Sacred Heart followed by another single-goal defeat to the College of Saint Rose. Our first win came in our third game, a 3-0 shutout over Bentley College. We finished that first season with a record of six wins and eight losses, scoring 31 goals while conceding 28.

There is a learning curve to be mastered in the coaching of women's soccer. Yes, it's the same game as the men's, with the same rules, but it is played differently. There is a much higher level of sporting behavior, less simulation, less diving, less attempting to get an opponent cautioned or sent off, less tactical fouling and less fouling overall. At least that is what I experienced, generally, in my first years as a women's college soccer coach. I also learned that playing the game seemed to, at times, outweigh the importance of winning. We were now a varsity college sport, and even if the university didn't expect us to win at first, I did!

I finally did get a role at the 1994 World Cup. I was hired by Jerry Langdon of the Gannett News Service to attend games at Giants Stadium (New Jersey) and sit with their reporters (John Ferro, Harry Frezza and Rich Libero) to answer any questions or otherwise advise as to what was happening on the field. I would alternate matches with Bob Reasso, who was a coach at Rutgers University at the time.

It so happened that the No.1 Soccer Camps session scheduled for the Los Angeles area coincided with the exact date of the World Cup final played in the Rose Bowl. Barbara and I took our tickets which were marked with a bold "WC" to the game on that very hot day. We, of course, thought that "WC" was meant to stand for the World Cup. When we tried to enter the stadium at the nearest gate, we were told that we had to take the elevator up to a certain level. When we located our seating area, we found that we did not have actual seats, because the "WC" on our tickets stood for "Wheelchair!"

My assistant coach for the women's team, Rick Schweizer, and I always made it a habit to stop at a local bagel shop to get a couple dozen bagels for the players on the weekends when the university cafeteria was either closed or had limited servings. Many of our players would come to training, therefore, without breakfast and looking forward to the still-warm bagels. I would also buy the local newspaper and catch up on a few things before entering the gymnasium, which housed our locker rooms.

On the inside cover of the Sports Page in the morning edition of the *New Haven Journal Courier's Notes Column* that Labor Day weekend was the small note that Wake Forest University and former US Men's Olympic and National Team coach, Walter Chyzowych, had died. Total shock! Walter passed away on the University's tennis court from a massive heart attack. He was only 57 years old.

I had tried to see Walter all summer long. I had learned that he had requested tickets for the World Cup from the Federation and was told that he had to buy them. He refused. I called him and offered to take him to a game or two. I had purchased extra tickets and didn't even go to all the matches for which I had tickets. He refused! A man of principle who, along with Werner Fricker, had done so much to grow and develop the game in the United States refused to purchase tickets to an event he helped in so many ways be awarded to the US. I asked him to join me at a game in Washington for which I had tickets, and he refused. As far as I know, he did not attend a single game.

After Walter's funeral mass in a Ukrainian Church in Philadelphia, there was a reception, a celebration of his life, held at a local restaurant. On short notice, so many of Walter's staff were in attendance. Bob Gansler, Lothar Osiander and so many others. Lenny Lucenko asked that I get up and speak about Walter's impact on my life and soccer in the US. I had no trouble finding the words in an emotional time. When the event was over, as people began to file out, John Kowalski and I found Werner Fricker at the bar. We stayed with Werner for at least another hour. The three of us were the last to leave.

The following January at the NSCAA (now United Soccer Coaches) Convention, there was a meeting of sorts to memorialize Walter and pay homage to the many roles he had in that organization, and his multifarious contributions for the good of the game. Walter's brothers, Gene and Ihor, both addressed the several hundred coaches who attended. But when Walter's wife, Olga, spoke there was not a dry eye to be found. She stated that Walter had not left but that he was only on an extended road trip, and he would always be with us. The meeting concluded with an announcement about the formation of a fund to honor Walter's life and legacy, and that its annual meeting would be held in conjunction with the Convention. It was decided that the fund would each year honor an individual's lifetime achievement with an award in Walter's name.

The first recipient of the Walt Chyzowych Fund Lifetime Achievement Award was Jerry Yeagley, a longtime successful coach at Indiana University. University of North Carolina and US women's national team coach Anson Dorrance received the second. When Lothar Osiander received the award in 2006, Dettmar Cramer himself was in attendance. The former national team coach had been invited to speak at the Convention, and I attended his presentation. Fewer than 50 people were in attendance in a room set up for more than 200. It should have been packed!

Barbara and I were asked to take over the management of the Walt Chyzowych Fund, which we have done as a labor of love with the help of Walt's nephew, Gene Chyzowych Jr., former Wake Forest soccer captain Thomas Finlay, Ronnie Gold, a former NASL staff member for the Washington Diplomats and the two Ralphs, Ralph Lundy and Ralph Polson. Ronnie Gold established and managed the fund's website, www.waltslegacy.com

and performs all the duties and responsibilities of organizing and managing our annual event. Each year Ralph Polson donates the Belfast Chrystal "trophy" emblematic of Lifetime Achievement and Lundy and I act as co-emcees keeping the event loose and fun as Chyzowych would have preferred. In 2012, the Walt Chyzowych Fund partnered with the United Soccer Coaches Foundation, which established the Walt Fund with a mission statement to honor Walt's life and legacy and assist aspiring young coaches through a series of scholarships and grants. In 2020, the fund honored both US women's national team coach Jill Ellis and legendary former NASL player, Howard University and Trinidad and Tobago coach Lincoln Phillips at the same function, which drew more than 500 attendees.

In 2017, the Walt Chyzowych Fund began to recognize distinguished playing careers as well as lifetime achievers. Landon Donovan was the first recipient, followed by the 1989 and 1992 Five-a-Side teams, then Michelle Akers, Ricky Davis and, in 2023, the players of the Philadelphia Atoms celebrating the 50th anniversary of their NASL Championship season.

In 2025, the Chyzowych Fund recognized the members of the 1980 US Men's Olympic Soccer team which qualified for Russia but were denied participation due to the US boycott of those games, and as the event was in Chicago, the legendary Chicago based player and coach, Willy Roy, was recognized for his lifetime achievements in the sport. There were fifteen members of the '80 Olympic team in attendance thanks mostly to the work of the team's captain Perry Van Der Beck.

It was at this meeting that we first showed a video clip of sportscaster Steven A. Smith talking with Howard Stern on his show about the contribution Walter made to Smith's career while he was a young reporter in Winston-Salem, NC and Walter was coaching at Wake Forest. Smith also mentions Walter in his book entitled: "Straight Shooter".

And this was also the meeting where the three coaches of the 1990 World Cup (Italia '90) team were together in the same room after so many years. Head Coach Bob Gansler and his assistants Ralph Perez and Joe Machnik received a standing ovation from the appreciative crowd which recognized that without the USA's participation in Italia '90, FIFA would have/could have withdrawn the 1994 World Cup from the United States and that would mean no MLS. Without MLS where would soccer in America be at this time?

The annual Walt Chyzowych Fund Award Ceremony and Reception is considered by many as one of the highlights of the Convention.

With a few more players, our second University of New Haven women's soccer season was a little better, finishing with an 8-9 record after a 4-0 start, all wins on the road. We even appeared in the NCAA DII Top 20 national rankings for a week or two. New Haven was now in the New England Collegiate Conference (NECC) which meant tough games against New Hampshire College, nationally ranked Franklin Pierce, Keene State and Le Moyne. We finished 2-4 in the conference in fifth place overall. Franklin Pierce was the class of the conference and won five NCAA DII National Championships between 1994 and 1999. So, losing to Pierce by a respectable 0-2 score in 1994 seemed like a reasonably positive result. We added No.1 Camps' standout staff member, Mike Potier, to the coaching staff, and he stayed with us in Branford until the completion of the season. Later, Clark Brisson helped along with his University of South Carolina teammate, Mike Gosselin. The players received a lot of individualized instruction during those times from some excellent former players.

I had always organized my teams with the idea that defense wins championships. Getting all players back on defensive corner kicks and building strong walls to defend against dangerous restarts was just the beginning. Often, there were individual player marking assignments designed to take the opposing best player off their game. Getting numbers back in a hurry was the foundation and launching counterattacks after luring opponents into a comfort zone had worked with the men's teams at LIU and during my first stint coaching men at New Haven. Two NCAA National Championship Game appearances in 1966 and 1976 at two different institutions would seem to validate the approach. The results were important. I will admit that giving up possession for long periods of time, chasing the ball and defending for much of the game, was not always the most fun to play or to watch.

During the summer of 1995, the World Special Olympics were hosted in New Haven at Yale University. Nearly 7,000 athletes participated in 21 sports. I was offered the position as Director of Soccer Officials for the tournament by long-time friend Stanley Startzell who was a player in the NASL first with the Cosmos and later Philadelphia Atoms when they won the league championship.

During the first organizational meeting I conducted for the Referees, a gentleman walked in the door unannounced. No one had told me that he would be attending the games as an official. Abraham Klein was one of the most famous soccer referees of his day. I watched him in person at the 1982 World Cup in Spain when he was in the middle for Brazil v Italy, a game during which Paolo Rossi scored a hat trick. And he was a linesman on the Final! Klein traveled all the way from Isreal to volunteer at the games. I was sure happy that I recognized him and immediately introduced him as a guest of honor at the meeting. A gentleman, indeed!

The 1995 season was our turnaround campaign. Although we lost our first game to Merrimack (0-1), we lost only two other matches while tying two others and had a record of 12-3-2 going into our final match, which was away to Franklin Pierce. I wanted the players to have the opportunity to decide if they could compete with Pierce in a more open game. Have some fun! They enthusiastically responded positively to the opportunity. We lost the game 9-0.

It was difficult to explain the heavy defeat back at the university. Debbie Chin was not happy. Neither were the hundreds of student and faculty supporters who had begun to follow us, including President Larry DeNardis and his wife, Mary Lou. We were going into that game having scored 54 goals with only 20 against. There were no reasonable explanations.

Regardless, I received a beautiful letter from DeNardis, dated November 29, 1995, congratulating the team. "The development of a nationally ranked team in three short years is a very significant achievement. I look forward to the next season and the team's future accomplishments." he wrote.

In the meantime, interest in the Management of Sports Industries program grew by leaps and bounds. So much so that I had been offered and accepted the position of Associate Professor and was now full-time.

When Allen Sack learned I had been in Zagreb, Croatia just prior to the revolution, he asked that I speak in Professor Zeljan Suster's Economics class. Suster would go on to write a *Historical Dictionary of the Federal Republic of Yugoslavia* (1999). My presentation, which included posters that I had brought back from Croatia, resulted in Sack and Shuster presenting a paper entitled, *Soccer and Croatian Nationalism – A Prelude to War*. Sack and Suster cited "Personal Communication," with me and Bob Gansler as resource material in their paper.

As a full-time faculty member, I served on several faculty committees. The most rewarding was when Debbie Chin appointed me and head football coach, Tony Sporano, to serve on the LGBTQ Task Force. Sporano was born in West Haven, CT, was a four-year letterman at UNH and after coaching at his Alma Mater, went on to an illustrious NFL coaching career, missing out by one vote on the Associated Press NFL "Coach of the Year" award in 2009.

Prior to the start of the 1996 regular season, we had arranged a Labor Day scrimmage with Wesleyan University in Middletown, CT. I volunteered to secure the officials. So, on the way up to the game, our two vans stopped in front of Lou Labbadia's house in Hamden, and he rode up with us to the game. After the match, we hosted a reception for the parents of our players at which Labbadia was invited, of course.

During that reception, our phone rang and Lou, being the closest, picked up the receiver to answer. "Joe, it's Sunil Gulati on the phone," he said. Gulati was now Deputy Commissioner of Major League Soccer (MLS) which was nearing the end of its first season. Gulati was calling from Mexico inquiring if I had interest in working to solve some of their officiating issues.

Despite having MLS constantly on my mind, 1996 was a banner year for the UNH women's soccer team. We finished the season with a record of 13-5-1 with an invitation to the ECAC post-season tournament.

We lost to Keene State for the second time that season in the ECAC tournament and didn't beat Franklin Pierce either. We did win against our former rival, Southern Connecticut, in their inaugural women's soccer season. I always believed the realization that I would be moving on to MLS and that the current season would be my last as their coach, inhibited me from doing the best that I could for this team and group of players. "Déjà vu all over again!"

I left the men's team to join MISL and now planned on leaving the women's team to join MLS.

I had recruited some significant players that year, none more important than Christine Huber, who attended UNH on a full scholarship to play both soccer and basketball. Christine was a High School All-American out of Maine and perhaps, coming from Maine, inhibited other schools from taking her soccer prowess seriously. I thought she could have been a legitimate DI player.

My four-year women's soccer coaching record finished at 39-26-3. When added to the men's soccer coaching record, the overall record at

UNH was 149-81-24. Far too many losses.

Still feeling bad about that last year, the least I can do at this time is provide a "thank you" by acknowledging the players' contributions both individually and as a team. Mireille DeRose was a terrific captain who provided leadership on and off the field. Our other players not mentioned previously include Marian Addotta, Nikki Demorro, Jennifer Leach, Beth Bailey, Maria Buonomo, Shannon Tosney, Anna Maria Uyar, Dawn Alderman, Marissa DiMatteo, Kristine Ganias, Candice Morgan, Michelle Orr, Jeanne O'Toole, Jessica Crandall, Christina Nuzzo, Michelle Hicks, Jessica Kmieczak, Paula Uscilla, Alycia Kowal, Sarah Cornelius, Stacy Wheller and Christel Thompson.

First-year recruit Kim Carillo left the team to concentrate on her studies in the Department of Criminal Justice. Sometime after the 9/11 attacks on the World Trade Center, I received a phone call from UNH's Alumni Office asking permission to give my contact information to a former student. It was Kim Carillo who, as a police officer working in New York City on the day of the attack on the Twin Towers, wanted to say "thank you" for the time she had spent on the team as it helped her understand the meaning of teamwork and coping with the stress of losing fallen officers. It was one of the best expressions of appreciation I had ever received.

Leaving UNH to accept the position of Vice President of Game Operations at Major League Soccer left a void in the Sports Management Department, which was solved, at least temporarily, by my being named Executive-in-Residence with a part-time teaching load. I held that university position for two more years before moving to South Carolina.

On December 16, 1998, I received a thoughtful and much appreciated letter from James W. Uebelacker, Vice President for Academic Affairs and Provost at the university. Uebelacker wrote: "Over the term of your stints here you have served students — both athletes and non-athletes alike — in a professional, compassionate and friendly manner. You were especially helpful on the academic side in the successful implementation of our Management of Sports Industries program. I'm sure that I join with your other colleagues here in stating that we will truly miss you."

My return to the University after nearly a decade!

In a short time we had developed very competitive women's soccer teams at the University of New Haven.

Chapter 13

Major League Soccer (MLS)
"Please Help Us"

It was Labor Day 1996. Major League Soccer (MLS) was in its first season of competition. The League office had moved from California to New York City on 42nd Street near Lexington Avenue, just across from Grand Central Station.

I had previously written to Commissioner Doug Logan (formerly of the Rockford Metro Center and AISA) about possible employment and was told to sit tight!

I was most pleased to receive Sunil Gulati's phone call that day! Sunil suggested that I contact MLS Executive Vice President of Operations, Bill Sage, for an interview. If employed, I would be working in Sage's department. I had never met him but was present at a talk he delivered to interested coaches at the NSCAA Convention a year before MLS got off the ground.

Several weeks later, Sage agreed to meet with me in the lobby of his hotel next to Giants Stadium, where the New York MetroStars would be playing later that evening. We would then attend the game together. It was the first game of the MLS playoffs, a best-of-three series against DC United, played on September 24th.

We sat in the press box area, and I got the feeling that many people were looking at me, even staring with seeming insight that I might be a potential hire.

The game was most interesting in that it finished 2-2 and the tie had to be broken via the MLS Shootout. Players would line up at a line 35 yards from the goal and upon a signal from an official via the dropping of a raised flag, have five seconds to score in a one v one breakaway of sorts against the opposing goalkeeper. Prior to the shootout, each coach had to give a list of their 11 shooters to the referee in exact shooting order.

FIFA had rid itself of that requirement prior to their tiebreaker known as "kicks from the mark" at the time; now known as "penalties". The new requirement stated that all eligible shooters (a player had to be on the field at the end of the game) report to the center circle to shoot in any order. Of course, a player could not take a second attempt before all the players on his team had taken their first.

Evidently, the MetroStars coaching staff had filled out their shootout card before noticing that defender Peter Vermes had injured himself just prior to the final whistle. Vermes was scheduled to shoot in an early round, but NY now claimed that he was unable. Chaos broke out as the MetroStars tried to change their shooting order. After much confusion and delay, referee Esse Baharmast allowed Vermes's name to appear last on the list in shooting position number 11. DC United suggested that they would protest!

As luck would have it, the shootout lasted 11 rounds. Tab Ramos missed the MetroStars' third attempt but then Raul Diaz Arce missed DC United's fourth. Then Damian Silvera and John Harkes missed on the fifth tries before Giovanni Savarese and Mario Gori both scored. Then three consecutive misses by both teams (Jeff Zaun, Tony Meola and Rob Johnson for NY and Richie Williams, Clint Peay and Eddie Pope for DC) led to the 11th round which pitted Vermes against DC United goalkeeper Jeff Causey. Vermes was receiving treatment throughout the entire shootout and managed to score his attempt after all, while the DC goalkeeper missed his! The game was won by the MetroStars 6-5 in the shootout. DC United won the series two games to one, with 1-0 and 2-1 scores at RFK Stadium in DC.

After the match, Sage and I were walking to his vehicle in the tunnel where the locker rooms were located. By chance, Esse Baharmast came out of the referee's locker room and upon seeing us said loud enough that Bill Sage could hear: "Please help us!" That sealed the deal. I knew I was going to be offered the job.

In an MLS document entitled *Referee Program-Preliminary Planning for 1997*, 17 bullet points outlined goals and objectives. The first was: "Secure services of person to manage game operations including all aspects of MLS Referee Program: including program development, budget, USSF and USISL program integration and the identification, training, assignment, and assessment of MLS game officials. Candidates shall have previous officiating, coaching and league administrative background."

The second bullet point reads: "Announce the appointment of Joseph A. Machnik, Ph.D. as MLS Vice-President of Game Operations with above duties and responsibilities."

The remaining bullet points included such items as reviewing at least two video tapes of each referee that worked in the 1996 season, writing a Referee Handbook, meeting with Gordon Hill, former NASL referee now in charge of officials in the USISL (second division) to set up a development league affiliation for officials; getting feedback from coaches and general managers on referee performance, setting up an evaluation system for the coaches post-game and meeting with USSF officiating staff in Chicago, where the USSF was now located.

The bullet points also included meeting with all ten MLS teams at their pre-season training sites regarding changes in the referee program, the expectations, rules and regulations and also the disciplinary process under my purview, paring down the list of officials to "a maximum 20 referees and 75 assistant referees", making sure each referee received a video tape of their game and providing each referee with a fax machine to promptly receive assignments and, lastly, participation in at least three referee training camps (one pre-season, one at the MLS Combine and one during the All-Star break).

Pairing down the officials list to 20 referees, 75 assistant referees and 30 fourth officials would mean the elimination of 77 officials from the total of 202 which worked that first MLS season.

Time was of the essence. The first MLS Cup Final was to be played just 10 days after I was announced. Commissioner Doug Logan smartly invited and paid for the top 20 referees based on the number of games each officiated in 1996 to come to the Final as guests of MLS and they were treated as VIPs.

I was also introduced to the media at the press conference involving both teams prior to the Cup match. DC United's coach Bruce Arena publicly acknowledged a "good move" by the League with my hiring. LA Galaxy goalkeeper Jorge Campos predicted a Galaxy victory because "they had the most stars".

The four officials assigned to work the final game were referee Esse Baharmast, assistant referees Paul Tamberino and Steve Olson, and fourth official Brian Hall.

I met with the 20 invited referees in attendance on the morning of the MLS Cup Final. They expressed their gratitude for being invited to the game and all the festivities. They then explained their disappointment with the game fee (referees were getting $185 per game, lower than what some college conferences were paying) and with their travel schedules. It was common for a referee from the West Coast to travel the day of the game across several time zones for instance. And then when I began to address the group as MLS referees, one of the senior officials stood up and corrected me: "We are not MLS referees, we are FIFA referees." I knew I had a problem.

One of the bullet points in the previously referenced document illustrated the need to change the culture whereby the referees took pride in working for the League and considered themselves part of the teamwork to make each game safe for the players and attractive for the spectators. Many of them had never dealt with games being broadcast on TV and all the protocol including dealing with start times etc. Most MLS matches had only a two-hour window for TV, which was one of the reasons that the game time was kept on a stadium clock and not by the referee. There could be no added time. And, for the referees, the shootout was horrible. A referee could have a strong 90-minute game and then the shootout became controversial due to penalty kick decisions that had to be made, or whether an attempt was made within five seconds.

Back at the MLS office, I asked why the game fees for the referees were so low? Bill Sage then informed me that the USSF suggested the fees. MLS was prepared to pay much more but was told it wasn't necessary.

The following week, Doug Logan, Bill Sage and I traveled to Soccer House in Chicago to discuss the future of officiating. We were greeted by Hank Steinbrecher, who introduced us to Julie Ilacqua, who Alan Rothenberg suggested overseeing the referee program as Chair of the Referee Committee. Ilacqua informed us that the USSF was prepared to hire Herb Silva as Director of Assessment and Al Kleinaitis as Director of Instruction, both working under department head Vinny Mauro (already in place), who would still have authority over assignments etc. During the meeting, I acted as if I had no previous relationship with Herb Silva. Herb and I had worked well together in the indoor leagues.

As soon as I got back to Connecticut, I called Herb from a pay phone in the cafeteria at UNH, where I was proctoring the study hall for the athletes. I told Herb of his impending appointment and strongly suggested that he lobby for being named Director of Assignment as I knew we could work together on this important element of getting the right official on the right game and making sure officials were not over-exposed in any market. Silva was successful in getting that done but it would lead to conflict with Mauro in the months to come.

The first organized pre-season referee clinic for the 1997 season would be held in Ft. Lauderdale on the last weekend in January. I knew I had to make a move to befriend the referees from the get-go. So, I immediately negotiated their pay raise with Commissioner Logan and Bill Sage. The senior referees (those with a FIFA international badge) would get $400 per game while all others $350. Senior assistant referees (bench side) would receive $ 200, junior assistants $150 and a fourth official $100. Only the referee and senior assistant would travel during which airfare, hotel and $41 per diem (which equaled the player's per diem) would be paid. For those not traveling, auto mileage at the going IRS rate and tolls would be reimbursed. For some, these fees represented greater than a 100% increase over the previous year.

I invited recently retired National Hockey League (NHL) referee Andy Van Hellemond to be guest speaker. After all, there were correlations between officiating hockey and soccer. Especially player management. Then Esse Baharmast gave a presentation on how he managed the 1996 MLS Cup final, which was a masterclass in player and game management. And, as a gesture, I gave out 50 MLS baseball-type hats with the hope that officials would wear a "MLS hat" during matches. Of course, this was just a symbolic suggestion, referees were not permitted to wear hats according to the Federation.

As part of the pre-season clinic, referees were required to pass a fitness test, which at the time consisted primarily of a "Cooper Test" and a series of shuttle runs. As officiating soccer was still a labor of love and for some an expensive hobby, the fitness test represented a serious challenge. The Cooper Test specifically required the completion of eight laps around a quarter-mile track within 12 minutes. At one such test I witnessed a referee of the highest-level step off to the inside of the track for a full lap and then join the group next time around. He then purported to have successfully completed the test. The Federation had begun videotaping the run and when I told them what I had witnessed, they at first would not believe me. But when they saw the tape at the finish line, they could only count seven laps for that official.

One of the toughest parts of the job initially was convincing Federation staff of the poor quality of some of the officials who had achieved the FIFA badge. The badge gave them a sense of entitlement which meant they had to be assigned. When I brought Herb Silva to a pre-season game with a FIFA referee in charge to show him in real time what I had seen on multiple video tapes of 1996 games, he was shocked, unpleasantly surprised to state the least. He had the most difficult task of informing an individual with the highest officiating credentials that he did not present sufficient talent to officiate in MLS. Herb was a US Marine Vietnam combat veteran who recognized authority and the chain of command, and removing a high-ranking official was tantamount to a court marshal. It did not sit well with him.

There was conflict even with the smallest issues. When a New England Revolution player suggested that officials wear colored socks different from the Rev's navy blue, the Federation resisted. This even though the referees in Italy were already wearing yellow socks when one of the teams wore black or navy socks. And when MLS purchased jackets emblazoned with a large MLS logo on the back for the fourth officials to wear, US Soccer protested with that same argument. "We are not MLS referees, we are FIFA (US Soccer) referees."

There always seemed to be a conflict of sorts with the Federation on MLS initiatives. To be fair, the Federation had FIFA concerns over the perception that once again, a US professional soccer league was not going to play by the established international rules. This goes way back to the NASL days where their use of a 35-yard offside line and post-game shootout to break regular season ties was highly criticized by FIFA as an attempt to "Americanize" the game. So, when MLS started with a shootout of its own and having the official time kept on the stadium scoreboard by a timekeeper not the referee, FIFA once again was critical of the concepts and the Federation felt threatened.

I was happy to lead the push toward MLS playing by international rules even though, for the 1998 season, I foolishly purchased ten gigantic shootout clocks which were rolled out to the side of the goal at which the shootout was to take place. The clocks cost $10,000 each and lasted only two seasons until the shootout was abandoned. Some of the clubs sponsored fundraisers whereby, for a donation, an incoming fan could take a swing at the clock with a sledgehammer.

Officiating was such an afterthought in the formation of the League that at the very first MLS Combine officials were not originally contacted to work on any of the games. It was reported that Sunil Gulati was pressed into service as a referee until enough certified officials could be recruited.

At one mid-season referee meeting during the All-Star Game break, I presented a breakdown of the referees into three categories. Type A were referees who officiated by the book, applying strict interpretation of the laws. And I listed the names of those referees on a whiteboard. Then there was Type C who bent the book as much as possible and were considered players' referees. And I listed those names. And of course, there was a Type B referee who was somewhere in between. For the most part the referees agreed with their placement. The presentation point being why we couldn't get all on the same page and consistently have referees who were neither Type A nor C but somewhere in between. Type B was a work in progress! But when MLS players and coaches were asked; Alex Prus, a former player and coach was the "Best Ref!"

In the second year of employment, I suggested that MLS help finance what the Federation was calling its National Referee Camp (NRC), a pre-season referee meeting outside of MLS at which more than 100 US national-level referees attended, many of whom did not work in MLS. The Federation agreed to our $100,000 contribution to hold the NRC in conjunction with the MLS pre-season tournament, which was being held in Orlando at the Disney Wide World of Sport. In this way, MLS would have input to the NRC program and the referees could simultaneously get multiple pre-season games to officiate and evaluate. It was important that the USSF assessors who would be working on MLS games be present as well.

The meeting room was packed with more than 200 soccer personnel, officials, assessors and administrators. In the back of the room, two booths were set up for the two companies that specialized in officiating uniforms and equipment: Official Sports and Law Five. I was scheduled to speak after a referee administrator from Scotland, whose presentation was filled with stories and jokes. Hardly anyone was paying attention, and sales were booming at the two booths at the back of the room. I knew I had to do something different to gain attention at the start of my presentation. So, I went to the back of the room and asked if both vendors could close their booths when I was introduced.

I had prepared 12 video clips of the worst challenges in MLS during the previous season, all of which deserved red cards. But none of the egregious plays resulted in a sending off and a few were called simple careless fouls, not even earning a yellow card.

So, I stood in the middle of the aisle between the two sections of seats and said in a very soft tone and low voice: "I have a stone in my shoe." A few seconds later, I repeated the phrase. And then a third time. Each time, more of the participants quieted down and on the fourth time there was complete silence.

The quote came from the 1990 movie *The Godfather Part III* when Eli Wallach's character Don Altobello whispers into the ear of an assassin that a stone could be removed from Altobello's shoe by the extermination of Michael Corleone. The stone that I needed to have removed was the unwillingness of the referees to apply the Laws of the Game correctly regarding excessive force and challenges which endanger the safety of the opponent. The message was received, finally.

Public criticism of the officiating was rampant in the early years of MLS, as was open and visual dissent directed to the officials on the field and especially to the fourth official who was stationed between the benches. At one NRC, I suggested that national team star Landon Donovan address the referees from a player perspective on several issues. When Donovan was asked why there was such blatant dissent directed to the officials he answered, "Because you let us!"

Dealing with dissent is a difficult issue for officials as they are "damned if they do and damned if they don't". The sanction for dissent is a yellow card but no one wants to see a player being sent off for his second caution or be suspended for his next game due to yellow card accumulation, the card for dissent being the determinative. There have been several different approaches to dealing with the issue but the most successful recently has been the "only the captain can talk to the referee" approach which was used in the 2024 European Championship, the Paris Olympics and the 2024-25 Bundesliga season.

As was done in the NASL years earlier, it was thought that bringing established referees from foreign countries to work in MLS would be a quick fix to some of the officiating issues. Herb Silva and the Federation would only agree to this if an exchange program could be set up where US referees would get to work at the equivalent level in the foreign country from which a referee would agree to work and for the same number of games. US Soccer would be in contact with other federations to secure such agreements. As a result, the following officials came to work in MLS: Spain's Jose Maria Garcia-Aranda, Japan's Toru Kamikawa, UAE's Ali Bujsaim, China's Baojie Sun, Brett Hugo from Australia, Kim Tae-Young from South Korea, Kazuhiko Matsumura from Hong Kong, Juan Paniagua of Bolivia and Stuart Dougal of Scotland. While several had World Cup experience and added to the overall quality of the game in MLS, others struggled with dissent and player management skills.

I was aided in the MLS office over the years by Melissa Bennett (now Mason), Cindy Solomon and later Nicole Ward. Each made it very clear that they were not my secretary, but rather my assistant. I had always made it a habit of handwriting memos on legal-sized yellow pads, sometimes scotch taping pages together. As this was not acceptable at MLS, I quickly learned how to use a computer.

But when Herb Silva told me that one day I would be traveling with a computer I told him, "No Way!" Herb had already learned how to hook his up to a phone line in a hotel to be able to access the internet. I had just learned how to turn mine on!

Commissioner Logan also organized a strategic planning meeting in June 1997 at a retreat on Long Island. The first item on the agenda was my report on the referee program which included the reduction of numbers, the international exchange program, our Thursday night conference calls with the officials and the relationship with the Federation. In the Meeting Plan Book was a copy of my April 16, 1997 letter to Vincent Mauro, referencing FIFA head Sepp Blatter's approval of the concept of full-time referees. As early as year two of MLS, we were putting pressure on the Federation to professionalize the referee program by providing full-time jobs to their top officials.

One of my Sport Management students, Jef Thiffault, had applied for an internship at MLS prior to my being hired. When I went to bat for him as Vice-President of Game Operations, he quickly got the job. Jef became my right-hand person at MLS full-time.

With the success of the US women's national team, the next step for US Soccer was to start a women's professional league. Two years before its launch, we were asked by the Federation to help prepare several female referees for the pro game by assigning them in MLS. So, during the 1998 season, Nancy Lay and Sandra Hunt each officiated two games, which increased to eight for Hunt and five for Lay the following year. Kari Seitz also took charge of several US Open Cup games involving MLS teams during that same time.

While in France at the 1998 World Cup, Esse Baharmast arranged for us to have lunch with Edgardo Codesal, the former FIFA referee who officiated the USA v Italy World Cup game in 1990 and who also took charge of the 1990 final. Codesal was now working for the world governing body and had responsibilities for officiating in Mexico. I had wanted to discuss the possibility of a referee exchange with our southern neighbors. Codesal indicated that if he could not get Baharmast to referee in Mexico then the only other referee he would accept was Brian Hall. The exchange never took place.

Baharmast himself had planned to retire after the World Cup and did so following the All-Star game which celebrated his homecoming from France and the historic penalty kick decision he made against Brazil which, after initially stirring controversy, made him an officiating legend after a photograph from behind the goal proved him right.

Soon after the 1998 World Cup, Baharmast replaced Vincent Mauro as Director of Officials at US Soccer. One of the first items on his agenda was to deal with a FIFA proposal to experiment with a five-official system, in essence the dual system of control that had been used in the college ranks but with assistant referees and a fourth official. Many of the officials who worked only for US Soccer did not work in the college game because it was not sanctioned by the national governing body or FIFA. So, it was all new to them. So new, in fact, FIFA sent in Codesal to conduct a seminar on the subject. During the on-field segment, I had several questions as it became obvious that Codesal knew less about the dual system and even cared less. After all, I had personal experience of implementing, with Herb Silva, a two-referee system for indoor soccer. By my fourth question, Codesal refused to recognize me.

For the record, 68 US Open Cup games were officiated by mid-season with five officials and with mixed reviews. As the tournament reached its final stages, it became clear that two whistles on the field did little to solve the issues of the day and only added confusion.

After the 1996 season, with its average crowd of more than 17,000, Commissioner Logan made a bold prediction that attendance would increase by 15% in year two. However, it ended up dropping by 16% to only 14,619.

Although I loved working in the MLS office, my duties and responsibilities as Vice President of Game Operations meant being present at the games, not in the office. So, I did not think it was a big deal when, in May 1998, I informed Bill Sage that my family would be moving to South Carolina. Under a new arrangement whereby I took a salary cut, I was able to maintain my job with MLS. I did fly up to NY on occasion when there were matters of importance to discuss in person.

Prior to the start of the 1999 season, my direct report, Bill Sage left MLS and took a senior position within US Soccer. I would now be reporting to Ivan Gazidis, an Oxford-educated attorney with a strong soccer background. Gazidis was comfortable with my relocation to South Carolina and the performance of my duties. He never questioned my qualifications nor my loyalty and dedication to the job. And we established a good working relationship.

It was therefore Gazidis who called me at my South Carolina home to inform me that Doug Logan was no longer the Commissioner and that he would be replaced by Don Garber, who was Senior Vice President and Marketing Director of NFL International at the time. So, it was like starting all over for the League and for me personally, as I would have to prove myself once again! I spent a lot of time in the office during the second half of the 1999 season. And the first time I got to speak with Commissioner Garber was one evening well after office hours, while I was reviewing game tapes, he came by to see about the noise. I explained to him that I watched every single MLS match.

At times, we had to wonder if Garber, as the new MLS Commissioner, knew what he was getting into. MLS's financial losses continued to pile up, estimated at $250 million during its first five years. As owners dropped out and the League folded the Tampa Bay Mutiny and Miami Fusion, only three owners were left standing to manage the remaining ten teams. Lamar Hunt, Philip Anschutz and the Kraft family, with Anschutz operating seven teams, kept the League alive. We were all asked to take a pay cut, which would be my second since joining MLS.

It was at this time that my working with industrial cleaning fluid in the days of my youth finally caught up with me. I was diagnosed with prostate cancer and underwent surgery which sidelined me for the whole of March just prior to the season.

My position with MLS afforded me a seat on US Soccer's Referee Committee, at which I kept up my pursuit of the full-time referee concept which FIFA continued to promote. Finally, US Soccer agreed and hired four officials on a full-time basis: Ricardo Salazar, Baldomero Toledo, Jair Marrufo and Terry Vaughn. It was proposed that each would work approximately 20 games during the MLS season. There was a problem, however, that each had a FIFA international badge and was away from the country for extended periods of time. When they returned from a CONCACAF or FIFA assignment, they were not the same referee as before they left. There was a marked difference with the expectations put on a referee by the international bodies as compared to the expectations of the pro league.

A Canadian-based FIFA referee explained at a meeting that CONCACAF prohibited a referee from touching a player while MLS encouraged officials to extend a helping hand to an injured player getting back on his feet. At times I wondered if our full-time referees were being groomed for the international game and perhaps a World Cup appearance rather than service to MLS.

Not everyone in the greater referee community was enamored with my work or the direction I was taking MLS on the field. A referee got hit by a free kick while standing just a few yards away and the ball changed direction and went to the opponents who broke away for a score. I publicly criticized the referee for not immediately stopping play. The Laws of the Game at the time stated that the referee was in play. But common sense should have prevailed. The referee, in my opinion, should have stated that the ball was not spotted correctly or was moving before the kick or that he had not properly given the signal for a restart. Several of the retired old-timers and assessors were incensed that I was instructing referees not to correctly apply the laws. They wrote a letter to Commissioner Garber insisting on my dismissal. In the letter they referred to me as a "hockey guy". I explained the situation to Garber, and he supported me. Many years later the Laws of the Game were changed, giving the referee authority to stop play when struck by the ball.

There was a very noticeable improvement in the fitness level of the full-time referees as US Soccer had afforded them training regiments and achievement standards as well as the services of its own physical trainers and coaches. Improved fitness meant being able to get into a better position and see a proper angle on a play, as well as being as strong in the closing minutes of a match as at the start. There could be no loss of concentration on the game due to a fitness issue.

In May 2001, Werner Fricker passed away at age 65. Bob Gansler, John Kowalski, Kevin Payne and I shared a hotel room near the location of his funeral. We had several beers that night in his honor. There were so many memories to rehash. Kowalski and I had been invited to go skiing with Werner on several occasions and had developed a strong bond. He was a strong skier who transversed the mountain while yodeling. His contribution to the growth and development of soccer in America cannot be overestimated. Like Walter Chyzowych, he passed way too early in life to see how soccer has become mainstream and part of the pop-culture in the US. He would marvel at the growth and sustainability of MLS, the numbers of boys and girls playing in soccer complexes with dozens of fields and how TV has embraced the game to the point that, with streaming, a game can be watched nearly 24 hours a day.

In July 2001, a subcommittee of MLS's Competition Committee composed of Clark Hunt, Kevin Payne, Sunil Gulati and Ivan Gazidis met during the All-Star break. The committee was assisted by coaches Octavio Zambrano and Bob Bradley. The committee was to study the policies and procedures of the MLS Disciplinary Committee, officiating in MLS games and the MLS game itself.

In preparation for the committee meeting, I was asked to prepare 25 video clips of key MLS incidents for distribution among all League coaches for the purpose of establishing consistency. "Consistency" is a word often used when criticizing officials. What is meant by it? Are we meaning consistency from the first half to the second, from one referee game to game, or consistency among all referees?

Each clip had a questionnaire at the bottom: "How do you see this challenge?" A) Worthy of a caution, B) A straight red card, C) Worthy of a second caution if the player is carrying a caution, D) Should be reviewed by the Disciplinary Committee for action beyond the referee's decision, E) Other ...please explain.

The role of the Disciplinary Committee under my supervision was also under scrutiny. I was charged with watching every MLS game and bringing plays to the Disciplinary Committee which needed further review, especially in player safety. While a red card was an automatic one-game suspension, a single game suspension for very serious foul play or violent conduct did not seem to be enough to modify player behavior.

The committee was shocked by the coaches' replies and the responses of its own members. There was no consistency! And as far as the Disciplinary Committee was concerned, there were many who believed that we were re-officiating the game "on Monday morning". They were of the belief that if a referee did not see an offense in real time, then it didn't happen. VAR was still many years away!

Life was made easier with the MLS hiring of Alfonso Mondelo, a pure soccer aficionado who grew up in Spain and had a true understanding of the game at many levels. He had a successful coaching career with the Long Island Rough Riders, winning the USISL Championship in 1995 with future MLS players Chris Armas, Tony Meola, Jim Rooney and Giovanni Savarese. He then served as assistant coach of the MetroStars under Brazilian Carlos Alberto Perreira, as an assistant to Bruce Arena with the USMNT, and as Director of Coaching with the ENYSA before taking a job with MLS in 2005.

With his soccer background, Mondelo was appointed as a member of the Disciplinary Committee and shared the watching of games over the weekend. And since I was not a regular in the office, he agreed that I could share his office space when I came to New York. Not only that, but we would also ride the subway together after he picked me up at my sister's house, where I stayed most times while in the city. All we did was talk about soccer. Alfonso also shared the duties of visiting with each team during the season and brought a lot of credibility to those meetings with his insight and feel for the game. He could have been an outstanding referee. Prior to every MLS Cup match we walked the field together. And he arranged for us to visit his beloved Real Madrid, touring their training facilities, meeting their officers and going to a game at the Bernabeu Stadium vs. Barcelona on the day Real were crowned champions.

It wasn't my only European trip endorsed by MLS. Ivan Gazidis arranged for Barbara and me to have full VIP treatment on January 12, 2002, being hosted by Fulham FC for their game against Middlesbrough. It was arranged for me to be in the referee's room before and after the match, to witness all the protocol going into gameday security etc. We watched the game from the Chairman's Box. The next day, my birthday, we celebrated at Arsenal for their match vs. Liverpool. Several years later, there was a three-game tour of referee operations in Germany along with then US Soccer head of officiating, Paul Tamberino.

The Federation was beginning to gain confidence in the professionalism of MLS employees, so much so that when Gazidis was asked to recommend two MLS staffers to attend a Match Commissioners Seminar in Trinidad and Tobago in September 2003, Nelson Rodriguez and I were recommended to attend the course, which was run by FIFA executive Walter Gagg.

Gagg seemed to recognize me right away, saying: "I know you." I had to explain to him that I was the assistant Five-a-Side US coach who challenged him in the Netherlands by stating that we came to win the tournament. Now, he remembered. And, of course, there was that speech at Coverciano.

It wasn't until May of the next year that I received my first Match Commissioner assignment. CONCACAF executive Ted Howard called Esse Baharmast asking who, if anybody, knew anything about Five-a-Side? The assignment was a playoff game between Panama and Canada in futsal (Five-a-Side). Esse suggested that I knew a lot about Five-a-Side. It was a relatively easy appointment for me based on my experience at the first Five-a-Side World Championship in 1989.

In June, I received a real challenge. A World Cup qualifier between Trinidad and Tobago and the host country, Dominican Republic. Fortunately, I had Esse Baharmast with me as Referee Assessor, who was able to get me through some of the logistics. The Match Commissioner's job is not an easy one. There is a checklist of duties and responsibilities. Among the items on the list are: check the field, check the loud speaker and national anthems, check the locker rooms, check the passports of each player individually in the presence of the player, ensure the safety and security of the game officials, check the ambulance and first-aid facility, make sure there will be stretcher bearers, prepare an area if there will be a FIFA doping test, attend the one-hour practice walk-through session of each team at the stadium, arrange police escorts for the teams and the referees. Then rehearse the FIFA walk out with the various flags and children escorts. And then believe what you are told that whatever is not ready on matchday minus one, will be ready on matchday. And of course, fax (if you can find one) the game report immediately after the match to FIFA and CONCACAF. All this would be explained to the teams and officials at the Match Coordination Meeting which usually took place on Match Day minus 2.

Then game day, two hours before the match, meet with the referees, collect the line-ups, check the uniform numbers against the line-ups, set up the flag bearers, rehearse the walk out again, allow the goalkeepers to come out and practice first, then the teams, then try getting them off the field in time for a timely game start. And, of course, it helps to be multilingual. I am not!

Nothing went right. The loudspeaker didn't work so the players sang their national anthems a cappella. The single in-stadium ambulance left in the middle of the game because there was an accident on a nearby highway. And of course, there was then a serious injury to deal with. A player was treated on the field and then moved to the side of one goal near the corner flag. There were no ambulances. Then, out of nowhere, a pickup truck came racing on the cinder track which surrounded the field, the driver leaving dust in his trail like a NASCAR dirt racer. The game had to be held up.

Fortunately, Esse was there to explain to CONCACAF President Jack Warner that this was my first real assignment and surely, I could do no worse. Added to the woes, the Trinidad players claimed they had money and jewelry stolen from their locker room.

After attendance at a U20 World Cup qualification tournament in San Pedro Sula, Honduras and a U17 tournament in Culiacan, Mexico, with multiple assignments, I had gotten some of the kinks out and exhibited a great deal more confidence and expertise as Match Commissioner.

I was now receiving several assignments a year. World Cup qualifiers and CONCACAF Champions League assignments in Costa Rica, Mexico, Bahamas, Canada, Jamaica, Honduras, St. Kitts and Nevis, El Salvador, Trinidad and Tobago, and a game in Houston where Belize was the host country.

In a game played on October 10, 2009, at Azteca Stadium in Mexico

City, I had to hold up the match as a swarm of wasps came out of one of the goalposts. Traveling home from that game, there was a message from FIFA that I was to travel to New Zealand to be the Match Commissioner for the final game of 2010 World Cup qualifying, in which the host would play Bahrain on November 14th in the second game of their home and away playoff series. The two teams had tied 0-0 in the first leg, which meant the winner of the "rubber match" would go on to the World Cup in South Africa. This was the second time that I had been involved in the final game of World Cup qualifying. It brought back memories of that 1989 USA v Trinidad match!

I couldn't travel halfway around the world without Barbara coming with me. And we planned to stay in New Zealand for a few days after the match before traveling to the MLS Cup Final which, conveniently that year, was being played in Seattle.

I was familiar with two players from the New Zealand squad who had MLS experience, namely captain Ryan Nelson, who had played at DC United, and Simon Elliot, who had played for the LA Galaxy and Columbus Crew.

New Zealand scored first when Rory Fallon delighted the crowd of 35,194 by heading in a corner midway through the first half. In the second period, Uruguayan referee Jorge Larrionda awarded a deserved penalty kick to Bahrain. The kick was poorly taken to Mark Paston's right side, and the goalkeeper was able to catch and hold the low drive. Had the penalty kick been scored, Bahrain would have advanced due to the away goals rule. The only way that extra time could have been played was if the final score of the return leg had also been goalless. It's a good thing the Match Commissioner knew the rules at the Match Coordination meeting.

Referee Jorge Larrionda had already worked four games in the middle at the 2006 World Cup, including a semi-final. He was considered one of the best in the world. He was selected for the 2010 World Cup and became infamous because in his second match, England vs. Germany, his assistant failed to see that a shot by Frank Lampard had clearly crossed the goal line which, if awarded, would have tied the score at two-all. Germany went on to win 4-1. The entire Uruguayan officiating team was sent home after that missed call and it was the beginning of serious discussions about the need for Goal Line Technology (GLT).

Before retiring as a Match Commissioner in 2016, I attended two more

FIFA/CONCACAF Match Commissioner Seminars (both in Miami) and had been assigned to 32 matches or tournaments. My last was Honduras vs. Canada, a 2018 World Cup qualifier where the major controversy was whether there would be water breaks as the kick-off time was 2pm!

When I arrived in Seattle for MLS Cup duty, I was informed that my attendance at a Board of Governors meeting was requested as officiating in MLS was once again a hot topic. At the meeting, Don Garber introduced me to the Board, which consisted of most owners present and/or their representatives. I was seated up front with the Commissioner when asked by representatives from Seattle what were my plans for the additional $400,000 that had been approved for the officiating budget. I had not been prepared for this question and was unaware that any money at all had been so approved. Regardless, I knew what had to be done and that was to add more full-time officials to the MLS officiating pool.

Esse Baharmast had recently taken a full-time job with FIFA as a referee instructor, leaving US Soccer, and MLS recommended that veteran referee Paul Tamberino take over his position. In essence, it would be Tamberino's job to manage the new money and decide which, if any, officials would graduate to full-time status.

When Toronto (2007), Vancouver (2011) and Montreal (2012) came into MLS; the Canadian Soccer Association (CSA) hired former English FIFA referee Joe Guest to further organize and manage their referee program. As such, MLS was obligated to utilize the services of Canadian game officials. At first there were difficulties with immigration, with US referees working in Canada and vice versa.

By 2007, MLS referees who were not full-time with US Soccer were getting paid as much as $800 per game depending on the number of MLS games officiated previously. The game fee in the first round of the MLS Cup playoffs paid $1,000, second round $1,200 and $1,500 for MLS Cup Final.

I found Joe Guest to be hard-working and dedicated to the task at hand. We developed a good working relationship once I remembered to always include the CSA in printed materials that I would distribute and in public speaking engagements.

The game of soccer seemingly always has officiating as a focus point. Even in modern times with Video Assistant Referees (VAR), Goal Line Technology (GLT), Semi-Automatic Offside Technology (SAOT) and a computer connected ball, there are still controversial decisions related to match-critical incidents and decisions relating to penalty kicks, send offs, and offside.

Each year, Alfonso Mondelo and I would travel to the respective MLS teams and explain the changes in the Laws of the Game and functions of the Disciplinary Committee. There was always a new initiative to start the season with the "Dissent Initiative" being repeated over several years. A particular bone of contention with the players was their opinion that the referees did not have enough playing experience, had little coaching knowledge and did not have a true feel for the game, what the Germans called "fingerspitzengefuhl". Each year, we promised that it would be better.

It was a good move to put a former player and former coach on the Disciplinary Committee. And I convinced US Soccer to develop a fast-track referee incentive program for an MLS player to move quickly up the Federation's ladder to work in MLS. It would be a two-year program during which the player would be paid $50,000 per year. There were no takers — no player wanted to be subjected to that level of abuse.

Once a month, MLS's Personnel Department would sponsor an "All Access Luncheon" whereby an individual staff member was chosen to speak about his/her duties and responsibilities within the League. In February 2009, it was my turn, and the conference room was packed, every seat taken and others standing in the back. Perhaps it was the free pizza lunch or maybe folks just wanted to find out what I did or who this person was that almost never was in the office? Or maybe MLS officiating was the hot topic within the office? I prepared a video and slide presentation of my background and experience and some video clips. One of the slides I presented was the iconic portrait of Walt Chyzowych that first appeared in US Soccer's *The Official Soccer Book*. I asked the attendees to identify him, and no one had the answer. It was shocking to me, as this was the office of Major League Soccer and the history of the game in America seemed of so little importance. It was not yet 15 years since Walter's passing. One could only imagine if I put up a photo of Dettmar Cramer.

My office, now called the Department of Officiating Services, was the sounding board for most, if not all, complaints coming from players, coaches, player's families, fans, agents, union representatives, general managers and in some cases team owners, so it was only natural for me to transfer as many of those complaints as possible to US Soccer. But in many cases, no one at the governing body had even watched the game or was familiar with the play in question. They were also so consumed with recruiting, training, assigning and assessing officials at so many other levels including at international games, in the emerging women's pro league and in the lower division pro and amateur leagues. There just wasn't enough time or resources to deal with MLS and all its issues. So, my office, in terms of handling all of the complaints, was serving as a buffer for US Soccer.

I had developed a Mission Statement for the Department of Officiating Services: "The promulgation of a consistent officiating mentality which enables the playing of a safe, fan friendly (family) entertaining game in which attacking soccer is encouraged in an atmosphere open to diverse and skilled players, playing styles and strategies." How could one argue with that?

The Technical Assessment Report written for MLS in 2008 indicates ongoing discussions with US Soccer to increase the number of full-time officials from four to six by 2009 and to ten in 2012. It also cites the failure of US Soccer's full-time referees to meet the required 20 MLS game assignments due to their international obligations.

When I traveled to Houston for the MLS All-Star Game in the middle of the 2010 season, I was met by Joe Guest before attending any of the referee meetings we had organized for the break. Guest, as a friend, warned me that US Soccer was taking a position that MLS was not welcome at the meetings, the referee program belonged to US Soccer, and to some extent the CSA, and that the League should not have contact with or play a role in the management and instruction of referees. Herb Silva joined the conversation in dismay.

Angered and upset, I left Houston without attending a meeting, reporting the events I had just experienced to Commissioner Garber. Ivan Gazidis had left MLS at the beginning of 2009 to become Chief Executive at English Premier League club Arsenal and Nelson Rodriguez had taken over many of his duties and responsibilities.

I announced to Don Garber that 2010 would be my last season working for MLS. I believed that I was at the end of my rope, so to speak. I could accomplish no more. The MLS game and the demands placed upon the officials were not getting any easier. The relationship with US Soccer and the CSA was not producing officials fast and qualified enough. The League was expanding, and the officials were not keeping up!

Commissioner Garber immediately charged Nelson Rodriguez with the development of a task force — onto which I had been invited — working with US Soccer and the CSA to find a new way forward.

At one of our first meetings, Nelson invited the head of NFL officiating, Mike Pereira, to address the task force which included Sunil Gulati, Joe Guest, Paul Tamberino, Jay Berhalter from US Soccer and US Soccer General Secretary Dan Flynn. The NFL officiating program was of interest to us because it was managed by the League and because of its short season did not have full-time officials. But neither did they have to answer to national, regional or global governing bodies.

During the meeting, Pereira addressed the issue of identifying officials who have "IT". I thought I was always able to recognize when an official had "IT" but could never put "IT" into words. So, I took notes and then modified his NFL outline to be more specific to soccer. So here "IT" is:

1. The referee sees a play with instant total clarity.

2. The referee applies the correct Laws of the Game with the most recent interpretation.

3. The referee relies on background and experience (playing/coaching/watching others work live and on TV).

4. The referee has a feel for the game (fingerspitzengefuhl).

5. The referee uses knowledgeable guesswork when not sure.

Referee Magazine also cites the elements of Passion, Competition Instinct, Command, People Skills, Situation Management and Investment as additional prerequisites for "IT".

It was at this meeting that Pereira announced to the group that he was leaving his position at the NFL for a new opportunity on the West Coast. He had us all guessing.

At a second meeting of the task force, this time in Chicago, Paul Tamberino brought in former English FA referee Keith Hackett to explain the workings of the Professional Game Match Officials Limited (PGMOL), the organization which was formed in 2001 when English referees became professional. The creation of a similar type of organization was what Rodriquez had in mind for the future of officiating in MLS. It seemed that Hackett and Tamberino had developed a relationship whereby Hackett was being considered for employment in the US.

After my role ended at MLS, I was offered a position as a consultant for another year to further advise on the development of officiating in MLS. Several additional task force meetings took place at which the Federation finally agreed with MLS. US Soccer had figured that it would be easier and more beneficial to help fund MLS's plans for a new officiating organization with what it was already spending on officiating at the top professional level and, by doing so, get rid of a myriad of headaches. The CSA liked the idea as well, but reportedly did not have any money to contribute.

In 2012, the Professional Referee Organization (PRO) was formed with the cooperation of US Soccer, the CSA and MLS. US Soccer President Sunil Gulati announced the formation by stating: "We've always understood that the development of referees is an important aspect to the growth of the game in the United States. PRO is another step toward the improvement and professionalization of our top referees. With the additional resources and funding provided by the formation of PRO, we continue to build upon the progress we've already made."

Englishman Peter Walton was hired to lead the new organization. I was fortunate enough that Walton considered it important that I still be involved, and I was selected to be one of the first chosen Coach Mentors. The plans for the new organization were ambitious indeed. Bi-monthly meetings in Dallas and elsewhere, full-time training staff to work on referee fitness and health, and computerized watches to monitor each referee's training routine and habits. All the officials and newly appointed Coach Mentors were fitted for customized tailored suits for travel. I even learned some new terms such as "cognitive dissonance" suddenly used to describe the discomfort a referee feels when their behavior does not align with their values, beliefs or expectations on the field.

I was pleased to be assigned as Coach Mentor to a young, up-and-coming referee, Ismail Elfath. The Moroccan-born official had a meteoric rise among the officiating ranks due to his imposing physical stature, his understanding of the game and his ability to engage players in conversation in a compelling manner where they appreciated his explanations and overall wherewithal.

I traveled with Elfath to Montreal for his first MLS assignment, a game played in the indoor Olympic Stadium which, because of the way the field was laid out, presented difficulties for the officials in terms of orientation within the building. It was not an easy match and Elfath was hampered in part by an over-aggressive assistant referee who wanted to impact the game beyond what was required. Elfath survived that first match and establish himself as one of MLS's better officials. He was appointed to the FIFA International Referee list in 2016 and in August of that year officiated the first match where VAR was being experimented with in a game between New York Red Bull II and Orlando City B.

Elfath was appointed to the 2019 FIFA U20 World Cup in Poland and then took charge of a semi-final in the FIFA Club World Cup in Qatar that same year. In 2021 Elfath officiated three games at the Covid-delayed Olympics and had three games at the 2022 World Cup in Qatar which included a round of 16 match. He was then honored to be assigned as fourth official on the World Cup Final.

I had a chance meeting with Don Garber on a pre-season soccer field in Florida where, referring to the creation of PRO, he asked: "What do you think of our new experiment?" I replied that experiments take time to get results, but I also knew the results would be positive if only because the fitness levels would be improved, as well as consistency with the bi-monthly meetings and the increase in the number of full-time referees. I also knew the experiment was going to be a lot more expensive than what had been previously budgeted for the referee program. But I was very happy to see that in so many ways, what I had hoped and asked for in the referee program over the years of my MLS employment was now taking place. The officials were no longer amateurs but full professionals deserving of their dedication, work ethic and performance.

Compounding the expense part was that the officials began organizing and, in 2009, formed the Professional Soccer Referee Association (PSRA) to unite all officials under one banner. And in 2013 the officials united to sign the first Collective Bargaining Agreement (CBA), putting them on the same plateau as officials in the NBA by having a recognized labor union.

One of my most prized possessions is a sterling silver Tiffany style plate which Don Garber presented to me following my retirement from MLS. The presentation was made at the MLS Draft at the NSCAA Convention in front of all the teams, their coaches, general managers and others, as well as assorted fan groups awaiting to see who would be selected with each team's first draft pick.

The plate has the logos of US Soccer, MLS and CONCACAF and reads:

"Joseph A. Machnik, Major League Soccer 1996-2010. With our deepest appreciation for your extraordinary service to MLS and the sport of soccer." It is signed with the signatures of Don Garber, Sunil Gulati, Joe Guest, Alfonso Mondelo, Nelson Rodriguez, Paul Tamberino and others.

Fifteen years later, by 2025, MLS is recognized as one of the top leagues in the world. It has five of the top twenty and 19 of the top 50 most valuable clubs globally.

It has attracted some of the world's top players to its 30 teams which now play primarily in soccer specific stadiums. A league office which once numbered less than a dozen employees now numbers several hundred. It has played a major role in soccer becoming part of the pop-culture in America. Commissioner Don Garber and the league's first employee, Mark Abbott, who wrote the business plan, have been inducted into the National Soccer Hall of Fame.

The growth and development of soccer in America has led both FIFA and CONMEBOL, the South American Confederation to conduct major tournaments in the United States. Two Copa America tournaments have been played, and two more FIFA World Cups (Men's 2026 and Women's 2031) have been awarded.

None of this happens without MLS. The proliferation of international soccer games led Commissioner Garber to state in an interview in THE ATHLETIC that there is "no question now that America has become the ATM for the soccer world".

News Release

For Immediate Release
http://www.MLSNET.COM

Contact: Dan Courtemanche or Aaron Helfetz
617/326-2960 – MLS Communications

JOE MACHNIK NAMED MAJOR LEAGUE SOCCER VICE PRESIDENT OF GAME OPERATIONS
Veteran Soccer Official To Oversee League's Referee Program

BOSTON, MA (October 18, 1996) – Longtime soccer executive, coach and referee Joe Machnik has been named Major League Soccer's Vice President of Game Operations, MLS Commissioner Douglas G. Logan announced today.

Machnik comes to MLS with a long list of achievements in all facets of the game. The 53-year-old Connecticut resident has more than 30 years of experience in soccer and collegiate athletics. Most recently, he served as an Associate Professor at the University of New Haven's School of Business, teaching courses in sports management.

Machnik's primary role with MLS will be to oversee the league's referee program and the game operations of all 10 MLS teams.

"The addition of Joe Machnik is a key step in Major League Soccer's plans to enhance the league's referee program," Commissioner Logan said. "His experience in all areas of the game will be invaluable. He is already working toward developing a comprehensive referee offseason training program."

Machnik's soccer experience includes serving as Long Island University's head varsity coach from 1966-69 where he advanced to two NCAA Final Fours. In addition to his tenure at Long Island University, Machnik's other collegiate sports management experience includes serving as an Athletic Director, Assistant Professor, Varsity Soccer Coach and Varsity Ice Hockey Coach during the 1970's at the University of New Haven.

Machnik first ventured into professional sports management in 1978 when he became Referee-in-Chief of the Major Indoor Soccer League. He later served as the league's Director of Operations and was the Head Coach of the New York Arrows during the 1983-84 MISL season. In 1985 he joined the American Indoor Soccer Association (now NPSL) as the league's Director of Operations and from 1986-88 served as the AISA's Commissioner.

Machnik's experience as a referee includes 13 years at the college and pro level. He officiated the 1988 NCAA Championship Game and numerous professional games, including the first MISL game in 1978.

A member of the National Soccer Coaches Association of America and the United States Soccer Coaches Association, Machnik was the Goalkeeper Coach of the U.S. National Team during 1990 World Cup qualifying. He also served as an Assistant Coach of the U.S. Five-a-Side Team which captured the bronze medal at the 1989 World Indoor Championship.

Machnik, who operates the No. 1 Goalkeeper Camps and No. 1 Striker Camps nationwide, will start immediately out of Major League Soccer's New York office.

###

2029 Century Park East, Suite 400 Los Angeles, California 9 0 0 6 7 Phone 310.772.2600 Fax 310.843.4836
110 East 42nd Street New York, New York 1 0 0 1 7 Phone 212.687.1400 Fax 212.687.6747

MLS Press Release announcing my appointment!

LAW FIVE — Referee's Corner...

Interview by Mike Woitalla

New MLS head ref

Joe Machnik's long resume includes U.S. 1990 World Cup goalkeeper coach, college coach, Major Indoor Soccer League referee-in-chief, AISA commissioner, camp director and decades of refereeing. In November, Major League Soccer named him vice president of league operations, a title that includes the responsibility of overseeing the league's referee program.

SOCCER AMERICA: How will you be working with MLS referees?
JOE MACHNIK: My immediate attention will be given to representing the league in the development program of referees with the U.S. Soccer Federation.

SA: Can we expect improvement in officiating next season?
JM: I don't know if the refereeing will get better because of anything I will do. But I want to assure that the referees at least have an understanding of what's expected by the league. That's where the shortfall was last season. When I interviewed the referees, they pretty much all said, "Please help. We don't know what the league wants."

SA: What were the problems during MLS's first season?
JM: The referees were very much handicapped because so many were trained by the USSF to do youth and amateur games. It was difficult for them to come in and referee professional games with that mindset and having very little experience in major stadiums with major crowds and huge pressure where lots of money is on line. Their performance will improve as they get comfortable with that level. That will come with experience.

SA: Coaches were highly critical of MLS refs, but I doubt you'd find positive critiques from coaches anywhere in the world.
JM: Pick up [the November] World Soccer and you'll find an article titled "Global Solutions" about three governing bodies, including UEFA, recognizing a refereeing crisis.

SA: But the barrage against MLS refs seemed to get a bit out of hand, and one had to doubt whether the league supported the referees in confrontations with coaches.
JM: The league admits it was a little unprepared for dealing with public criticism of referees, not only by coaches but from players.
At the referees' breakfast at MLS Cup, commissioner Doug Logan opened with an apology to the referees saying the league in its first year was somewhat unprepared to deal with behavior control.
I think my appointment has something to do with addressing that.

SA: What will you do?
JM: I will be watching tapes of every game, in addition to ones I attend, and evaluating the referees and the coaches and expect fines and suspension for indecent behavior.
One thing I want to accomplish is taking a much stronger stand against public criticism.

SA: I suppose it's not as simple as just forbidding coaches to criticize.
JM: The league has to provide an avenue to get criticism and allow coaches to evaluate referees and to use that evaluation in training, retraining and assignment selection.
Coaches are part of the formula of the total professional soccer experience. Obviously, after each game, one coach is happy

> 'The league has to provide an avenue to get criticism.'

because he won and the other isn't. We want input from both, even the happy coach who may also be able to point out certain things.
I'll be forming a committee that will meet monthly, bimonthly or however often is needed. We will constantly be reviewing the referee program to see where training is needed.

SA: Has U.S. refereeing improved during the three decades that you've been involved in U.S. soccer?
JM: If I think back to NASL days, American referees with high credentials, like John Davies, Toros Kibritjian, Gino D'Ippolito and Bill Maxwell, come to mind. Then the NASL died, which meant American referees had few opportunities for high level games at home.
If you referee college games, for example, the pace may be fast, but games rarely have over a 1,000 fans and the whole atmosphere is different.

SA: Any chance of using foreign referees in MLS?
JM: We would consider an exchange program, where, for example, we invite one, two or three officials to referee in our league, but we would only do that if their federation allowed our referees to officiate in their league. In interviews with MLS referees, they indicated to me they would love such a program.

For Immediate Release
Contact: Carrie Goldberg, MLS
Communications, (212) 450-1227

FEMALE REFEREES MAKE MLS DEBUT IN MIDDLE
Nancy Lay and Sandra Hunt Run the Middle on August 29

NEW YORK (Thursday, August 20, 1998) — Nancy Lay and Sandra Hunt, two of the five women who are Major League Soccer assistant referees for the 1998 campaign, have graduated to the next level of officiating and will make their debuts on August 29 as the first female senior referees in MLS history. Commissioner Douglas O. Logan announced today.

Major League Soccer joins the National Basketball Association (NBA) as the only major professional sports leagues in the United States to have women rank as senior game officials.

"Sandra Hunt and Nancy Lay have distinguished themselves as game officials at the highest levels of soccer in the United States," said Joe Machnik, MLS Vice President, Game Operations. "Each have performed well in recent U.S. Open Cup competitions involving MLS teams and have had outstanding performances as assistant referees in MLS matches. We welcome them and wish them the best."

Hunt, a United States Soccer Federation registered referee since 1987, has been assigned to officiate the Chicago Fire at Kansas City Wizards game on August 29. Lay, a referee since 1985, will step into the middle for the MetroStars at Dallas Burn match.

Hunt has officiated close to 1,000 games in her 11-year career at the youth, collegiate, amateur, professional and national team levels. During the past 14 months Hunt, who recently worked as the senior referee for the U.S. Women's National Team vs. Canada game at the 1998 MLS All-Star Weekend in Orlando, has run the middle in eight A-League games, four friendlies for the U.S. Women's National Team and the Columbus Crew's 3-1 win over the Miami Fusion in a U.S. Open Cup quarterfinal on July 22. In addition, Hunt has served as a referee's assistant in nine MLS games this season.

"It is an honor to be appointed to officiate this game," said Hunt, a Western Washington University soccer alumnus. "I am very grateful for the opportunity to pay tribute through my performance to all of my mentors, past and present, who have made and continue to make themselves available and spend a considerable amount of their time improving my performance."

Lay, who has served as the senior referee in three matches for the U.S. Women's National Team in 1998, has been on the pitch for many 1,000 matches as a referee since her career was initiated 13 years ago. Lay, who has experience at the youth, men's collegiate, amateur, national and professional ranks, has run the lines in three games during her first season with MLS. In addition, she has run the middle in 10 A-League games, and the Nashville Metros' (A-League) 3-1 win over the Kansas City Wizards in a third-round U.S. Open Cup match on July 8.

"I want to walk away with respect as a referee, not just as a woman referee," said Lay, a former member of the U.S. Women's Select Team, the precursor to the current U.S. Women's National Team. "I want to know that I am competent to officiate at the MLS level."

Both Hunt and Lay have been selected as referees for the Nike U.S. Women's Cup '98 featuring the United States, Brazil, Mexico and Russia. Lay will take center stage when the U.S. faces Mexico as part of a doubleheader with the New England Revolution at Foxboro Stadium in Foxboro, Mass. on September 12. Hunt will serve as an official for the U.S. vs. Brazil on September 20 at the University of Richmond Stadium in Richmond, Virginia.

Hunt, who played in Seattle's Division I Open League from 1980-1995, lives in Seattle with her husband, Jeff, along with their three children: Kris, Griffin and Heidi.

"I enjoy very much the players, the passion and the spirit they inject into the game," Hunt said. "As a player it's what keeps you coming back and I get the same feeling as a referee."

Lay, who led the University of Central Florida women's soccer team to the 1981 AIAW Championship Game and the first-ever NCAA Championship Game in 1982 only to lose both games to the University of North Carolina, lives in Ft. Lauderdale where she teaches physical education to kindergarten-through-fifth-grade students. Lay is single and lives with her cat, FIFA.

"I enjoy being a referee because it's a challenge," Lay said. "As an athlete you go out and you try to perfect yourself physically and mentally each game. I feel the same way today as a ref as I did when I was the one who was playing."

Kari Seitz, Sharon Wheeler and Susan Cicchinelli round out the elite group of five women serving as MLS senior assistant referees for the 1998 season.

Certificate of Attendance at my first Match Commissioner's Course. I attended two refresher courses and worked at 32 FIFA and CONCACAF games and Tournaments as a Match Commissioner.

With MLS Commissioner Don Garber on the occasion of my retirement from the League after 15 years!

SOCCER

MLS referee exchange with Japan ruled success

By Jerry Langdon
USA TODAY

Toru Kamikawa of Japan's J-League got high grades for his month-long stint as a referee in Major League Soccer.

"In four of the five games, he was exceptional," MLS vice president of game operations Joe Machnik said before Kamikawa's final game Thursday night in Tampa.

"He's young (34), he was a player, he recognizes fouls. He's consistent, he calls games tight, he expects fair play off the ball, that the wall be 10 yards..."

He was part of an exchange program in which Tim Weyland went to Japan for seven games this summer. "Tim got very good scores there," Machnik said.

Kamikawa was involved in the nine yellow-card game Sept. 10 between the Los Angeles Galaxy and Colorado Rapids, including the ejections of Galaxy defender Paul Caligiuri and Rapids defender Steve Trittschuh.

"I thought the second yellow cards given both of them was a little harsh, but overall Toru did a superb job," Machnik said.

An exchange program with Spain is under consideration for 1998.

improved with forward Joe-Max Moore back in form. Forward Giuseppe Galderisi and defender Francis Okaroh are ready. The MetroStars are 0-3 at Foxboro Stadium. Key matchup: New England midfielder Alejandro Farias vs. New York/New Jersey midfielder Tab Ramos (groin), whose status could be decided on game-day. Referee: Arturo Angeles.

Sunday's games

▶ **Tampa Bay at (Washington) D.C.**, ESPN: This game is important for Mutiny psyche, since they are 1-8 against the United the last two years. They are hopeful of getting untracked, even against likely reserves, before playoffs. Key matchup: Tampa Bay defender Frank Yallop vs. D.C. forward Raul Diaz Arce, in renewal of Sunday's Canada-El Salvador World Cup qualifier, won by El Salvador on Diaz Arce goal. Referee: Brian Hall.

▶ **Los Angeles at San Jose (Calif.), Univision**: Another do-or-die game for the Clash, who must win in regulation to stay in the playoff hunt. Whether it's an important match for the Galaxy depends on whether they beat Dallas on Friday. Key matchup: Los Angeles forward Eduardo Hur-

Kamikawa: Spent month as MLS ref.

Article illustrates the Referee Exchange program MLS had in its early years.

Chapter 14

Fox Sports TV Rules Analyst
"The Doctor Is In The House"

Early in my time at Major League Soccer, as Vice President of Game Operations, I was approached by Michael Cohen for a meeting to discuss ways and means to enhance the television broadcasts of MLS games. Cohen oversaw everything televised at MLS and had some innovative ideas. These included putting TV cameras on the goal posts or support stanchions, microphones on the corner flags and embedded into the turf, putting body cams on the referees and microphoning the officials so that the TV audience could share in their communications.

In addition, Cohen wanted a cameraman to come onto the field during the MLS shootout, 35-yard line tiebreaker scenario. By having a handheld camera placed behind the shooter, viewers could get the best angle on the play and see the shootout clock which was placed to the side of the goal. Somehow, we were able to get Federation approval for this request, perhaps because FIFA was permitting a cameraman on the field for kicks from the mark now known as "penalties".

While Cohen and I often "butted heads" on these and similar issues, we always did so with the mutual respect of knowing that all we each wanted was for MLS to be successful despite the history of every other professional soccer league in America failing.

Michael Cohen realized that there were very few soccer "play by play" and color commentators with previous high level refereeing experience. Most were unfamiliar with the intricacies and interpretations of the Laws of the Game. Cohen took the opportunity to invite me to a pre-season broadcaster's meeting and gave me the assignment of updating the "talent" on the latest interpretations of the Laws but also to speak about the role of the Disciplinary Committee.

In watching the video tapes of MLS games played in its first season, I realized how much work was needed in this area. Especially on local, rather than national, broadcasts. Not only did some announcers not fully understand the intricacies of the offside law, but they also couldn't discern the differences in the flag signals from assistant referees (foul or offside) or make the most of interpreting the body language or signals from the center referee. A clear example of the latter point is the similarity of the signal for penalty kick (pointing to the spot) and goal kick. One would only have to be familiar with the reaction of the players as to what happens next.

At one such meeting, I used the word "IFAB" to describe the International Football Associations Board, which was then followed up by a question from those to whom I was addressing, to explain what I was talking about. The term itself was not familiar nor was the knowledge that FIFA did not make up the Laws of the Game.

It was especially disheartening when an official got a call correctly, but the local broadcast team for whatever reason, went out of their way to prove the official wrong sometimes with improper use of video replay or no replay at all. This added to the public perception that the officiating in MLS was not up to par and added to the public criticism of officials which was plaguing the League in its early years.

Whenever I worked the broadcaster meetings, Michael Cohen would always schedule me to present right after lunch. He believed my presentations were lively enough with the use of video and props to wake up a sleepy group. He said that I knew how to "read the room". At times I would bring a referee with me just to further introduce the official to the group and to illustrate that the officials were a professional and caring group who had the game at its best interest, even when they had to make a "controversial call".

Once I asked a former coach, now color commentator, to come up to the front of the room to draw on the whiteboard what he was trying to explain in relation to offside. I made the comment that he must have watched Sunday morning telecasts of *Learn to Draw* with Jon Gnagy and only one other person in the room knew what I was talking about.

The news of the entertaining sessions that I was conducting somehow got to Don Garber and on one occasion both he and MLS President Mark Abbott, the man who wrote the business plan for MLS and saw it through, came to see the entertainment value for themselves. After that,

I was assigned by the Commissioner to make similar presentations to fan groups attending MLS Cup or All-Star weekends.

It was seemingly natural then that Cohen and his company Bizzy Signals Entertainment would be hired by Fox Sports when that company decided to launch their two sport channels, FS1 and FS2, which would contain significant soccer coverage. Fox Sports had huge success introducing Rules Analyst Mike Pereira, the former person in charge of NFL officials, to explain certain situations and otherwise controversial calls made by officials during NFL games on TV. This was the assignment Pereira would not reveal to us at the MLS Task Force on Officiating meeting he addressed.

Among Cohen's challenges was to recommend soccer personalities for the various positions on air, both "play by play" and color commentators and in-studio hosts and contributors. Fox had secured the English language TV rights from FIFA for the 2015 Women's World Cup and 2018, 2022 and 2026 Men's World Cups. In addition, Fox had the current rights to UEFA's Champions and Europa Leagues, as well as Bundesliga games each Saturday morning and some MLS games.

Upon Cohen's recommendation, I was interviewed over Skype for the position of Fox's first soccer Rules Analyst. During the interview, I relayed the story of how I met Mike Pereira during the task force meeting which led to the formation of the Professional Referee Organization (PRO). I thought I had a good interview but heard nothing back for several months. I became aware that Fox was interviewing other candidates, including former FIFA and MLS referees.

Cohen was apprised of the situation that Fox was prepared to go with another candidate. By coincidence, I was assigned by PRO to be in Los Angeles to assess and work as coach/mentor for an MLS LA Galaxy game. Cohen convinced the executives at Fox to give me an in-person interview the afternoon prior to the Saturday night game. Fox sent a car to my hotel and drove me to their studios in Century City. As it turned out, I arrived at their studios just as they were wrapping up a soccer broadcast. To my surprise, I was greeted by commentator Rob Stone and asked to sit at the desk and participate in what amounted to a screen test.

I was then shown a video of the US men's national team's World Cup qualifier against Costa Rica in Colorado, which has become known as "the snow game". I was asked to comment on what should have been a penalty kick awarded to the US and then further opine on the playing conditions and whether the game should have been postponed. It was then that my Match Commissioner's experience came into play. I knew that the Match Commissioner was from a warmer CONCACAF nation, and I jokingly suggested that he probably did not even bring a coat and was most likely bunkered up in a locker room.

The "screen test" lasted all of ten minutes, after which, I was greeted by several executives including Jonty Whitehead, who was assigned to Fox by Sky Sports in England to assist in the production of FS1 and FS2's soccer broadcasts. I was then told that a video tape of my work would be sent "upstairs" to be evaluated, and I was driven back to my hotel to get ready for the MLS game.

Several weeks went by before I received a phone call from Whitehead, who practically had to re-introduce himself as our previous meeting had been so brief. By this time, I was not expecting to hear anything further from Fox Sports. I was thoroughly surprised to hear Whitehead explain that I "got the job" and the reason was that the executives upstairs believed I "was a teacher" and that was what they were looking for at the time.

Within a matter of weeks, I was flown out to LA again, this time to sit in front of a bank of monitors in what was known as the "Pereira Room" where Mike Pereira worked every Sunday. Thereafter, I traveled to LA every other week. I would leave South Carolina on Monday afternoon to work UEFA Champions League games on Tuesday and Wednesday and a Europa League match on Thursday. I would then fly back to South Carolina on a "red eye" through Atlanta getting home late Friday morning.

The entire experience was brand new to me. Each broadcast day started with an hour-long production meeting where the "talent" was given a breakdown, minute by minute, of the pre-game, half-time and post-game schedules. If there was a controversial play, I would be asked to comment during the game. Since I was in the studio, there were times when I would be part of the pre-game show or even post-game. Often, we would pre-record a segment about a particular play or on-field incident, and it was sometimes marveled on how we could get it done in "one take".

In time, I was given an assistant who would operate an "EVS" (sometimes referred to as an Elvis) machine which enabled us to stop play, rewind, see the action in slow motion or make a still frame shot, which greatly assisted in my ability to correctly analyze a given situation. Did handling take place? What was the point of contact? Was there excessive force? And many other variables. With that help, I was able to inform the producer that we may have caught something not picked up in the regular speed broadcast. This was all before the introduction of VAR.

In fact, the first introduction of goal-line technology (GLT) happened at the 2015 FIFA Women's World Cup. Fox had stationed us all in Vancouver, Canada, taking over a facility right on the harbor and in walking distance to the stadium. FIFA was beginning to realize the importance of having broadcasters fully aware of the latest technology and instructions to game officials as transparency was becoming the order of the day. Spectators were beginning to attend games with their cell phones or tablets and were able to see video replays that FIFA was not yet permitting to be shown on a stadium's giant screen.

As such, all the broadcast teams that were headquartered in Vancouver were invited out to the stadium to witness the testing process and utilization of GLT. In addition, FIFA scheduled a media day with the referees, and we watched them train and were able to interview the officials of our choice. It was at this event that I met, once again, Toru Kamikawa, the former MLS exchange referee from Japan who was now the head of the Japanese referee program and a FIFA referee instructor.

The Fox Sports studios and production center in Vancouver were within walking distance of our hotel. I had been assigned a young producer from Fox's local LA channel by the name of Micah King. We had a small room with a bank of monitors and a camera in case there was a play so important or egregious that they wanted to bring me into the broadcast live. I had plastered the walls with information about all of the referees garnered from various websites which tracked their games, number of cautions and send-offs etc. We kept a running tally of each referee's assignment in the tournament so we could assist the broadcasters in describing the history and background of each official, not only in this tournament but in their entire international careers. I also made "cheat sheets" with word-by-word quotations of the appropriate Law on the critical match decisions of offside, careless, reckless and excessive force challenges, stopping a promising attack (SPA), denial of an obvious goal or goal scoring opportunity (DOGSO), serious foul play and violent conduct etc.

In the opening game, Ukrainian referee Kateryna Monzul awarded Canada a penalty kick against China two minutes into added time, from which they scored what turned out to be the match's only goal. There had always been subjective commentary that the home team would get the benefit of doubt on 50/50 decisions because FIFA wanted the home teams to advance so that local interest in the tournament would be maintained. I was brought on to the post-game show and explained how any one of three — holding, charging and kicking — fouls could have been applied, making the decision entirely legitimate.

Later in the tournament, I had to correct a previous comment I had made on an offside decision when Jonty Whitehead came to our room asking me to look at another angle that had surfaced. I used the opportunity to explain how unless one is in position with the second to last defender, or has a TV angle that is perfect, one should not jump to conclusions regarding offside.

And when a game was held up due to lightning, I quickly got out my Match Commissioner's Handbook and was able to quote the exact 30/30 guidelines which would be used to determine when the game would restart.

Fox always did a great job providing accommodation and opportunities on days off for their talent and staff, and Vancouver was no exception. Because we were in Canada for the Fourth of July and could not celebrate that day, Fox hired a tour boat and scheduled their own fireworks show on the first available day off. I was happy that, by this time, Barbara and grandson Ryder were able to join us. Micah King and Ryder hit it off and did some adventurous things together, hiking in the nearby hills and mountains.

The following summer, the US hosted Copa America Centenario, and working in LA, I was able to comment on the impending use of VAR which FIFA was testing and how, if we had it for the Copa, several goals would have to be disallowed. At the studio desk, I had an exchange with former English international Ian Wright, during which he argued that if offside was going to be called this close with the use of video replay, then half of his 248 goals scored in league and international play would have to be disallowed. He had a valid point.

After the Women's World Cup of 2015, Fox installed a "Home Cam" system in my home office where I was able to be involved in broadcasts of games produced from all over the world. I would be required to sit in my chair which was wired to a headset and mic and speak with the producer before contacting the announcers wherever they might be, regardless of whether they were working from monitors in LA or at the actual game. This meant not having to travel to LA or the venue of the game unless there was a major tournament.

But I did get to travel to some of the matches of the 2017 CONCACAF Gold Cup. The final was to be played in Santa Clara, CA on July 26th. I was woken at 5am by a phone call from a number I did not recognize so I let it ring. There was no message. Several hours later, a second call came in from the same number. This time after letting it ring there was a voicemail message. It was Hank Steinbrecher, from US Soccer, asking that I return the call as he had some news for me. I immediately called back, and Mr. Steinbrecher informed me that I was elected to the National Soccer Hall of Fame in the Category of "Builder". This came as a complete surprise as it was totally unexpected.

Later that evening there was a Fox staff dinner, during which I signaled for attention by knocking my glass with my spoon, similarly as they do at a Polish wedding when the groom is expected to kiss the bride. I then announced my Hall induction at the dinner to my Fox family before telling anyone back home, even Barbara. Rob Stone then announced it on a Fox soccer pre-game show introducing it with the words: "I hope you've told Barbara by now."

The National Soccer Hall of Fame originally opened in Oneonta, New York, which gave itself the title of "Soccer City USA" due mainly to the results of Hartwick College, and to some extent, Oneonta State University. I was inducted into the NISOA Hall of Fame in a ceremony in Oneonta in 2003.

The Hall in Oneonta had fallen on hard times, even with its proximity to Cooperstown and a replacement was being built in Frisco, Texas, with the support of the Hunt family, owners of MLS' FC Dallas. Since the Hall would not be ready for my induction in 2018, I was inducted at US Soccer's AGM in Orlando along with fellow former goalkeepers Briana Scurry and the late great Tony DiCicco. In my acceptance speech, I commented that three goalkeepers were being honored because, "There was a lot to save at the Federation."

Six tables of family and friends attended the induction and Barbara also planned pre and post induction get togethers, including a dinner amongst the shark tanks at Sea World. Swimming with sharks was a skill I had to learn repeatedly during my career.

Earlier in 2017, I learned of the passing of Earl Foreman at the age of 92. Herb Silva and I had last seen him upon the occasion of the second MLS Cup Final in Washington, DC in 1997. We invited him to dinner at a restaurant of his choosing in DC and we all reminisced about the good old days of indoor soccer.

He did not live long enough to see the success of Major League Soccer, or the premiere of a film dedicated to his ownership of ABA's Virginia Squires which revolutionized basketball with their run and gun style, the red, white and blue ball and the play of Julius Erving. The film was entitled *The Dream Maker – the Earl Foreman Story*, produced by Eric Futterman. John Kowalski had been contacted by Stuart Foreman, Earl's son, to attend the premiere at a theater in Norfolk, VA. Kowalski could not attend and asked if I would represent him. Barbara and I traveled to Norfolk to get to the designated hotel about 4pm in time for the 7pm premiere. We had no itinerary and asked at the front desk for directions and whether there would be transportation to and from the theater. The front desk person directed us to talk with the tall person at the back of the room. I introduced myself and then the person said, "Hello, I am Julius Erving." Flabbergasted, I asked Barbara to take our picture. "Dr. Joe meets Dr. J." I will never forget it. Just before boarding the bus, we met with Stuart, who had worked on occasion at various MISL positions and Phyliss, Earl's wife, as well as other family members. At the premiere, I requested to speak representing the soccer community. I was the only "soccer person" there. And I also got to meet Al Bianchi, the legendary coach who Earl Foreman said I reminded him of, and I shared that story with him. We shared a few other Earl Foreman memories.

In 2018, Fox traveled our entire production crew to Moscow for the FIFA Men's World Cup. Fox set up an elaborate studio in Red Square in walking distance from our hotel. Although I taped a segment on the use of VAR at the studio prior to the first game, I did not return to the studio as I was headquartered at the International Broadcasting Center (IBC) where telecasts for every country in the world would originate. It was also the home of the VAR. It would be the first time the video review concept would be used at a World Cup, and everyone knew that no matter how much the officials and technicians would prepare, there was sure to be controversy.

MLS and PRO had been using the VAR concept, Commissioner Garber being convinced that such ability to correct clear and obvious errors on the field would be good for the game and solve some of the officiating issues that had plagued the League from its outset. As such, I contacted Howard Webb, who was now at the head of the VAR program at PRO and asked his permission to join the PRO officials at one of their meetings where VAR was to be used and evaluated.

Although I was not expecting him to remember, I met with Webb in 2007 when MLS and the Mexican Federation began the Superliga tournament which pitted the top four teams from MLS and Liga MX in a knockout competition. Ivan Gazidis and I wanted the best possible referee at the time to handle the final, which we all thought would be a classic game between a MLS team and a team from Liga MX.

We contacted Webb and offered a game fee of $1,000 for the final, which he graciously accepted, with of course full transportation, a per diem, hotel and other expenses. As it turned out, the final was played between two MLS teams, Houston and New England, and we could have asked Webb not to come. We did not renege on our offer, and I met with Webb at his Boston area hotel and paid him the money in cash prior to the match, which went to penalties after the game ended 2-2 in regulation time.

I was sitting in the PRO referee meeting room in Minneapolis, where I would spend several days learning the ins and outs of VAR. When Howard Webb walked into the room, he looked at me and loudly proclaimed: "There's royalty present." So classy! He immediately acted to make sure I was welcomed by all the referees and for the next several days I worked as a VAR on simulated game situations under the direction of Mark Geiger, who was also to be a referee at the World Cup.

Prior to going to Russia, we had a lengthy security meeting on Zoom where we were advised not to bring our cell phones or computers to Moscow. Fox would supply each of us with the necessary equipment. The cell phone we were given would have a tracking device so that Fox security would know where we were at all times. We were then advised not to go to any policemen in Moscow if we got lost or were in any kind of difficulty for fear of being "shaken down". Instead, Fox security would be with us within five minutes after alerting them with our special cell phone.

Each morning in Moscow, I would be transported by van to the IBC located 30 minutes out in the suburbs, where a separate studio was set up just in case there was a power outage or other problem at the Red Square location. The entire Fox IBC set-up was organized by Kevin Callahan, who was a five-year goalkeeping camper at No.1 Goalkeeper's Camp. Kevin welcomed me and made the set-up as comfortable as possible. The location was also the site of each morning's production meeting, during which I was able to present my point of view on officiating to all present and those on set in the main studio. At the IBC, I had a battery of monitors which could be used as a split screen because there would be occasions when I would work two games at the same time, such as when the final group games were played simultaneously. And each morning there was a new wardrobe set up for me to wear just in case I was asked to be on screen.

Because everyone knew that FIFA's new VAR system was going to be the talk of the tournament, a special meeting for me was arranged with Roberto Rosetti, the former FIFA and World Cup referee who now had the title of VAR Project Leader at the 2018 World Cup. Rosetti spent over an hour with me in private conversation and then later, again, when our entire broadcast team was invited to tour the VOR (Video Operations Room). In addition, FIFA held a media briefing conducted by former referees Collina, Massimo Busacca and Rosetti, in which the entire VAR procedure was again detailed in length. If anything, I thought I now knew as much about VAR as anyone in the world.

FIFA was smart to have the officials in the VOR in full uniform so they would feel part of the officiating team, and as much as possible, have the VAR come from the same country and/or speak the same language as the referee on the field.

I spent much of the first half of the World Cup explaining the VAR procedure and concept on air as almost every game had an official on-field review in which the referee would go to the monitor to hopefully see a better angle on a play that, at least in the VAR's opinion, represented a decision that was a "clear and obvious error".

The highlight, for me at least, came in the final match. I had been encouraged by Fox executives to start the practice of predicting the referee's final decision as he was reviewing a play on the VAR monitor and before rendering the final decision to the players and coaches with a signal. With the score tied 1-1 between Croatia and France, referee Nestor Pitana went to the monitor to get a better angle to judge whether there was handling in the penalty area by Croatia's Ivan Perisic. The decision was a difficult one as Perisic's arm seemed to be at his side as the ball, which came from a corner kick, hit his arm after a possible deflection off the heads of players directly and closely in front of him. Pitana spent a long time at the monitor. The decision had the possibility of being critical to the outcome of the match. Then, he walked away from the monitor, paused and then went back for a second look. I did not know at the time that the monitor had failed while he was watching it and then came back on while he was walking away. Advised of the occurrence, Pitana spent some more time in front of the monitor. I took a chance, reading his body language and with knowledge of the other handling decisions that were made throughout the tournament, I stated on air that Pitana was going to award a penalty kick. Alas, he turned away from the screen, walked onto the field and signaled to the spot. After the match, Fox executive Ben Grossman came to me to congratulate me on the "educated guess" and stated the hope that I would be able to continue the practice in any such tournaments in the future.

I continued to work as a Rules Analyst exclusively for Fox, mostly with the use of the Home Cam, which can be a challenge as it is not connected to an EVS machine, and I therefore must rely only on the replays that are shown to the general TV audience. I do have a TV in the room with the Home Cam but use satellite TV which presents the picture some 17 seconds later than what I have seen on the home cam monitor. Usually that is far too late.

In 2019 the FIFA Women's World Cup was being conducted in France at the same time as CONCACAF's Gold Cup and Fox had the rights to both. Fox brought all the talent into LA for preparations, and I was introduced to Cristina Unkle, who would handle the women's tournament from LA off a monitor while I worked the Gold Cup from the home cam. I did my best to mentor Christina over those three days to get her ready for the challenge ahead. She did a fantastic job which led to her being offered several similar positions, both on network and streaming services, for international and domestic competitions.

The 2022 Men's World Cup was held in Qatar. Fox hired former FA and FIFA referee Mark Clattenburg to also work the tournament. I had done all 64 games by myself in Russia, as many as three a day, but the tournament in the Middle East was condensed over a shorter period and four games a day was a new challenge. Mark and I would split the coverage.

There was a great advantage to having Clattenburg with us, as he had worked with so many of the officials who were assigned to the tournament and could be in direct contact with them throughout. In addition, he was on a first-name basis with Collina, which of course could be useful.

I had never met Clattenburg before, but he introduced himself as if he knew me when we both boarded a bus in Qatar for our first orientation meeting.

Getting to Qatar was an adventure, indeed. JP Dellacamera, Tom Rinaldi and I were stuck at JFK as we were not permitted to board our flight due to perceived difficulty with our previously approved "Hayya Card" which was tantamount to a Visa. There were several hours of haggling, including being in touch with Fox's travel consultant, the US Embassy in Qatar, Qatar Airlines and representatives of Qatar immigration. As my personal telephone was being used for all these international calls, I accumulated some $700 in phone charges which Fox later reimbursed.

Clattenburg and I attended the FIFA media briefing prior to the tournament at which the concept of Semi-Automatic Offside Technology (SAOT) was introduced. In essence, 12 additional cameras were in place to monitor parts of every player's body, 50 hits per second which, when used with a computer connected ball, could determine at a much faster rate whether a player was in an offside position at the moment the ball was played by a teammate.

I was assigned to the first game and, sure enough, SAOT would come into play within the first four minutes. Ecuador scored a goal which looked to the naked eye to be valid. There was a situation where the Qatar goalkeeper left his line to play a crossed ball from a free-kick and then a scramble with defenders on or near the goal line. All players seemed onside, and I could not understand the long delay after Ecuador scored. I knew every goal would be reviewed but this one hardly seemed necessary. I tried to explain on air the situation whereby there must be two defenders closer to the goal line when the goalkeeper is not the last defender. After what seemed like an eternity, the goal was disallowed because at the taking of the free kick, an Ecuadorian attacker had his foot ahead of the line of Qatari defenders. SAOT picked up what the human eye could not see in real time. And as I was prepared to talk about SAOT, I, instead, was focused on the wrong aspect of play.

After about ten games, Mark Clattenburg and I convinced those in charge that we needed an EVS machine and, when it finally arrived, there was smooth sailing the rest of the way.

The 2023 Women's World Cup was hosted by Australia and New Zealand, and I had the pleasure of working that tournament from the home-cam in South Carolina. Because of the time zone difference, it meant working games in the middle of the night and trying to get some sleep during the day. Barbara managed my schedule, mealtimes etc. in order to accomplish the task.

I believed I had a strong tournament, enhanced by predicting that referee Tori Penso would award a penalty kick for Spain after VAR had recommended that she go to the monitor to see an angle showing that an England defender deflected the ball with her hand. My view was that there was movement of the hand to the ball and the position of the hand made her body bigger. After a lengthy review, the penalty kick was awarded and saved. Spain won the final 1-0.

During the summer of 2024, Fox had secured the rights for the European Championship and the Copa America, which was again going to be played in the United States. The tournaments overlapped and I assisted Mark Clattenburg by calling five games at the Euros before focusing entirely on the Copa.

In the summer of 2025, Fox had both the CONCACAF Gold Cup and UEFA Women's "Euros" Tournaments. Once again, Mark Clattenburg and I shared the Rules Analyst responsibilities with Mark covering the Euros while I focused on the Gold Cup. We each now had Home Cams.

The Gold Cup Final between Mexico and the USA drew 3.73 million viewers on Fox which was up 239% over the 2023 Final. The game peaked at 5.2 million viewers during its last 15 minutes.

Also, the expanded FIFA CLUB World Cup was being played simultaneously on another network and drew huge crowds to its more significant matchups.

And with less than a year to go, all attention was being turned to the 2026 FIFA World Cup expanded to include 48 teams: 104 matches with 78 of those matches being played in the United States.

All this from the "Sandlots"!

One can only speculate what Walter Chyzowych and the early US Soccer Coaching School candidates, many of whom have passed, would think about the rewards of their pioneering efforts.

I feel fortunate to be able to reflect on the growth and development of soccer in America from the INSIDE. And to share with the reader and anyone else who will listen, how soccer in America was mostly a Sunday League sport played in ethnic communities. And how over seven decades, the passion and dedication of players, coaches, referees, investors, administrators, and others in love with the beautiful game, all builders in their own way, have step by step brought soccer into mainstream American life.

From the early days at parks like McCarren and ovals like New Farmers to multi-field soccer complexes and soccer specific stadiums to the crescendos of the Rose Bowl and Met Life. From TVs "Soccer Made in Germany" to national network coverage to exposure to nearly every league and competition streamed and otherwise.

We may never call the game Football, Futbol or Fussball because it will always be soccer to us! It has gained an American Foothold!

And, as Rob Stone said when he first introduced me on Fox Sports: "The Doctor is in House!"

The National Association of Sports Officials (NASO) brought together the Rules Analysts from all sports for their National Convention and then published this article in their Referee Magazine.

With "Dr. J" Julius Erving at the debut of *"The Dream Maker"* a film about Earl Foreman's ABA Virginia Squires.

Staying on top of the latest changes to the Laws of the Game and their interpretations is key to providing a quick and accurate analysis of any officiating decision.

Some thirty-five years later, the 1990 coaching staff got together at a Walt Chyzowych Fund event at the United Soccer Coaches Convention in Chicago.

On a day off in Qatar, I got to ride a camel. I don't recommend it!

Joseph & Barbara

Throughout this journey from the Sandlots to the World Cup, Barbara has always been at my side! The journey does not take place without her presence and support. Barbara and I would like to thank you for being part of this adventure. We sincerely hope that you have enjoyed it, whether you participated in some way in real life or are reading about it for the first time.
The sandlots are gone! The beautiful game has captured us all!
While the photo above can be interpreted at the sunset, it actually is sunrise. Because this is just the beginning!

APPENDIX A
HALLS OF FAME
1. Long Island University (1975/2001/2008)
2. University of New Haven (1978/2001)
3. Connecticut State Soccer Association (2002)
4. New England Soccer Hall of Fame (2002)
5. National Intercollegiate Soccer Officials Association (2003)
6. Ukrainian Sports Hall of Fame (2017)
7. National Soccer Hall of Fame (2017)
8. Eastern New York State Association (2023)
9. United Soccer Coaches formerly NSCAA (2024)

AWARDS
1. Eastern College Athletic Conference for Scholarship and Athletic Prowess (1964)
2. Long Island University: Outstanding Alumnus Award (1987)
3. University of New Haven: Outstanding Service Award (2001)
4. Walt Chyzowych Fund: Lifetime Achievement Award (2005)
5. National Soccer Coaches Association of America (NSCAA): Letter of Commendation (2011)
6. New York City Soccer Gala Award (2014)
7. National Intercollegiate Soccer Officials Association (NISOA) - Ray Bernabei Award (2017)
8. Walt Chyzowych Fund - Distinguished Coaching Career (2018)
9. University of Utah, Department of Parks, Recreation and Tourism - Outstanding Alumnus (2024)

PLAYING HONORS - Long Island University
1. All New York State Soccer Team (1961/1962/1963)
2. All Metropolitan Intercollegiate Soccer League Team (1962/1963)
3. All-American Honorable Mention (1962)

COACHING HONORS
1. Long Island University: Metropolitan Intercollegiate Soccer League – Coach of the Year (1966/1967)
2. University of New Haven: New England Intercollegiate Soccer League Division II – Coach of the Year (1977)

OFFICIATING AWARDS
1. NCAA Division I Championship Game (1988)
2. New England Intercollegiate Soccer League – Outstanding Official Award (1991)

APPENDIX B
FIFA / CONCACAF Match Commissioner Assignments
1. Panama/Canada Futsal Playoff – Panama City, Panama (May 15, 2004)
2. Dominican Republic/Trinidad & Tobago – 2006 WC Qualifier – Dominican Republic (June 13, 2004)
3. U20 WC Qualification Tournament – San Pedro Sula, Honduras (May 2005)
4. Trinidad & Tobago/Mexico – 2006 WC Qualifier – Port of Spain (September 8, 2005)
5. U17 WC Qualification Tournament – Culiacan, Mexico (March 2005)
6. Costa Rica/Panama – 2006 WC Qualifier – San Jose, Costa Rica (March 26, 2005)
7. Guatemala/Panama – 2006 WC Qualifier – Guatemala City, Guatemala (August 17, 2005)
8. Guatemala/Mexico – 2006 WC Qualifier – Guatemala City, Guatemala (October 8, 2005)
9. Pachuca/CD Marquense – 2007 CONCACAF Champions Semi-Final – Pachua, Mexico (February 22, 2007)
10. Chivas Guadalajara/Pachuca – 2007 CONCACAF Champions Cup – Guadalajara, Mexico (April 18, 2007)
11. Bahamas/British Virgin Islands – 2010 WC Qualifier – Nassau, Bahamas (March 26, 2008)
12. Belize/Mexico – 2010 WC Qualifier – Houston, Texas USA (June 15, 2008)
13. Montreal Impact/Real Esteli Nicaragua – 2008 CONCACAF Champions League – Montreal, Canada (August 27, 2008)

14. Canada/Honduras – 2010 WC Qualifier – Montreal, Canada (September 6, 2008)
15. Santos Laguna/CSD Municipal – CONCACAF Champions League – Torreon, Mexico (September 17, 2008)
16. Jamaica/Mexico – 2010 WC Qualifier – Kingston, Jamaica (October 11, 2008)
17. El Salvador/Mexico – 2010 WC Qualifier – San Salvador (June 6, 2009)
18. Toluca/Marathon – CONCACAF Champions League – Toluca, Mexico (September 17, 2009)
19. Mexico/El Salvador – 2010 WC Qualifier – Mexico City, Mexico (October 10, 2009)
20. New Zealand/Bahrain – 2010 WC Qualifier Playoff – Wellington, New Zealand (November 14, 2009)
21. Bahamas/Turks & Caicos – 2014 WC Qualifier – Nassau, Bahamas (July 9, 2011)
22. Antigua & Barbuda/Curacao – 2014 WC Qualifier – Antigua & Barbuda (September 2, 2011)
23. Grenada/St. Vincent & Grenadines – 2014 WC Qualifier – Grenada (October 15, 2011)
24. St. Kitts & Nevis/Canada – 2014 WC Qualifier – St. Kitts & Nevis (November 11, 2011)
25. Alajuelense/Tigres – CONCACAF Champions League – Alajuela, Costa Rica (August 29, 2012)
26. Monterrey/Xelaju – CONCACAF Champions League – Monterrey, Mexico (March 12, 2013)
27. Costa Rica/Honduras – 2014 WC Qualifier – San Jose, Costa Rica (June 7, 2013)
28. Panama/Jamaica – 2014 WC Qualifier – Panama City, Panama (September 6, 2013)
29. Grenada/Haiti – 2018 WC Qualifier – Saint-Georges, Granada (September 4, 2015)
30. Vancouver MLS/Olympia Honduras – CONCACAF Champions League – Vancouver, Canada (September 15, 2015)
31. Monterrey/Arabe Unido – CONCACAF Champions League – Monterrey, Mexico (August 17, 2016)
32. Honduras/Canada – 2018 WC Qualifier – San Pedro Sula, Honduras (September 2, 2016)

APPENDIX C
PUBLICATIONS
1. "Intramural Handbook" (Long Island University, 1965,1966)
2. "The New York Diary of Badu & Tejan - United States News Information Agency - Documentary Film (1968)
3. "The Goalkeeper" - The Coaching Clinic (Prentice-Hall, Inc., August 1973)
4. "Motivational Aspects of Soccer" - The Coaching Clinic (Prentice-Hall, Inc., August 1973)
5. "A Goalkeeping Philosophy - An Analysis & Evaluation of Modern Trends in Coaching Soccer" (Azusa Pacific College Press, 1973)
6. "Recreation in Planned Retirement Villages" Doctoral Dissertation (University of Utah, 1973)
7. "Some Thoughts About Soccer's Goalkeeper" - The Coaching Clinic (Prentice-Hall, Inc., June 1974)
8. "Motivating the Soccer Player" in conjunction with Dr. Leonard Lucenko - The Coaching Clinic (Prentice-Hall, Inc., July 1974)
9. "Analysis Reveals LA's Free Kick Strategy" NASL - Soccer America (June 28, 1977)
10. "The Goalkeeper" Newsletter - Reusch/No. 1 Goalkeeper's Club (1985)
11. "For Soccer's Most Important Player" - Reusch/No. 1 Goalkeeper's Club (1985)
12. "Indoor Goalkeeping" - USYSA Network (1987)
13. "Indoor Goalkeeping" as Commissioner, AISA - American Soccer Magazine (1987)
14. "A Message to AISA Soccer Fans" - American Soccer Magazine (1987)
15. "AISA Referee Signal Roster" - American Soccer Magazine (1987)
16. "Extending The Range Of The Goalkeeper" - USYSA Network (1989)
17. "World Cup Report" - ALIX Uhlsport Monthly Update (February 1990)
18. "Machnik Analyzes Goalkeeper's Future in Soccer" - United States Coach, Vol 2 Issue 6 (Nov/Dec 1991)
19. "Overload Training For Goalkeepers: Double Goal Theory" - NSCAA Coaching Soccer, edited by Tim Schum (1996)
20. "Complex Training Drills For Goalkeepers" in conjunction with Frans Hoek - NSCAA Coaching Soccer, edited by Tim Schum (1996)
21. "Machnik Appointed Executive-in-Residence" - Sports Industries Management - University of New Haven (Fall 1997)

APPENDIX D
SPEAKING ENGAGEMENTS, CLINICS, APPEARANCES AND POCASTS

1. "Adjusting Defense to Offense with Walter Chyzowych", National Soccer Coaches Association of America (NSCAA) Annual Convention, New York NY (January 1969)
2. Nassau County Soccer Coaches Association Clinic, NY (1968)
3. Valley Stream North High School Clinic, NY (1968,69)
4. Commack High School Varsity Club Dinner, NY (1968)
5. Hamden High School Varsity Club Dinner, CT (1969)
6. Civitan Association of Greater New Haven CT (1969)
7. New Jersey Soccer Coaches Association Clinic, NJ (1969,75,77)
8. American Legion Post #71 Sports Night, West Haven CT (1970)
9. Queens College, Physical Education Majors Club, NY (1971)
10. "The Goalkeeper", NSCAA Convention, St. Louis MO (January 1972)
11. West Haven High School Varsity Club Dinner, CT (1972)
12. Milford Park & Recreation Department Soccer Banquet, CT (1973)
13. Kutcher's Country Club Mid-Winter Sports Clinic, Monticello NY (1974)
14. Northeast Urban-Suburban Recreation Conference - Chairman, Panel on "Recreation for the Aging in an Urban Setting, New Haven CT (1974)
15. George Washington Lodge No.82, Ansonia CT (1975)
16. New Jersey Interscholastic Coaches Association Annual Coaches Conference, NJ (1975)
17. National Soccer Coaches Association of America - Development Staff Clinics: Bridgeton Academy, ME (May 1974) - Suffolk County Community College, NY (June 1974) - SUNY Binghamton, NY (August 1974) - Minneapolis MN (June 1975) - Milwaukee WI (June 1975) - Colorado Springs CO (May 1976) - Cincinnati OH (May 1976) - Alexandria, VA (March 1977) - Shippensburg, PA (1977,78) - Westchester PA (1979)
18. Sociology of Leisure Seminar, Southern Connecticut State College, CT (1976)
19. Northwest Indiana Soccer Clinic, IN (1977)
20. Hamden High School Banquet, CT (1977)
21. Guilford High School Banquet, CT (1977)

22. First Congregation Church, East Hartford CT (1977)
23. Southern New York State Soccer Association Clinic, NY (1977)
24. West Chester State Soccer Academy, West Chester PA (1977)
25. "Goalkeeping" NSCAA Annual Convention, Philadelphia PA (January 1977)
26. Sportcraft Coaching Clinics, Poughkeepsie NY (March 1978), Alexandria VA (April 1978)
27. UNCAS Spring Soccer Jamboree, Albany State, NY (May 1978)
28. ProKeds Coaching Clinics, Los Angeles CA (January 1979)
29. West Haven "Rotary" – West Haven CT (December 1979)
30. Ohio State Soccer Coaches Association Annual Meeting, OH (March 1980)
31. Empire State Games Coaching Clinic, NY (Spring 1980)
32. Illinois Soccer Referee Association, IL (December 1985)
33. AIAC and UEFA International Coaches Association, Coverciano, Italy (October 1990)
34. Commonwealth Soccer Officials Association Clinic, MA (1992)
35. Charles E Murphy School – "Be All It Can Be", Waterford CT (Spring 1992)
36. 14th Annual Westchester Soccer Clinic, Rye NY (January 1993)
37. USISL Referee Clinic "Climbing the Pyramid" (January 1997)
38. MLS Rock 'n Soccer Celebrity Game – Disney's Wide World of Sports Complex (July 1998)
39. MLS All Access Luncheon (February 2009)
40. SCISOA – Soccer Officiating "The College Game", Charleston SC (August 2013)
41. Allen Sack Lecture Series on Sports and Social Issues – "Sixty Years Around the Beautiful Game", University of New Haven, CT (October 2017)
42. Planet Futball Podcast "The Long and Winding Soccer Journey of Dr. Joe" (February 2018)
43. Greater New Haven Soccer Officials Association – Annual Awards Banquet, CT (November 2018)
44. Modern Soccer Coach Podcast "Video Assistant Referee" (March 2020)
45. Soccer Coaches Summit "Conversations with Legends of Indoor Soccer" (May 2020)

46. We the Peeps Podcast "The Incredible Soccer Journey of Dr. Joe Machnik" (January 2021)
47. Whales Certified Podcast "Soccer Goalkeeping" (August 2024)
48. World Football Summit Podcast, Episode 109 "The Evolution of Soccer in North America (September 2024)
49. Episode 161 – 343 Podcast "These Stories About American Soccer History from Dr. Joe Machnik Will Blow You Away"
50. James Island Youth Soccer AGM (August 2025)
51. An American Game Podcast, Lone Eagles "A History of Goalkeeping in America" (August 2025)

APPENDIX E
THE PRESS

1. "State Soccer Takes Big Step: Oklahoma Soccer Association Given D-Level Program" – USSF National Coaching Staff – *Tulsa World* (August 1981)
2. "AISA Survives Growing Pains Under Machnik" – David Tanner – *Soccer America* (March 17, 1988)
3. "Only 20, But USA's Meola Is A Keeper" – Ray Jordan – *St. Louis Post Dispatch* (November 3, 1989)
4. "Helpful Tips" – *The Royale Gazette* (February 13, 1990)
5. "U.S. Benefits from Connecticut Connection" – Jerry Trecker – *The Hartford Courant* (May 18, 1990)
6. "Good in Goal" – Jerry Trecker – *The Hartford Courant* (May 20, 1990)
7. "A Coaches Eye-View of Meola" – 1990 World Cup – Michael Lewis – *Soccer Week* (May 24, 1990)
8. "Be All That You Can Be" – Student Awareness Day – Charles E. Murphy School – Oakdale CT (December 14, 1991)
9. "Joe Machnik Q & A" – Shots on Goal (June 1991)
10. "The Doctor Is In!" – Pete Zanardi – *Trackside* (October 16-19, 1992)
11. "Young, Rondeau, Holdridge Honored at Waterford Banquet (Joe Machnik Sportsman of the Year) – *Speedway Scene* (March 13, 1992)
12. "Machnik Excited About Prospects at UNH" – Paul Marslano – *New Haven Register* (September 3, 1993)
13. "Win Over Argentina a Long Time in Coming" – Jerry Trecker – *The Hartford Courant* (July 18, 1995)

14. "It's A Kick" George School, Newtown PA – Sports & Money, *Bucks County Courier Times* (August 7, 1996)
15. "Joe Machnik, University of New Haven D-II Women's Soccer" (Non-Revenue Sports) – *The Recruiting Struggle* by Lee Carter (1996)
16. "Joe Machnik Named Major League Soccer Vice President of Operations" – News Release – MLS (October 18, 1996)
17. "MLS Referee Exchange with Japan Ruled Success" commentary by Joe Machnik as Vice President of Game Operations – *USA TODAY* (September 19, 1997)
18. "Blowing … The Whistle" – *Soccer New England* (December 1998)
19. "Entering Its Fourth Season, MLS is Far From Measuring Up" – The Parting Shot – Frank Dell'Apa – *Soccer* (March/April 1999)
20. "Blowing … The Whistle" – Mike Jones – *Soccer New England* (April 2000)
21. "MLS to Crack Down on Dissent" – Backline – *Soccer America* (December 18, 2000)
22. "Wallach, Machnik set to enter Soccer Hall of Fame" – *Branford Review* (January 23, 2002)
23. "90 Minutes with Joe Machnik" – Joyce Furia – *Soccer New England* (2005)
24. "5 Minutes with Joe Machnik, Ph.D./Fox Sports Rules Analyst" – *REFEREE* (September 2016)
25. Dr. Joe Machnik: American Soccer's Renaissance Man" – Michael Lewis – *The Guardian* (April 2017)
26. "Not Your Ordinary Joe: Machnik Elected to the National Soccer Hall of Fame" – Michael Lewis – *Front Row Soccer* (August 2, 2017)
27. "5 Minutes with Joe Machnik, Ph.D./Fox Sports Rules Analyst" – *REFEREE* (November 2022)

Index

A

Abbott, Mark, 297, 303
Addotta, Marian, 263, 271
Agnolin, Luigi, 235
Agoos, Jeff, 251
Aiken, Carole, 94
Akers, Michele, 267
Aladren, Emilio Soriano, 232
Alberto, Luis, 152
Alderman, Dawn, 271
Alexander, Gary, 92
Allen, Kara, 263
Allen, Marcus, 242
Allen, Steve, 13
Alvarez, Fernando, 148
Alvarez, Leonel, 241
Ambrose, Darren, 196
Amoros, Sandy, 200
Anderson, Dave, 202
Anderson, Ole, 121
Andrews, Jeff, 80
Andrulis, Greg, 8, 97, 192, 203
Andrulis, Lorrie, 8, 203
Andrulis, Maggie, 8
Andrulis, Rob, 8, 203
Anschutz, Phillip, 284
Ardiles, Osvaldo, 186
Arena, Bruce, 212, 253, 276, 287
Arias, Oscar, 234
Armas, Chris, 287
Armstong, Desmond, 227, 240
Arrowsmith, Gordon, 236
Ashburn, Richie, 13
Ashley, John, 50
Aston, Harry, 9
Avelon, Henry, 65

B

Babb, Carl, 8, 93, 98
Babij, Jerry, 53, 54
Bacon, Danny, 201
Baharmast, Esse, 8, 145-157, 170-71, 275-91
Bahr, Walter, 92, 184
Bailey, Beth, 271
Balboa, Marcelo, 235, 240, 251
Banks, Glen, 83
Banks, Jimmy, 240, 245
Baresi, Franco, 246
Barrios, Alvaro, 93, 95-97
Barry, Bob, 8, 184, 190-94
Batata, 178
Bathgate, Andy, 13
Bean, Joe, 55
Beauregard, Dick, 214
Beckenbauer, Franz, 82
Beckham, David, 202
Bellinger, Tony, 110
Benevento, Joan, 98
Benevento, John, 98, 100, 142
Benko, Steve, 83
Bennett, Melissa, 282
Bentley, Doug, 19
Bentley, Max, 19
Bergamo, Nelson, 34
Bergamo, Giuseppe, 246
Berhalter, Jay, 294
Bernabei, Ray, 212

Bernstein, Alex, 111
Berti, Nicola 246
Bertrand, Paul, 29, 43
Best, George, 114
Bianchi, Al, 135, 309
Bilardo, Carlos, 249
Bilek, Michal, 245
Bilous, Len, 100, 130, 134
Birenbaum, Dr. William, 50, 65-66, 91
Bishop, Joe, 166, 173
Black, Jay, 52
Black, Marvin, 47
Blatter, Sepp, 230, 245, 282
Blazer, Chuck, 229, 230
Bliss, Brian, 227, 234, 236, 239-240
Bodinet, Eric, 192
Boring, Ryder, 307, 345
Boring-Sturgis, Adeline, 345
Boring-Sturgis, Joan, 345
Boring-Sturgis, Wesley, 345
Bourdeau, Paul, 55
Boyle, Silas, 192
Bradley, Gordon, 28-29, 32, 108-14, 188, 286
Bramble, Todd, 8, 116
Brawner, Scott, 345
Brcic, David, 115-117
Brewster, Ben, 34
Brisson, Clark, 8, 198, 201-03, 213, 268
Brisson, Olivia 22, 202, 345
Broner, Jurgen, 22
Broun, Heyward Hale, 56
Brown, Neville, 83, 86, 88
Brown, Rupert, 46

Bruce, Bob, 217
Buckley, John, 121
Bucyk, Johnny, 19
Budish, Jim, 146, 172
Buffallini, Dave, 92
Bujsaim, Ali, 282
Buonomo, Maria, 271
Busacca, Massimo, 311
Busch, Guy, 56
But, Richard, 146, 191

C

Calabrese, Scott, 196
Caliguri, Paul, 172, 227, 237-38, 240-41, 244, 253
Cambell, Terry, 145
Callahan, Kevin, 310, 311
Callahan, Tom, 42, 55
Callas, Charlie, 52
Campos, Jorge, 276
Cannuscio, Vincent, 45
Cantillo, Ringo, 121
Carbognani, Toni, 169
Carillo, Candice, 263
Carillo, Kim, 263, 271
Carli, Peter, 193
Carnevale, Andrea, 246
Carter, Jack, 31
Carter, Jimmy, 118
Caruso, Andy, 197
Carvacho, Eddy, 198
Cassidy, Jerry, 151
Causey, Jeff, 275
Chabot, Lorne, 116
Chacon, Raul, 236
Chacurian, Chico, 34, 263
Charles, Hutson, 235

Charlton, William "Billy", 184
Childs, Ted, 50, 54
Chin, Debbie, 8, 94, 101, 142, 262-63, 269
Christopher, Brother, 14
Chyzowych, Gene, 27, 33, 59, 98, 108, 114, 132, 266
Chyzowych, Ihor, 98, 266
Chyzowych, Ihor Jr, 98, 100
Chyzowych, Olga, 115-16, 266
Chyzowych, Walter, 7, 22, 27-34, 44-64, 80-98, 109-22, 129-56, 170, 182-93, 212, 226-51, 262-67, 286, 292, 314
Cila, Renato, 152, 155
Cirino, Tony, 117
Clattenburg, Mark, 312, 313, 314
Clavijo, Fernando, 154, 251
Clemente, Roberto, 116
Codesal, Edgardo, 245, 283
Coffee, Paul, 146, 191
Cohen, Michael, 8, 302-04
Cohen, Mickey, 8, 53-54, 187
Cohen, Tony, 110
Collina, Pierluigi, 311, 313
Collins, Michael, 155
Collins, Peter, 155
Connolly, Ray, 83
Constantine, Gus, 145, 147, 211
Contiguglia, Dr. Bob, 119
Corbett, Cornelia, 171
Cornelius, Sarah, 271
Cornell, Bob, 79
Cosgrove, Tommy, 14, 26
Couto, Dimas, 93, 97
Covone, Neil, 240, 241, 243
Cox, Bill, 28

Cramer, Dettmar, 106-21, 129, 186, 251, 266, 292
Crandell, Jessica, 271
Crouse, Artie, 79, 81, 93
Crow, Kevin, 227
Cruyff, Johan, 114, 139
Cunningham, Mike, 48
Curran, Richard, 78

D

Dachniewski, Yaro, 198
Daft, Bobby, 80
Dale, Francis, 158
Dangelo, Paul, 170
Dasayev, Rinat, 131
Davies, John, 145
Davis, Rick, 117, 122, 227-29, 267
Dayes, Hylton, 198, 201
DeCarlo, Dr. Thomas J., 89
Decker, Mary, 136
de Hoog, J. Walter, 60
DelGobbo, Paul "Topsy", 78
Dell, Gabe, 13
Dellacamera, JP, 313
Dellarocco, Rick, 80
DeMarsh, Nick, 196
Demers, Isabel, 263
Demling, Buzz, 133
Demorro, Nikki, 263, 271
DeNardis, Larry, 269
DeNardis, Mary Lou, 269
DeRose, Mireille, 8, 202, 263, 271
D'Errico, Dave, 152
Devaney, Nikki, 263
DeWeese, Don, 145, 171
DeWeese, Rita, 171
Diaz Arce, Raul 275

DiCicco, Tony, 36, 199, 308
DiCostanzo, Joe, 65, 83, 86
DiFlorio, August, 52, 93
Dikranian, Bob, 95
DiMatteo, Marissa, 271
D'Ippolito, Gino, 133, 140-41, 143-44
Dodd, Mark, 240, 251
Dolinsky, John, 143, 178, 201
Donadoni, Roberto, 246
Donnely, George, 109
Donovan, Landon, 267, 281
Dorrance, Anson, 212
Dougal, Stuart, 282
Dowler, Mike, 141
Doyle, John, 227, 237-38, 240, 245
Duback, Jeff, 227, 234, 235
Dyak, Troy, 240, 251
Dykes, Dave, 214
Dziurzynski, Stanley, 83

E

Ebert, Don, 141
Eck, Ted, 240
Eddy Bruce, Skye, 194, 195
Edwards, Gene, 114, 121
Eichmann, Eric, 172, 198, 227-29, 236-37, 240
Elfath, Ismail, 295, 296
Elliot, Simon, 290
Ellis, Betty, 145
Ellis, Jill, 267
Ely, Alex, 27
Engl, Paul, 60, 64
Ercoli, Pat, 134, 140
Everone, Claudio, 263
Erving, Julius, 90, 129, 309

Eskenazi, Gerald, 134
Etherington, Gary, 117, 155, 157

F

Fallon, Rory 290
Fanning, Jim, 64, 78
Farrell, Colleen, 202
Farrell, Sam, 50, 53, 55, 60, 63
Faulkner, John, 217
Favellato, 30
Feger, Bob, 47
Ferro, John, 265
Ficken, Dieter, 43, 44, 66
Fillol, Ubaldo, 186
Finlay, Thomas, 266
Firmani, Eddie, 66
Fisher, Terry, 137
Flanders, Mario, 95
Fleck, Tom, 120
Flo, Tore Andre, 149
Flynn, Dan, 294
Flynn, Melissa, 263
Fontella, Jonah, 33
Foreman, Earl, 7, 90, 118, 129-32, 135-38, 140, 141-48, 150-53, 157-58, 167-68, 247-48, 309
Foreman, Phyliss, 129, 309
Foreman, Stuart, 309
Fortin, Bill 121, 211
Foster, Jim, 138
Fraiture, Guy, 132
Francis, Emil 13
Franklin, Joe, 32
Frezza, Harry, 265
Fricker, Werner, 121, 149, 170, 226, 226-51, 262-66, 286
Friedel, Brad, 198, 253

Fuchs, Steve, 227
Fuksman, Felix, 145
Funes, Juan Manuel, 236
Furillo, Carl, 200
Furman, Krys, 8, 93-95, 97, 100, 134
Futterman, Eric, 30

G

Gabarra, Jim, 169, 172-73, 198, 227, 229, 231, 234
Gagg, Walter, 230-31, 248, 288
Gallaro, Louis, 50, 53, 60, 63
Ganias, Kristine, 271
Gansler, Bob, 7, 110, 118, 232-33, 235-36, 238-39, 245, 247-48, 249, 251, 262, 266-69, 286
Garafano, Gigi, 34
Garber, Don, 8, 284-85, 291-93, 296-97, 303, 309
Garcia-Aranda, Jose Maria, 282
Gardner, Phillip, 97
Garrett, Mike, 170, 171
Gaspar, Dan, 97, 187, 199
Gazidis, Ivan, 8, 284, 286-88, 293, 310
Geiger, Mark, 310
Gilbert, Ron, 184
Glanville, Brian, 46
Glavin, Tony, 150
Glenn, Rudy, 172
Glisovic, Svetislav, 113
Gmoch, Jacek, 113
Gnagy, Jon, 303
Godfrey, Steve, 214
Gomez, Omar, 152
Gold, Ronnie, 266

Goldman, Danny, 142, 145
Gooding, Peter, 36
Gordon, Billy, 203
Gori, Mario, 275
Gosselin, Mike, 201, 268
Goulet, Brent, 172, 227, 229, 234
Gourash, Dan, 93, 95
Graham, Tony, 111
Granitza, Karl-Heinz, 178
Green, Peter, 44
Greenberg, Mrs., 18
Gretzky, Wayne, 138
Grgurev, Fred, 155, 156, 157
Grossman, Ben, 312
Guest, Joe, 291, 293, 294, 297
Gugliotti, Nikki, 263
Gulati, Sunil, 8, 219, 228, 239, 270, 280, 286, 294, 295, 297
Guzman, Javier, 82

H

Hackett, Keith, 294
Hadfield, Vic, 13
Hagen, Ron, 173, 174
Hagler, Marvin, 246
Hall, Brian, 276, 283
Harkes, John, 227, 234-35, 240-41, 244, 275
Harris, Paul, 191-92
Hauan, Ellen, 263
Haug, Gunther, 21
Havelange, Joao, 232
Hayashi, Dr. Melvin, 229
Hazzard, Kelvin, 83, 86
Heddergott, Karl-Heinz, 119, 120-21
Heideman, Phylliss, 173

Heideman, Richard, 173
Hellenkamp, Chris, 172-73, 198
Henderson, Chris, 240, 243, 251
Henni, Geza, 28
Herberger, John, 114
Hermans, Vic, 231
Hernandez, Manny, 136, 137
Herrick, George, 187
Hess, Bob, 47
Hickersberger, Josef, 248
Hicks, Michelle, 271
Higuita, Rene, 241, 246, 249
Hill, Gordon, 154, 276
Hislop, Shaka, 213
Hites, Sandor, 57, 58
Hoek, Frans, 8, 191, 193-95, 229-30, 240
Hogan, Mike, 54-55, 60
Holzenbein, Bernd, 169, 171
Hood, Bruce, 5
Horton, Randy, 183
Horvath, Bronco, 19
Howard, Ted, 288
Hoxie, R. Gordon, 58, 65
Huber, Christine, 8, 202-03, 270
Hughes, Charlie, 185
Hugo, Brett, 282
Hulcer, Larry, 110
Humphrey, Scott, 96
Hunt, Clark, 286
Hunt, Lamar, 284
Hunt, Sandra, 283
Hunter, Ken, 47,
Hyde, Jessica, 263

I

Ibrahim, Ibrahim M, 212
Idland, Michael, 196
Ilacqua, Julie, 277
Irwin, Ivan, 13
Ivanow, Mike, 57
Izaquirre, Peggy, 263

J

Jabusch, Ron, 50, 53, 55, 60, 63, 110-11
Jago, Gordon, 114
Jares, Joe, 58
Jedrelinic, John, 94
Jeffrey, Bill, 114
Jelacic, Ban, 250
Jenei, Emerich, 249
Jensen, Dr. Gwen, 87, 91
Johnson, Denis, 83
Johnson, Keith, 87
Johnson, Peter, 132, 187
Johnson, Rob, 275
Jolly, Melissa, 263
Joseph, Glen, 93, 95

K

Kalyna, Jarapolk (Jerry), 20, 22, 43, 50
Kane, Paul, 80
Kaplan, Martin, 79
Kaplan, Dr. Phillip, 88, 91-92, 100 142, 146
Kamikawa, Toru, 282, 306
Karbiner, Ewald, 22
Kasper, Dave, 198
Kehoe, Bob, 114
Keller, Kasey, 233, 239-40, 242-43, 253

Kelly, Brian, 55
Kennedy, John F, 45
Kennedy, Steve, 216
Kenny, Gene, 57
Kentling, Bill, 158
Keough, Ty, 110, 122, 136
Kessel, Dick, 184
Kessel, Rick, 8, 93-95, 134, 184, 190
Keyes, Tony, 56, 61
Kibritjian, Toros, 145, 175
Killen, Bill, 114, 121
King, Alan, 211
King, Micah, 306, 307
Kinnear, Dominic, 251
Kitson, Paul, 154
Kittleberger, Jim 229
Klein, Abraham, 269
Kleinaitis, Al, 145, 277
Klivecka, Giedris (Gerry), 44, 47, 50, 66, 111
Klivecka, Rimantis (Ray), 7, 20-21, 29, 41-44, 47, 54, 66, 111, 120-21, 147
Klopas, Frank, 227, 234
Kluszewski, Ted, 13
Kmieczak, Jessica, 271
Knotts, Don, 13
Kohen, Brian, 202
Kopelman, Harriet, 49
Kopelman, Milt, 49
Kostecki, TJ, 66
Kowal, Alycia, 271
Kowalski, John, 7, 79, 88, 95-100, 130, 134, 145-46, 172, 177, 185-87, 190, 192, 197-98, 219, 226, 228-30, 251, 253, 266, 286, 309

Kowalski, Tom, 7, 79
Kraft, Robert, 284
Kramig, Bobby, 196
Kreitlein, Rudolf, 106
Krul, Tim 231
Krumpe, Paul, 227, 240, 241
Kulba, Jaroslaw, 26
Kulishenko, Yuri, 29
Kullman, Jim, 34
Kulmann, Jenn, 202, 263
Kurowycky Jaroslaw (Jerry), 29

L

Labbadia, Lou, 213, 270
Lachowecki, AJ, 8, 172, 191-92, 229, 230-32
Lampard, Frank, 290
Langdon, Jerry, 264
Lai, William T "Buck", 40-41, 53, 57
Lalas, Alexi, 251
Lane, Steve, 87, 93
Lane, Susan, 263
Lapper, Mike, 251
Laprade, Edgar, 19
Larrionda, Jorge, 290
Laschev, Mike, 155
Lataby, Russell, 235
Latimer, Madelyn, 9, 193
Launi, Marcello, 47, 50, 53, 57, 60
Laventure, Perry, 83
Lavery, Art, 29
Lawson, Doc, 95, 155, 229-30
Lay, Nancy, 283
Lazaroni, Sebastiao, 249
Leach, Jennifer, 263, 271
Lear, Norman, 135

Le Bec, Marcel, 61
Leibovich, Leon, 170
Leite, Paul, 46, 60, 61
Leite, Marcio, 198
Leitner, Otto, 46, 60
Leiweke, Terry, 139, 151
Leiweke, Todd, 152 158
Leiweke, Tracey, 139-40, 151-53
Lemieux, Bob, 167, 168, 169
Lennox, Jim, 111, 233
Leoniak, Steve, 50
Levy, Jon, 49
Lewis, Michael, 34
Libero, Rich, 265
Liddle, Chad, 203
Lieberman, Ike, 83
Liekoski, Timo, 110-11, 130, 147
Limberis, John, 50, 53, 55, 60
Lischner, David, 155
Liveric, Mark, 121, 155-57
Lockhardt, Andrea, 202
Logan, Doug, 8, 167, 170, 274, 276-78, 282-84
Logan, George, 110
Loomis, Aubrey, 189, 190
Lopera, Ernesto, 183
Loske, Walter, 21
Loustau, Juan Carlos, 237-38
Loustau, Patricio, 238
Lucenko, Lenny, 59, 81, 83, 85-6 106, 108, 121, 182-84, 266
Lund, Flemming, 137
Lundergan, Fr. Barnabas, 190
Lundy, Ralph, 266, 267
Lundy, Ralph Jr, 266
Lyons, Elizabeth, 201

M

Machnik, Barbara (Otlowski), 6, 8, 9, 15, 35, 41-65, 79-99, 121, 152, 168-71, 186-203, 215-19, 242, 243-53, 265-66, 288-90, 307-11, 345
Machnik, Colette Powell, 8, 35, 62-63, 80-90, 168, 192-215, 345
Machnik, Janine Brawner, 9, 35, 62, 80- 90, 168, 192-202, 215, 217, 345
Machnik, Ellie, 62
Machnik, Leon, 62
Machnik, Josef, 28
Machnik, Joseph Sr, 6
Machnik, Viola, 6
Maessner, John, 251
Magyar, Kalman, 53
Mahlock, Peter, 166, 171
Maier, Sepp, 185
Maierhofer, Ron, 148
Maldini, Paolo, 246
Malin, Seamus, 213
Mandelbaum, Dr. Bert, 252
Mantel, Jeff, 144
Maradona, 243
Markus, Dov, 8, 50, 53, 55-56, 58, 60-63
Marrufo, Jair, 285
Marsh, Rodney, 171
Marslano, Paul, 263
Martin, Dean, 52
Masopust, Josef, 108
Matavuli, Nick, 132
Mate, Andrew, 29
Matsumura, Kazuhiko, 282
Maturana, Francisco, 249

Maurice, Michael, 237
Mauro, Vinnie, 241, 277-78, 282-83
Maxi, Paul, 147
Maxwell, Bill, 132, 140-41, 144, 146, 157
Mayer, Alan, 146
Mazurkiewicz, Ladislao, 82
Mazzola, Sandro, 248
McCormick, Tom, 82, 97
McFadden, Gene, 136
McGeough, Jim, 158
McGuire, Gary, 240
McKeon, John, 44, 183
McLaughlin, Benny, 184
McLaughlin, M L, 264
McNulty, Bob, 81, 83, 106, 108, 184
McPhatter, Clyde, 98
Meagher, Tara, 263
Megaloudis, Nick, 155
Melendi, Ursula, 112
Melnick, Merrill, 88
Mendez, Rodolfo, 234
Meola, Tony, 198, 235-53, 275, 287
Mephem, Denis, 147
Meskill, Mike, 79
Meskill, Tom, 79
Messing, Roy 188
Messing, Shep, 131-34, 152-58, 188
Michia, Juan Carlos, 154
Miller, Al, 114, 118, 183
Miller, Noel, 83
Mills, Jimmy, 114, 183, 184
Milutinovic, Velibor "Bora", 251, 252, 262
Mondelo, Alfonso, 8, 287, 292, 297
Monroig, Dr., 116
Monson, Lloyd, 184
Montero, Mauricio, 234
Monzul, Kateryna, 306
Moracik, Lubomir, 249
Morgan, Candice, 271
Morris, Noreen, 219
Morrone, Bill, 115
Morrone, Joe Jr, 115, 116
Morrone, Joseph, 108-09, 115, 190
Mrakovic, Darko, 94
Muller, Gerd, 82, 114
Mulroy, Tommy, 110, 155
Munn, Biggie, 57
Murray, Angelique, 263
Murray, Bruce, 227, 229, 234, 236, 240-42, 245-47, 251
Muse, Bill, 110, 118, 121
Musial, Stan, 13, 136, 143
Myernick, Glenn, 139
Myers, Greg 84
Myers, Wilbur, 108

N

Nagy, Steve, 29
Namath, Joe, 241
Nanchoff, Louis, 122
Nemickis, Bruno, 20
Nevers, Thomas, 108, 109
Newman, Doug, 240
N'Jie, Tejan, 60
Nikaci, Jako, 94, 96
Noha, Mike, 27
Noonan, Mike, 169
Norman, Mr., 20
Northcutt, Allen, 166, 173
Northway, Jennifer, 263
Notaro, Pete, 96

Nowak, Dan, 263
Nugent, James A, 146, 177
Nussbaumer, John, 6, 20, 22, 26, 29, 50
Nuttal, Bill, 84, 262
Nuzzo, Christina, 271
Nye, Louis, 13

O

Ooft, Hans, 113, 193
O'Leary, Tom, 53
Olivia, Mario, 8, 94
Olson, Steve, 170, 276
O'Neill, Georgie, 130, 131
Ormrod, Don, 64-5, 78, 91
Orr, Graham, 203
Orr, Michelle, 271
Osiander, Lothar, 57, 118, 226-28, 233, 266
Osim, Ivica, 248
O'Toole, Jeanne, 271
Otto, Ed, 14

P

Palmer, Bud, 13
Palencia, Carlos, 8, 93, 95
Palone, Joe, 51
Panagoulias, Alketas, 119, 120
Panczak, Wasyl, 26
Paniagua, Juan, 282
Papelo, Joe, 198
Parli, Steve, 108
Parseghian, Ara, 87
Paston, Mark, 290
Patrick, Lester, 116
Paxos, Steve, 169, 174, 177
Payne, Kevin, 286

Paz, Mario, 28
Peay, Clint, 275
Pecher, Steve, 137
Peck, Arthur, 6, 19, 21
Pele, 82, 93, 114, 151
Penso, Tori, 314
Pereira, Delfim, 79, 83
Pereira, Mike, 294, 304
Perenchio, Jerry, 135
Perez, Hugo, 236, 240
Perez, Ralph, 227, 233, 239, 262, 267
Perisic, Ivan, 311
Perodin, Eddy, 53
Perrault, Alix, 50, 53
Pesa, Njego, 116, 155, 158
Peterson, Dr. Marvin K, 83
Pfeil, Roy, 111
Phillip, Bernadette, 263
Phillips, Lincoln, 267
Picariello, SJ, 41
Pierce, Tony, 8, 172, 192, 203
Pitana, Nestor, 311, 312
Plamondon, Ted, 190, 200
Plante, Jaques, 13
Podoloff, Nate, 81
Pope, Eddie, 275
Polis, John, 229, 240, 252
Pollihan, Jim 13
Polson, Ralph, 266, 267
Poole, Richard, 202
Popovic, Don, 152
Popovich, Anatol, 33, 50, 141, 144, 151
Popovich, Mr., 24
Poston, Tom, 13
Potier, Mike, 8, 203, 268

Powell, Andy, 345
Presley, Elvis, 129, 169, 187
Pringle, Alex, 134
Prus, Alex, 192, 202, 280
Pugh, Trevor, 108
Puleo, Eddie, 214, 219
Puleo, Ignazio, 214, 219
Puleo, Jonathan, 219
Purdon, Ted, 28, 31, 32, 188

Q

Quackenbush, Debra, 9, 47, 193
Queiroz, Carlos, 97

R

Rahn, Dominic, 108
Ramirez, Arnold, 8, 64, 66, 110, 111
Ramos, Tab, 227, 229, 234-36, 242, 246, 275
Ramsey, Graham, 111
Rand, George, 83
Rangel, Eduardo, 56, 57
Rattin, Antonio, 106
Reasso, Bob, 265
Reed, JD, 136
Reed, Tim, 114
Reich, Norbert, 29, 43
Reid, Hugh, 53
Reid, Ian, 96
Reinhardt, Steve, 53, 54
Rendon, Osar, 94, 95
Rennie, John, 212
Rhoden, Giberto, 234
Rhoden, William C, 152
Riehl, Rich, 240
Rigby, Bobby, 128
Ringbloom, Sheila, 202, 263

Ritcey, Robert, 108
Riva, Gigi, 82
Rivera, Gianni, 82
Robbie, Joe, 167
Roberts, Kirk, 80
Robson, Robert, 137
Rocha, Claudio, 155
Rodax, Gerhard, 246
Rodriguez, Nelson, 288, 290, 293, 294, 297
Roethlisberger, Kurt, 245
Rogers, Carl, 46
Rosetti, Roberto, 311
Roitman, Len, 227
Rooney, Jim 287
Rose, Pete, 133
Rosenstein, Joel, 121
Rosenthal, Allen, 47
Rosenthal, Gary, 6, 21, 41-67, 91, 135, 189, 192
Rosenthal, Ira, 48
Rosenthal, Lynne, 48, 49, 52
Rosenthal, Robert, 47
Rossi, Paolo, 269
Rote, Kyle Jr, 169
Rothenberg, Alan, 247, 251, 262, 277
Roxburgh, Andy, 249
Roy, Willy, 33, 113, 267
Rubin, Roy, 53
Rubinson, Dave, 189
Ruck, Don, 116, 130

S

Saar, Arvi, 184
Sack, Dr. Allen, 8, 87, 90, 264, 269
Sack, Gina, 87

Sagastume, Luis, 57
Sage, Bill, 8, 274, 275, 277-78, 284
Salas, Julio, 145
Salas, Reuben, 86
Salazar, Ricardo, 285
Sallah, Alieu, 60
Sampson, Steve, 253, 262
Samuels, Howard J, 150, 151
Sanchez, Manny, 198
Santel, Mark, 251
Santomier, James, 85
Saunders, Harry 107, 108, 109
Saunders, Scott, 187
Savarese, Giovanni, 275, 287
Savic, Zoran, 172
Scandrett, Scully, 211
Schum, Tim, 111
Schapp, Dick, 242
Schellscheidt, Manfred, 108, 114
Schmidt, Heinrich, 136
Schmotolocha, Walter, 26, 30
Schneider, Johnny, 29
Schneider, Walter, 29
Schoen, Helmut, 107, 113
Schoenstadt, David, 151, 157
Schwart, Uwe, 28, 32
Schwarz, Erno, 114
Schweizer, Rick, 8, 169, 192, 198, 265
Schwink, Hans, 132
Scully, Kevin, 93-94
Scurry, Briana, 201, 308
Segota, Branko, 152
Seitz, Kari, 283
Sheparovich, Andrew, 6, 20-22, 24, 43, 95, 145, 192
Sheparovich, Michael, 22, 192

Sheska, Jerry, 184
Shilton, Peter, 185
Shoemaker, Layton, 108
Silva, Dr. Herb, 8, 136-37, 141, 170, 277-79, 281-83, 293, 309
Silvas, Tom, 172
Silvera, Damian, 275
Single, Erwin, 109
Skov, Art, 50
Skuhravy, Tomas, 244, 245
Slagle, Sammy, 45
Slaten, Kevin, 143
Smart, David, 193
Smethurst, Peter, 28, 30, 32
Smile, John, 134
Smith, Charles, 94
Smith, Greg, 79
Smith, Joyce, 169, 171
Smith, J Wise, 169, 171
Smith, Karyn, 263
Smith, Pat 85
Smith, Peter, 229
Smith, Steven A, 267
Smithson, Rod, 170
Snider, Duke, 200
Snyder, Ed 128, 129
Snylyk, Zenon, 27, 33
Soas, Cliff, 42
Sobieski, Krys, 146, 198
Socha, David, 210
Solomon, Cindy, 282
Sommer, Jurgen, 239
Soprano, Tony, 270
Soria, Albert, 54
Soskic, Milutin, 252, 253
Sparwasser, Jurgen, 183
Stam, Garth, 111

Stamatis, Jimmy, 116
Stanaitis, Otto, 20
Stankovic, Mike, 156
Stanisic, Scoop, 198
Startzell, Stanley, 268
Steffans, Diane, 155
Steffans, Mark, 155
Stein, Jon, 91
Steinbrecher, Hank, 85, 251, 262, 277, 308
Steinsdoerfer, Reinhold, 83
Stern, Howard, 267
Stevenson, Cliff, 182, 211
Stollmeyer, John, 227, 234, 240
Stone, Rob, 253, 304, 308, 315
Straut, Ann, 263
Stritzl, Sigi, 21
Sullivan, Chris, 240, 241, 242
Sullivan, Danny, 49
Sun, Baojie, 282
Sunderland, Wayne, 59, 182
Suri, Caleb, 198
Suster, Zeljan, 269

T

Tabarez, Oscar, 249
Tae-Young, Kim, 282
Tamberino, Paul, 276, 288, 291, 294, 297
Tarantini, George, 212
Taylor, Roberto, 8, 88, 92-93
Templin, Marty, 145
Tepper, Ed, 118, 128, 129-31, 133, 135, 145
Thau, Roland, 43
Theiss, Reinhold, 20
Thompson, Billy, 240

Thompson, Christel, 271
Thompson, Simon, 9
Tieman, Barry, 56
Tierney, Nikki, 263
Toledo, Baldomero, 285
Toplak, Ivan, 113
Tortorella, John, 79
Tosney, Shannon, 271
Toth, Zoltan, 146, 155, 191
Toye, Clive, 151
Tozer, Keith, 134, 169, 173
Tramontozzi, Carlo, 8, 47, 49, 50, 53, 54, 55, 56, 60, 66, 246
Tremble, Ed, 248, 250
Trittschuh, Steve, 227, 229, 234, 235, 240, 241
Tuksa, Dunja, 250
Tuksa, Val, 155, 156, 157, 250
Turner, Roy, 139

U

Udvari, Frank, 50
Uebelacker, James W, 271
Uhl, Karl, 192
Ulrich, Joe, 152, 155
Unkle, Cristina, 312
Urbanski, Barry, 80
Uscilla, Paula, 271
Uyar, Anna Maria, 271

V

Valderrama, Carlos, 241
Van Den Brink, Andre, 99, 100
Van Den Brink, Denis, 98
Van Der Beck, Perry, 116, 121, 267
Van Eron, Kieth, 133
Van Gaal, Louis, 194

Van Hellemond, Andy, 50, 278
Van Ness, Keith, 93-94, 97, 234-35
Vanole, David, 191-92, 227, 229-32, 236, 239-40
Vaughn, Terry, 285
Vecsey, George, 238
Veee, Juli, 152, 229
Venglos, Josef, 248-49
Verfaille, John, 55
Vermes, Peter, 227, 229, 232, 234-35, 240-42, 245, 251, 275
Vialli, Gianluca, 246
Vicini, Azeglio, 249
Vieira, Frank, 7, 79, 89-92, 95, 101
Vigliotti, Ray, 155
Visnyei, Gyula, 229
Vizvary, George, 110, 111
Vogelsinger, Hubert, 34, 36, 106, 108-09, 182-83, 185, 190
Vogt, Randy, 219
Volpi, Piero, 249
Voyevidka, Dr., 26

W

Wachter, Artie, 132, 145
Wadley, George, 92
Walker, Keith, 251
Walker, Paul, 94
Wallach, Eli, 281
Walls, Art, 226, 233, 262
Walton, Peter, 295, 296
Nicole Ward, 282
Warner, Jack, 289
Washington, Dante, 251
Webb, Howard, 310
Weiss, Ira, 46, 53, 60, 83
Wheller, Stacy, 271

White, Vanna, 170
Whitehead, John, 136
Whitehead, Jonty, 305, 307
Windischmann, Mike, 172, 227, 229, 231, 234, 240
Wismer, Harry, 241
Wolmerath, Heinz, 142, 145
Wood, John, 114
Wooles, Jan M, 240
Woosnam, Phil, 81, 114, 119, 150
Wozniak, Max, 114
Wright, Don, 97
Wright, Ian, 307
Wynalda, Eric, 240, 241, 244-45, 249
Wynschenk, Don, 34, 64, 78-79, 132-33, 144, 189-90, 194

Y

Yannis, Alex, 134
Yashin, Lev, 131
Yeagley, Jerry, 266
Yebleski, Nelson, 30, 32
Young, John, 188
Yrfeldt, Anders, 28

Z

Zambrano, Octavio, 286
Zanardi, Pete, 100, 216
Zaun, Jeff, 275
Zelinske, Craig, 192
Zenga, Walter, 245
Zlatar, Nick, 111, 121
Zimmerman, Bernard, 100
Zimmerman, Peter, 8, 93, 94, 95
Zungul, Steve, 133, 142, 150, 152, 156

Testimonials

"I've known Joe Machnik for 50+ years with my first interaction when I was in high school and he officiated several of my games. Over those 50 years Joe has been involved in every phase of the game—as a referee, as a coach, as an administrator and most importantly as a true friend of the sport. I can think of no one better positioned to write about that period in American Soccer history than Dr. Machnik."

Sunil Gulati, President of US Soccer (2006-2028), FIFA Executive Committee (Council) (2013-2025)

"I have known Joe Machnik from my first game as a referee in the Major Indoor Soccer League (MISL) over 45 years ago and our friendship has been a wonderful gem to treasure. As Referee-in-Chief of the MISL, Dr. Joe worked with us on the field and mentored us through the nuances of the indoor game. His work as an administrator in three professional leagues (MISL, AISA, MLS) and with US Soccer and PRO contributed immensely to the success of our refereeing family. His seven-decade memoire takes the reader INSIDE those special times and moments and the memories we all share."

Esse Baharmast, FIFA Referee (1993-1998) 1998 World Cup Referee, Director of Officials, US Soccer, FIFA Referee Instructor

"More than anything, Joe Machnik can be considered modern US soccer history. After all, he has lived the game and seen the sport grow for decades. He has played so many roles, whether it has been as a player, coach, administrator, athletic director, referee-in-chief, or more recently as Dr. Joe on TV, commenting about officiating decisions. As I wrote in The Guardian years ago, he is soccer's renaissance man. Joe's passion for the game is unrivaled and that was paid back when he was inducted into the National Soccer Hall of Fame. His memoir is a history lesson for everyone in sport, on how the game has exploded in the USA over the past seven decades, thanks to Joe's memory, copious note taking and his ability to put those thoughts to the page in an educational and entertaining way. Congratulations on your book, Joe!"

Michael Lewis, Publisher, Editor, **Front Row Soccer, Covered 13 World Cups**

"Dr. Joe Machnik played an important role in shaping Major League Soccer's early years. bringing energy, experience, and a deep understanding of the game to the league. Over his seven-decade journey through nearly every corner of the sport, Joe has earned the respect of players. coaches, referees and executives alike. His perspective is as unique as it is insightful, and there is no one better to take readers inside the evolution of American soccer. I am proud to call him a colleague and a friend."

Don Garber, Commissioner, Major League Soccer (MLS) (1999 to present)

"Joe Machnik is a giant in US Soccer history. His influence has helped shape the game into what it is today, and I'm proud to say I am one of the many players he impacted along the way. At age 13, I attended his No.1 Goalkeeper's Camp. That camp taught me what it truly means to be a goalkeeper—how to lead from the back, have self-confidence, and embrace the responsibilities of the position. Those lessons stayed with me throughout my professional career and were a big part of what led to my induction into the National Soccer Hall of Fame. Thank you, Joe for everything you've done for me and the game."

Nick Rimando NCAA National Champion 1997, MLS Cup MVP 2009, Holder of MLS goalkeeping records for appearances (575), wins (223) and shutouts (154). Member of the 2014 USA World Cup team.

"'It's Great to be Alive'! These words were often repeated at Joe Machnik's No.1 Goalkeepers Camp in 1980 when I attended as a 16-year-old at Chapman College (CA). I was so inspired by these and other messages which not only led to success on the field but much more in professional life. The importance of targeted preparation, mental training and toughness and failure analysis provided foundational confidence walking into pressure situations as a corporate attorney. On behalf of nearly one hundred thousand No.1 Campers, I want to express my extreme gratitude to Dr. Joe for sharing his gifts and keys to success. 'From the Sandlots to the World Cup' is another example."

Daniel Bauch, Esq. Corporate Attorney for Multinational Companies.

"Joe Machnik's remarkable seven-decade journey—as a player, coach, referee, league administrator and commentator—is nothing short of legendary. His memoire offers a deeply personal and unique perspective on the beautiful game, capturing the incredible growth of soccer in the U.S. from humble grassroots beginnings all the way to the World Cup stage. As one of the very first graduates of the Ph.D. program in Parks, Recreation and Tourism at the University of Utah, Dr. Joe has always exemplified passion and dedication. We are incredibly proud to call him one of our most distinguished alumni and are honored to recognize him as our 2024 Outstanding Alumnus. Congratulations, Dr. Joe—your legacy is an inspiration!"

Dorothy L. Schmalz, Ph.D. Professor and Chair, Department of Parks, Recreation and Tourism, College of Health, University of Utah.

About the Author

JOSEPH A. MACHNIK (Ph.D)

With a soccer career spanning seven decades, Dr. Joe Machnik has been recognized for his contributions to the growth and development of American soccer.

His 1973 achievement of a doctoral degree from the University of Utah led to the nickname "Dr. Joe" as promulgated by his role as Rules Analyst for Fox Sports soccer TV coverage.

Machnik has had a notable career as a player, coach, referee, league administrator, referee coach/mentor and broadcaster which led to his 2017 induction into the National Soccer Hall of Fame as a "Builder".

An Honorable Mention All-American goalkeeper at Long Island University, Machnik later coached his Alma Mater to two NCAA Finals achieving runners-up status in 1966.

He later coached the University of New Haven to two NCAA Division II Finals achieving runners-up status in 1976. At New Haven, he also coached ice-hockey, served as Director of Athletics, started the women's soccer program in 1991 and contributed to the start of the Management of Sports Industries program.

Machnik has the unique distinction of being the only individual to have played in the NCAA soccer tournament (LIU 1963), coached in two NCAA Tournament Championship Games (LIU '66 and New Haven '76) and served as Referee for a NCAA Division 1 Final (1988).

In 1997 Machnik started the No.1 Goalkeeper's Camp the first of its kind on a national level. Operating today as No.1 Soccer Camps, No.1 has a camper alumni list approaching 100,000 and has employed over 20,000 coaches.

After attending the first US Soccer Coaching Schools in 1970 and achieving the coveted "A" coaching license in 1974, Machnik served as a Staff Coach for the United States Soccer Federation and Assistant Coach for the 1989 US Five-a-Side team which won a FIFA Bronze Medal and Assistant Coach for the 1990 US World Cup team which qualified for its first finals in forty years at Italia '90.

In 1978 Machnik was appointed Referee-in-Chief of the Major Indoor Soccer League (MISL) and later Vice President of Operations. He served as Commissioner of the American Indoor Soccer Association (AISA) and in 1996 was appointed Vice-President of Game Operations for Major League Soccer (MLS), a position he held for fifteen years.

As Rules Analyst for Fox Sports, Machnik has covered two Men's and two Women's World Cups, two Copa Americas, multiple CONCACAF Gold Cups, UEFA Champions and Europa Leagues, FA Cup and a variety of other competitions including Bundesliga, Liga MX, MLS and US Men's and Women's World Cup Qualification games.

"Dr. Joe" Machnik resides in Mount Pleasant, SC with his wife Barbara near to his daughters, Colette with husband Andy, Janine with husband Scott, granddaughter Olivia and grandson Ryder with spouse Joan and great grandchildren Adeline and Wesley.

SUMMER 1990 A PUBLICAT

U.S. Team Ready fo at Italy's 1990 FIFA

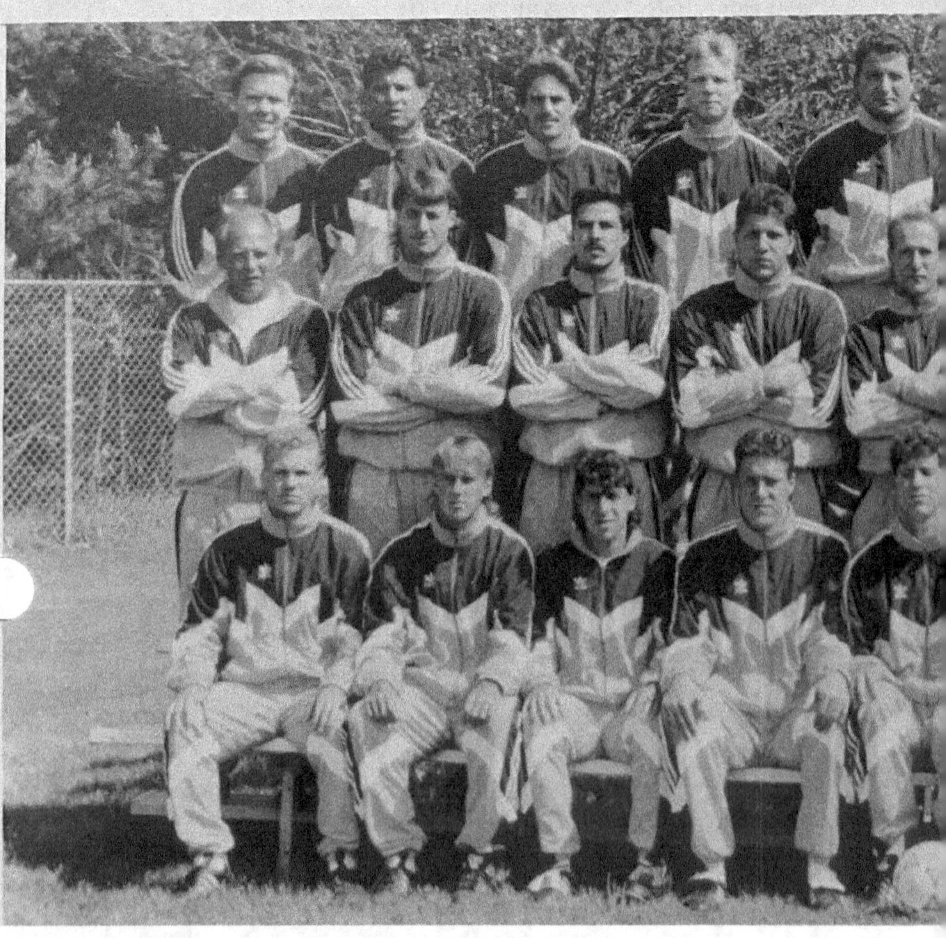

RATION NEWS

ON OF THE UNITED STATES SOCCER FEDERATION

or Ultimate Test
A World Cup

MAKING WAVES

www.ingramcontent.com/pod-product-compliance
Lightning Source LLC
Chambersburg PA
CBHW060941230426
43665CB00015B/2018